The Dictionary of Music Business Terms

By Tim Whitsett
Edited by Sarah Jones

MIX

6400 Hollis Street
Emeryville, CA 94608

The Dictionary of Music Business Terms

Library of Congress Catalog Card Number: 98-67691
ISBN 0-87288-684-0

Production staff: Mike Lawson, Publisher; Sarah Jones, Editor; Linda Gough, Cover Design

6400 Hollis Street
Emeryville, CA 94608
510-653-3307

Also from MixBooks:
The Studio Business Book
The Songwriter's Guide to Collaboration
How to Run a Recording Session
500 Songwriting Ideas
Critical Listening and Auditory Perception
Keyfax - Omnibus Edition
The Audio Pro Home Recording Course Vols. I, II and III
Modular Digital Multitracks - The Power User's Guide
Live Sound Reinforcement
Music Publishing - The Real Road to Music Business Success
I Hate the Man who Runs this Bar - The Survival Guide For Real Musicians
How to Make Money Scoring Soundtracks and Jingles
The Art of Mixing
Hal Blaine and the Wrecking Crew
The Home Studio Guide to Microphones
Professional Microphone Techniques
The Mix Reference Disc
Concert Sound
Sound for Picture
Music Producers

Also from EMBooks:
Making the Ultimate Demo
Anatomy of a Home Studio
Making Music with your Computer
Tech Terms - A Practical Dictionary for Audio and Music Production
The Independent Working Musician

Also from the publishers of *Mix* and *Electronic Musician*:
The Recording Industry Sourcebook
Mix Master Directory
Personal Studio Buyer's Guide
Digital Piano Buyer's Guide

PRIMEDIA
Intertec

AAA
(1) Abbreviation for *Adult Album Alternative*. (2) Abbreviation for *American Arbitration Association*.

A Cappella
A vocal performance without instrumental accompaniment.

A-Side
One of two sides of a *single* recording, the "A-side" is the track chosen by the record company as the one most likely to achieve commercial success. It is the side promoted by the record company and the one normally played on the air by disc jockeys. Tracks with less immediately obvious commercial potential are relegated to the *flip side* or *B-side*.

A-Side Protection
In a record producer's contract with a record company, this is a provision that prohibits the company from *prorating* the producer's royalties on an *A-side* with royalties due another producer who produced the *B-side*. Singles sales are driven by the A-side. It is the A-side producer's work, therefore, that motivates consumers to buy the record, and the producer does not want his or her royalty rate diminished. For example, if the producer's royalty is 3% of the retail price of the single, and if the royalty rate were to be prorated, the producer would receive only 50% of 3% (1.5%).

A&B Comparison
(1) To play two versions of a recording back-to-back, or to play alternating segments of the two versions, in order to compare performances, *mixes*, and/or recording quality. (2) To play alternating segments of the same recording on different playback systems in order to compare sound systems or to insure that a mix holds up on different types of speakers. Also called an A/B comparison.

A&R
Abbreviation for *Artists & Repertoire*.

A&R Administrator
Person who manages business details arising from the creative process of record production. The A&R administrator oversees the flow of contracts, budgets, studio bookings, master deliveries, invoice payments, and compliance with union regulations, etc. The position involves coordinating the functions and requirements of record company personnel in accounting, legal, marketing, and business affairs, etc. with those of A&R staff, artists, producers, studios, and others involved in the production of an album.

A&R Department
Division of a record company that auditions, signs, and develops recording artists; matches song material and producers with recording artists; plans, budgets, and oversees recording sessions; and coordinates release schedules and marketing campaigns with the company's production, marketing, sales, and promotion departments.

A&R Director
Person in charge of *A&R department*.

A&R Person
Staff employee of a record company or record production company who carries out A&R functions. This role involves checking out new talent, signing artists to the company, finding songs for artists signed to the company, and matching producers with artists. An A&R person normally has direct responsibility for certain artists on a label's roster, and motivates other departments of the company to aggressively market and promote product by those artists.

A&R Scout

Person employed by a record company, music publisher, or record producer to find new artists and song material with commercial potential. See also *talent scout*.

A/V Film

Abbreviation for *audiovisual film*. See *videogram*.

ABA

A term for analyzing a song section by section, or to describe the structure of a song. For instance, the first section is *A*, the next section is *B*, and then the first section (*A*) is repeated. Of course, there can be numerous combinations (i.e., *AABA*, *ABCA*, *ABACABA*, etc.).

Abandonment of Copyright

A copyright owner may voluntarily relinquish all rights to a copyright without selling or giving it to another party by "dedicating it to the public" (i.e., allowing its public usage without permission, license, restriction, or claim for compensation, etc.). A copyright may also be involuntarily abandoned if the owner knowingly allows its public usage without permission, license, restriction, or claim for compensation, etc. An abandoned copyright is said to be in the *public domain*.

Abandonment of Trademark

A *trademark* may be considered as abandoned if it falls into disuse, if its owner fails to renew its registration, and/or if its owner knowingly allows its public usage without permission, license, restriction, or claim for compensation, etc.

Above the Line Expenses

Expenses in a production budget for creative services (talent) and above-*scale* payments to musicians, technicians, arrangers, singers, etc., and other special payments for facilities, equipment, etc. See also *below the line expenses*.

Abridge

To cut the length of a work or performance; to shorten, condense, abbreviate, reduce, cut out, or cut off.

Abridgment

A work or performance that has been shortened, condensed, abbreviated, reduced, cut out, or cut off.

AC

Music format abbreviation for *adult contemporary*.

ACA

Abbreviation for *American Composers Alliance*.

Academy Award

An award presented annually since 1928 by the *Academy of Motion Picture Arts and Sciences* for meritorious work in film. Known as an *Oscar*, each award is represented by a gold-plated bronze statuette, ten inches tall and weighing seven pounds.

Award categories include best motion picture, actor, and actress, supporting actor, supporting actress, direction, screenplay based on material not originally written for the screen, original screenplay, art direction, cinematography, costume design, set decoration, film editing, sound, sound effects, song, original music score, score of a musical picture, live-action short subject, cartoon short subject, documentary feature, documentary short subject, special visual effects, make-up, and foreign-language film.

Nominees for awards in each category are selected from five entrants nominated by academy members active in that particular field. The entire academy membership then chooses the winners by secret ballot, and the results are publicly announced at the formal awards ceremony each spring. See also *Oscar* and *Academy of Motion Picture Arts and Sciences*.

Academy of Country Music (ACM)

Trade association founded in 1964 for creative and business professionals active in country music. The ACM's mission is to promote and expand the market for country music. It produces the annual Academy of Country Music Awards television show, stages seminars for members and runs industry-related charity events. Located at 6255 Sunset Blvd., Hollywood, CA 90028. Tel: (213) 462-2351.

Academy of Motion Picture Arts and Sciences (AMPAS)

An organization of approximately 3,000 members active in the performing, technical, and administrative branches of the motion picture industry. The academy was founded in 1927 in Hollywood to promote the cultural and technical standards of the industry.

To carry out its mission, the academy supports technical research, maintains an extensive film archive and library of film books, and issues bulletins of credits, etc. It also produces the annual *Academy Awards* presentations. The academy is located at 8949 Wilshire Blvd, Beverly Hills, CA 90211. Tel: (310) 247-3000. See also *Academy Award* and *Oscar*.

Academy of Television Arts and Sciences (ATAS)

A non-profit corporation founded in 1946 to advance telecommunications arts and sciences and develop creative leadership in the telecommunications industry. ATAS presents the *Emmy Awards* annually to recognize outstanding achievements in television. In addition, the organization sponsors meetings, repertory groups, conferences and activities, to bring people together from within and without the industry to share ideas and information. ATAS also publishes *Emmy* magazine; and is responsible, through the Academy Foundation, for the ATAS/UCLA Television Archives, ATAS Foundation Library, College Television Awards, Internship Program and the Faculty Seminar. ATAS is located at 5220 Lankershim Blvd., North Hollywood, CA 91601. Tel: (818) 754-2800; Fax: (818) 761-2827.

ACAM
The *performing-right society* in Costa Rica.

Acceptance
(1) In contract law, the agreement to all terms of an offer (as opposed to a *conditional* or *qualified* acceptance). Without complete acceptance, a contract is not binding. A *letter of acceptance* of a contract offer is complete upon depositing the letter in the mail. (2) A *waiver* of a contract requirement by allowing performance different from that called for in the contract. (3) An unspoken agreement or "silent consent" to a transaction by failing to reject it or object to it. (4) The acceptance of product received through a sales or licensing transaction without rejection or objection to its quality or quantity.

Access
A means of entry or approach. In a *copyright infringement* case, where the *defendant* is alleged to have copied another work, the *plaintiff* usually seeks to prove that (1) the offending work is *substantially similar* to the original, and (2) the defendant had "access" to the original work whereby he or she could have heard or seen it prior to creating the offending material. If it can be shown that the defendant did have access, and the offending work is deemed substantially similar to the original, the plaintiff's case is strengthened, whether or not the copying was intentional.

Accessory
Non-essential item or device to supplement or enhance a performance or sound.

Account
(1) To provide a detailed summary of financial transactions. (2) To justify or explain. (3) To take into consideration or make an allowance for. (4) A detailed summary of financial transactions allocated to a particular activity, person, or group (i.e., a songwriter's royalty account, a recording expenses account). (5) A customer or client who has a credit relationship with a company.

Account Executive
Usually, (1) an advertising agency employee assigned to develop campaigns for clients; but also, (2) sales reps assigned to oversee customer accounts.

Account Servicing
To call on retailers in order to solicit sales orders, set up *POP* displays, restock display bins or racks, deliver product, etc.

Accountant
Person who maintains and audits financial records, and prepares financial statements and tax returns. See also *certified public accountant (CPA)*.

Accounting
(1) A detailed summary of financial transactions. (2) A justification or explanation. (3) Process of bookkeeping and maintaining financial records of business transactions. (4) Process of preparing financial statements summarizing assets, liabilities, and operating profits/losses.

Accounting Period
The time period covered by financial reports and/or the time period for which licensees must report monies accrued and render monies due for sales or performances during the period. Accounting periods are usually stated as annual (yearly), semi-annual (6 months), quarterly (3 months), and monthly; not to be confused with *collection period*, which is the average number of days a company normally takes to collect monies owed for sales made on credit or *consignment*.

Accounts Payable
Monies owed for goods or services received.

Accounts Receivable
Monies due but not yet received for goods sold or services rendered.

Accrual
(1) The process of accumulating, increasing and/or becoming due. (2) A gain. (3) Something that has accrued (accumulated, increased, or been added).

Accrual Based Accounting
A method of accounting that includes cash actually received and spent during an accounting period as well as *accounts receivable* (payments, royalties, or fees owed *to* the company) and *accounts payable* (payments, royalties, or fees owed *by* the company). See also *cash based accounting*.

Accrue
(1) To gain, increase, and accumulate over a period of time; to become due over a period of time. *Example*: as an artist's recordings are sold, royalties "accrue" to the artist's royalty account and are due to be paid at the end of the agreed *accounting period*. (2) In legal disputes, when something happens to justify a legally enforceable *claim* or *cause of*

action. Example: a record company's cause of action against a *counterfeiter* "accrues" when the company's copyrighted works are illegally copied and sold as genuine.

ACDAM
The *performing-right society* in Cuba.

ACE
A searchable database available online from *ASCAP*, which contains information on all compositions in the ASCAP repertory that have appeared in any of ASCAP's domestic surveys, including foreign compositions licensed by ASCAP in the United States.

Acetate
A metal disc coated with lacquer made from cellulose resin, used in the *disc mastering* process as a reference to check the transfer quality of sound from a master tape to disc before approving the manufacture of vinyl records. Acetates are fragile; their sound quality deteriorates noticeably with repeated playings. Also called a *reference lacquer* or *test pressing*.

Acid
A musical genre *aka* "acid rock," particularly associated with the late 1960s and psychedelic experiences.

Acid House
A music genre geared toward dance clubs and lifestyle that gained favor in the late 1980s and early '90s. It is a variant of *house music*, and is sometimes called *new punk*, since it represented a reaction to status-conscious dress codes and superstar recording artists of the earlier 1980s.

Acid Jazz
Gaining popularity in the late 1980s/early 1990s, a music genre concurrent with *acid house*. Acid jazz marries elements of *hip-hop*, rap, jazz, and samples of vintage jazz recordings.

Acknowledgment
(1) A formal declaration of compliance with the terms of an agreement. (2) The formal admission of an obligation. (3) A formal recognition of some thing (such as a contract) as legally valid. (3) A formal recognition of another's claim, authority, or right. (4) A formal response to some act or compliance. (5) A public expression of thanks or appreciation for help, support, friendship, etc. given by an author, producer, artist, and/or songwriter in the acknowledgments section of a book, film, or album liner notes. See also *credits*.

Acknowledgment Letter
A legally binding letter of acceptance to, or compliance with, the terms of an agreement or settlement. *Example*: A songwriter under exclusive agreement to a music publisher is usually required to sign an acknowledgment letter as new songs are written during the term of the agreement in order to document that each new song is assigned to the publisher as per terms of the agreement.

ACM
Abbreviation for *Academy of Country Music*.

ACODEM
The *mechanical-right society* in Colombia.

Acoustic
Unamplified, non-electric music or musical instruments.

Acoustics
(1) The character and physical qualities of a space, a room, or an enclosed area that have an impact on the properties, production, and transmission of sound, and on the ability to hear sounds clearly. (2) The study, experimentation, technology, and application of the properties, production, and transmission of sound. (3) The architectural science of designing and building structures (such as studios, auditoriums, and theaters) in order to achieve the optimum conditions for propagating sound.

Acquire
To obtain the rights to product, such as masters, songs, or catalogs. *Example*: a record company acquires a master when it licenses or buys a finished master from an independent producer.

Acquired Master
A master recording licensed or purchased by a record company from an independent producer or other *third-party* source, as opposed to being produced *in-house*.

Acquisition
(1) The process of acquiring product. (2) An addition of product to a company's catalog. (3) An addition of songwriters, artists, or producers to a company's roster. (4) The purchase, lease, or licensing of copyright assets, such as masters, songs, or catalogs.

Act
(1) A performer or group of performers, such as a singer, vocal group, or band (i.e., a recording act, nightclub act, cabaret act). (2) A statute, decree, or law enacted by a legislative body (i.e., The *Copyright Act of 1976*). (3) A major division of a theatrical performance. (4) To play or assume a dramatic role in a theatrical performance. (5) A deed or action or activity (i.e., *counterfeiting* copyrighted material is a criminal *act*).

Act of God

A *force majeure*. An earthquake, flood, violent storm, or other natural disaster that prevents a company from benefiting from a contract. Most contracts have a force majeure provision allowing the duration of the agreement to be extended by the same number of days during which the company was unable to benefit due to any event or effect of any event that could not be reasonably anticipated or controlled. In addition to acts of God, examples of force majeure events include fires, strikes, riots, war, government decrees, shortages, breakdowns, or failures of delivery of supplies, materials, labor, or equipment, etc.

Activate

(1) To promote a song or copyright catalog in order to generate sales, airplay, and other revenue-producing usages. (2) To organize and put into effect a marketing campaign. (3) To set up and operate an organization, a company, or a division of a company.

Active

(1) A song, recording, or catalog that is currently being promoted and achieving a degree of commercial success. (2) A company that is currently in operation. (3) A person or group currently engaged in a professional career.

Activity

(1) A degree of sales, radio airplay, or chart movements attained by a song, record, or catalog. See also *chart activity*. (2) A field of endeavor, a process, or an organizational function.

Actors Equity Association (AEA)

Commonly called *Equity*. An *AFL-CIO* affiliated trade union for actors, singers, and dancers professionally active in theater. Headquartered in New York City, the organization has approximately 40,000 members. Its mission is to promote professional theater generally, and, more specifically, to protect members' interests through establishing conditions of employment, compensation, and contracts. An employment contract with a qualified theatrical producer is required for Equity membership.

ACUM

The *performing-* and *mechanical-right society* in Israel.

Ad

Abbreviated reference for *advertisement*.

Ad Agency

See *advertising agency*.

Adapt

To edit, tailor, translate, rearrange, condense, or cut a work in order to make it suitable for a specific use, market, or situation.

Adaptation

A work that has been edited, changed, tailored, translated, rearranged, condensed, or cut for a specific use, market, or situation.

Adaptation Rights

Permission granted by a copyright owner to edit, change, tailor, translate, rearrange, condense, or cut a work in order to make it suitable for a specific use, market, or situation.

ADC

Abbreviation for *analog-to-digital converter*.

Add

An addition of a new recording to a radio station *playlist* or a *new entry* to a best-seller *chart*.

Addendum

An addition, extension, attachment, or supplement to a contract or license.

Addendum to a Regional Memorandum of Understanding (MOU)

A 1997 agreement reached between *Fox Agency International (FAI)* and six multinational record companies for the establishment of *mechanical royalty* rates and payment of mechanical royalties arising from use of FAI's publisher-clients in nine Southeast Asian Countries (China, Hong Kong, Indonesia, Malaysia, the Philippines, Singapore, South Korea, Taiwan, and Thailand). The importance of this agreement to US music publishers arises from the fact that these nine *Pacific Rim* territories generated nearly $2 billion in sales of recorded music in 1996, of which Anglo-American repertoire accounted for 30% - 40%.

Adjudicate

To hear, study, arbitrate, mediate, and settle a dispute or controversy by judicial procedure.

Adjudication

A binding judicial ruling in the settlement of a dispute or controversy.

Ad-Lib

Extemporaneous remarks; an impromptu, unrehearsed performance or speech; something improvised on the spur of the moment, such as a singer spontaneously adding lyrics to a song, or an instrumentalist departing from a prepared arrangement.

Admin

Abbreviated reference for *administration, administrative,* or *administer.*

Administer

(1) To manage the business affairs of a company, estate, or trust. (2) To manage business affairs relating to copyrights, contracts, and licenses.

Administration

The business management of companies, estates, trusts, copyrights, contracts, and licenses.

Administration Agreement

An agreement whereby one party undertakes to *administer* the business affairs of another party. In the music business, administration agreements commonly refer to arrangements where a full-service music publisher or copyright administration company handles copyright registrations, song clearances, contracts, licenses, and royalty collections for a small publisher or songwriter. *Administrators* do not normally pay advances or provide promotional or creative services. Administrators usually retain 5% to 15% of gross income collected on the other party's behalf as a catchall *administration fee,* though the administrator might also insist on recouping any *direct costs.* See *administration costs,* below.

Administration Costs

Expenses incurred in the process of managing the business affairs of a company or copyright catalog. There are two types of costs: *direct* and *indirect.* Indirect costs include overhead, rent, and salaries. Indirect costs cannot be precisely attributed to any one copyright, whereas *direct costs* (i.e., copyright registration fees, lead sheets, demos, advertising, collection costs, etc.) can easily be itemized and allocated to individual copyrights.

Administration Department

Division of a music publishing company that manages copyright-related business affairs, including licensing, collections, contracts, registrations, and clearances.

Administration Fee

Compensation paid to an *administrator.* In music publishing, this is typically a 5% to 15% retention of gross income collected on behalf of a copyright owner, although, in some administration agreements, the administrator also recoups out-of-pocket expenses incurred for such *direct costs* as registration fees, postage, copying, lead sheets, etc.

Administration Rights

Copyright owners are vested with statutory rights giving them exclusive control over their work's production, reproduction, manufacture, sale, publication, distribution, display, or performance. The management of these rights is called copyright administration. Some copyright owners have an *administrator* manage their copyright affairs. When this is the case, a copyright owner enters into an *administration agreement* with an administrator, assigning the administration rights to the administrator. Administration rights do not include ownership of the copyrights.

In a *copublishing* deal (or *split*), where a copyright is jointly owned by two or more parties, one copublisher may assign administration rights of its share to one of the other owners. Justification for claiming full administrative rights arises where one publisher has a larger share of the copyright (i.e., one publisher has two writers in a three-way split and thus owns 66.66%); or, where one publisher is an established, full-service company, while the other is insufficiently staffed to properly administer and promote the work. See also *joint-administration.*

Administrator

(1) Person in charge of administering a copyright catalog. (2) In an *administration agreement,* the company that has been assigned *administration rights.* (3) In a *copublishing* deal, the publisher that has administration rights has the sole right to license and collect all royalties and fees earned by the song on behalf of all other copublishers. The administrator must account to copublishers for their royalty shares (including their respective writers' shares).

Adult Album Alternative (AAA)

Radio station format, usually called *Triple A,* geared to appeal to young adults with white-collar jobs and college educations who came of age in the 1970s.

Adult Contemporary (AC)

Market segment or musical *genre* usually geared toward *baby boomer* audiences. Typically, a soft, melodic pop/rock musical style, often with romantic storylines. Radio formats geared to this audience may mix in other genres, such as soft rock, *oldies, easy listening,* and *MOR.*

Advance

(1) To pay a sum of money before it is due. (2) Money loaned on account, to be repaid from future earnings. (3) Money paid for goods or services before they are received or rendered.

Record companies and music publishers frequently offer *royalty advances* as *inducements* for songwriters and recording artists to assign their works to the company. Royalty advances are interest-free loans with no fixed repayment schedule. They are *recoupable* against royalty income that may or may not materialize. Advances are recouped piecemeal as royalties are earned by artists, writers, and producers over rather indefinite periods of time. Furthermore, royalty advances are usually *non-returnable*—there is no recourse if not enough royalties are earned, because recipients aren't obligated to repay unrecouped royalty advances. In effect, when a company pays a royalty advance, it guarantees that the songwriter, artist, or producer will earn at minimum an amount equal to the advance, since the sum is non-returnable.

Example: When a publisher advances a songwriter $1,000 as an inducement to assign a copyright, the publisher is entitled to withhold (recoup) the first $1,000 from the songwriter's royalties. The songwriter receives royalties only after the advance is repaid, but doesn't have to pay the publisher back at all if the song never earns a dime.

A royalty advance differs from a conventional loan, because conventional loans obligate borrowers to repay certain sums by certain dates. They are also normally made on terms that include interest and some type of collateral that is forfeited if the loan isn't repaid as agreed.

Advert
Shorthand reference for *advertisement*, particularly in Great Britain.

Advertise
To publicly announce, proclaim, or promote the desirable qualities and benefits of a product, company, or event, in order to generate or increase sales, or to maximize attendance at an event, such as a concert.

Advertisement
An announcement, promotion or proclamation made to increase sales of a product or attendance at an event. Advertisements are normally paid for, as opposed to free notices resulting from *publicity* generated through press releases, press conferences, interviews, reviews, editorials, news reports, and *public service announcements*.

Advertising
The process of placing paid announcements and notices in public places or in the media in order to increase sales of a product or attendance at an event. Means of advertising include billboards, posters, display and classified space in magazines, newspapers and Web sites, radio and television spots, *trailers* included on home video releases or shown with feature films at movie theaters, etc.

Advertising Agency
A company employed to create advertising concepts, develop strategical and tactical advertising plans, design and produce advertisements, and carry out ad campaigns.

AEA
Abbreviation for *Actors Equity Association*.

AEPI
The *performing-right society* and *mechanical-right society* in Greece.

AES
Abbreviation for *Audio Engineering Society*.

Affiliate
(1) To become a member, subordinate, subsidiary, employee, or associate of an organization. (2) A person, group, or company associated with another person, group, or company as a subordinate, subsidiary, or member. (3) Music publishers and songwriters who assign *performing rights* to *Broadcast Music, Inc.* (BMI) are called *affiliates*. (Music publishers and songwriters whose performing rights are assigned to ASCAP are called *members* of that society.) (4) A television or radio station linked to one of the major broadcasting networks and having exclusive programming rights for that network in a city or region.

Affiliated
To be a member, subordinate, subsidiary, employee, or associate of an organization.

Affix
To add, attach, or join. *Examples*: To add a signature to a contract; to attach a schedule of song titles to a contract; to place a copyright notice on a publication.

Affixation
Something attached, joined, or added (i.e., a schedule of titles attached to the end of a contract).

AFIM
Abbreviation for *Association For Independent Music*.

AFL-CIO
Abbreviation for American Federation of Labor and Congress of Industrial Organizations, an umbrella confederation of approximately 90 autonomous trade unions, including the *AFM*, *AFTRA*, *AGVA*, *AGMA*, *AEA*, *SAG*, and *SEG*.

AFM
Abbreviation for *American Federation of Musicians*.

AFM Defaulters List
A *blacklist* warning *AFM* union members not to accept work from the listed individuals and companies who have failed to pay agreed wages, dues, or fees to other union members. Union members who work with defaulters are subject to fines or other

disciplinary action. The defaulters list is published monthly in *International Musician*.

AFM Employers Pension & Welfare Fund
Under the *Phonograph Record Labor Agreement*, employers of union musicians for recording sessions are required to pay up to 10% of the gross scale wages paid for each session into this fund, which provides pension benefits to participating members.

AFM Health & Welfare Fund
Under the *Phonograph Record Labor Agreement*, employers of union musicians for recording sessions are required to pay certain amounts into this fund, which provides health insurance for participating members. Certain eligibility requirements apply before a member can be covered.

AFM Local
A district chapter or branch office of the *American Federation of Musicians*, which has oversight and direction of members within that district. See *local*.

AFM Phonographic Record Labor Agreement
An agreement regulated by the *AFM*, which binds record labels who sign the agreement to pay *union scale* to musicians on recording sessions. Union wage scales vary according to the number of songs recorded, type of session (i.e., masters, demos, film scores, etc.), number of instruments played, time of day session takes place (i.e., after regular business hours, weekends, holidays), number of hours the session lasts, etc. Union members are prohibited from working for record companies who don't sign the agreement, and are also prohibited from working with non-union musicians on recording sessions. See also *National Code of Fair Practices for Phonograph Recordings*.

AFM Phonographic Trust Agreement
An agreement between the *AFM* and *signatory* record labels requiring the record companies to pay a small percentage of the price of each recording sold into the *Music Performance Trust Fund*. The purpose of the fund is to employ union musicians to perform in public places, such as parks, veterans' homes, schools, etc. These performances provide free entertainment for public benefit, promote live music, and provide income for union members.

AFM Special Payments Fund
A provision of the AFM agreement with record manufacturers requires manufacturers to pay a percentage of income received from sales of records by union members into a trust fund. After trust fund expenses are deducted, the funds are ultimately distributed to union members who participated in the recordings.

AFM Television, Video Tape Agreement
Under the AFM Television, Video Tape Agreement, musicians receive 75% of the basic scale amount paid for the original work when a program is re-broadcast the second and third time, 50% of scale for the fourth, fifth, and sixth reruns, 10% for the seventh rerun, and 5% for each additional rerun thereafter. Such payments are called *reuse fees* or *residuals*. *AFTRA* members receive *replay fees* for rebroadcasts of recorded performances, formulated on a *sliding scale* similar to AFM reuse fees.

Aftermarket
Follow-up sources of income for films, television productions, stage plays, record releases, etc. after primary release or publication.

AFTRA
Acronym for *American Federation of Television & Radio Artists*.

AFTRA Local
A district chapter or branch office of *American Federation of Television & Radio Artists*, which has oversight and direction of members within that district. See *local*.

AGAC
Abbreviation for *American Guild of Authors & Composers*.

AGADU
The *performing-right society* in Uruguay.

AGAYC
The *performing-right society* in Guatemala.

Agency
(1) A business or service authorized to represent and act for another. *Examples*: advertising agency, booking agency, talent agency. (2) The means by which something is accomplished.

Agent
Person authorized to represent another. A representative empowered to act on behalf of a company.

AGMA
Abbreviation for *American Guild of Musical Artists*.

AGVA
Abbreviation for *American Guild of Variety Artists*.

AIMP
Acronym for *Association of Independent Music Publishers*.

Air
To broadcast on radio or television.

Air Time
(1) The time a broadcast is scheduled to start. (2) The amount of broadcast time allotted for a record, concert, performance, or program.

Aired
A program, record, concert, interview, etc. broadcast on radio or television.

Airline Music
Also called *in-flight entertainment* or *in-flight programming*. Music provided by airlines for passengers to listen to on headsets. The nature of the usage more closely resembles *syndicated* radio programs than background music, because it is intended for entertainment rather than mood enhancement. Therefore, *transcription licenses* issued for airline music programming are similar to those issued to radio syndicators, as opposed to licenses issued to *background music* services. The transcription license is akin to a *mechanical license* that authorizes the packager to duplicate the work, and is issued by the publisher or the publisher's *mechanical-right society*. Rights to perform songs on the transcribed program are obtained from *performing-right societies*.

Airplay
The broadcast of a *sound recording* on radio.

Airplay Monitor
Weekly hardcopy reports published by *Billboard* in magazine format issued to subscribers of *BDS*. Several versions of *Airplay Monitor* are available, each of them dedicated to a specific market segment (R&B, Top 40, Country, etc.). See *Broadcast Data Systems*.

AKA
Abbreviation for "also known as." *Example*: Joe Jones, *aka* Joe Superstar.

AKM
The *performing-right society* in Austria.

Album
(1) A *sound recording* containing several musical selections and/or more *playing time* than can be contained on a *single* recording format. Albums of sound recordings are typically packaged in protective cases, slipcases, or cardboard jackets and issued in various *formats*, including compact discs (CDs), 12-inch long-playing records (LPs), and audiocassettes. A recorded album may also consist of two or more discs or tapes packaged together in the same binding (a "double album" or "boxed set"). (2) A printed edition of musical selections bound together.

Album Cut
One of several recorded performances included on an *album*.

Album Network
Weekly *trade publication* reporting chart and *playlist* summaries from radio stations focusing on rock and *alternative* music. Also publishes annual *trade directory* called *Yellow Pages of Rock*. Located at 120 North Victory Blvd., Burbank, CA 91502. (818) 955-4000.

Album-Oriented Rock (AOR)
A market segment, radio station format, or chart designation of a particular genre characterized by rock music styles.

Album Tour Cycle
Most artists embark on tours timed to start with the release of a new album in order to promote the recording. An album tour cycle is generally defined as starting the date of an album release and ending either with the start of recording for the next album or on the date of the last scheduled performance on a tour connected with the album. Most *merchandising agreements* made with artists are structured to coincide with album tour cycles.

Album Track
See *album cut*.

Alignment
(1) An adjustment or *calibration* of mechanical parts (such as recording *heads*) so that they are in proper position relative to each other. When tape heads aren't properly aligned, tracks on the tape are out of phase with each other; loss of audio information may also occur. (2) An arrangement or positioning, such as the sequence in which songs are placed on an album. (3) A lineup of musicians on a recording session or the composition of a band. (4) A group of performers appearing separately on the same bill.

Allegorical Lyrics
Using an image to represent or illustrate another. In popular Christian music, for instance, allegories are frequently used to make the genre more appealing to mainstream audiences. The lyrics might be akin to love songs, where the word "you" is capitalized in reference to Jesus.

All-In Advance
An advance paid to a producer that includes the costs of producing finished masters. The producer retains any surplus after recording costs. By combining the producer's advance with money slated for production costs, the record company forces the producer to control recording costs, since any overrun reduces the amount of the producer's royalty advance. See also *recording fund*.

All-In Royalty Rate

(1) A royalty payable to an artist, from which the artist must pay the producer's royalty and royalties entitled to any other performers or personnel involved in producing the masters (2) A royalty payable to a production company, from which the production company must pay the artist and any other performers or personnel involved in producing the masters.

Allowances

Price deductions, discounts, rebates, or reductions given for special circumstances. *Examples*: (a) A record company discounts 5% of its product price to a distributor who pays cash within 30 days; (b) a retailer discounts 50% off the price of an album to customers who purchase two albums at full price; (c) a record company pays artists' royalties on 90% of sales; the remaining 10% represents "allowances" for product lost, warped, or broken in storage or shipment and/or product shipped on credit that is returned unpaid for or that has to be written off for nonpayment.

Alteration

(1) In a contract or license: a correction, an amendment, a change, or revision. (2) In a musical work: an adaptation, such as a translation, or a change in lyrics or melody, etc.

Alternative

Youth-oriented music genre seemingly indicative of the cutting edge in popular music (away from or ahead of the mainstream), often incorporating varying degrees of other styles, such as punk, grunge, house, industrial, heavy metal, pop, world, reggae, techno, thrash, and/or new wave. Also called "alternative rock."

AM

Abbreviation for *amplitude modulation*, the broadcast airwave band signal used by AM radio stations. Approximately 5,250 radio stations broadcast on AM in the United States, compared with around 7,750 *FM* stations. See also *amplitude modulation*, *FM*, and *frequency modulation*.

Amateur

(1) A person who does something as a hobby rather than as a profession; a writer or performer who does not earn a living by those pursuits. (2) An unpolished writer or performer who lacks the skill and experience of a professional.

Ambience

The aura, setting, atmosphere, feel, or mood created by a work, audio or visual effects, lighting, decor, etc. Also spelled *ambiance*.

Ambient

A music genre pioneered by Brian Eno in the late 1970s, characterized by soothing, "spacey" instrumental variations of other forms of music.

Ambient Music Performance Royalty

A performance royalty paid by local television stations who opt for *per program performance licenses* for each *ambient music usage*.

Ambient Music Use

Music of 15 seconds or less picked up from the background of television broadcast coverage of an event, such as a parade, football game half-time show, fashion show, political rally, etc.

AMC

Abbreviation for *American Music Conference*.

AMCOS

Abbreviation for *Australian Mechanical Copyright Owners Society*.

Amend

To formally correct, improve, or otherwise change a contract, license, or law by adding, deleting, or rephrasing certain provisions, words, terms, conditions, stipulations, or clauses.

Amendment

A formal correction, addition, deletion, or other change to a contract, license, or law.

American Arbitration Association (AAA)

A nonprofit service that refers parties involved in contract disputes to professionally qualified *arbitrators*.

American Composers Alliance

An organization formed in 1937 to promote the interests of *serious music* composers. It operates *American Composers Edition*.

American Composers Edition

A *BMI*-affiliated music publishing company operated by the *American Composers Alliance* to publish works by contemporary *serious music* composers, making scores available for sale and rental to symphony and school orchestras and opera companies.

American Federation of Musicians (AFM)

AFL-CIO affiliated union formed to protect and promote interests of musicians in the United States and Canada. The AFM negotiates terms of employment for session musicians with record companies, setting union scale and pension contributions for recording sessions. National headquarters are located at 1501 Broadway, Suite 600, New York, NY 10036. Tel: (212) 869-1330; Fax: (212) 764-6134.

American Federation of Television & Radio Artists (AFTRA)

AFL-CIO affiliated union formed to protect and promote interests of actors employed by radio and television production companies in the United States and Canada, though some musicians and vocalists affiliate with AFTRA rather than the *AFM*. AFTRA negotiates terms of employment for actors and announcers with broadcasting networks, local stations, and production companies, setting union scale and pension contributions for broadcast work. National headquarters are located at 260 Madison Ave., New York, NY 10016. Tel: (212) 532-0800; Fax: (212) 532-2242. See also *National Code of Fair Practices for Phonograph Recordings*.

American Guild of Authors & Composers (AGAC)

Founded in 1931 as the *Songwriter's Protective Association*, the organization later changed its name to AGAC, then changed again in the 1980s to the *Songwriter's Guild of America* (*SGA*).

American Guild of Musical Artists (AGMA)

An AFL-CIO affiliated trade union promoting and protecting the interests of singers and dancers working in opera, ballet, and concert performances.

American Guild of Variety Artists (AGVA)

An AFL-CIO affiliated trade union for nightclub, cabaret, and other live-music-venue performers, located at 184 Fifth Avenue, New York, NY 10010.

American Music Conference (AMC)

Trade association comprising music instrument manufacturers, print music publishers, distributors, and retailers. The association promotes music education and amateur music making.

American Society of Composers, Authors & Publishers (ASCAP)

One of three US *performing-right societies* (*BMI* and *SESAC* are the others). ASCAP is the oldest American performing-right society, founded in 1914 by Irving Berlin, Jerome Kern, et al. ASCAP collects some $400 million annually from broadcasters, jukebox operators, and all venues where music is performed or played, on behalf of more than 60,000 writer/publisher *members*. Together, ASCAP and BMI license the performing rights for approximately 99% of all song copyright repertoire in the United States. As a non-profit organization, ASCAP retains an average 18% of its gross collections for administrative overhead and distributes the balance to its members. Headquartered at One Lincoln Plaza, New York, NY 10023. Tel: (212) 595-3050.

AMOA

Abbreviation for *Amusement & Music Operators Association*.

Amp

Abbreviation for (1) *amplifier* and (2) ampere (a unit of electrical current).

AMPAS

Abbreviation for *Academy of Motion Picture Arts and Sciences*.

Amplifier

An electrical device that increases the volume, power, or amplitude of a signal. Amplifiers are rated in watts (the amount of power the amplifier can produce). Most amplifiers today are solid-state (equipped with integrated circuits). Sound-signal voltages that are too small for the amplifier to read are boosted by a *preamplifier*.

Amplitude

In a *sound wave*, amplitude refers to the intensity (volume) of the sound. When the wave is represented graphically, the degree of amplitude is seen as peaks and valleys, from the height of a crest to the depth of a trough.

Amplitude Modulation

A method of altering radio waves to transmit broadcasting signals, used by *AM* radio stations. Though the *frequency* is constant, AM waves vary in transmission according to the broadcast signal. See also *FM*, *frequency*, *frequency modulation*, and *AM*.

Amusement & Music Operators Association (AMOA)

Trade organization formed in 1948 to promote and protect the interests of the coin-operated amusement industry (i.e., arcade video games and jukeboxes). See also *jukebox* and *Jukebox License Office* (*JLO*). AMOA is headquartered at 401 B. Michigan Ave., Chicago, IL 60611. Tel: (312) 245-1021.

Analog

A method of conveying or storing audio signals in which the signals vary continuously, thus being subject to interference or distortion. On a vinyl phonograph record, for instance, the grooves represent sounds in the form of a mechanical analog; the phonograph's *pickup* device converts the sound information from mechanical to an electrical analog signal, which is then reproduced by the record player's speakers. See also *digital*.

Analog-to-Digital Conversion

The process of converting continuously varying electronic or audio signals from an *analog* source into discrete "off-on" digital signals. See also *digital-to-analog converter*.

Analog-to-Digital Converter (ADC)

A circuit, switch, or device for changing continuously varying electronic or audio signals from an analog source into discrete "off-on" digital signals, which can be entered into a computer for processing or manipulation. See also *digital-to-analog converter*.

Ancillary Income

Additional royalties and fees earned by a copyrighted work from secondary sources as an indirect result of the work's primary licensed usage. For instance, a song licensed for use as a movie theme may earn additional income from a variety of spin-off usages, such as *mechanical royalties* (from sales of the movie soundtrack album and home video sales), and *performance royalties* (when the soundtrack recording is played on radio and/or when the movie is broadcast on television and/or shown in European cinemas).

Ancillary Rights

The rights to participate in secondary or indirectly derived income or other benefits of copyright ownership beyond a copyright's primary usage. For instance, the *grand right* to a *Broadway musical* is normally shared between the composer, lyricist, author, and the producer of the play. The producer, however, does not always share in the "ancillary rights" (i.e., royalties and fees earned from *mechanical, performance, synchronization*, and *print* licenses when a song from the musical is extracted from the play and licensed on its own for nondramatic usages).

Angel

Person or company providing financial backing for a *Broadway musical*, record or film production, or small, start-up company.

Anne, Statute of

The first real copyright law in an English-speaking country, enacted in 1710 by the British Parliament. The Statute of Anne forbade the unauthorized printing, reprinting, or importing of books for a limited number of years.

Annual

Something that occurs or recurs once each year. *Examples*: An annual accounting, a financial or shareholders report, a contract renewal option, a royalty advance payment, etc.

Anon

Abbreviation for *anonymous*.

Anonymous

(1) A work authored by a person or persons unknown. (2) A work whose authorship is unnamed or unassigned.

Answer Record

A recording produced in response to a previously released recording. See *answer song* below.

Answer Song

A song written in response to a previously released recording. Typically, the "answer" is an adaptation of the first release, with melodic and lyrical similarities, and therefore requires permission from the original work's copyright owner. Answer songs normally are created only in response to a work that has achieved a degree of success and public recognition, in order to capitalize on the original work's demonstrable commercial appeal. An answer song may either be a serious response (i.e., "I Love You Too" in answer to a song called "I Love You") or comedic (i.e., "I Hate You" in answer to a song called "I Love You").

Anthem

An inspirational, uplifting musical composition used by or identified with a person, group, institution, movement, cause, or country.

Anthology

A collection of songs or recordings representing a songwriter's or artist's work over time, or a collection of works that are representative of a genre or an era (i.e., "An Anthology of Delta Blues", "Love Songs of World War II").

Antitrust Laws

Legislation enacted to regulate, restrict, limit, or break up business *monopolies*, in order to prevent *unfair competition*.

AOR

Abbreviation for *album-oriented rock*.

APA

The *performing-right society* in Paraguay.

APDAYC

The *performing-right society* in Peru.

Apparent Authority

The power of *agency* or the accepted authorization to represent and act for or on behalf of another, which is not expressly granted but which is recognized as clearly evident and obvious from a record of established precedents wherein one party has allowed another to so act on his or her behalf. See also *express authority*.

Appraisal

An estimate or assessment of something's value or worth. Formal appraisals are normally professional judgments made by experts after careful analysis of the item under appraisal.

Appraise

To estimate or assess the value of an asset, an artistic quality, or a professional competency.

Appraiser

An expert who evaluates and reports on the value, quality, or worth of an asset, a property, an artistic work, or a professional ability. Appraisers normally have demonstrable professional qualifications, such as a degree or license.

APRA

Abbreviation for *Australian Performing-Rights Association*, the *performing-right society* in Australia.

Arbitration

A process of settling a dispute out of court by which the parties involved submit their differences to a *third party* appointed by mutual agreement, whose judgment in the matter will be binding.

Arbitration Clause

A contractual provision that requires the contracting parties to submit any dispute to a mutually agreed *third party* for *arbitration*.

Arbitrator

A person mutually selected by parties to a dispute who will hear and weigh both sides of the argument, then render a judgment to settle the dispute. An arbitrator is normally selected on the basis of impartiality and knowledge of the business issues in dispute.

Arbitron

A broadcast audience rating service provided by the Arbitron Company, which surveys radio and television audiences to determine which stations (and programs) are tuned in at any given time, and who is listening to those stations.

Arbitron Ratings

Survey results supplied by the *Arbitron Company* showing which radio and television stations (and programs) are tuned in at any given time, and who is listening to those stations.

Arcade

Rows of coin-operated pinball machines and video games located in malls, shopping strips, and other commercial establishments. Formerly, "Penny Arcade."

Video games enjoy popularity in arcades where pinball machines once ruled supreme. Software for arcade games is not a mass market item, although game users do constitute a mass market. Game machines cost arcade operators upwards of $3,000 each.

Royalties to music copyright owners, whose works are *synchronized* in arcade video games, are calculated against the cost of the machine, and usually range between 1/2-of-one percent to 1% of the machine's price ($150 to $300). Or, a *prorated* royalty of between $10 to $15 per song per unit might be considered. In either case, a *fixation* or *synchronization fee* is usually required, which might be anywhere from $150 to $600.

The use of music in video arcades also amounts to a *public performance*. The copyright license issued to the machine manufacturer does not include the right of public performance, but requires the machine to be authorized for use only to arcade operators who have valid *blanket licenses* from the *performing-right societies*.

Archives

A repository, storage place, or collection containing tapes, records, catalogs, documents, or other materials of value or interest. The stored material is usually indexed, cross-referenced, or cataloged to enable ready access to individual items within the collection.

Arena

(1) A large *venue* for concerts, such as a coliseum, a stadium, or an auditorium. (2) A particular specialty or field of activity (i.e., "She was successful in the songwriting arena").

Arm's Length Transaction

Dealings between two or more parties who are not connected by a close relationship (such as shared ownership, partnership, or other relationship) that might pose a *conflict of interest* for one of the parties.

Arrange

(1) To *orchestrate* a musical work for instruments or voices. (2) To modify a musical work for another style of performance. (3) To write orchestral or vocal parts for a musical composition. (4) To *score* a musical work. (5) To settle a dispute or bring about an agreement.

Arrangement

(1) Written orchestral or vocal parts for a musical work. (2) Musical directions for the performance of a composition, given either to a full orchestra or for a particular instrument or voice. (3) A *score* or *orchestration*. (4) An agreement or settlement.

Arranger

Person who scores, orchestrates, or writes individual instrumental and vocal parts for a musical composition, and/or who provides directions for the composition's musical performance.

Art Music

Reference to *serious* or *classical music*, which includes opera, operettas, ballet, symphonies, chamber music, etc.

ARTIJUS

The *performing-right society* in Hungary.

Artist

Often, a shorthand reference for *recording artist*: A singer or musician whose creative ability, talent, and skill are applied to creating and recording works of aesthetic value and/or commercial appeal.

Artist Development

Process of grooming a singer's or musician's creative ability, talent, and skill to the level required for commercial success as a recording artist. When undertaken by a management, production, or publishing company, the process can include recording demos and masters, staging showcase performances, and negotiating contracts with record companies, etc., in order to get a recording deal for the artist. See also *artist development deal*.

Artist Development Deal

An agreement between a performer and a manager, producer, music publisher, or record company whereby the performer's creative ability, talent, and skills are groomed to the level required for commercial success as a recording artist. Usually, such deals are undertaken by companies or individuals before a record company is approached. For instance, a singer-songwriter might enter into an agreement with a music publisher, where the publisher finances or produces an agreed number of demos or masters to showcase the act to record labels. The publisher might directly negotiate record deals for the artist, or it might team the artist with an artist-management firm to handle record company negotiations.

Artist development deals are tailored to meet specific objectives of the parties involved, but they typically cover the following points: the recording budget; the number of songs to be produced, the time frame for recording sessions, the amount of the advance or advances paid to the writer (and the payment schedule); publisher's options in the event a record deal is not made within the allotted time. See also *demo deal*.

Artist Management

Overseeing the business and creative affairs of an artist, including negotiating contracts for recording, publishing, and personal appearances, liaison with record companies, publishers, booking agents, publicity agents, etc., and handling financial matters.

Artist-Owned Label

A record company owned and operated by a recording artist whose works are released by the label.

Artist-Owned Publisher

A music publishing company owned and operated by a recording artist, usually to acquire copyright interest in works written and/or recorded by the artist.

Artist-Producer

A recording artist who produces or co-produces his/her own recorded performances.

Artists Relations

A department or person within a record company who acts as liaison between artists and their managers and the various other departments and personnel within the company. In a sense, the position is that of artists' advocate within the company.

Artist-Songwriter

A recording artist who writes or co-writes much of the material he/she records.

Artistic Control

Same as *creative control*: The creative direction, choice of producer and material, and/or final judgment as to whether or not an artistic work or performance meets acceptable commercial and aesthetic standards. In a recording contract, creative control may also extend to approval of album artwork, advertising materials, and video production.

Artistic License

The creative range of artistic expression in speech, writing, performance, or interpretation, which may bend the rules of common practice, tradition, expectation, or author's original intent, and which is employed to achieve a certain effect on an audience. Also called *poetic license* and *literary license*.

Artists & Repertoire (A&R)

Also called *Artists & Repertory*. Process of scouting, signing, grooming, and guiding the recording careers of artists, of selecting material for them to record, assigning producers, booking recording sessions, and developing marketing campaigns for recorded releases in cooperation with artist managers and other record company departments, such as marketing, press, promotion, advertising, sales, international, etc.

Artwork

The composite graphics, illustrations, line drawings, photographs, and text used in print advertising and on covers of record albums, CDs, CD-ROMs, audiocassettes, music folios, sheet music, books, home videos, etc.

ASCAP
Acronym for *American Society of Composers, Authors & Publishers.*

Assign
To transfer an ownership claim, right, copyright, interest, title, or other property from one party to another.

Assignability
The right to transfer an ownership claim, right, copyright, interest, title, or other property from one party to another. See also *assignment clause.*

Assignable
A condition of right, title, claim, or benefit that can be lawfully assigned or transferred from one party to another; something that is transferable.

Assignee
(1) One who receives interest, rights, or ownership in a copyright or other property from another party. (2) Someone authorized to act as an agent or representative for another.

Assignment
(1) The transfer of an ownership claim, right, copyright, interest, title, or other property from one party to another. (2) The license, contract, or other instrument transferring an ownership claim, right, copyright, interest, title, or other property from one party to another.

Assignment Clause
A licensing provision prohibiting the *licensee* from assigning, transferring, or *sublicensing* the license or any of its rights or obligations to any *third party* without the consent of the *licensor.*

Assignor
Party who transfers, or makes an assignment of, certain rights or interests to another party.

Associated Actors and Artists of America (The Four A's)
A cooperative alliance of six show business unions affiliated with the *AFL-CIO: Actors Equity Association (AEA), American Federation of Television and Radio Artists (AFTRA), American Guild of Variety Artists (AGVA), American Guild of Music Artists (AGMA), Screen Actors Guild (SAG),* and *Screen Extras Guild (SEG).*

Association
An unincorporated group of people or companies formed to pursue a common goal, such as protecting and promoting the interests of its members. Associations may operate either on a for-profit or nonprofit basis, but they have no legal existence independent of their members.

Association For Independent Music (AFIM)
Formerly called *National Association of Independent Record Distributors (NAIRD).* A trade organization consisting of non-major, independent record distributors and record labels. Founded in 1972, the association's mission is to strengthen the clout of *indie* operations, offering information and co-op support on marketing, promotions, advertising, and manufacturing activities. AFIM stages a convention every spring where distributors and labels can solidify relationships, exchange views, attend educational seminars, buy and sell product, etc. Located at PO Box 568, Maple Shade, NJ 08052-0568. Tel: (609) 547-3331.

Association of Independent Music Publishers (AIMP)
Located at PO Box 1561, Burbank, CA 91507. Tel: (818) 842-6257.

Assumed Name
A *pseudonym* (*aka* stage name, pen name, *non de plume*). A fictitious name adopted to hide the true identity of an author.

At Arm's Length
See *arm's length transaction.*

ATAS
Abbreviation for *Academy of Television Arts and Sciences.*

At Source
Term used to describe a method of calculating and paying royalties. It usually applies to situations where publishers or record companies *sublicense* copyrights or masters. An "at source" contract provision requires the publisher or record company to pay royalties based on all gross income earned and collected by a *licensee* (the source of the income) as opposed to calculating and paying royalties on *net receipts* (income received after the licensee has deducted its percentage).

For instance, if a songwriter's contract calls for 50% of all the publisher's net receipts, and the publisher's German *subpublisher* retains 25% of earnings in that country, then the writer would receive 50% of 75% of income earned in Germany. But, if the writer is paid based on earnings at source, and the German publisher retains 25%, the original publisher must factor the subpublisher's share back into net receipts and pay the writer 50% of all income earned in Germany. The effect is that of all earnings in Germany, the writer receives 50%, the subpublisher retains 25%, and the original publisher is left with 25%—instead of 37.5% (50% of 75%). See also *receipts-basis royalties*.

Atonality
Musical term meaning lack of central tone or key.

Attenuation
The reduction or weakening in force or volume of a sound signal with little or no distortion.

Attorney
A person qualified and licensed as a lawyer who is appointed to act for or represent another in business transactions, negotiations, and legal proceedings.

Attorney At Law
A licensed lawyer or legal counsel employed as an advocate or agent to act in legal matters.

Attorney In Fact
A lawyer employed as an agent to represent a client for specific business transactions *but not* legal matters.

Audience Share
Determination of a specific broadcast program's viewing or listening popularity derived from dividing the program's *rating* by the number of radio or television receivers in use at the time. See *Arbitron* and *Nielsen*.

Audio
(1) Sound perceived by humans. (2) A sound signal that is electronically generated, broadcast, received, or reproduced. (3) That part of an *audiovisual* recording or broadcast that contains sound.

Audio Engineering Society (AES)
Trade association comprising recording audio equipment designers, studio owners, managers, producers, engineers, and technicians. AES stages annual conventions featuring new technologies and equipment. It also presents seminars and promotes educational and training standards in recording technology. Located at 60 E. 42nd Street, Room 2520, New York, NY 10165; Tel: (212) 661-8528; Fax: (212) 682-0477.

Audio Home Recording Act
A 1992 Congressional amendment to the *Copyright Act of 1976*, requiring a 3% tax on the wholesale price of blank digital audiotapes, a 2% tax on the wholesale price of nonprofessional digital recorders, and a *serial copyright management system* (SCMS) encoded on every digital recorder so that digital copies can't be made of digital recordings. The tax provides compensation to copyright owners for *home taping* of digitally recorded product.

Two-thirds of tax revenues collected go into the *Sound Recording Fund* for distribution to copyright owners of the sound recording, featured artists, and nonfeatured backing vocalists and musicians. One-third of the tax goes into the *Musical Works Fund* for distribution to song copyright owners and songwriters. See *Digital Audio Recorders and Tape (DART)*.

Audio Visual Licensing Agency (AVLA)
Canadian *copyright collective* that licenses the exhibition and duplication of over 95% of all audio recordings and music videos produced and/or distributed in Canada over television, airline in-flight programs, video pools, etc.

Audiocassette
A magnetic *cassette* tape that records and plays back sound only.

Audiotape
A cassette or reel of *magnetic tape* that records and plays back sound only.

Audiovisual
Information, entertainment, or data presented with sound and pictures combined. Films, tapes, discs, and broadcasts containing both visual and audio information.

Audition
(1) A try-out by an artist or musician to demonstrate performing skills. (2) To evaluate a performance or a performer's talent and skill.

Audition Reel
An audiotape or a videotape of performances or songs prepared for submission to record companies, music publishers, etc. so that a performer's (or songwriter's) talent can be evaluated.

Audition Tape
See *audition reel*.

Audit
(1) To examine and verify financial records and accounts. (2) To check records of financial transactions and accounts for accuracy. (3) An adjustment or correction of financial records after examination.

Audit Trail
The tracing of accounting records and bookkeeping entries step-by-step back to their source in order to determine their accuracy by reviewing the sequence of events from which the final figures were derived.

Australian Mechanical Copyright Owners Asscociation (AMCOA)
Mechanical-right society in Australia, which also covers New Zealand, Fiji, Pacific Island Territories,

and Papua/New Guinea. Located at 14th Floor, 56 Berry Street, North Sydney, NSW 2060, Australia. Tel: (02) 954-3655; Fax: (02) 954-3664.

Australian Performing Rights Association (APRA)

Performing-right society in Australia, located at 1A Eden Street, Crows Nest, NSW 2065, Australia. Tel: (02) 922-6422.

Austro-Mechana

Mechanical-right society in Austria.

Author

(1) The originator or creator of a musical or literary work. (2) A writer, songwriter, or composer. (3) A publisher or producer who commissions someone to write a *work made for hire* and who is then designated the "author" of the work for copyright purposes, and who is thus responsible for the content of the work.

Authority

(1) The power to negotiate, transact business, enter into agreements, issue licenses, sign contracts, collect income, distribute funds, etc. (2) A person or company invested with the power to act for another party in financial and/or legal matters.

Authorship

(1) The creative source of a musical or literary work. (2) The instigator of an idea leading to the production of a creative work. (3) The commissioner of a creative *work made for hire*. (4) The assumption of responsibility for the content of a creative work. (5) The process of writing or composing.

Automated Radio

Radio station broadcasting prerecorded musical programs, usually programmed and fed from another location, as opposed to controlling material by an in-house programmer or live dee-jay.

AVLA

Abbreviation for *Audio Visual Licensing Agency*.

B
Music format abbreviation for *blues*.

BG
Music format abbreviation for *bluegrass*.

B Side
One of two sides of a *single* recording. While the A side is the track slated for promotion by the record company as the one most likely to achieve commercial success, the B side is usually a track deemed to have less obvious commercial potential. Also called the *flip side*.

B/W
Abbreviation for backed with when listing the flip or *B side* of a single recording together with the *A side*; same as *c/w* ("coupled with"). *Example*: "I Love You" *b/w* "Do You Love Me?"

Baby Act
New signing to a record company; an artist or band that is evolving from the "introductory" and "nurturing" stages of a product *life cycle* and is primed to enter the "growth" phase.

Baby Boomer
Member of the generation born between 1946 and 1964, which comprised over 75 million Americans in 1998.

Back Announce
Broadcasting segment of radio announcements and record identifications after a series of recordings has been aired uninterrupted.

Back Catalog
The non-current repertoire of songs, masters, or recordings belonging to a recording artist, songwriter, music publisher, or record company. A back catalog (or portions thereof) may still be *active* in terms of usage, popularity, and income generation.

Back End Money
The final profits, or true net, of a recording, play, film, etc., after all expenses.

Backed With (B/W)
See *b/w*.

Background Music
(1) Music played in commercial establishments to provide an ambiance or desired atmosphere, but not as primary entertainment. It is sometimes called piped music or *elevator music*. See *background music service*, below. (2) A music track without vocal overdubs. (3) Film, television, or theatrical music used to enhance a scene's action or mood, but not as the primary focus, as opposed to *foreground* music (an onscreen musical performance by a singer or musician). (4) Music used in a documentary, or advertisement, underneath a *voice-over* narration.

Background Music Service
A company, such as *Muzak*, that provides *background music* to subscribers through special broadcast links (i.e., cable, FM, or telephone lines), or on prerecorded tapes. Background music services offer dozens of different musical formats to suit different types of clients and the ambiance they want to create for their customers and/or employees. The most widely used format is *easy listening*.

Background music services typically commission

special arrangements of existing popular works and record their own versions, which require *electrical transcription licenses* from song copyright owners. Background music service firms also usually obtain master or *block licenses* from the *performing-right societies*, which require annual fees based on the number of franchised establishments where the *transcribed* programs are used. In licenses that combine both *mechanical* and *performance rights*, a specified royalty is paid per composition for each program sold or rented to users. These royalties are usually broken down as 40% representing payment for mechanical-right usage and 60% for the performance right. Thus, if the stated royalty were 5¢ per song per copy, 2¢ would cover the mechanical right and 3¢ the performance right.

Background Rendition
Also called background use, the use of a musical work in a film or television program where no one is seen onscreen performing the work. A *synchronization license fee* for a background rendition is generally less than that charged for a *foreground use*.

Background Score
Music composed to underlay a film or theatrical presentation, as opposed to a featured performance onscreen or onstage. Background scores contain mostly instrumental musical segments that set the mood of a scene, introduce scenes, segue between scenes, punctuate dramatic actions, etc.

Background Singer
A vocalist who backs up a featured or lead vocalist with harmonies, responses, and choruses onstage or on a recording. See also *session singer*.

Backing
(1) Instrumental and vocal support given to a featured performer. (2) Financial sponsorship.

Backing Band
Band of professional musicians whose primary work comes from supporting a featured performer.

Backing Card
Also called an *inlay card* or *tray card*. A card cut to be inserted in a jewel box with a booklet and *compact disc*. It contains printed material corresponding to the backside of an album cover (i.e., song titles, *bar code*, etc.), and shows through the back of the transparent jewel box.

Backward Compatibility
A new technology that is compatible with earlier technologies.

Baffles
(1) Portable soundproof partitions used to acoustically separate singers, instruments, and amplifiers in a studio or onstage in order to prevent sounds being picked up from other singers, instruments, or amplifiers. (2) Partitions used to eliminate conflicting sound waves in loudspeakers.

Balance
(1) In recording or listening, the distribution of sounds between two or more channels or speakers. (2) The blending of individual sounds, or combined groups of sounds. (2) Symmetry, equilibrium, compensation. (3) To equalize, harmonize, offset, compensate. (4) In accounting, the amount of royalties due after deductions (i.e., administration charges, recoupment of outstanding advances, etc.). (5) The amount still owed on an advance after applying royalties earned to the advance account. (6) The amount of money still owed after subtracting previous payments. (7) The bottom line of an account summary, showing profit or loss during an operating or accounting period.

Ballet
(1) An elaborately choreographed, formal dance form. (2) A theatrical dance presentation with musical accompaniment, normally including scenery, costumes, and having an underlying storyline or dramatic theme. (3) A musical work specifically composed for ballet. (4) A dance troupe formed to perform ballet.

Bankable
Descriptive term for a performer whose demonstrable popularity assures commercial success of a concert, recording, film, etc.

Banker Publisher
A music publisher who pays substantial royalty advances to acquire copyrights from established songwriters or writers having existing recording deals with guaranteed releases. The banker publisher's deal is based on the calculated commercial success of song catalogs; it is more of a financial consideration than a creative one, since less development and marketing are required to offset investment risks.

Bankruptcy
A legal judgment that a debtor is insolvent and unable to pay creditors. Under court supervision, the debtor's assets are administered for, or distributed among, the creditors. Most music business contracts contain provisions that terminate one party's obligations should the other party declare bankruptcy. There are several classes of bankruptcy, including voluntary, involuntary, business, and personal. See also *cash flow*.

Bar Band

An ensemble of professional musicians whose primary work comes from extended bookings in nightclubs, cabarets, and bars, as opposed to recordings, one-nighters, concerts, etc.

Bar Code

Also called *product code* or *universal product code*. A computer coding system used for inventory control, to identify products and customer accounts, and to track and facilitate delivery of mail and packages. Bar codes are patterns of vertical lines or bars representing a string of unique identifying numbers or letters that are assigned to each product, account, or mailing piece. Bar codes are read by computer-linked optical scanners, which provide and record information, such as price or quantity sold, etc. Most retailers require manufacturers to supply product with bar codes so that inventory control, pricing, and sales can be tabulated by in-house databases.

Base Price to Dealer (BPD)

A method of calculating royalties (to artists, music publishers, etc.) formulated on a percentage of the price retailers pay to buy recorded product from the manufacturer or distributor. Many countries outside of the United States and Canada have abandoned the concept of allowing a manufacturer to establish, suggest, or recommend a retail selling price. Therefore, many overseas licensing agreements provide for royalty payments calculated on the base price (per unit) to dealers.

Basic Cable

Standard range of *cable television* channels offered to subscribers by a local cable television company. Subscribers may elect to upgrade this service upon additional subscription payments to receive various *premium channels* (HBO, Disney, et al) and even more sophisticated services, such as interactive *Videotex* communication and information channels, burglar- and fire-alarm protection, and radio reception. See also *cable television* and *community antenna television*.

Basic Track

A foundation *track*, or group of tracks, laid down in a recording session by rhythm musicians, which will be used later to overdub vocals, *sweetening*, etc. Also called *rhythm track*.

Bassing

Street slang term for turning up the volume on a radio, tape player, stereo, etc., particularly increasing the sound of the bass.

BBS

Abbreviation for (electronic) *bulletin board service*.

BDS

Abbreviation for *Broadcast Data System*.

Beat Frequency

Term used in musical acoustics to describe the fluctuating sound made when two or more notes of roughly equal pitch are played simultaneously. The beat frequency between the two sound waves equals the difference in the frequency of the notes.

Beat Sheet

A scene-by-scene production summary of a television show or film.

Beats per Minute (BPM)

A unit of measure used to set the tempo of a musical performance, or to measure the rhythmic pace of a recording, especially of recordings produced for the *dance* or *disco* market.

Beaux Arts

Same as *fine arts*. Those art forms used as creative expressions of beauty or aesthetics, rather than for practical application. Examples include music, poetry, painting, sculpture, etc.

Bed

Term used by ad agencies and broadcasters to describe the music background for commercial advertisements.

Below the Line Expenses

Budgeted production costs for studio and equipment rental and supplies, union scale payments to musicians, copyists, technicians, etc. See also *above the line expenses*.

Belt

Term used to describe an energetic vocal performance (to "belt out a song").

Benchmark

A recognized measure or *standard* by which something may be compared for quantity, quality, or value.

Beneficiary

One that receives, or has the right to receive, monies, property, or other benefits from a will, insurance policy, or assignment of interests, etc. See also renewal assignment.

Benelux

Acronym for the economic union of *Belgium*, the *Netherlands*, and *Luxembourg*. In overseas copyright licensing situations, the three countries are usually grouped as one territory.

Berliner, Emile (1851-1929)

German-American inventor of the *Gramophone* and a method of duplicating disk records in 1887. See also *Edison*, *Thomas* and *Phonograph*.

Berne Convention (Berne Union)

Named after the capital of Switzerland where it was held, and which is the seat of the *International Copyright Union*, the Berne Convention or Union is one of three major international copyright treaties (see also *Universal Copyright Convention* and *Buenos Aires Convention*). The full title of the Berne Convention is the "Berne Convention for the Protection of Literary and Artistic Works."

The United States joined the Berne Convention effective March 1, 1989, and from that date US copyrights are automatically protected in all member nations of the Berne Union. Likewise, foreign copyrights owned by nationals of any other country belonging to the Berne Union are automatically protected in the United States.

While US copyright law continues to govern the protection and registration of works in the United States, joining the Berne Union required certain changes in US copyright law. These changes are not retroactive and are effective only with regards to works created on and after March 1, 1989. One of the more notable changes deals with requirements for a *copyright notice* on published materials in order to affect copyright protection.

For detailed information about the amendments to US copyright law under the Berne Convention agreement, request circulars 93, "Highlights of US Adherence to the Berne Convention," and 93a, "The United States Joins The Berne Union" from the *Copyright Office*. See also *Berne Convention Implementation Act of 1988*, *copyright*, *Copyright Act of 1976*, and *copyright notice*.

Berne Convention Implementation Act of 1988

An act passed by the US Congress in order to comply with terms of the *Berne Convention*. The act made certain changes in the United States copyright law. These changes are not retroactive and are effective only on and after March 1st, 1989. For detailed information about the amendments to US copyright law under the Berne Convention agreement, request circulars 93, "Highlights of US Adherence to the Berne Convention," and 93a, "The United States Joins The Berne Union" from the Copyright Office. See also *Berne Convention*, *copyright*, *Copyright Act of 1976*, and *copyright notice*.

Best Boy

A *gofer*-type assistant on a film production crew.

Best Edition

The *1976 Copyright Act* requires copyright claimants to deposit two copies of the "best edition" of a published work with the Library of Congress within three months of publication date. A best edition is a copy of the commercially published format at the time of copyright registration-i.e., printed sheet music as opposed to a handwritten *lead sheet*, or a commercially released disc as opposed to a *demo* tape. (A compact disc would be considered the best edition if a song or recording was published simultaneously on audiocassette.)

Best Efforts

A contractual agreement by a party to do its best to achieve some goal or perform some act, without an absolute guarantee that the goal will be achieved or the act performed. *Examples*: An attorney may promise "best efforts" to secure a recording deal for a client; a record company may promise its best efforts to promote a release nationally; a booking agent may promise its best efforts to get bookings for an act at or above a stated price.

Best Of

Similar to a *greatest hits compilation*: an album collection of songs or recordings by one or more artists, containing the top-selling songs or recordings by that artist or those artists. May also pertain to an album collection of songs or recordings representing a genre, era, theme, etc., such as "best of bluegrass banjo music" or "best of Irish drinking songs."

Best of Knowledge

A qualified representation or warranty. Rather than a statement of fact, an assertion in a contract or license that something is true "to the best of my knowledge" leaves a degree of ambiguity which may not be acceptable to the party to whom the statement is made.

BET

Abbreviation for *Black Entertainment Television*.

Beta

Abbreviated reference for *Betamax*, a half-inch videocassette format that is encased in a smaller cassette than the now-standard *VHS* format.

Beta Test

Hands-on testing of a new technology product, such as computer hardware or software, in order to find and eliminate any previously undiscovered glitches or bugs before the product is mass-marketed to consumers.

Betamax

A half-inch videocassette format that is encased in a smaller cassette than the now-standard *VHS* format. Betamax was introduced by the Sony Corp., and was ultimately overshadowed in the American marketplace by consumer preference for the *VHS* videocassette format introduced by JVC.

Bias

In recording, the amount of fixed voltage applied to an electrode in order to establish a reference level. Bias is the adjustment of the strength of a magnetic field applied during the recording process to a *magnetic tape*. High-frequency voltage combined with an audio signal reduces distortion in tape recording. See also *ferric*, *high bias*, and *normal bias*.

Bid

(1) A contract offer or deal proposal, particularly with regard to the financial terms thereof. (2) A firm offer or proposal. (3) The financial terms of an offered deal. (4) To make a firm offer or proposal in competition with others.

Bidding War

Fierce competition between two or more companies to acquire the services or copyrights of a third party, causing the competing companies to try and outbid each other, thus driving up the price of the deal. See also *buzz band*.

BIEM

Acronym for *Bureau International des Societies Gerant les Droits D'Enregistrement et de Reproduction Mecanique*.

Big Band

(1) Pertaining to an era (c.1930s) when popular music was dominated by dance orchestras led by musicians such as Glenn Miller, Tommy Dorsey, Benny Goodman, Harry James, etc. (2) The genre of orchestrated *swing music* popularized by the "big bands."

Bilateral Agreement

A mutually beneficial or reciprocal agreement between two parties that is equally binding on both.

Bill

(1) A detailed list of charges or fees for goods sold, services rendered, or damages caused. (2) To submit for payment an itemized statement of such charges, damages, or fees. (3) A listing of performers appearing in concert or entertainment offered by a theater, cabaret, etc. (4) To place the name of an act or performer on a concert program, or on an advertisement for a concert, etc. (5) A publicly displayed poster, notice, or advertisement. (6) A legislative proposal or law enacted. (7) A list of formal complaints or particulars presented to a court, representing a case submitted for judicial consideration.

Billboard

(1) A large outdoor display panel for advertisements. (2) A list of highlighted features to be found in a program, magazine, or broadcast.

Billboard

A weekly *trade magazine* for the music industry, located at 1515 Broadway, 39th Floor, New York, NY 10036. Tel: (212) 764-7300; Fax: (212) 536-5358.

Billboard Information Network (BIN)

An online database service operated by the publisher of *Billboard* magazine. Information includes radio playlists; a weekly electronic newsletter; advance sight of all US and European Billboard charts the Friday before newsstand distribution of the magazine; availability of territorial music publishing rights to all charted songs; national and regional record sales reports; rental, club, and airplay activity on audio and video releases; and chart share reports for labels and artists. Located at 1515 Broadway, New York, NY 10036. Tel: (212) 536-5319 or (212) 536-5040; Fax: (212) 536-5351.

Billboard International Buyers Guide

A trade directory for the music industry published annually by Billboard magazine. Listings include companies in all major countries involved in record manufacturing, distribution, recording, video production, music publishing, etc., along with their principle executives, addresses, branch locations, fax and telephone numbers, e-mail addresses, web sites, etc.

Billboard Online

An online service offered by the publisher of *Billboard* magazine, providing access to text and chart data from past and current issues of *Billboard* magazine. Subscribers can scroll through headlines to find subjects of interest. More efficiently, subscribers can search for keywords such as the name of a company, artist, industry issue, or product. Full text or charts can be downloaded.

Information offered includes 15 categories of singles charts, 7 album charts, 5 video charts, and 2 European charts, all covering airplay and sales. Subscribers can search *RIAA* statistics and consumer profile information, and find all RIAA-certified *gold* and *platinum* audio and video releases since 1958.

Also available are *box office* and touring data, regional breakout charts (searchable by artist, title, label), and creative and production credits for music videos. The text archives go back to the beginning of

1991; the charts go back to 1985. The archives are updated weekly. New editions of *Billboard* are available electronically each Friday prior to newsstand distribution. Located at Billboard Electronic Publishing, 1515 Broadway, New York, NY 10036. Tel: (800) 449-1402 or (212) 536-5341. Fax: (212) 536-5310.

Billing

(1) A detailed list of charges or fees for goods sold, services rendered, or damages caused. (2) The submission for payment of an itemized statement of such charges, damages, or fees. (3) A listing of performers appearing in concert or entertainments offered by a theater, cabaret, etc. (4) The placing of the name of an act or performer on a concert program, or advertisement for a concert, etc.

BIN

Acronym for *Billboard Information Network*.

Bin

A divided or partitioned container for display storage of recorded product in retail stores.

Bin Card

A divider card placed in *bins* for recorded product in order to identify the specific musical genre contained in that section of the bin and/or the name of an artist whose product is contained therein.

Bin-Loop

A *high-speed duplication system* used to mass-produce audiocassettes. The master tape is spliced *heads to tails* to form a loop. Blank tape is loaded onto large pancake reels. As the master tape plays, the sound is transferred to the blank tape. A tone signals the start and stop of the master recording, so that the copies are automatically cut and loaded into individual cassette shells. See also *in-cassette duplication*.

Binary

A number system usually associated with computer code, consisting of combinations of only two digits, 0 and 1. Binary code is used in digital sound recordings. For instance, digital information is etched onto the surface of a compact disc in the form of microscopic pits, which are read optically by a laser beam passing over the disc.

Bind

(1) To legally compel or obligate by virtue of contract or license. (2) To secure pages of a book, folio, proposal, or report (or the front and back covers of an album), with a *binding*.

Binding

(1) A legally enforceable obligation. (2) An action that *binds* one to an agreement or obligation, such as the signature to a contract or license. (3) A cover that secures or holds pages of a book, folio, proposal, or report (or the front and back covers of an album). (4) The strip along the edge of a book, folio, report, proposal, or album cover that protects and reinforces the contents.

Bio

Slang for *Biography*.

Biography

An account of professional accomplishments, usually fleshed out with personal anecdotal information to present a profile for publicity purposes, as opposed to a *résumé*, which is a brief summary of professional qualifications, experience, and accomplishments only.

Black Box

Term used to describe the disposition of copyright royalties collected by overseas rights societies when the society can not identify to whom the copyrights belong. If a foreign society can not identify a song's owner, royalties earned by the work are put into escrow (the "black box"). Monies accumulated in the black box are held until such time as (1) the copyright owners are identified and paid, or (2) the royalties are declared unclaimed, and are distributed to that society's own members. See *Warsaw Rule*.

Black Entertainment Television (BET)

A cable-only television channel featuring music, news, interviews, documentaries, and commentary geared to the interests of African-Americans. Headquartered at 1232 31st Street NW, Washington, DC 20007. Tel: (202) 337-5260; Fax: (202) 342-7882.

Black Music

Catch-all designation for music created by and appealing to African-Americans; variously called R&B, soul, and urban contemporary.

Black Rock Coalition (BRC)

Association of African-American musicians formed in 1985 to promote opportunities and audiences for rock music performed by Black musicians.

Blacklist

The AFM "defaulters list" published monthly in *International Musician*, warning union members not to accept work from the listed individuals and companies who have failed to pay agreed wages, dues, or fees to other union members. Union members who work with defaulters are subject to fines or other disciplinary action.

Blanket Catalog Agreement

A contract or license between a copyright owner and a music user, distributor, subpublisher, producer, or manufacturer, etc. covering all works in the copyright owner's catalog. Such an agreement may be *exclusive*, as in the case of a *subpublishing* agreement, or *non-exclusive*, as in the case of *blanket licenses* issued by *performing-right societies* to radio stations. See *blanket license*, below.

Blanket License

License issued by a copyright holder to a music *user* that applies to several or all of the copyright holders' works, covering all instances in which the works may be used and under what conditions or terms. *Example*: *Performing-right societies* issue blanket licenses to broadcasters and venues where music is used or performed, which permit licensees to use or perform any work in the society's repertoire, so that the user doesn't have to seek individual permissions for each and every title. Blanket license performance fees for broadcasters and some other types of music users are based on a percentage of the adjusted gross receipts of the user.

Bleed

(1) In broadcasting or recording, leakage occurring when sound emanating from one source (i.e., an instrument or amplifier) is picked up by a microphone placed to pick up sound from another source. (2) In printing, a method of printing that carries artwork off the edge or edges of a page after trimming.

Bloc

(1) Group of countries treated as one territory for licensing purposes. See also *block*, below. (2) A group of individuals, companies, and/or organizations who join together to support or promote a common interest or goal, usually through political lobbying. *Example*: authors, composers, songwriters, music publishers, book publishers, record companies, et al, lobbying for copyright reform legislation.

Block

(1) A grouping of related or similar items, treated, licensed, or sold as a single unit. *Examples*: shares of stock, copyright repertoire, etc. (2) A group of countries treated as one territory for licensing purposes. See *English Block* and *Continental Block*. (3) To bar, stop, prohibit, or prevent something from happening. *Example*: an injunction to prevent the release of a record because of a contract dispute.

Block License

A license covering the entire *repertoire* of the *licensor* (or a number of works identified in the license), so that the *licensee* can use any work in that repertoire under terms covered by the license, without having to negotiate numerous, separate licenses for individual works in the same repertoire. Also called *blanket license* and *master license*.

Background music service firms, such as *Muzak*, usually obtain a master or block license from *performing-right societies*, which enables them to use virtually any work in the performing-right societies' repertoire without having to locate innumerable copyright owners to negotiate individual licenses for specific works.

Block Rate

An agreement between a *licensor* and *licensee* whereby the licensee pays one stated royalty rate for all copyrights covered by, and used under the terms of, the agreement.

Blockbuster

A song or recording that dominates sales and airplay charts in a given period.

Blue Note

The slight, intentional flattening of a musical pitch (usually the 3rd or 7th note on a scale) by a vocalist or instrumentalist in order to achieve a "bluesy" effect. See also *blues*.

Blue Screen

A monochromatic screen used as a performer's backdrop in video, film, or television production when the performer's image is to be later superimposed on a scene filmed or taped elsewhere.

Bluebird

Term sometimes used by music publishers in reference to a licensing request for a song that comes without any marketing effort by the publisher. Usually, this happens with *standards* or *evergreens* (hit songs that have been *covered* by numerous artists over time), which tend to perpetuate their own momentum in the marketplace. Ad agencies, artists, record producers, and audiovisual producers frequently decide to use one of these works on their own initiative, without any marketing effort by the publisher. When these unexpected but welcome usages occur, they are like the bluebirds in the old Disney film "Song of the South" that land, unbidden, on Uncle Remus's shoulder.

Bluegrass

Style of music originating in the southeastern United States from folk music traditions of Scotch-Irish settlers, featuring uptempo, improvisational performances on banjos, guitars, fiddles, and/or mandolins.

Blueline Proof

A blue printer's proof of artwork negatives made on photosensitive paper showing placement and size of images, type, cuts, and folds, as well as color separations markings. The proof is submitted to the printer's client for final checking before the artwork is printed.

Blues

Type of music originating in the southeastern United States from Black American folk traditions and life experiences, usually featuring a 12-bar construction of moderate to slow tempos. Lyrically, blues songs tend to reflect the downside of life (i.e., unhappiness in love, work, income, etc.) and are expressed in pithy, earthy language. See also *blue note*.

Blurb

Advertising term referring to personal endorsements, testimonials, quotes from favorable reviews or satisfied customers, publicity notices, and copy appearing on book jackets, album covers, and other merchandise packaging designed to promote a product.

BMDA

The *performing-right society* in Morocco.

BMI

Abbreviation for *Broadcast Music, Inc.*

Board

The *console* or *desk* in a recording studio that hosts the sound recording, routing, and mixing controls operated by recording engineers.

Board of Directors

A group elected and empowered by shareholders of a corporation to appoint and oversee senior management, authorize issuance of additional shares, declare dividends, etc. The composition of a board usually includes the most senior corporate executives (called "inside directors"), and frequently includes "outside directors" with expertise in other businesses that may be useful in advancing the corporation's interests. Directors are ultimately responsible to shareholders for the success of the corporation.

Bobbybrown

Street slang term for leaving a band or group to go solo.

Bof

Slang for "best of," as in a compilation album of an artist's biggest hits.

Boilerplate

Term for language contained in standard provisions of most contracts, which rarely cause controversy or need for negotiation. See also *whereas clause*, *recital*, and *legalese*.

Bomb

(1) In the United States: a flop, failure, dud. (2) In Great Britain: a smash, a huge success.

Bona Fide

Good faith. A bona fide offer is one that is genuine, sincere. Something that is bona fide is genuine, authentic, not counterfeit, fraudulent, forged, or deceitful.

Bona Fides

Evidence of authenticity, good faith, or genuineness.

Bonus

A reward, an incentive payment, a premium. See *signing bonus*, *bonus payment*, and *bonus record*.

Bonus Payment (BMI/ASCAP)

In addition to distributing performance royalties to music publishers and songwriters, BMI and ASCAP award bonus payments for songs that receive a certain number of broadcasting plays. The BMI bonus formula ranges from 1.5-times base rate for works receiving 25,000 plays to 4-times base rate when a work has achieved 1 million plays. ASCAP songwriters and music publishers receive bonus awards that amount to roughly an additional 44% for songs that log more than 5,000 feature radio performances in any one quarter.

Bonus Record

A free recording given to *record club* members for purchasing a certain number of other recordings at full club price. While record company contracts generally specify that artist royalties will not be paid on records given away for free, this agreement is usually narrowed to apply to those records given away for promotional and sales incentive purposes. With regards to bonus records given away by record clubs, however, record companies are more willing to negotiate some form of royalty compensation, such as 50% of the normal royalty rate.

Book

(1) To engage an entertainer or entertainment act for a performance. (2) To hire a studio or other facility for a recording or performance. (3) To reserve time. (4) To schedule an appearance or make an appointment. (5) A script or *libretto* of a play.

Booking

(1) A scheduled appointment, appearance, or performance. (2) Time reserved.

Booking Agency

An agent or service authorized to represent performers in booking personal appearances. Its function is much like that of an employment agency, finding work, negotiating terms of engagements, administering the flow of contracts for appearances, etc. It is compensated by the performer with a commission based on a percentage of each engagement fee. See also *talent agency*.

Book Value

The value of an asset as shown on a balance sheet, and which is the cost of the asset less any accumulated depreciation. Book value thus accounts for the cost of asset acquisition and usage, and does not reflect the asset's value to the company, its cost of replacement, or its *market value* (what the asset might bring on the open market).

Booklet

In CD packaging, a small book of four or more pages cut to be inserted in a *jewel box* with an *inlay card* and *compact disc*. The first page contains album cover artwork and shows through the front of the transparent jewel box. Additional pages contain album credits, song titles, playing times, copyright information, and additional information, such as liner notes, biographical data, lyrics, etc.

Boom

An overhead microphone, supported by a tube-like, telescoping arm extending from a stand or tripod.

Bootleg

(1) To make, produce, distribute, sell, or transport copyrighted product (such as recordings or videos) without permission. (2) To record performances and reproduce copies of the recording for sale without compensation to, or permission from, the performer. (3) A copyrighted product or performance that is reproduced and sold without compensation to, or permission from, the copyright owner or performer. See also *counterfeit* and *piracy*.

Bottom Line

(1) Entry at end of a financial statement that shows whether there is profit or loss in a venture. (2) The end result; the last word. (3) The upshot of one's efforts.

Bounce-Back Card

A self-addressed, stamped postcard-sized *response card* included with mailouts of promo recordings, especially those sent to radio stations. Typical bounce-back cards request the program director or music director to return the card indicating whether or not the recording has been added to the station playlist. Other information may also be requested on the card, such as whether the station reports to any trade magazines, names of personnel to whom future promo copies should be sent, etc. See also *response card*.

Boutique

Term originally used for a small specialty shop or department in a large store, but now also applicable to a small specialized business. For instance, a boutique record label, which may either be independently owned and operated, or set up as a division of a larger company to focus on a certain genre or market segment, or as an outlet for the work of one producer.

Box Office

A ticket office; place where admission to concerts and other events is purchased. The term is also applied to describe the appeal of a concert or tour in terms of revenue raised by ticket sales ("big box office receipts").

Boxed Set

A cardboard box (often an anthology) holding two or more discs or cassettes packaged together with a book or *booklet*. CDs and cassettes contained inside boxed sets generally are also individually packaged in *jewel boxes* or cassette cases.

BPD

Abbreviation for *base price to dealer*.

BPI

Abbreviation for *British Phonographic Industry*.

BPM

Abbreviation for *beats per minute*.

Branch Operation

(1) A wholly-owned subsidiary established by a record company as a separate business entity for the purpose of distributing product. A major record company's branch operations may distribute product from other labels as well as that of the parent company. Branch operations are normally structured to operate on two levels: regional promotion and sales. The promotions division employs promotion people to coordinate marketing activities with staff promotion personnel of the distributed labels. The sales division employs salespeople or *route people* to service retail accounts in the territory. (2) A wholly-owned subsidiary established by a domestic record company in an overseas location to coordinate overseas releases of domestic product in the territory and to acquire local product. Typically, overseas branch operations maintain *A&R*, *marketing*, and *administrative* functions while entering into *P&D* arrangements with local record companies for manufacturing and distribution.

Brand

(1) A *trade name* or *trademark* used to identify a product, product line, service, or manufacturer. (2) A type or category, as in "brand of music."

Brand Name

A name (which may or may not be *trademarked*) under which a company operates, which identifies a product or service, or by which a service or process is known to the trade.

Brass

(1) Generic reference for wind instruments (also called *horns*), although, technically, the term should only apply to the group of wind instruments made from brass or some other metal, and using metal-cup mouthpieces (i.e., trumpets, trombones). (2) Slang for top management of a corporation.

BRC

Abbreviation for *Black Rock Coalition*.

Breach

(1) To break a contract, promise, agreement, or obligation by acting contrary to what was agreed. (2) The failure to fulfill an agreed obligation, duty, or promise.

Breach of Contract

The failure to fulfill a contractual obligation, duty, or promise or by acting contrary to what was agreed.

Break

(1) An opportunity. (2) Unexpected good luck. (3) An intermission; an interruption, pause, or interval in a piece of music, performance, or broadcast. (4) A commercial announcement that interrupts a broadcast. (5) A rest during a rehearsal. (6) A musical improvisation taken by a solo instrument between the arranged sections of a melody (i.e., a sax break). (7) A favorable price reduction. (8) A breach of contract or severing of ties. (9) A break-even point at which a film or recording recovers costs and begins to make a profit for the distributor.

Breakage

A contractual allowance for product loss or damage. *Example*: a record company pays artists' royalties on 90% of sales; the remaining 10% represents allowances for "breakage" (product lost, warped, or broken in storage or shipment and/or product shipped on credit that has to be written off for nonpayment).

Break Dance

A vigorous, gymnastic style of dancing usually associated with, or performed to, the accompaniment of *Rap* or contemporary *Urban* music.

Break Down

(1) To divide into sections or parts for analysis. (2) A segment in a live musical performance where the volume is lowered in order to feature a particular instrument or voice.

Break Out

A commercially released recording seeing chart and sales activity in a regional area, indicating sufficient popular acceptance to pyramid similar success in other regions.

Break Through

To gain notice. To achieve commercial success or popularity.

Bridge

Musical term referring to the passage between a chorus or *hook* and a verse, or between a hook and a repeat of the hook; a transitional passage between two sections of a song. Also called a *middle eight*.

Brill Building

Building located at 49th Street and Broadway in New York City where several record labels and music publishers operated during the *Tin Pan Alley* era. The building was a hive of hitmaking activity during the 1950s and '60s, generating hits from artists, songwriters, and producers like Carole King, Neil Diamond, Phil Spector, et al.

Bristol Sound, The

Descriptive characteristic of those artists and music styles associated with the port city of Bristol in southwestern England, which is considered a breeding ground for various Jamaican-oriented musical genres, such as *drum-n-bass* and *trip-hop*.

British Institute of Recorded Sound

Now called *National Sound Archive*, a British organization founded in 1948 as an archival depository for sound recordings. The organization's mission is to obtain, catalog, and preserve copies of every recording produced in every genre, and to make them available for research.

British Invasion

Term associated with the period of 1964 - 1966 when numerous British bands led by the Beatles overwhelmed American charts and radio airplay, influencing Pop styles and youth culture.

British Phonographic Industry (BPI)

Trade association for record companies in the United Kingdom, formed to advance and protect the interests of its 200 members, which collectively generate over 90% of record sales in the UK.

BritPop

A British music genre and lifestyle surfacing in the mid-1990s as a reaction to American-oriented *grunge* culture. Termed the "British music renaissance," mainstream BritPop acts were reminiscent of earlier British bands like the Beatles and Rolling Stones.

Broad Rights

A comprehensive package of rights covering the use of a copyright in a variety of interrelated usages. For instance, a motion picture producer negotiating a *synchronization license* with a music publisher to use a song in a film will seek broad rights allowing the song to be exhibited, as part of the completed film, in all media, including *free television*, *cable*, satellite and pay television, and promotional clips.

Broadcast

(1) To send out, transmit, or communicate information, news, or entertainment to the general public by means of radio or television. (2) To publish or make known over a wide area. (3) To *air* a program, performance, message, or recording. (4) A program aired on radio or television. (5) A radio or television signal transmitted to the general public. (6) To take part in a radio or television program.

Broadcast Data System (BDS)

Billboard magazine *online* service that monitors radio, television, and cable *broadcasts* nationally and instantaneously updates a central databank as songs, records, videos, and commercials are aired. Through this service, labels, publishers, managers, producers, and others associated with a particular release can get the details of each play.

BDS generates reports that include specific stations playing a song, their locations, the size of the listening audience, the dates and times of each play, and the recording's ranking on each station's *playlist* during the reporting period. BDS offers tailored summaries of stations adding a release during the current period, the number of stations dropping it from their playlists, the total number of stations playing it, and the total number of plays it received.

Because the airplay reports are 100% accurate and up-to-the-minute, they can be used to find out exactly what's being played where and when. Thus, informed decisions can be made about deployment of promotion and marketing resources with maximum effect; and the results of those promotion and marketing efforts can be quickly evaluated.

BDS subscribers can order a variety of individually tailored reports, including: (1) Song Activity Report, (2) Song By Station Report, (3) Song By Daypart Report, (4) Station Logs, (5) Station Playlists, (6) Video Logs, (7) Video Playlists, (8) National Airplay Chart, (9) Hot 40 Markets, (10) Market Activity Report, and (11) Artist Activity Report.

BDS has had an impact on the way labels use independent promoters to get records added to radio station playlists. Because BDS reports the exact date and time of each play on over 550 radio stations in more than 100 markets (with more being added), label execs can monitor and verify the results of promoters' efforts. Accordingly, some labels now pay promoters by the number of actual *plays*, rather than by the number of *adds*.

BDS is located at Billboard Electronic Publishing, 1515 Broadway, New York, NY 10036. Tel: (800) 449-1402 or (212) 536-5349; Fax: (212) 536-5312.

Broadcast Music, Inc. (BMI)

One of three American *performing-right societies*. (ASCAP and SESAC are the others.) BMI was founded in 1939 by radio station owners to break ASCAP's virtual monopoly on rights to perform copyrighted song material. BMI now represents more than 140,000 writers and publishers (called affiliates), collecting more than $300 million annually in performance royalties from broadcasters, jukebox operators, and venues where music is played or performed. Together, ASCAP and BMI license the performing rights for approximately 99% of all song copyright repertoire in the United States. As a nonprofit organization, BMI retains an average 18% of its gross collections for administrative overhead and distributes the balance to affiliates. Located at 320 West 57 Street, New York, NY 10019. Tel: (212) 586-2000.

Broadcaster

(1) A company that operates a radio or television station, or network of stations. (2) A person who announces or produces programs over radio or television.

Broadway

The premiere US theater district, located on the West Side of midtown Manhattan in New York City. Also known as the "Great White Way" because of the vast array of flashing electric lights, signs, billboards, and theater marquees.

Broadway Musical

A dramatic play set to music, produced on *Broadway*, and usually staged with choreography, costumes, and scenery, and characterized by catchy, memorable songs with lyrics interwoven into the storyline. See also *musical*, *musical comedy*, *dramatic performance*, and *grand rights*.

BSDA

The *performing-right society* in Senegal.

Bubbling Under

Term used for commercially released recordings primed to enter the *Billboard* Top 100 singles and albums *charts*.

Budget

(1) An itemized list of projected or intended expenditures for a specific project or period of business operations. (2) A proposal or plan for financing a specific project or period of business operations.

(3) The total sum of money set aside to finance a specific project or a period of business operations. See also *recording budget* and *recording fund*.

Budget Album

Also called "budget line." A recorded album marketed at less than 75% of the customary retail price of *full line* or *top line* albums. Budget albums usually consist of *sound-alikes*, or of older, previously released material, and/or *compilations* of material by different artists. Record company contracts with artists often provide that artist royalties for budget album releases will be based on around 50% to 66-2/3% of the royalty paid on top line albums. See also *midline album*.

Buenos Aires Convention

A multilateral treaty signed in 1910 by the United States and the nations of Central and South America that provides copyright protection in all member countries for any work meeting copyright requirements in any of the other *signatory* countries. For copyright protection under terms of the treaty, the statement "All Rights Reserved" should be included in the *copyright notice*. See also *Berne Convention* and *Universal Copyright Convention*.

Buff

An enthusiastic follower, an *aficionado*, a devotee, or a fan.

Buffalo Broadcasting Case

A lawsuit filed against *BMI* and *ASCAP* alleging that the *performing-right societies'* requirements that local television stations obtain *blanket licenses* to use music in the societies' *repertoires* constituted an unreasonable restraint of trade in violation of antitrust laws. The *plaintiff* wanted the freedom to negotiate individual performing-right licenses directly from copyright owners (see *source license* and *direct license*). The court found in favor of the plaintiff in 1982, effectively barring ASCAP and BMI from licensing music for local television. The decision was immediately appealed, because local television generated approximately 33% of performance royalty collections. Pending the appeal's outcome, BMI and ASCAP ended the practice of paying royalty advances to music publishers and songwriters, to offset the potential financial setback. Though the appeal was won in 1984, and the lower court's decision was reversed, neither BMI nor ASCAP has resumed paying advances.

Bullet

A symbol (•) used by *Billboard* magazine to indicate significant sales and/or airplay activity by specific recordings listed in the publication's best-seller charts. The bullet is placed on the left side of the title listing on the charts for each recording that has generated such activity.

Bulletin Board Service (BBS)

An online computer network, generally catering to users who share specific interests. Using modems, BBS subscribers or patrons dial into the network in order to exchange e-mail, post information, or download information or software programs. See also *transmission* and *reproduction license*.

BUMA

The *performing-right society* in The Netherlands.

Bundle of Rights

Five specific rights inherent in copyright ownership. These rights are automatically vested in the author or creator of the work, and include the rights to (1) *reproduce* copies of the work (i.e., sheet music, phonorecords, etc.), (2) *distribute* copies of the work to the public by sale, rental, lease, or lending, (3) *prepare derivative* works (adaptations, translations, arrangements, dramatizations, etc.), (4) *perform* the work publicly, and (5) *display* the work publicly.

A songwriter owns this bundle of rights by virtue of, and immediately upon, writing a song. Only the copyright owner may make and sell copies of the song-or authorize others to do so-in any format existing now or hereafter. Only the copyright owner may use or perform-or authorize others to use or perform-the song live, on film, radio, television or by any other method existing now or in the future.

When a songwriter assigns the bundle of rights by contract to a music publisher, the publisher in effect acquires every conceivable right in the territory covered by the agreement to use, license, and authorize the use of the song, or any part of the song (including title, lyrics, melody, chorus, storyline, etc.), for every conceivable purpose in any conceivable media or technology whether existing now or in the future.

Bureau International des Societies Gerant les Droits D'Enregistrement et de Reproduction Mecanique (BIEM)

An international organization of *mechanical-right societies* from 30 countries, which meets to arbitrate issues between societies, and to promote and protect the international interests of copyright owners where mechanical rights are concerned. BIEM negotiates mechanical royalties and mechanical-licensing terms with the *IFPI* for most of Europe and Latin America, though not for the United States, the United Kingdom, or Canada.

BURIDA

The *performing-right society* in the Ivory Coast.

Burlesque

(1) A theatrical entertainment featuring short comic skits and sometimes striptease acts. (2) A musical work or parody written for such a theatrical entertainment. (3) A literary work employing humorous exaggeration, mockery, ridicule, and caricature.

Business Affairs Department

Division of a company responsible for negotiating and administering contracts and licenses, and for corporate matters (legal, insurance, financial, taxation, governmental regulatory compliances, etc.).

Business Manager

Person who looks after the business affairs of a recording artist, producer, or songwriter. Functions include oversight of bookkeeping and accounting, collecting income, auditing, investment advice, insurance, business and personal budgeting and tax planning, etc. See also *personal manager*.

Buyer

See chain *buyer*, *talent buyer*, and *time buyer*.

Buyout

(1) An outright purchase of the rights to use a copyright in a particular manner, as opposed to paying royalties based on *per use* or *per unit* sale of *derivative works*. (2) The purchase of a contract. An artist, for instance, might buy back his or her contract from a record company in order to sign with another label. See *buyout rights*, below. Also see *cash pay-out* and *contingent pay-out*.

Buyout Rights

In an exclusive contract, a provision giving an artist, songwriter, producer, etc., the right to repay any unrecouped advances and terminate the agreement. Buyout rights might also be contingent upon other contractually stated provisions, such as paying interest on the amount of the unrecouped advance, paying a premium over and above the unrecouped advance, paying for unsold inventory, etc. Buyout payments are frequently made by other companies wishing to acquire the exclusive services of an artist, songwriter, or producer seeking to get out of his or her current obligations. Therefore, buyout provisions are usually coupled with *matching rights* or *rights of first refusal*, which gives companies the right to match any third-party offer.

Buzz Band

An unsigned recording act being pursued by several record labels. Competition between labels to sign an act creates a *bidding war* and gives the act negotiating clout to demand bigger advances, higher royalty rates, and other contractual concessions, such as guaranteed *tour support*, *reversion of masters*, *creative control*, nonrecoupable marketing expenditures, more favorable *mechanical royalty* rates (see *controlled composition*), etc.

C
Music format abbreviation for *country*.

C/W
Abbreviation for *coupled with* when listing the *flip side* of a *single* recording together with the *A side*. *Example*: "I Love You" *c/w* "Do You Love Me?" Same as *b/w* (*backed with*).

C&W
Music format abbreviation for *country & western*.

CA Form
Form supplied by the *Copyright Office* for filing corrections or additional information about copyright claims previously registered. See *copyright formalities* and *copyright registration*.

Cabaret
(1) A nightclub or restaurant that features live *floor shows* and *variety* acts. (2) A type of live act appearing in nightclub floor shows.

Cable Television
A method of television broadcasting that transmits programming to paid subscribers via either coaxial or fiber-optic cable instead of through the airwaves, thus eliminating the need for antenna reception and reducing atmospheric interference. Originally, cable served mostly rural areas where local broadcasting was nonexistent or reception was poor. However, since the mid-1970s, with newer technologies, government deregulation, and expanded programming, cable broadcasting has become the predominate method of home television reception. In addition to providing local television programming, cable services offer additional cable-only channels featuring movies, music, sports, news, weather, home-shopping, entertainment, documentaries, pay-per-view, and interactive information services. See also *basic cable* and *community antenna television*.

Cablecast
A television broadcast via cable transmission.

Cablevision
See *community antenna television*.

Cadence
(1) A measured beat, flow, or rhythmic balance in the performance of music, recitation of poetry, or delivery of a speech. (2) A musical chord progression or resolution ending a phrase, verse, chorus, or section of a work.

Calibrate
(1) In recording, to check, make adjustments, or tune by means of comparing one tone or frequency with another used as a standard. (2) To *align* tape heads.

Calibration
(1) The process of calibrating or *aligning* a recording device or instrument. (2) A gradation showing the position or value of a tone or frequency.

Call Letters
Same as *call sign*: A unique combination of letters or letters and numbers assigned to radio and television stations for identification purposes, as in WABC, WGN, K101, etc. Typically, call letters for broadcast stations east of the Mississippi River begin with W; west of the river, the letters start with K.

Call Sign
Same as *call letters*.

Camcorder
Hand-held combination video and sound recorder.

Cameo
A brief appearance or limited participation in a performance, scene, or recording, usually by a well-known performer.

Camera Ready
Final artwork or graphic layout material ready for the printer's camera. See also *mechanical*.

Campaign
(1) A series of tactical steps planned and carried out for the purpose of accomplishing a strategic goal. *Example*: a marketing campaign to break a record or launch a recording artist's career. (2) To carry out a plan designed to accomplish a purpose or goal.

Can
(1) To shelve. (2) To discharge or fire from a job. (3) To cancel a project or production. See also *in the can*.

Canadian Academy of Record Arts & Sciences (CARAS)
Trade organization of companies and individuals professionally active in the Canadian recording industry, including ancillary professions, such as management, music publishing, songwriting, music videos, album artwork, etc. Presents the annual *Juno Awards*, which are the Canadian equivalent to the *Grammy Awards* in the United States. CARAS is located at 124 Merton Street, Ste. 305, Toronto, ON, M4S 2Z2, Phone: (416) 485-3135; Fax: (416) 485-4978.

Canadian Content
Under Canadian law, music programmed on radio stations must include a minimum percentage of music that is of Canadian origin. Canadian Content ("CanCon") is defined as meeting at least two of the following four conditions: (1) the music was written by a Canadian composer; (2) the lyrics were written by a Canadian; (3) the artist or performer is a Canadian; (4) the production is Canadian. At least 30% of all music broadcast on private FM and AM stations each week must meet CanCon guidelines; at least 50% of all music broadcast each week over the CBC network must meet CanCon guidelines; and at least 10% of all music broadcast each week over "special interest and traditional" stations (i.e., classical and jazz) must meet CanCon guidelines. It should be noted that France has similar broadcast regulations mandating French content.

Canadian Musical Reproduction Rights Agency (CMRRA)
A *mechanical-right licensing agency*, CMRRA is the Canadian counterpart of the *Harry Fox Agency*.

CMRRA charges music publishers a 5% fee for *mechanical royalty* collections and 10% for *synchronization* license fees. American publishers affiliated with Fox usually affiliate separately with CMRRA. But it is possible to affiliate with one of the agencies and not the other. CMRRA is headquartered at 56 Wellesley Street West, Suite 320, Toronto, Ont. M5R 2S7, Canada. Tel: (416) 926-1966.

Canadian Recording Industry Association (CRIA)
Trade association established in order to promote and protect the interests of Canadian record companies, particularly with regards to counterfeiting, bootlegging, and piracy. The organization also certifies sales of recordings in order to officially award *gold* and *platinum* discs, and provides extensive research on the markets for recorded music product.

CanCon
Abbreviated reference for *Canadian Content*.

Canned
(1) Shelved, not used. (2) Prerecorded, not live, as in "canned laughter" or *canned music*. (3) Fired or discharged from a job. See also *in the can*.

Canned Music
Prerecorded music tracks available from *recorded music libraries*. Also called *needledrop music*, *library music*, or *production music*. Producers of low-budget films, documentaries, training films, television programs, commercials, etc. frequently license canned music tracks from library services, which provide master quality recordings and rights to use the track and the underlying music copyright, all at one relatively low cost fee.

Canned Release
Generic *bio* or *press release*, as opposed to specifically tailored releases written for special occasions or targeted to specific media outlets.

Canned Spot
Prerecorded commercial announcement or *PSA* used for broadcasting.

Canned Track
Prerecorded instrumental material used in whole or in part to complete or enhance another work, or as a backing track for a live vocal performance.

Cap
A *ceiling* or upper limit. For instance, the *statutory mechanical royalty* rate "caps" the amount of royalty per unit a music publisher receives from a record company, though publishers and record companies may agree on a royalty rate lower than the statu-

tory amount. Or, two parties may agree on a rate of compensation based on performance or sales up to a "capped" maximum amount. Another example of a cap is a *controlled composition clause* in a recording artist contract, which "caps" the amount of mechanical royalties the record company will pay to music publishers-any aggregate amount of mechanical royalties accruing to publishers above that cap will be paid for out of the artist's royalties.

CAP
Abbreviation for *Catalog Administration Plan.*

CAPAC
Canadian *performing-right society,* an affiliate of *ASCAP,* which was merged with *BMI*'s Canadian affiliate *PROCAN* into *SOCAN* to form a single Canadian performing-right society.

Captions
(1) Subtitles for a motion picture. (2) Brief explanation, title, or identifying description accompanying a visual image. (3) Paragraph headings or section titles of a contract, license, legal pleading, or article.

CARAS
Acronym for *Canadian Academy of Record Arts & Sciences.*

CARP
Acronym for *Copyright Arbitration Royalty Panel.*

Card
Reference to a *screen credit.* A *shared card* is when two or more people are simultaneously given credit on screen; a *separate card* is when only one person's credit appears on screen. See also *union card.*

Cart
A cassette tape containing one looped track, which can be easily *cued.* Used by radio stations to play commercials, *PSAs, station IDs,* frequently played records, etc.

Cartage
(1) The process of transporting equipment, musical instruments, or other property. (2) A charge added to a musician's fee to compensate for transporting musical instruments or equipment to a recording session or performance.

Cartridge
(1) Case containing a reel of *magnetic recording tape.* (Also called a *cassette.*) (2) On a record player *tone arm,* a removable case that contains electric conversion circuitry and the *stylus.*

CASH
Abbreviation for *Composers & Authors Society of Hong Kong.*

Cash
Compensation for services, sales, or performances in the form of currency, check, certified check, money order, or bank draft.

Cash Basis Royalty Accounting
Method of accounting for royalty revenue and royalty payments that recognizes royalties only upon actual receipt and royalty expenses only when cash is actually paid out. In contrast, *accrual*-based royalty accounting recognizes royalty income and expenses when product is sold, though income from product sales has not yet been received.

Cash is a real-time method of accounting, but it doesn't factor *accounts receivable* (royalties or fees due the company) and *accounts payable* (royalties owed by the company to artists, songwriters, producers, co-publishers, etc.). Thus, cash-based accounting does not show ultimate net profits.

Suppose, for example, that using the cash method of accounting, $1 million was received during the past year and $250,000 paid in royalties, ostensibly leaving a net of $750,000. *But*, an additional $250,000 is owed in royalties, though not due to be paid for another 3 months. The true net is then actually $500,000, which would be evident if the accrual basis were used.

Cash Box
A weekly music industry *trade magazine,* located at 157 W. 57 St., New York, NY 10019. Tel: (212) 586-2640.

Cash Flow
A measure of solvency or liquidity; the amount of cash coming in during an accounting period as opposed to the amount of cash going out. When more cash comes in than goes out, there is "positive cash flow"; "negative cash flow" occurs when not enough money comes in to meet expenses. See also *insolvency* and *bankruptcy.*

Cash In
(1) To sell off assets, pay off creditors, and withdraw from a business activity. (2) To score profits on an investment or activity.

Cash on Delivery (C.O.D.)
A transaction in which a seller requires a customer to fully pay for product by cash or the equivalent (certified check, money order, or bank draft), at the point of delivery. Also called *collect on delivery.*

Cash Pay-Out

In a *buy-out* situation, a method of structuring payments from the party buying out a contract. For instance, if a band or partnership is buying out the share of a leaving member, the assets (of the band or partnership) are valued, a *prorated* share price established, and payment is made in installments over an agreed period of time. Say, for example, the assets of a four-way partnership are valued at $200,000, the buyout price of one leaving member is $50,000, which may then be paid in 10 quarterly payments (more than 2 and 1/2 years) of $5,000 each. See also *contingent pay-out*.

Cassette

A small plastic, rectangular-shaped flat case containing *magnetic tape* that spools between two reels when used to record or play back audiotape or videotape. Also called *cartridge*. See also *audiocassette* and *videocassette*.

Cassette Deck

A device used for recording or playing cassette audiotapes.

Cassette Memory

A *cartridge* containing *magnetic tape* that stores computer programs.

Cassette Player

An audio playback device designed to play prerecorded audiotapes in cassette format. Cassette-tape players vary in size, from small portable Walkman® types to nonportable units built into *high-fidelity* systems.

Cassette Recorder

A recording device designed to record sound onto audiotape cassettes. Cassette-tape recorders vary in size, from small portable micro devices to nonportable units built into *high-fidelity* systems.

Cassingle

A commercially released recording in audiotape cassette format containing two tracks only, corresponding to the traditional vinyl disc *single*.

Cast

(1) To choose songs for a recording artist or recording session. (2) To *pitch* or *plug* songs for a recording artist or recording session. (3) To select actors or other performers for parts in a film, teleplay, or other theatrical production. (4) The actors or performers in a film, teleplay, or other theatrical production.

Cast Album

A recorded album of music or acting sequences featuring the cast of a play, movie, teleplay, or other theatrical production in which the material was originally performed.

Casting

(1) The act of choosing songs for a recording artist or recording session. (2) The act of *pitching* or *plugging* songs for a recording artist or recording session. (3) The act of selecting actors or other performers for parts in a film, teleplay, or other theatrical production.

Casual

A *one-nighter*. Typically, an engagement by a performer in a privately booked club or other venue for a one-night event, such as a party, convention, prom, etc.

Catalog

(1) Itemized or alphabetized list of items, such as books or records, in a collection, usually including brief summaries or other identifiers for each item. (2) In the music business, "catalog" most often refers to the *repertoire* of product released by a record company or recording artist, or the titles of songs controlled by a music publishing company.

Catalog Administration Plan (CAP)

Optional copyright administrative service provided to members of the *Songwriters Guild of America (SGA)*.

Catalog Agreement

Also called *catalog deal*. A contract or license dealing with the entire *catalog* of a music publisher, songwriter, or record company. While catalog deals include all works owned or controlled by the publisher, songwriter, or record company as of the agreement's *effective date*, they may also cover new works created or acquired in the normal course of business by the *assignor* or *licensor* during the term of agreement.

An acquisition outside the "normal course of business" would be the purchase of another copyright catalog that significantly increases the *licensor*'s or *assignor*'s revenue stream. Major acquisitions that skew the dynamics of the original deal should be subject to new and separate negotiations as and when they arise. Such acquisitions shouldn't change the original catalog agreement, which remains in effect. The *licensee* or *assignee* can negotiate to represent the acquisition, which might mean paying an additional advance, or be content to represent only the catalog currently under contract.

For instance, ABC Publishers makes a *subpublishing* deal with DEF Ltd. in London. ABC then purchases XYZ Music, thereby doubling its catalog size and annual revenues. The original subpublishing agreement with DEF was negotiated without considering the infusion of income and activity the addition of XYZ would make.

ABC would then approach DEF and offer to add the XYZ catalog to the subpublishing deal in return for an additional advance commensurate with the value of the acquisition. If DEF passes on the offer, ABC can then license XYZ to another subpublisher. Of course, ethics and common courtesy require ABC to at least give DEF *first refusal*. See also *blanket agreement*, and *exclusive agreement*.

Catalog Number

The identifying number used by manufacturers and distributors to distinguish one product from another for the purposes of licensing, accounting, inventory control, shipping, sales, invoicing, manufacturing, etc. See also *record number*, ISWC, ISBN, ISRC, and master number.

Catch Action

To prepare a musical segment as a *cue* to *synchronize* with a filmed action scene.

Catch All

A phrase or provision in a contract or license to cover a broad range of issues not otherwise specifically detailed elsewhere in the agreement. For example, a catch all provision might state "all rights not specifically granted herein are reserved by the licensor," or "no royalties or other monies shall be paid to licensor except those expressly provided herein."

Category

A classification or class designating a specific type, quality, concept, or genre, such as *country* music, *adult contemporary* market segment, *urban contemporary* radio station format, etc.

Cattle Call

Auditions for a film or theatrical production (usually), which are publicly announced and open to all-comers.

CATV

Abbreviation for *community antenna television*.

Cause

The reason or grounds for a lawsuit or other legal action.

Cause of Action

See *cause*, above.

CCTV

Abbreviation for *closed-circuit television*.

CD

Abbreviation for *compact disc*.

CD5

A five-inch compact disc containing a single track (or, perhaps, two or more versions or mixes of one song), which is used primarily for promotional purposes. Typical CD5s are sent to radio stations in clear plastic jewel boxes with no color artwork or insert. All pertinent information (i.e., name of artist, song title, performing-right affiliation, etc.) is on the disc label. When released commercially, CD5s may also include a color *tray card* and *insert*.

CD-I

Abbreviation for *compact disc-interactive*.

CD Mastering

See *compact disc mastering*.

CD-Plus

An enhanced CD that not only plays audio on a standard CD player, it can also be used in a CD-ROM drive to display multimedia files (text, graphics, video).

CD-Quality Sound

The minimum standard for recording compact discs, whereby sound is digitized at 44.1kHz/16-bit resolution, which is capable of reproducing sounds across the range of normal human hearing.

CD-R

Abbreviation for compact disc-recordable, a device that can record onto blank compact discs; also, recordable compact disc media.

CD-ROM

An *optical laser disc* read by a computer using a CD-ROM drive. CD-ROM is an acronym for Compact *Disc-Read Only Memory*, which means the stored data can be played back but not altered or recorded over. CD-ROMs can contain any combination of data, including text, audio, and video. A standard CD-ROM can contain as much as 500,000 pages of text. See also *CD-Plus*.

CD Single

A commercially released compact disc containing two tracks, as opposed to a complete album, corresponding to the traditional vinyl disc *single* or audiotape *cassingle*. See also *CD5*.

CD-WORM

Name for a type of *optical laser disc*, meaning Compact *Disc-Write Once-Read Many*, which can record text, audio, or visuals, but, recorded data can only be altered by obliterating the original entry to store the changes on a previously unused portion of the disc.

Ceiling

See *cap*. A maximum amount placed on royalty rates or other forms of compensation (as opposed to *floor*, which is a minimum amount).

Central Licensing

The *European Union* (*EU*) is eliminating trade barriers so that Western Europe will for all practical purposes be one commercial entity without cross-border red tape inhibiting the free movement of funds or goods. There has been a trend towards a centralized record industry (i.e., manufacturing at a German plant, for instance, for product ultimately intended for sale in France, Britain, Holland, Italy, etc.), This has given rise to the concept of central licensing whereby the *mechanical-right society* in, say, Great Britain (*MCPS*) can license and collect mechanical royalties for a recording released anywhere within the EU (as opposed each individual EU country's mechanical-right society having sole licensing authority for sales within its borders). Since the early nineties, major record companies like Warner Bros. and PolyGram have been promoting central mechanical licensing for European releases.

CEO

Abbreviation for *chief executive officer*.

Certified Mail

Uninsured first-class mail for which the recipient signs a receipt to confirm delivery.

Certified Public Accountant (CPA)

A public accountant who, having passed a state licensing exam, is certified by the state's examining board as meeting legal requirements for the practice of accountancy.

Certificate of Recordation

Document filed with the *Copyright Office* to make a public record of a *copyright transfer*.

CFO

Abbreviation for *chief financial officer*, a senior corporate position charged with management of company financial affairs.

CH

Music format abbreviation for *Christian*.

CHA

Abbreviation for *Copyright Holders Association*, the *performing-right society* in Taiwan.

Chain

Two or more retail stores, selling the same lines of merchandise, which are owned and operated by the same company. Each individual store in the chain is managed by an employee-manager who typically must follow policies laid down by corporate management. In the music business, the term "chains" may refer either to chain stores focusing only on music product, or on department stores and other retailers who sell music product along with a great variety of other merchandise. In recent years, chains have come to dominate the retail market for music product. Because they purchase product in large quantities from centralized distribution centers, they can command big discounts from record manufacturers, which in turn enables them to offer lower prices to consumers at the expense of independent retailers, or mom & pop stores.

Chain Buyer

Person in charge of buying a line of merchandise for a chain-store system. Chain buyers can negotiate discounts from manufacturers, wholesalers, and distributors, because their centralized buying procedures and buying efficiency enables them to purchase product in large quantities for redistribution to individual stores within the chain.

Chain of Title

Documentation supporting a claim of copyright ownership. The chain of title originates with the *author* of a work who is automatically *vested* in all *statutory* rights to the copyright. When the author makes an *assignment* of any or all of those rights, the assignment is a link in the chain of title (from author to *assignee*). As each assignee further assigns the statutory rights the chain is lengthened. A chain of title, then, documents each assignment of statutory rights from the author through to the ultimate assignee (the final link in the chain of title).

Changes

(1) Alterations of an original work (i.e., new lyrics, translation, revised melodic structure, adaptation, etc.). (2) Alterations, deletions, or additions to the provisions of a contract or license. (3) Progression of chords ("chord changes") in a melodic structure.

Charge

(1) A cost or an item of expense that is allocated by a record company or music publisher to the royalty account of a songwriter, recording artist, or producer, and which is *recouped* by the company through deductions from any royalties earned. (2) An allegation or claim by one party to an agreement that the other party has failed to honor the agreement. (3) To authorize or empower someone to manage or take care of something.

Charge-Back

To set off of one debt against another. *Example*: A recording artist's recording costs are recouped

Chart — CIC

(charged back) by the record company from royalties the company owes the artist.

Chart
(1) Tabulation of best selling recordings, videos, sheet music, radio airplay, etc., as in *Top 100*. The definitive national charts are compiled by or for trade magazines such as *Billboard* by means of surveys of retailers (for sales) and radio stations (for airplay). Charts are frequently compiled to reflect most active sales or airplay in specific genres or market segments (i.e., Top 100 Country Singles; Top 100 R&B Albums, etc.). Large retailers often compile charts of in-store sales activity charts for display to customers. Many radio stations also compile and publish charts reflecting most requested or most played releases. (2) *To chart* is the term used describe a product that enters a chart after generating sufficient surveyed sales and/or airplay activity. (3) Chart is also a term used to describe a written *arrangement* (or *part*) for musical instruments or instrumental sections, such as "horn charts."

Chart Activity
Success of a recording measured by its performance on recognized national best-seller and/or airplay *charts*.

Chart Entry
A recording or other product that has just achieved sufficient surveyed sales and/or airplay to be placed on the latest *chart*.

Chart Topper
A recording or other product that has achieved sufficient surveyed sales and/or airplay to reach the number one position (the "top of the chart").

Cherry Pick
To select the best from the rest. ("The *A&R director* cherry-picked songs from all the *demos* submitted.")

Chief Executive Officer (CEO)
Appointed by the board of directors, a CEO is the highest-ranking corporate executive, charged with carrying out the policies of the board of directors on a daily basis.

Chief Financial Officer (CFO)
A senior corporate executive charged with managing the financial affairs of a company.

Chief Operating Officer (COO)
A senior corporate executive charged with managing the day-to-day operational affairs of a company.

Children's Music
A musical *genre* appealing to the preteen and/or preschool *market segment*.

Chitlin Circuit
Slang for a series of engagements at bars, taverns, or roadhouses that feature blues and soul music.

Choice of Forum
A contractual provision setting out the legal *jurisdiction* in which any disputes between the parties will be adjudicated. (A jurisdiction is a legal district, such as a city, county, state, territory, or country in which the laws of the district apply to contracts made, actions taken, or disputes that arise within the district.)

Choice of Law
A contractual provision stating that the laws of the legal *jurisdiction* governing the agreement (see *choice of forum*) will define the construction and enforcement of the agreement between the parties.

Chorus
(1) Singing group. (2) The *refrain* or *hook* of a song.

CHR
Abbreviation for *contemporary hit radio*, a radio station format that focuses on playing recordings from the current Pop charts (i.e., Top 40).

Christian Music
Musical genre blending spiritually uplifting, inspirational lyrics with more *secular*-sounding modern pop and soft rock music styles, rather than straightforward *gospel* or *spiritual* music.

Christian Rap
Spiritually uplifting, inspirational lyrics rapped to hip-hop beats.

Chrome Cassette
One of three basic types of cassette tape (the others being *ferric* and *metal*). Ferric tape is the most common, but chrome and metal offer higher-quality recording and playback. However, chrome and metal each require cassette players that are *calibrated* to play them, because of their higher *bias* and *EQ* requirements. In addition to being more expensive than ferric, chrome and metal cassettes are abrasive, which causes wear on the recording and playback *heads*.

Chron Files
Method of filing correspondence and other documents chronologically, by dated sequence.

CHUrban
Acronym for *contemporary hit urban*, a radio station music programming *format*.

CIC
Abbreviation for *Creative Incentive Coalition*.

CIRPA
Acronym for Canadian Independent Record Producers Association.

CIS
Abbreviation for *Common Information System*.

CISAC
Acronym for *International Confederation of Societies of Authors & Composers*, based in Paris. An organization of "creators societies" (mechanical- and performing-right societies) from over 60 countries that meets every 2 years to govern matters of international and reciprocal concern to the member societies, and to address copyright issues arising from new technologies. See also Warsaw Rule.

Cite
To quote an authoritative source in order to support a position, prove a point, or illustrate a meaning.

CL
Music format abbreviation for *classical*.

Claim
(1) To assert something as a fact, to state something as true. (2) To maintain a right or an ownership. (3) To maintain the right to benefit from something. (4) The basis by which a right is maintained, such as authorship or assignment. (5) To demand one's just due by right of performance, ownership, assignment, or authorship. (6) A title or right derived from authorship, assignment, or fulfillment of an agreed requirement. (7) A demand for compensation on the basis of a formal agreement.

Claimant
(1) A party who asserts something as a fact. (2) Party who maintains a right or an ownership interest. (3) Party who claims a right to benefit from something. (4) Party demanding just due by right of performance, ownership, assignment, or authorship. (5) Party making a formal complaint, especially in court. (6) A *plaintiff* or *complainant*.

Clam
A wrong note, musically.

Class A Commercial
Type of *residual* paid for television commercials aired in 21 or more cities. Class B commercials are those that are aired in more than six and up to 20 cities; Class C commercials are aired in five or fewer cities.

Classic
(1) A song or performance accepted as being of the highest artistic merit. (2) A song or performance having enduring significance or popularity. (3) A definitive song or performance. See also *evergreen* and *standard*.

Classic Jazz
Jazz music performed in the traditional manner, usually instrumental, *improvised*, and using *acoustic instruments*. Sometimes called *pure jazz*.

Classic Rock
Traditional, late 1950s to early 1960s rock-and-roll music as typified by Elvis Presley, Chuck Berry, The Beatles, Buddy Holly, *et al.*

Classical Music
(1) General reference to *serious music*. (2) In musical teminology, the period beginning around 1750 near the birth of Haydn, and ending around 1820, near the deaths of Beethoven and Schubert.

Clause
In a contract or license, a distinct *stipulation* or *provision*.

Clean
(1) To erase a magnetic recording tape. (2) A blank recording tape or videotape.

Cleans
Phonorecords that are not marked as promotional or discount merchandise.

Clearance
(1) Permission from a rights holder or copyright owner to use a work, usually given in the form of a license. (2) Official declaration or certification of acceptance or suitability.

Clearance Form
Form used by *BMI*-affiliated songwriters and music publishers for registering new works with BMI.

Clearing House
An independent agency that tracks down music-rights owners on behalf of clients (such as film and television production companies), and negotiates licenses for the use of the music needed in a production. This process is called *music clearance*. Clearing houses normally are paid for their services by the clients that use them on a per song, per use basis.

Clearing House Ltd, The (TCH)
A music rights *clearing house* (see above), located at 405 Riverside Drive, Burbank, CA 91506. Tel: (213) 469-3186.

Clef
Symbol used in musical *notation*. A clef is placed at the beginning of each *staff* to mark the note values

of lines and spaces. There are five clefs used in Western musical notation: The Treble clef, or G clef (the note G placed above middle C on the second line); the Bass clef, or F clef (the note F is placed below middle C on the fourth line); the Alto clef places middle C on the middle line; the Tenor clef places middle C on the fourth line; and the Soprano clef places middle C on the first line.

Click Track

One track on a multitrack tape dedicated to an electronically set tempo of rhythmic clicks. Click tracks are used (1) to facilitate *scoring* and *synchronizing* music with film; or (2) as a guide track to record or overdub music in *sync* on a recording; or (3) to help percussionists keep tempos steady when laying down *rhythm tracks*.

Clip

(1) A brief segment or extract taken from a complete videotape or film, used for promotional purposes, review, commentary, or news reporting, etc. Also called *film clip*, *video clip*, *promo clip*, or *sample footage*. See also *music video* and *promotional music video*. (2) To cut an article, photo, review, or news item from a newspaper or magazine.

Clipping

An article, photo, review, or news item cut out of a newspaper or magazine.

Clipping Service

An organization hired to scan publications and *clip* articles, photos, reviews, and news items that refer to their clients, and to send clippings of all relevant items.

Clipsheet

A single sheet of newsprint paper containing publicity material for clipping and reprinting.

Close

(1) To finalize terms of an agreement; to sign a contract. (2) A *finale*; the final movement in a work of several movements; the final act or closing theme of a play, film, or program. (3) To end a show (a closing act or closing number). (4) The resolution or conclusion of a musical phrase or theme.

Close-Miking

Placing a microphone as close as possible to the source being recorded in order to reproduce the original sound in its most intimate quality.

Closed-Circuit Television (CCTV)

A local or short-distance television transmission system linking camera, controls, and display terminals or receivers by cable. Used for in-house programming at hospitals, educational institutions, and large companies, and to monitor premises for internal and external security.

Closed Corporation

An incorporated company owned by relatively few people who are restricted from selling their shares of stock to outsiders. Also called "close corporation."

Closed Session

A recording session (or meeting) closed to all but those who are invited and/or directly involved in the proceedings.

Closed Shop

A business whose employees are required to be union members. Also called *union shop*. See also *open shop*.

Closing Act

The star attraction on a bill of several performers. See also *close*.

Closing Credits

Acknowledgments of work done, services rendered, and rights licensed, displayed at the end of a motion picture, television show, or publication, or announced at the end of a broadcast. See also *acknowledgments*, *credits*, and *opening credits*.

Cloud on the Title

Legal term referring to an unresolved dispute or conflicting claim of copyright ownership somewhere in the *chain of title*, thereby reducing the copyright's market value or prohibiting its assignment. See also *defective title*.

Club

(1) Shorthand reference for *record club*. (2) Shorthand reference for nightclub, particularly when referring to venues that feature dee-jays playing Dance or Disco records.

Club Band

Band hired for engagements in nightclubs, whose repertoire focuses on current dance-oriented Top 40 material and/or material previously recorded and released by other acts.

Club Culture

Term describing fashions and lifestyles of teens and young adults whose social lives center around dance-oriented nightclubs and proponents of the latest subgenres of dance music.

Cluster

A series of recordings broadcast without interruption by dee-jay patter, announcements, or commercials. Also called "cluster programming."

Clutter

(1) Jumbled noise on a recording; (2) back-to-back airing of a series of short commercial spots during a programming break in a broadcast.

CMA

Abbreviation for *Country Music Association.*

CMI

Abbreviation for *Copyright Management, Inc.*

CMJ Music Marathon & Music Fest

Annual trade showcase for new artists and hot new bands. Sponsored by *CMJ*. Contact CMJ at 811 Middle Neck Road, Suite 400, Great Neck, NY 11021-2301, Tel: (516) 466-6000; Fax: (516) 466-7159.

CMJ New Music Report

Weekly trade magazine focusing on alternative, rock, rap, reggae, world, metal, and jazz. Reports on airplay at over 1,000 radio stations, particularly college stations, and sales activity from retailers. Also sponsors annual *CMJ Music Marathon & Music Fest* and publishes CMJ New Music Monthly for music consumers, which includes a compact disc in every issue, featuring over 70 minutes of new music. CMJ is located at 811 Middle Neck Road, Suite 400, Great Neck, NY 11021-2301, Tel: (516) 466-6000; Fax: (516) 466-7159.

CMPA

Abbreviation for *Church Music Publishers Association.*

CMRRA

Abbreviation for *Canadian Musical Reproduction Rights Agency.*

CMT

Abbreviation for *Country Music Television.*

Co-author

An author who collaborates with another author to create a work of *joint-authorship.*

COD

Abbreviation for *cash on delivery* or *collect on delivery.*

Coin-operated

Reference to a device such as a *jukebox* or *video arcade game* that plays music or games upon insertion of a coin or token.

Cold

(1) A quick, unrehearsed run-through of a performance. (2) A commercial announcement without musical backdrop. (3) As opposed to "hot," an act or a recording that loses popularity or fails to gain popular acceptance.

Collaborate

To work together to create something; to make a joint effort towards achieving a common goal; to participate in creating a work, such as a song or book.

Collaboration

(1) A joint work, such as a cowritten song. (2) A joint effort or action toward a common end. (3) A participation in the creation of something or the pursuit of a common goal.

Collaborator

(1) One who participates in the creation of a work, the pursuit of a goal, or the formulation of a plan or design. (2) A *cowriter, coproducer, co-author.*

Collateral

Something pledged or given to hold as security in order to guarantee repayment of a loan or the performance of an obligation. See also *cross-collateralize.*

Collateral Contracts

Contracts entered into simultaneously by the same parties to deal with separate, but related, issues. For instance, a singer-songwriter might enter into a recording contract with a record company and a publishing contract with the record company's music publishing division at the same time. See also *conterminous.*

Collateralize

To secure a loan by pledging some property as *collateral* in order to guarantee repayment. See also *cross-collateralize.*

Collect

(1) To accumulate or gather objects of a related type, such as a record collection. (2) To receive royalties or fees owed by *users* of licensed works. (3) To enforce payment of monies owed through appropriate legal action. (4) To *recoup* an advance, expenditure, or investment.

Collect on Delivery (C.O.D.)

A transaction in which a seller requires a customer to fully pay for product by cash or the equivalent (certified check, money order, or bank draft), at the point of delivery. Also called *cash on delivery.*

Collection

(1) An accumulation of objects of a related type, such as a record collection. (2) The receipt of royalties or fees owed by *users* of licensed works. (3) The receipt of money owed, either through voluntary payment or through enforced legal action. (4) The sum collected during a set period.

Collection Agent

(1) A person or company employed and empowered by another for the purpose of collecting royalties, fees, and other payments due from users of licensed works. (2) A person or company employed and empowered by another to enforce payment of debts owed by customers in default. See also *collection agreement*, *mechanical-right society*, and *performing-right society*.

Collection Agreement

An agreement between a *copyright holder* and another person or company in which the copyright holder appoints the other party as its *collection agent* or representative in a specified territory for a specified period of time. A collection agreement normally empowers the agent to license the copyright holder's works in the territory, and to collect all monies arising from such licensing, retaining a percentage of such collections for its services. Collection agreements do not normally require any promotion, marketing, or sales activities on the part of the agent. As a consequence, the collection agent's percentage of retained income is smaller (5% to 15%) than with full-service licensing agreements. For the same reason, collection agreements do not normally require agents to pay advances for the right of representation.

Collection Deal

Same as *collection agreement*.

Collection Period

The average number of days a company normally takes to collect monies owed for sales made on credit or *consignment*. A company's collection period is calculated by dividing its total *accounts receivable* by its average daily sales made on credit or consignment. The shorter a company's average collection period is, the greater its cash *flow* and the more cash the company has available for reinvestment and operating costs. A collection period should not be confused with *accounting period*, which is the time covered by financial reports and/or the time period for which licensees must report monies accrued and render monies due for sales or performances during the period. Accounting periods usually are stated as annual (yearly), semi-annual (6 months), quarterly (3 months), or monthly.

Collective Work

(1) A group of works assembled or accumulated into a whole, such as a *medley*. (2) A work resulting from *collaboration* by two or more people in which distinct copyright exists in the individual contributions of each collaborator. Unless there is an agreement between the collaborators to merge the collective work into one, shared copyright, each collaborator has copyright only in his or her individual contribution.

Collector

(1) A person or company employed to collect royalties, fees, and other payments. (See *collection agent*.) (2) A person who collects related items as a hobby, such as a "record collector."

College Radio

Radio stations on college campuses, operated by college students under sponsorship of their colleges and supervised by college instructors. College stations are noncommercial and normally operate on relatively low power. Because their programming is usually discretionary (as opposed to the rigid formats of commercial stations), and they are generally more liberal about *playlisting* new releases by less established recording artists, and, because the college population is an important market segment, college radio is a viable area for promoting new artists.

College Rap

Generic term applied to various types of stylistically diverse hip-hop acts of the early 1990s marketed to *alternative* and *college radio* audiences.

Color Match

A full-color proof of artwork printed from a negative in order to check the accuracy of ink colors before a print run is started. See also *Pantone Matching System* and *rainbow*.

Color Separations

In the printing process for posters, album artwork, and other printed matter using color photographs, the photographs must be converted into four *halftones* separating or filtering the primary colors (red, yellow, and blue, plus black), which are then printed over each other to reproduce the photograph in all its original colors.

Columbia House

Unit of Sony Music, which operates the *Columbia Record Club*. Located at 1221 Avenue of the Americas, New York, NY 10020. Tel: (212) 596-2000, and 1400 N. Fruitridge Ave., Terre Haute, IN 47811. Tel: (812) 466-8111; Fax: (812) 466-8836.

Columbia Record Club

A division of *Columbia House*. See *record club*.

Commercial

(1) Pertaining to a work created or marketed for appeal to a mass market for the purpose of returning a profit. (2) A song, recording or other work that has achieved popular success in the consumer market. (3) An advertisement broadcast on television or radio.

Commercial Agreement

Also called commercial contract; a contract to produce, write, perform, direct, or tape a television commercial.

Commercial Bed

Term used by ad agencies and broadcasters to describe the music background for commercial advertisements.

Commercial Code

Abbreviated reference for *Uniform Commercial Code (UCC)*: a set of laws, adopted by and applicable in most states, dealing with commercial transactions, particularly involving the sale, lease, and licensing of tangible and intangible goods, as well as financial transactions such as deposits, collections, securities, negotiable instruments, warranties, documents of title, lending, and investments, etc.

Commercial Load

The proportion of broadcast *air time* allocated to *commercial spots* and announcements as opposed to program content.

Commercial Quality

A work, such as a song or recording, created to professional standards and likely to appeal to a paying audience or retail customers.

Commercially Released

A song, recording, film, or other work distributed for sale to the public.

Commercial Slot

A segment of broadcast time allocated for a commercial announcement or advertisement.

Commercial Spot

An advertisement or commercial announcement broadcast during a *commercial slot*.

Commercial Station

A for-profit radio or television station supported by selling broadcast time to advertisers, as opposed to a *noncommercial* station, which is sponsored by private or public donations.

Commercial Synchronization License

Permission to reproduce and *synchronize* a copyrighted musical work with visual images for broadcast advertising promotions of commercial products.

Commission

(1) To employ a person, group, organization, or company to carry out a particular task, such as to write a song, produce a recording, etc. (2) The task or duty of one so employed (a "commission to compose a film score"). (3) A percentage of income derived from a service rendered. *Example*: An artist's *personal manager* might receive a commission of 15% of the artist's earnings.

Commissioned Work

A work produced or created by someone as a specific condition of employment. See also *work made for hire* and *employee for hire*.

Commissioning Fee

Sum paid to someone employed to write, create, or produce a *commissioned work*.

Commitment

(1) A promise, an obligation, a duty. (2) Under contract, pledge, obligated, duty-bound.

Commitment Fee

(1) A fee paid as a *commitment* to do something. (2) A fee charged to hold open an *option*, or to hold open a line of credit. See also *earnest money*.

Common Information System (CIS)

A joint-project undertaken by major music rights societies throughout the world to combine their individual database entries into one centrally accessible database of copyright information. It has been estimated that each major rights organization's database contains millions of works and each of those works has an average of 3 entries regarding rights owners or interested parties (i.e., music publishers, songwriters, etc.). Further, each work may be re-entered under various records in each database up to 100 times, leading to countless opportunities for erroneous data input. The CIS project, therefore, is an effort to give each individual creative work a unique, identifying digital code number that can be accessed and checked via one international data exchange network. (See *WorksNet, ISWC,* and *ISRC*.)

Common Law

System of laws developed over the centuries in England, which forms the basis of laws in the United States and most other English-speaking countries. Common Law is based on time-tested customs and traditions and has generally been perpetuated by court decisions and general usage, rather than *statutory* regulation initiated by legislative bodies.

Common Law Copyright

The *Copyright Act of 1976* provides copyright owners with *statutory* legal protection of songs *fixed* in *tangible* form. But there is also protection for songwriters under *common law* for songs that have not yet been recorded or written down.

No formal copyright registration is required under common law; copyright protection begins the moment a work is created and continues until the work is fixed in tangible form. The work can be performed live if the performance is not recorded whereby someone may later have access to the recording. No one may use a song protected by common law copyright for commercial purposes without the owner's authorization. As long as a song is not fixed, common law copyright protection can continue virtually forever. Once fixed, a song's term of protection is subject to the *Copyright Act of 1976*, as amended.

Common Market
See *European Union*.

Community Antenna Television (CATV)
Television programming distribution system that captures television station signals using elevated antennas, then relays the signals by cable to subscribers' receivers. Also called *cable television* and *cablevision*.

Comp
Abbreviation for complimentary ticket or complimentary copy. See also *free copy*, *freebie*, *pass*, and *paper the house*.

Compact Disc (CD)
A type of *optical disc*, coated with a transparent plastic film, which stores digitalized information. Although CDs were originally developed to store and playback audio as an alternative to phonorecords and audiotapes, they are now also commonly used to store text data and video. CDs offer several advantages over vinyl phonorecords and audiotapes. The sound quality is superior; they are relatively small and light, thus requiring less physical storage space; the digitalized method of storing sound enables CDs to encode more audio material so that one compact disc can contain as much material as two or more 12-inch vinyl LPs; and, since the encoded data is "read" by an infrared laser, the disc suffers no physical wear and tear during the playing process. See also *laser disc*, *optical disc*, *CD-quality sound*, *CD-ROM*, *CD-WORM*, *CD-I*, and *videodisc*.

Compact Disc-Interactive (CD-I)
A type of *optical laser disc* capable of storing any combination of text, audio, and visual images, which can be manipulated (interacted with), added to, or altered by the user.

Compact Disc Mastering
In manufacturing compact discs, a master recording is first *premastered* and converted to *U-Matic* video tape. The mastering stage follows next, involving either one of two processes: *glass mastering* or *direct metal mastering* (DMM).

In the glass mastering process, a polished glass master disc containing a layer of photo-sensitive material is exposed to a laser beam controlled by digital information encoded on the U-Matic master tape. The exposure creates approximately 3 billion microscopic pits on the disc surface. These pits represent the audio information to be read by a CD player.

The glass master is next coated with a metal layer to make the pit surface electroconductive. An electroforming process then takes place to make negative and positive metal masters (*fathers* and *mothers*, respectively). The metal masters are used to produce the finished compact discs, serving much the same purpose as *stampers* in the process of *pressing* vinyl records.

In the direct metal mastering process, microscopic pits are embossed on copper layered over a glass base, then galvanized to prepare stampers for manufacturing.

Companion Folio
Also called *matching folio*. A published collection of song arrangements issued in conjunction with a recorded album release, reproducing the album cover on the folio cover, and including all the songs contained on the album.

COMPASS
Abbreviation for *Composers & Authors Society of Singapore*.

Compensate
To make a payment or reimbursement in exchange for services rendered or goods provided.

Compensation
A sum given or received in payment or reimbursement for services rendered or goods provided.

Competent Party
Person qualified to enter into an agreement or carry out an agreed act, and who is deemed of sound mind and body, and who is not prevented from acting responsibly or accepting responsibility by reason of medical or legal disability.

Compilation
(1) An assembly of separate works into an organized *collection*. (2) A collection or assortment of literary or musical works, such as an anthology or best of album. A collection of musical works organized by some theme or linked by some concept into a single album or folio. Examples: "Top 10 Pop Hits of 1975," "Country Love Songs," "Great Movie Themes," etc.

Compilation Copyright
A copyright in a *compilation* as a whole, as opposed to copyrights pertaining to the individual works contained within the compilation.

Compile

To assemble several works from various sources into a single book, folio, or album.

Compiler

(1) A person who assembles and edits several works from various sources into a single anthology, book, folio, or album. (2) A company that conceptualizes, compiles, and markets compilation albums.

Complainant

Party who makes or files a formal *complaint* or *charge*. See also *plaintiff* and *claimant*.

Complaint

A formal accusation or charge of contract violation, negligence, failure, malfeasance, malpractice, etc.

Completion Date

A contractual *commitment* by one party to complete a project or service by a certain date.

Compose

To create, arrange, write, or produce a literary or musical work.

Composer

A person who *composes* a musical work.

Composers & Authors Society of Hong Kong (CASH)

The *performing-* and *mechanical-right society* in Hong Kong, which also covers Macao.

Composers & Authors Society of Singapore (COMPASS)

The *performing-right society* and *mechanical-right society in Singapore*.

Composite

(1) A work made up of separate and distinct parts, such as a *medley* or *compilation*. (2) A blending of two or more styles. (3) A combination, fusion, or mixture of two or more distinct elements.

Composition

(1) A musical or literary work; a song, an instrumental piece, etc. (2) The artistic structure or arrangement of a musical work. (3) The make-up or organization of a musical group, orchestra, or band (i.e., the combination of distinctive parts or individuals to form a unified entity). (4) The end-product of a combination of different elements.

Compression

The process of limiting the range of dynamic responses from sound sources in order to present a more even, less erratic volume level.

Compression Method

One of two methods used to *press* vinyl phonograph records (the other process is called the *injection method*). The compression method hydraulically compresses semi-molten *polyvinyl chloride* (PVC) into a *stamper*. Depending upon the quality of *vinyl* used, the compression method generally produces records that last longer and have a cleaner sound than those molded through injection. The disadvantage is that the compression method is slower and more expensive.

Compressor

A *signal-processing* device used in recording and mixing to limit the range of dynamic responses from sound sources in order to present a more even, less erratic volume level. See also *limiter*.

Compulsory Licensing

Under the *Copyright Act of 1976*, both *published* and *unpublished* copyrightable works are subject to a single system of statutory protection giving copyright owners exclusive rights to reproduce their works for distribution to the public by sale, rental, lease, or lending, and to perform, display, or broadcast the works to the public. Copyright owners also are given exclusive rights to prepare *derivative works* based upon the original copyrighted work. All of these rights are subject to certain exceptions, including the principle of *fair use* and *compulsory licensing* for (a) the recording of musical compositions; (b) *noncommercial transmissions* by *public broadcasters* of published musical and graphic works, and the *secondary transmission* on *cable television systems*; and (c) voluntary licensing of jukebox performances. See *compulsory mechanical license*, below.

Compulsory Mechanical License

A *mechanical license* issued under terms of the *compulsory licensing* provision of the *Copyright Act of 1976*, which states, in effect, that once a song is recorded and commercially released, the copyright owner can not prevent others from also recording and releasing it, as long as new *users* (a) serve a *notice of intention* on the copyright owner (before any recordings are distributed and within 30 days after recording the work); (b) pay *mechanical royalties* at the *statutory rate* by the 20th of each month for all recordings distributed in the preceding month; (c) make each monthly accounting sworn under oath; (d) make cumulative, annual statements, certified by a CPA.

If monthly payments and annual accountings are not made on schedule, and the default is not *cured* within 30 days of a written *demand* from the copyright owner, the compulsory license can be *terminated*.

If the notice of intention is not served, no compulsory license will be issued. Anyone who makes and distributes recordings of a copyrighted song without a license may be subject to prosecution for *copyright infringement*. But if the person wishing to make the recording cannot locate the copyright owner, and the *Copyright Office* is unable to provide a current address, notice of intention can be sent to the Copyright Office with a $6 filing fee.

If the copyright owner has not registered a *claim* to the work with the *Library of Congress*, no compulsory license is necessary, and there is no obligation to pay the owner. The owner can still register a claim and demand statutory compensation for all copies made and sold after registration, but cannot claim royalties on copies sold before registration.

It must be emphasized that the compulsory mechanical licensing provisions do not apply to the first recording of a song. Copyright owners have full discretion over who may first record and release a song under the concept of *first use*. After a publisher authorizes the first recording's manufacture and distribution, then anyone can record and distribute the work if the compulsory licensing provisions are followed. See also *negotiated mechanical license*.

Computer Game

A game encoded on software written for personal computers or specially devised hardware such as Nintendo and Sega. Computer games frequently include music background, which may require *synchronization licenses* and/or *mechanical licenses* from copyright owners. See also *video game* and *arcade*.

Conceive

To form, devise, develop, dream up, or conceptualize a project, plan, theme, or intellectual work, such as a song.

Concept

An idea, thought, theme, plan, vision, or impression.

Concept Album

A collection of songs or recordings linked to each other by some common theme. *Example*: "The London Symphony Orchestra Plays the Beatles."

Concept Folio

A printed book containing orchestrations or arrangements of different songs unified by a single theme or related to each other by some link. *Example*: "Great Movie Themes for Piano."

Concert

A musical performance given for a live audience by one or more singers, instrumentalists, orchestras, bands, etc. See also *recital*.

Concert Edition

A musical work arranged for concert bands and orchestras.

Concert Master

Usually, the leader of an orchestra's string section who is second only to the conductor in authority over the orchestra.

Concert Promoter

Person or company who stages a concert by booking a venue and performers, and advertising the performance to the general public.

Concerto

A composition written for one or more solo instruments with orchestra, usually consisting of three movements.

Condition

(1) A provision in a contract or license that limits, restricts, or modifies rights and obligations granted by one party to the other. (2) Something required to be done or complied with by one party before the other party is required to do something else. (3) The status, shape, or state of something.

Conditional

Something (such an offer, option, or acceptance of an offer, etc.) that is contingent upon a modification of terms, conditions, or clarification, or the performance of some action or fulfillment of some obligation, or upon the acceptance of certain qualifications, limitations, or restrictions.

Conditional Contract

A contract that has no force unless and until a certain condition has first been met or a certain condition has first occurred.

Conference of Personal Managers

Officially called the *National Conference of Personal Managers* (NCOPM). A trade association of personal managers in the United States, comprising regional and national offices. The organization sets professional standards of conduct for personal managers and provides model contract forms.

Confidentiality Clause

(1) A contract provision or agreement of *nondisclosure* in which one party acknowledges it is, or will be, entrusted with another's *proprietary* information (such as financial position, product development and marketing plans, contractual terms with artists or songwriters, etc.), and agrees not to disclose such information to any other party without permission. Such a provision often is part of a business plan, sale prospectus, financing proposal, private stock place-

ment, employment agreement, or partnership agreement. (2) A contractual provision in an agreement between an artist, songwriter, producer, or other party and a record company, music publisher, etc., which prohibits either party from disclosing the terms of the agreement to anyone other than their respective legal and financial advisers and government agencies. The reason for such a clause, from the company's viewpoint, is that the size of an advance and/or royalty given to one artist (or songwriter, producer, etc.) may upset other signees who received less, or may be used as benchmark negotiating positions by others the company wants to sign in the future.

Configuration

The physical form, format, or composition of an object. A sound recording might be manufactured in several "configurations," such as *audiocassette*, *compact disc*, vinyl 12-inch disc, *DAT*, etc.

Confirmation Letter

A letter usually having legal weight as documentary evidence that the sender agrees to terms of a proposal, accepts an offer, acknowledges being bound to the terms of a specified agreement, offer, or proposal, and/or supports, substantiates, or corroborates a certain position.

Conflict of Interest

A conflict between the private interests of one party and its obligations to another, or a conflict of professional interests arising when one party represents the individual interests of two or more other parties to an agreement or a dispute. *Example*: An attorney who represents a recording artist in negotiations with a record company he also represents has a conflict in trying to impartially advocate the best interests of both parties.

Consideration

A payment or promise that serves as an *inducement*, motive, or reason for one party to enter into a contract with another. Considerations can include one or more of the following: cash payments, advances against royalties, promises of royalty payments, promises to perform certain acts. A consideration is a material reason for entering into a contract, and failure to deliver any consideration promised constitutes a *breach* of contract, which can result in the contract being *voided*.

Consideration of Agreement

See *consideration*, above.

Consent

Approval, permission, acquiescence, acceptance.

Consent Decree

A court order, having the force of law, summarizing a voluntary agreement between parties to a suit, particularly where one party, typically the *defendant*, agrees to compensate the *plaintiff* and/or cease those activities that caused the complaint and/or cure a failure to perform to the plaintiff's satisfaction. Both *BMI* and *ASCAP* operate under consent decrees entered into with the Justice Department, which, among other things, govern how the *performing-right societies* license *performance rights*. For instance, instead of movie theaters being subject to *blanket licenses* covering performance rights for music used in movies, motion picture producers must obtain performance licenses directly from each music rights owner. In addition, television broadcasters and owners of television programs may opt to bypass blanket licenses from performing-right societies by negotiating *direct licenses* and *source licenses* directly from music rights owners.

Consequential Damages

The loss of potential profit opportunities suffered by a *licensee* through the direct or indirect actions or negligence of the licensor.

Consign

(1) Usually, to deliver product on trust to a retailer or wholesaler on a *sale-or-return* basis. (The merchandiser pays for the product after its sale, and/or returns all unsold product.) (2) Also, to *assign* certain rights or property to another for a specific purpose or use.

Consignment

Product accepted by or shipped to a retailer or distributor on a *sale-or-return* basis (i.e., payment is made only on completed sales and all unsold items are returned).

Console

(1) The *board* or *desk* in a recording studio that hosts the sound controls operated by recording engineers. (2) An array of audio controls, such as faders, manuals, stops, pedals, levers, buttons, knobs, etc., arranged in front of or to the side of a musician playing an organ, synthesizer, etc.

Constructive Notice

Legal term meaning public notice is given of a set of facts. *Example*: a *recordation of transfer* registered with the *Copyright Office* serves notice of a change of ownership to a copyright.

Consumer

The *end-user* of a product or service, being a person who buys goods or services for his/her own use rather than for the purpose of resale or for use as a raw product for manufacturing.

Consumer Price Index (CPI)

Also called the "cost-of-living index," the *CPI* is an index of prices of selected goods and services, which is used to measure changes in costs of living over a fixed period of time.

Contact

A business acquaintance. See *networking*.

Contact Sheet

A sheet of photo paper containing thumbnail shots developed from a roll of film from which selections can be made for enlargements.

Container Charge

Also called *packaging deduction*. A charge against an artist's royalties by a record company for the costs of packaging a record album, including the costs of covers, *J-cards*, *O-cards*, envelopes, slipcases, sleeves, *jewel boxes*, jackets, inserts, shrink wrapping, etc. Record companies typically deduct around 25% from the price of a CD before calculating royalties payable (see *royalty base*). Packaging deductions for cassette tapes are in the 20% range. Record companies defend this deduction by contending the artist should only be paid on sales of the recording, not of the packaging.

Contemporary

(1) A word used to define a musical genre, song, or artist as being current, modern, new, up-to-date, fashionable, the latest thing, etc. *Examples*: contemporary *rock* (as opposed to 1950s *rock & roll*) or contemporary *country* (as opposed to traditional *country & western*). (2) Also used to describe styles or artists whose years of productivity or popular acceptance occurred during the same period of time. *Examples*: Elvis Presley and Jerry Lee Lewis were contemporaries, as were J.S. Bach and G.F. Handel.

Contemporary Hit Radio (CHR)

A radio station format that focuses on playing recordings from the current *Pop* charts (i.e., Top 40).

Content Testing

A marketing testing technique to gauge audience reaction before a creative product, such as a recording or film, is commercially released, so that necessary changes can be made to strengthen the product's potential for commercial success.

Conterminous

Same as *coterminous*. Two or more contracts or licenses sharing the same termination date. *Collateral contracts* are often conterminous.

Contingency Fee

See *contingent fee*, below.

Contingent Fee

A fee paid only if and when a deal is made or a service is successfully rendered. A contingent fee is often percentage-based. For instance, an attorney might get 10% of the monetary advance he is able to negotiate on behalf of a client, but is paid nothing if no deal is concluded.

Contingent Pay-Out

A method of structuring payments from a band or partnership to a leaving member. Instead of a *buyout* or *cash pay-out*, the departing member continues to receive a *prorated* share of all earnings from all contracts, licenses, product, and/or activities in which he or she participated before leaving. Say, for example, an album recorded by a four-member band earns $200,000 after one member leaves the group. The leaving member receives 25% ($50,000). Of course, the former member receives nothing from earnings generated on product recorded by the group after the departure date. A contingent pay-out may also be used to compensate a personal manager or other party whose contract with an artist terminates. See also *sunset clause*.

Contingent Scale

The royalty payable to *AFTRA* members whose performances are included on commercially released recordings. The amount of earnings paid is contingent upon the number of recordings sold.

Continental Block

Though the distinction has blurred somewhat in recent years, Western Europe has traditionally been thought of as two distinct blocks of countries from a cultural and marketing perspective when it comes to licensing creative works. The *English Block* consists of countries where English-language music tended to be successful without the necessity of lyric translations. Aside from Great Britain and Ireland, this block includes Scandinavia (Denmark, Sweden, Norway) and the Netherlands. Music licensed in the Continental Block, on the other hand, tended to need translations into local languages. This block consists of the GAS territories (Germany, Austria, Switzerland), France, Belgium, Italy, Spain, and Portugal.

Contract

A legally binding agreement between two or more parties, which may be oral but is more often written. A contract that is enforceable by law normally summarizes in detail the entire understanding between the contracting parties, spelling out each party's duties and obligations, commitments and pledges, warranties and assurances, as well as detailing the *consideration of agreement*, amounts and methods of *compensation*, the *jurisdiction* in which disputes will be settled, the term of agreement, options for renewing the term of agreement, etc. In order for a contract to be legally binding, the party that agrees to do, or refrain from doing, a particular thing must receive "adequate consideration," the undertaking must be lawful, the agreement must be mutual and voluntary, obligations must be reciprocal, and the parties must be legally *competent*.

Contractor

Person engaged by a producer or record company to hire session musicians, and who serves as the go-between for payments, compliance with union regulations, and arrangement of working conditions. Contractors' fees are double the minimum *union scale* for a musician. Often, a session musician will also act as contractor, in which case he or she is paid double the minimum scale.

Contractual Dispute

Disagreement between two parties to a contract as to the meaning or interpretation of the contract or a portion thereof, or as to whether one of the parties violated the terms of the agreement.

Contractual Limitation

A clause or provision in a contract that limits one or both of the parties to a specific role, a stated amount or method of compensation, or restricts the contract's application to a specific time, place, or type of activity.
.

Contractual Prohibition

A clause or provision in a contract that prohibits one or both of the parties from engaging in a specific act.

Contractual Relationship

The relationship between two or more parties to a contract as defined by the contract's provisions. *Example*: A *work-made-for-hire* agreement between a music publisher and a songwriter defines the relationship between the parties as employer (music publisher) and employee (songwriter).

Control

The authority to manage, license, direct, or exercise dominating influence over a copyright, company, person, or event by virtue of authorship, agreement, assignment, ownership, or contract.

Control Room

A soundproofed room separated by a large glass window from a studio area, which contains the *console* and recording or broadcasting equipment, and in which the engineer, producer, and/or director oversee the recording, taping, or broadcast of a performance.

Control Sheet

A work sheet used by concert promoters/producers to summarize details of a planned concert, including names, addresses, telephone and fax numbers, costs, and requirements of talent, agents, personal managers, road managers, technicians, publicists, advertising and ticketing outlets, crews, facilities, transportation, equipment, union reps, etc. Control sheets also list assignments of personnel responsibilities, lead time requirements, flow of contracts, deliveries, etc. Variations of control sheets are also used by record, film, and television producers to reduce planning and responsibilities to a quick reference form.

Control Unit

Nerve center of a hardware system. For instance, in a *high-fidelity system*, the control unit contains various devices used to adjust sound reproduction, such as a scratch filter (to reduce surface noises of old records); a rumble filter (to reduce low-pitched vibrations from a turntable motor); volume and tone controls, which balance relative levels of treble and bass tones, etc.

Controlled Composition

Term used for songs included on a recording session that are written, published, or in any way *controlled* by the recording artist. See *controlled composition clause*, below.

Controlled Composition Clause

Provision in a recording contract used by record companies to reduce their liability for *mechanical royalties*. A controlled composition clause might state that the *mechanical rate* will only be 75% of the *statutory rate* for songs written or *controlled* by the artist.

Such a clause might also state that the total mechanical royalties payable for an album shall not exceed 10 times the three-fourths statutory rate for all the songs on the album. This means that if an album contains 12 songs, for which the normal, aggregate statutory royalty is 85.2¢ (12 x 7.1¢), the record company actually pays only 63.9¢ (7.1¢ x 75% x 10). Some new artists, lacking the bargaining clout of more established artists, have had to agree to 50% of statutory rate on controlled compositions. And virtually all controlled composition clauses call for 50% of the statutory mechanical rate on *record club* and *budget-priced* releases.

Another variation of the controlled composition clause is when a record company requires royalties to be calculated as if every song is less than 5 minutes in playing time, regardless of any song's actual length. Under the current (1998) statutory rate of 1.35¢ per minute, if one track is 10 minutes long, the mechanical royalty would be 13.5¢. But under this provision, the track would be calculated as if it were less than 5 minutes, for which the statutory rate is 7.10¢. And, if the rate is further reduced to 75%, the royalty payable would only be 5.325¢, or more than 50% off the statutory requirement.

Still another controlled composition provision

might base the statutory mechanical royalty rate as of the date of recording. That means that if the statutory rate goes up before the release date (or date of manufacture), the royalty calculation is applied to the older, lower statutory rate.

Controlled composition clauses generally state that *additional mechanical royalties will be paid out of the artist's share of royalties.* The discrepancy between the statutory rate and the controlled composition rate must be made up from the artist's royalty share. Since songs written and published by *third-parties* over which the artist has no control are not subject to a reduced rate, artists must either reduce the number of songs on their albums, or pressure third-party publishers to grant reduced rates to the record company in order to prevent mechanical royalties being deducted from their own royalties.

Controlling Interest
Having more than 50% ownership of something, either as an individual, or acting together in combination with other partial owners.

Converted Master
In the vinyl record manufacturing process, a negative impression of the *master lacquer* (an aluminum disc into which the grooves are cut and which is coated with lacquer) is made, then converted directly into a stamper used to press the records. Converted masters are delicate and easily damaged, so are only used for short press runs.

Converted Stamper
(See *converted master.*) Stampers are used to press vinyl records in the manufacturing process. Converted stampers are made from the original negative master, and deteriorate after press runs of 1,500 to 2,000 discs, after which they must be replaced.

COO
Abbreviation for *chief operating officer*, a senior corporate executive charged with managing the daily operational affairs of a company.

Cooling Records
Same as *curing records*. During the manufacturing process of vinyl discs, either vinyl or hot liquid styrene is poured into a mold then baked and cooled (cured). Improper cooling results in warped discs.

Co-Op Advertising
A cooperative advertising effort by two or more companies sharing the costs of ads or mailings featuring their respective products or services. A common example is where a record label and record retailer split costs of local newspaper ads to tout the availability of the label's new album releases at the retailer's locations.

Co-Owned Copyright
Ownership of a copyright can be shared by any number of parties, and ownership shares need not necessarily be equally distributed. The *co-authors* of a *joint-work* are automatically vested with copyright in the work upon *fixation*. Co-authors are thus co-owners of the copyright; each co-owner may independently transfer his or her ownership share to another party. Absent an agreement between the owners to the contrary, a co-owner may also license nonexclusive uses of the copyright, insuring that the other rights' owners are properly accounted to; but no co-owner can issue exclusive licenses for the work without the consent of other owners. See also *joint-administration*, *copublishing*, and *administration rights*.

Copies
Reproductions of an artistic work. Copies are fixed tangible representations, which transmit or communicate an artistic work either directly or through a machine or device, such as a tape player.

Copr.
Abbreviation for *copyright*.

Coproducer
A producer whose production responsibilities, credit, and compensation are shared with one or more other producers on a recording project. While some coproducers work together on all facets of production in committee fashion, other coproducers may divide tasks according to individual strengths and preferences. For instance, one coproducer's forte might be creative (arranging, directing musicians and vocalists, etc.), while a partner's expertise is technical (engineering and mixing, etc.).

Copublish
To publish a work together with one or more other publishers. See *copublishing*.

Copublisher
One of two or more music publishers who share ownership of a song copyright. See *copublishing*, below.

Copublishing
Copublishing (or *split publishing*) is when two or more music publishers share ownership of a song copyright. Every active publisher's catalog contains split copyrights, and negotiating copublishing arrangements is a common occurrence, though not always an easy one.

Copublishing typically comes about when: (1) two or more writers signed to different publishers collaborate on a song; (2) a record company, producer, or an artist acquires interest in a copyright in return for recording a song; (3) a film or television production company acquires interest in a copyright in return for using a song; (4) a small publisher splits copyrights with a *full-service publisher* in return for an advance or other financial consideration; (5) a small publisher splits copyrights with a full-service publisher who can handle promotion, administration, and licensing.

Copy

(1) An exact reproduction of an original work. (2) To reproduce or duplicate an original work. (3) To imitate or be derivative of something else.

Copy Protection

A software code used to prevent a program from being copied without compensation to the copyright holder. See also *serial copy management system* and *DART*.

Copyist

Person engaged by an arranger to copy out individual parts of a musical score.

Copyright

The legal statutory right granted to the creator of an original literary, musical, dramatic, or artistic work by which the creator has exclusive control over the work's production, reproduction, manufacture, sale, publication, distribution, display, or performance. The creator of the work may be an author or a composer, but in copyright law a person or company, such as a publisher, producer, or distributor, may also be deemed the *author* of the work if the person or company *commissions* the creation of the work as a *work made for hire*. In any event, the author can assign, give, sell, or transfer copyright ownership in the work to another person or company. The copyright owner (or *copyright holder* or *copyright proprietor*) maintains the exclusive right to reproduce the work or license others to do so, and receives payments for each performance or royalties for each copy sold.

In the United States, copyright protection is subject to the *Copyright Act of 1976* as amended. Protection extends for the life of the creator plus 50 years, or, in the case of *works made for hire*, for 75 years from the date of first publication. (As of 1998, Congress was considering legislation to extend the term of copyright protection.) International copyright protection is provided through treaties with other nations, such as the *Universal Copyright Convention*, the *Buenos Aires Convention*, and the *Berne Convention*, all of which the United States signed. See also *common law copyright*.

Copyright Abandonment

A copyright owner may voluntarily relinquish all rights to a copyright without selling or giving it to another party by "dedicating it to the public" (i.e., allowing its public usage without permission, license, restriction, or claim for compensation, etc.). A copyright may also be involuntarily abandoned if the owner knowingly allows its public usage without permission, license, restriction, or claim for compensation, etc. An abandoned copyright is said to be in the *public domain*.

Copyright Act of 1790

See also *Statute of Anne*. The United States Constitution authorized Congress to promote the arts, "by securing for limited times to authors...the exclusive right to their respective writings..." (Article I, Section 8). Under this constitutional provision, the first Congress enacted the first US copyright law in 1790. The statute was revised and expanded over the years and eventually underwent major revision with the *Copyright Act of 1909*.

Copyright Act of 1909

Statutory act passed by Congress for the purposes of regulating copyright procedures and protection in the United States, superseding previous acts, and remaining in effect until superseded by the *Copyright Act of 1976*, which took effect on January 1, 1978. Notable provisions of the Act of 1909 included: (a) copyright protection for a term of 28 years; (b) opportunities to renew protection for a further 28 years, making maximum protection 56 years; (c) a statutory mechanical royalty rate of 2¢ per song per record sold; (d) requirement that a *notice of copyright* be placed prominently on all published copies of songs, with failure to place such notice resulting in automatic loss of copyright; (e) registration of unpublished works to be made with the Library of Congress using an *EU Form*, with re-registration required when a work was published, using an *EP Form*.

Copyright Act of 1976

Copyright law in the United States is governed by Title 17 of the United States Code, which was amended by the enactment of a statute for its general revision, Public Law 94-553 (90 Stat. 2541), and which is referred to as The Copyright Act of 1976. The 1976 Act supersedes the *Copyright Act of 1909*, as amended, as of January 1, 1978.

The US Copyright Act of 1976 (effective January 1, 1978) replaced the Copyright Act of 1909. Revision became necessary because of technological advances not dreamed of by the framers of the old law-tape recorders, photocopiers, television, radio, long-playing records, piped music, synchronization of music onto film, etc. (And since 1976, of course, there have been further technological advances not dreamed of by the revisers of the 1909 law-CDs, DAT, MIDI, CD-ROMS, etc.) Copyright laws in other countries have undergone revisions and amendments for the same reason.

Under the 1976 Act, both published and unpublished copyrightable works are subject to a single system of statutory protection giving copyright owners exclusive rights to reproduce their works for distribution to the public by sale, rental, lease, or lending, and to perform, display, or broadcast the works to the public. Copyright owners also are given exclusive rights to prepare *derivative works* based upon the original copyrighted work. All of these rights are subject to certain exceptions, including the principle of fair use and *compulsory licensing* for the recording of musical compositions, *noncommercial transmissions* by *public broadcasters* of published musical and graphic works, and the *secondary transmission on cable television systems*; and voluntary licensing of jukebox performances.

Copyright protection is given only to original works of authorship *fixed* in a *tangible* medium of expression, from which they can be "perceived, reproduced, or otherwise communicated, either directly or with the aid of a machine or device." Works eligible for copyright protection include literary works, musical compositions, dramas and dramatico-musical compositions, pantomimes and choreographic works, motion pictures and other audiovisual works, sound recordings, and visual arts.

The United States joined the *Berne Convention* effective March 1, 1989, and from that date US copyrights are automatically protected in all member nations of the *Berne Union*. Likewise, foreign copyrights owned by nationals of any other country belonging to the Berne Union are automatically protected in the United States.

While US copyright law continues to govern the protection and registration of works in the United States, joining the Union required certain changes in US copyright law, which were put into effect by the *Berne Convention Implementation Act of 1988*. These changes are not retroactive and are effective only with regards to works created on and after March 1, 1989. One of the more notable changes deals with requirements for a *copyright notice* on published materials in order to affect copyright protection. Another change deals with compulsory licensing for jukeboxes, which is now "voluntary." (See *Jukebox licensing*.)

For detailed information about the 1976 Copyright Act and subsequent amendments to US copyright law, contact The Copyright Office, Information Section, LM-401, Library of Congress, Washington, D.C. 20559. Tel: (202) 707-3000.

Copyright Administration

(1) The management of business affairs related to copyrights, including copyright registration, contracts, licenses, royalty accounting, etc. (2) The system of managing and protecting copyright assets.

Copyright Administrator

Person in charge of *copyright administration* for a *copyright owner*.

Copyright Asset

An *intangible* property having monetary value, which is owned by a firm or an individual, and which is protected by statutory copyright law. The assessed value of a copyright or copyright catalog is entered in the balance sheet portion of the financial statement listing a company's or individual's assets.

Copyright Arbitration Royalty Panel (CARP)

Until 1993, the *statutory mechanical royalty* rate was set by the *Copyright Royalty Tribunal* (CRT), and periodically adjusted to reflect changes in the *consumer price index* (CPI). The Copyright Royalty Tribunal was abolished in 1993. The mechanical rate is now periodically adjusted by the *Copyright Arbitration Royalty Panel* (CARP), which is appointed by the *Librarian of Congress*. In addition to setting the statutory mechanical royalty rate, CARP holds hearings on copyright royalty matters and distributes mechanical royalties to copyright owners that have previously been deposited with the *Copyright Office* by copyright users.

Copyright Claim

(1) To maintain a right or an ownership in a copyright. (2) The basis by which a copyright ownership is maintained, such as authorship or assignment.

Copyright Claimant

Person or company claiming copyright ownership by virtue of *authorship* or *assignment* of ownership from the original or previous *copyright owner*.

Copyright Collective

A music rights organization, such as a *performing-rights society* or *mechanical-rights society*.

Copyright Control

(1) The authority to manage, license, direct, or exercise dominating influence over a copyright, such control being derived from *authorship* or by virtue of an agreement, assignment of ownership, a license or a contract. (2) In the United Kingdom, "Copyright Control" is printed on published works and record labels instead of the *copyright notice* when there is no music publisher to credit or when publishing rights are in dispute.

Copyright Convention

International conferences held by authorized representatives from various countries to establish or amend reciprocal copyright protection treaties. See *Berne Convention, Universal Copyright Convention, Rome Convention, Geneva Phonograms Convention*, and *Buenos Aires Convention*.

Copyright Deposit

One of the *formalities* of establishing a claim of copyright ownership under the *Copyright Act of 1976* is the requirement that claimants deposit two complete copies of the *best edition* of a work in the *Copyright Office* of the *Library of Congress*. A deposit is not the same as *registering* a work, which is a separate formality. Section 407 of the Copyright Act states that deposit must be made within three months of publication, although failure to do so does not invalidate a copyright claim. However, the Copyright Office is authorized to demand copies be deposited, and failure to make a deposit after receiving such a demand may result in fines ranging from $250 to $2,500. For more information about deposit procedures, contact the Copyright Office and request Circular 7d.

Copyright Duration

Same as *copyright term*, the period in which a work is protected by statutory copyright. Under the *Copyright Act of 1909*, copyright protection was given for an initial term of 28 years with the right to renew for a further 28 years. This offered a maximum duration, or copyright life of 56 years.

The *Copyright Act of 1976* (effective January 1, 1978) as amended by Public Law 102-307 (effective June 26, 1992), makes renewal of works published or registered between January 1, 1964, and December 31, 1977, automatic. Filing a renewal claim in the Copyright Office is now optional. Copyrights in their renewal term as of January 1, 1978 are automatically extended up to a maximum of 75 years. *Unpublished* works in existence on January 1, 1978, which were not protected by statutory copyright, but had not fallen into *public domain*, now have automatic copyright protection for the duration of the author's life, plus 50 years, or, at minimum, for a term of 25 years (until December 31, 2002). For works *published* before January 1, 1978, copyright protection is automatically extended for an additional term of 25 years.

Works created on or after January 1, 1978 are granted a term of copyright protection equal to the author's life, plus an additional 50 years. (As of 1998, Congress was considering legislation to extend the term of copyright protection.) For *works made for hire*, and for *anonymous* and *pseudonymous* works, the term of protection is 75 years from publication or 100 years from creation, whichever is shorter. All terms of copyright protection run through the end of the calendar year in which they expire. See also *copyright renewal*.

Copyright Fee

Fees charged by the *Copyright Office* of the *Library of Congress* for the registration of copyright claims, *recordations of copyright transfers*, and recordations of amended copyright information. Fees vary depending upon the type of filing. For instance, a $20 fee is the cost of registering a claim of copyright, a $10 fee is imposed for filing a *mortgage recordation*, etc.

Copyright Forms

When registering copyright claims, a *copyright claimant* fills out one of the following forms and sends it to the *Copyright Office* along with the *filing fee* and two copies of the best edition of a the work (one copy if the work is *unpublished*):

• *Form PA* for registering both published and unpublished songs.

• *Form SR* for published and unpublished sound recordings. (When registering a recorded performance *and* the songs rendered on the recording, both claims may be registered on this one form-rather than separately filing an SR for the recording and a PA for the song).

• *Form TX* for nondramatic literary works.

• *Form CA* for filing corrections or additional information about works previously registered.

• *Form VA* for registering visual arts (photos, models, prints, posters, album covers, designs, advertisements, etc.)

See also *copyright formalities* and *copyright registration*.

Copyright Formalities

Term used for procedures required to establish a valid copyright claim. Under the *Copyright Act of 1976*, copyright claimants in the United States were required to affix a *copyright notice* on all copies of published works, deposit two copies of the best edition of the work, and register the claim to copyright with the *Copyright Office*. But, with the *Berne Convention Implementation Act of 1988*, these formalities are no longer required for establishing a copyright claim to works published on or after March 1, 1989. However, voluntary compliance with these formalities is strongly recommended, because they aid in validating a claim in the event of *infringement*, and, unless the formalities have been undertaken, the copyright claimant may not be eligible for all statutory civil remedies and damage awards that are otherwise available.

Copyright Holder

A person, company, organization, or entity vested with ownership in a copyright, or authorized to act for the copyright owner in matters relating to the copyright.

Copyright Holders Association (CHA)

The *performing-right society* in Taiwan.

Copyright Holding Company

Generally, a holding company owns or controls partial or complete interest in another company or other companies; a holding company exists primarily to invest in and exercise control over other companies. The holding company's earnings are entirely derived from earnings of those companies it controls. A copyright holding company, therefore, might be formed to invest in other companies that own copyrights, but the copyright holding company itself does not actively operate as a full-service music publisher (promoting and directly acquiring copyrights.) However, the term "copyright holding company" might also loosely be applied to operations that actively spark the creation of music, but aren't necessarily full-fledged publishing companies, because they don't develop songwriting talent or market songs outside their own area of business. Examples include television, film, jingle, and record-production companies who *commission* works specifically for in-house productions. They can also include recording artists and producers who acquire copyright interests in songs they record, but who don't actively exploit those works to other users.

Copyright Income
Monies earned from licensing permissions to use copyrighted works. In music publishing, for instance, copyrights earn income from royalties and fees derived from sales of sound recordings, home videos, printed music, and from broadcast, live, and background music performances, and from music used in advertising and films, etc. See also *mechanical royalties, synchronization fees, performance royalties, transcription fees, print, reprint, subpublishing*.

Copyright Infringement
The violation of rights belonging to a copyright owner. Copyright infringement occurs when someone makes any unauthorized use of a copyrighted work. It also occurs when someone uses enough elements of a copyrighted work to be considered *substantial similarity*. In other words, infringement is not limited to cases where copies are made note-for-note or word-for-word.

Infringement is a violation of copyright law, and is usually handled through civil lawsuits brought by the aggrieved party in federal court. In order to sue for copyright infringement, the copyright must first be registered with the *Library of Congress*. If a case is proved, the court can issue an injunction against the defendant to cease and desist any further infringement. Criminal penalties can be imposed if the injunction is ignored.

The court can also order all copies of the infringing work to be destroyed, and the defendant to reimburse the *plaintiff* for all financial loss incurred by the infringement. This can include an amount equal to all profits the infringer has made from the usage.

If someone uses a copyrighted work as a movie theme or TV jingle, the plaintiff can have expert witnesses testify as to what the fair market value of a *synchronization license* would be in similar usages to establish how much money should be awarded in damages. In addition, the copyright owner may be awarded *statutory* damages for each work infringed (usually between $250 and $10,000), plus all court costs and reasonable attorney's fees.

Infringement doesn't necessarily have to be intentional. Indeed, cases abound where the guilty party wasn't consciously aware of copying an existing work. The situation is different, however, when someone, such as an organized counterfeiting organization, knowingly infringes a copyright for profit. Although infringement is normally treated as a civil matter, cases of blatantly intentional infringement might constitute criminal activity. In such cases, the copyright owner can bring criminal charges, and, if proven, the court can levy criminal penalties of imprisonment and fines of as much as $50,000 for each work infringed.

One defense against a charge of infringement is the principle of *fair use*. This concept is incorporated into copyright law, and permits the reproduction of small amounts of copyrighted material for the purposes of critical review, parody, scholarship, news reporting, etc. The amount of copying must have no practical effect on the market for, or value of, the original work, and must be used only for purposes of teaching, illustration, comment, criticism, quotation, or summary.

Copyright in Sound Recordings
Since 1972, when an amendment to the then-operative copyright law (The *Copyright Act of 1909*) took effect, sound recordings have been eligible for *statutory* copyright protection similar to protection afforded other types of *intellectual* works. For sound recordings, *copyright notice* consists of the symbol (P) (the letter P in circle), the year of first publication, and the name of the copyright owner, visible on the surface of the phonorecord, its label, or container. Example: (P) *1998 Smith Record Corp.*

Under the amendment to the Copyright Act of 1909, which provided for copyright registration of sound recordings after January 1, 1972, copyright claimants submitted their claims to the *Copyright Office* using *Form N*. Under the *Copyright Act of 1976* (effective January 1, 1978), however, copyright claimants for sound recordings use *Form SR* when registering claims with the Copyright Office.

Copyright Life
The term during which a copyright is in effect. See *copyright protection, copyright duration*, and *public domain*.

Copyright Management
Usually, the same as *copyright administration*: The management of business affairs related to copyrights, including copyright registration, contracts, licenses, royalty accounting, etc. (2) The system of managing and protecting copyright assets.

Copyright Management, Inc. (CMI)
Nashville-based company, which claims to currently collect the equivalent of 15% of all US *mechanical licensing* revenue on behalf of its publisher and songwriter clients. But, apart from mechanical li-

censing, CMI provides clients the option of letting it handle complete *administrative* services worldwide. Its administration package includes registering songs with the *Copyright Office*, filing *clearances* and *cue sheets* with *performing-right societies*, preparing and managing songwriter agreements, copublishing contracts, *synchronization licenses*, and other related documents, contracts, and licenses, overseas collections, and preparation of royalty statements to songwriters.

CMI's service charge to clients is two-tier: 5% of gross collections for US and Canadian mechanical licensing only, or 10% of gross collections for publishers who elect to use its complete, international administration package.

CMI is located at 1102 17th Avenue South, Suite 401, Nashville, TN 37212. Tel: (615) 321-0652.

Copyright Manager

Usually, the same as *copyright administrator*: Person in charge of *copyright management* or *administration* for a *copyright owner*.

Copyright Notice

Under the copyright law in effect before 1978 (The *Copyright Act of 1909*), all published copies of a work were required to bear a *copyright notice* affixed in such manner and location as to give reasonable notice of the owner's *copyright claim*. The *Copyright Act of 1976* continued this requirement, but it is no longer mandatory for works published on or after March 1, 1989 as a result of the United States joining the *Berne Convention*. Notice of copyright is still required on all copies of works published before March 1, 1989, however.

Copyright notice (except for sound recordings) consists of the symbol (c) (the letter C in a circle), the word "copyright," or the abbreviation "copr.," the year of first publication, and the name of the copyright owner. *Example: (c) 1998 Smith Music.*

For sound recordings, copyright notice consists of the symbol (P) (the letter P in circle), the year of first publication, and the name of the copyright owner, visible on the surface of the phonorecord, its label, or container. *Example: (P) 1998 Smith Record Corp.*

If the copyright notice is omitted or given with erroneous information, copyright will not immediately be forfeited, but it must be corrected within certain time limits. However, persons or companies misled by copyright notice omissions or errors may be immune from liability for infringement.

Prior to the effective date of the 1976 Act (January 1, 1978), if a work was published without the required notice, copyright was lost immediately (though some works were granted "ad interim" protection). Once copyright is lost, it can only be restored in the United States by special legislation.

Though the required notice of copyright has been abolished for works published on or after March 1, 1989 under the accords of the Berne agreement, voluntary use of notice is strongly recommended. When a copyright notice is displayed, an infringer cannot claim to have "innocently infringed" a work, and may then be liable for damages the *infringement* caused the copyright owner.

The *Berne Convention Implementation Act of 1988* is not retroactive, meaning that all works published before March 1, 1989 must comply with the notice requirements of the 1976 Act. If a work was first published without notice between January 1, 1978 and February 28, 1989, it must be registered within five years after publication and the notice added to all copies distributed in the United States after discovery of the omission.

Copyright Office

Section of the *Library of Congress*, headed by the *Register of Copyrights*, which is charged with dealing with copyright matters. The Copyright Office is located at 101 Independence Avenue S.E., Washington, DC 20559; Tel: (202) 707-3000; Fax: (202) 707-8366.

For copies of publications explaining copyright matters, and for copies of *copyright registration forms*, call the Forms and Publications Hotline, (202) 707-9100, or write: The Copyright Office, Publications Section, LM-455, Library of Congress, Washington, DC 20559.

To talk directly with an information specialist or to request further information, call (202) 707-3000, or write: The Copyright Office, Information Section, LM-401, Library of Congress, Washington, DC 20559.

Copyright Organisation of Trinidad & Tobago (COTT)

The *performing-right society* in Trinidad & Tobago.

Copyright Owner

A person, company, organization, or entity vested with ownership in a copyright, or with any of the five exclusive rights that comprise a copyright. Copyright ownership derives initially from *authorship*. The *author* of a work is automatically vested with copyright ownership upon creation of the work. An author is not necessarily the creator of the work, however. A person, company, organization, or entity may *commission* a songwriter, for instance, to create a work as a *work made for hire*, in which case the commissioning party is classed as the author of the work and owns the copyright therein.

Copyright ownership bestows five exclusive rights, known as the *bundle of rights*, which include rights to reproduce copies of the work, publicly perform the work, prepare *derivative works* based on the original, distribute copies of the work to the public, and publicly display the work, or to authorize others to do any of these acts.

Copyright ownership pertains only to ownership in the intellectual property from which copies are made (i.e., the song or the performance); it does not pertain to the physical property embodying the copyrighted work (i.e., discs, tapes, film, sheet music, etc.).

Copyright Proprietor
Same as *copyright owner*.

Copyright Protection
The *statutory* protection of all rights vested in the owner of a copyright during the copyright's life. A copyright is a perishable asset. There is a statutory limit to a copyright's life, after which legal protection ends. At that time, the song enters the *public domain* and can be used by anyone without need of a license or payment of royalties. However, copyright life is long enough to be considered a long-term asset.

Copyright protection is in effect from the time a work is fixed in permanent form (recorded or written down) until 50 years after the author's death, or for a period of 75 years from publication or 100 years from the date of creation in the case of a *work made for hire*. In the case of a work jointly created by two or more authors, copyright remains in effect until 50 years after the death of the last surviving collaborator. (As of 1998, legislation was being considered to extend copyright protection to 70 years after the author's death.)

Any original work is automatically copyrighted once it has been "fixed in any tangible medium of expression." A "tangible medium" is any format "now known or later developed" from which the work "can be perceived, reproduced, or otherwise communicated, either directly or with the aid of a machine or device."

Copyright protects the way a work is expressed, not the idea behind the work. For instance, if a song is about lost love, the lyrics and music are copyrightable, but not the subject matter. The theme of lost love has been, and will be, applied to thousands of songs.

Copyright doesn't protect the physical property used to fix a work. When a person purchases a CD, he owns the disc, but not the songs, nor the artist's performance of the songs on the disc. The owner of the CD may not, therefore, make copies of the CD, or even play it publicly for profit without authorization from the copyright owners.

The copyright owner is paid on the *first sale* of the product (i.e., a CD) embodying the copyright. The purchaser then is the owner of the physical product, though not the copyright. But, as owner of the physical product, the purchaser can resell the product without additional payment to the copyright owner. Which means a person can sell his CD collection without having to compensate the music publishers or recording artists.

The concept of *first sale* is the legal basis video stores use to buy videos that they in turn rent out and ultimately resell as used videos. Many record stores also buy and sell used CDs on the same legal grounding.

Copyright does not protect the title of a work. Though a lot of thought often goes into choosing a song title, dozens of copyrighted songs might share the same title. (Titles of motion pictures can, however, be protected by registration.) However, certain works ultimately become so famous that the Library of Congress refuses to accept a copyright registration claim with a title that can easily be confused with the established work. For example, the doctrine of *unfair competition* might apply if someone were to register a new song called *Rudolph the Red-Nosed Reindeer*.

Copyright Registration
One of the *formalities* of establishing a claim of copyright ownership under the *Copyright Act of 1976* is the registration of claims of copyright in the *Copyright Office* of the *Library of Congress*. A registration is not the same as making a *deposit*, which is a separate formality. Registration may be made at any time during the term of copyright. Under the accords of the *Berne Convention*, which the United States joined effective March 1, 1989, registration is not required to establish a copyright claim, nor is it any longer a prerequisite for bringing a court action against alleged infringers. However, copyright claimants may not be fully eligible for awards of statutory damages and attorney's fees for acts of infringement that occur before a registration is made. For this reason, it is recommended that copyright claims be registered with the Copyright Office at the first opportunity. See also *copyright formalities*.

Copyright Renewal
The *Copyright Act of 1909* provided copyright protection for a maximum of 56 years (an initial term of 28 years with the right to renew for a further 28 years). To renew a copyright, the *claimant* had to file a renewal claim (*Form R*) with the *Copyright Office*. Copyright protection could be lost through errors and oversights when it was time to file a renewal claim.

Under the *Copyright Act of 1976* (effective January 1, 1978), and subsequent legislation (Public Law 102-307, the *Copyright Renewal Act of 1992*, effective June 26, 1992), copyright renewal of works published or registered between January 1, 1964 and December 31, 1977 is automatic. Filing a renewal claim in the Copyright Office for this class of pre-1978 works is now optional.

Moreover, copyrights in their renewal term as of January 1, 1978, are automatically extended up to a maximum of 75 years. *Unpublished* works in existence on January 1, 1978, which are not protected by statutory copyright, but have not yet fallen into *public domain*, now have automatic copyright protection for the author's life plus 50 years, or, at minimum, for a term of 25 years (until December 31, 2002). For works *published* before January 1, 1978, copyright protection is automatically extended for an additional term of 25 years.

For works created on or after January 1, 1978, the Copyright Act of 1976 provides a term lasting for the author's life, plus an additional 50 years. For *works made for hire*, and for *anonymous* and *pseudonymous* works, the term of protection is 75 years from publication or 100 years from creation, whichever is shorter. (As of 1998, legislation was being considered to extend copyright protection to 70 years after the author's death.) All terms of copyright protection run through the end of the calendar year in which they expire.

Works already in the public domain are not protected under current law. There is no way to restore protection to works which have gone out of copyright for any reason, except through special legislation.

Copyright Renewal Act of 1992

See *copyright renewal*, above.

Copyright Renewal Assignment

Under the *Copyright Act of 1909*, creative works were given *statutory* copyright protection for an initial period of 28 years, which could be renewed for an additional 28 years. A copyright owner could assign (give, sell, transfer) the copyright to another party during the original term, just as any other type of property right could be transferred. However, a copyright owner had no rights per se in the work beyond the original term unless and until those rights were renewed for a renewal term. Therefore, the copyright owner had only an "expectancy" of continuing rights beyond the original copyright term, contingent upon renewal. In order, then, to assign those future rights before they existed, the copyright owner could only make an assignment of *renewal expectancy*.

Assuming the copyright owner made such an assignment, and was still living at the expiration of the original copyright term, the original owner was bound by the terms of the assignment. The rights vested in the copyright upon the renewal date would then become the property of the *assignee*. If, however, the copyright owner died before expiration of the original term, the rights vested upon renewal belong to the *statutory beneficiaries* of the deceased's estate.

If, for example, a music publisher wished to obtain renewal rights from a songwriter, the publisher would have to also obtain the renewal expectancies of the writer's statutory beneficiaries (normally, the spouse and children) at the same time. Even this was not foolproof, because, if the writer *and* the spouse and children had died by the time of renewal, the expectancies would pass to *their* statutory beneficiaries. The issue could be further complicated by the writer having additional children or re-marrying after the publisher had received assignments of renewal expectancy from the original statutory beneficiaries.

The *rule of expectancy* applies only to songs in their original terms of copyright as of the effective date of the Copyright Act of 1976 (January 1, 1978). Works created after that date are provided with one term of copyright protection, and there are no renewals.

Copyright Restoration

Under the *Copyright Act of 1909*, the term of *copyright protection* in the United States was limited to 56 years maximum (a 28-year term plus a 28-year renewal). Many foreign copyrights thus fell into *public domain* in the United States, either because renewal *formalities* weren't taken properly or because 56 years lapsed, even though the works were still under copyright protection in their countries of origin. Since the United States joined the *Berne Convention* in 1989, copyright owners of songs originating in countries that are signatories to the Berne Convention (or which are members of the *World Trade Organization*) can have copyright protection restored to works that fell into the public domain, as long as those works are still in copyright in their countries of origin. Copyright restoration is accomplished by filing a *GATT form* with the *US Copyright Office*.

Copyright Reversion

(1) The return of a copyright and all rights therein to its original or previous owner or to the previous owner's heirs or successors after a copyright assignment has expired or otherwise been terminated. (2) The right to succeed to a copyright and all rights therein after a copyright assignment has expired or otherwise been terminated.

Copyright Revision

(1) The act or process of revising, editing, changing, or adding to the content of a copyrighted work. (2) The act or process of revising information pertaining to copyright ownership or its change of copyrightable content. (3) A revised or new version of a copyrighted work. (4) A correction of information pertaining to copyright ownership or its copyrightable content. (5) A change, revision, or amendment to statutory copyright law.

Copyright Royalty Tribunal (CRT)

Until 1993, the *statutory mechanical royalty rate* in the United States was set by the *Copyright Royalty Tribunal* (CRT). The CRT adjusted the statutory mechanical royalty rate every two years to reflect changes in the *consumer price index* (CPI). The Copyright Royalty Tribunal was abolished in 1993. The mechanical rate is now periodically adjusted by the *Copyright Arbitration Royalty Panel* (CARP), which is appointed by the *Librarian of Congress*.

Copyright Search

The process of researching registrations of copyright claims in the *Copyright Office* in order to ascertain ownership of rights. A copyright search is a prerequisite when purchasing copyrights in order to verify the status of rights claimed by a seller. Records in the Copyright Office provide detailed listings of registered titles, their owners, authors, remaining terms of protection, recordations of assignments, liens, mortgages, counterclaims, corrections of previously filed information, etc. Exhaustive copyright searches are usually carried out by attorneys or research specialists and may ultimately be expensive due to the time-consuming nature of the process. See also *search organization, clearing house, title search,* and *due diligence.*

Copyright Symbol

In a *copyright notice*, the copyright symbol (except for sound recordings) consists of the symbol (c) (the letter C in a circle). This is followed by the year of first publication, and the name of the copyright owner. *Example: (c) 1998 Smith Music.* For sound recordings, copyright notice consists of the symbol (P) (the letter P in circle), followed by the year of first publication, and the name of the copyright owner. *Example: (P) 1998 Smith Record Corp.*

Copyright Term

Same as *copyright duration*, the period in which a work is protected by statutory copyright. See *copyright life, copyright duration, copyright protection,* and *copyright renewal.*

Copyright Termination

(1) The date on which statutory *copyright protection* ends. For works created on or after January 1, 1978, termination occurs on December 31st of the 50th year from the date of the last surviving author's death; or on December 31st of the 75th year from the date of a *work made for hire's* first publication. (As of 1998, legislation was being considered to extend *copyright protection* to 70 years after the author's death.) (2) The loss of *copyright protection*. See also *copyright renewal* and *copyright reversion.*

Copyright Transfer

The assignment, gift, or sale of a copyright from one party to another. Although all rights of copyright (the *bundle of rights*) are automatically vested in the author of a work upon its creation, the *author* may give, sell, assign or "transfer" some or all of these rights (or a percentage thereof) to another person, company, organization, or entity at any time during the *term of copyright*. Most songwriters assign their copyrights to music publishers, for instance. And many music publishers ultimately sell their catalogs of copyrights to other publishers. Each such assignment or change of copyright ownership requires a written agreement detailing the transfer of rights. When assignment is made of a work that has previously been registered with the *Copyright Office*, the new copyright owner generally files a copy of the transfer agreement with the Copyright Office, which then issues a *Certificate of Recordation*. See also *chain of title.*

Copyright User

A person, company, organization, or other entity that performs, broadcasts, records, prints, reproduces, distributes, or sells a copyrighted work under license from the copyright owner.

Copywrite

To write copy for advertisements, publicity, promotional materials, album liner notes, etc.

Copywriter

Person who writes copy for advertisements, publicity, promotional materials, album liner notes, etc.

Corp.

Abbreviation for *Corporation.*

Corporation

Corporations are legal entities separate and apart from their owners. They have a life of their own, may enter into agreements, purchase property, make investments, raise money, sue and be sued, all in the name of the corporation. Even a corporation owned 100% by one person continues to exist after the owner dies-the deceased's shares pass to his estate. The corporation exists so long as it remains solvent, or until it is voluntarily dissolved by its owners. And as long as it exists, no matter how often it changes hands, it remains bound by any contracts, licenses, debts, and obligations entered into by previous owners.

Corporations are chartered and regulated by the states in which they operate. Some types of corporations must also comply with federal regulations, particularly those that sell stock to the public. A corporation may be owned by individuals, partnerships, other corporations, or any combination thereof.

One of the principle advantages of a corporation is that its owners have *limited liability*; the personal assets of owners are shielded from any liabilities incurred by the business. In the event of business failure, liquidation, or bankruptcy, the most any owner can lose is the amount of capital they have already invested in the business.

The extent of ownership or equity a person has in a corporation is represented by shares of stock. Each shareholder has a "security" interest, or a claim on the assets of the company equal to the value or percentage of shares owned. If a corporation is wound up or sold, liquidated assets pay (1) accrued taxes, (2) creditors in order of security, and (3) accrued salaries. Any remaining balance is distributed to shareholders in proportion to the amount of stock owned.

To maintain corporate status as a separate legal entity, personal affairs of shareholders and directors must not spill over into corporate activities. Otherwise, the IRS may declare the corporation as an "alter ego" of the owner(s) and nullify the corporate status for tax purposes. Mixing personal and business records may also pierce the corporate veil of limited liability for shareholders, exposing personal assets to claims from creditors and winners of law suits.

Corporation for Public Broadcasting (CPB)
Founded in 1967, CPB is a federally funded organization that created and helps fund the operations of *National Public Radio* (*NPR*) and television's *Public Broadcasting Service* (*PBS*). CPB develops public telecommunications services (radio, television and new media such as online programming), investing in nearly 1,000 local radio and television stations that reach virtually every household in the country. It is the largest single source for funding for public programming. Congress appropriates federal tax dollars for the public broadcasting system in three-year advance cycles and appropriates these funds two years ahead of the fiscal year in which they are to be spent. (Appropriation for fiscal year 1996 was $275 million.) CPB also receives grants from foundations and corporations for specific projects. CPB distributes more than 95% of its budget to local station producers and service providers for operations, community service grants and programming. CPB's overhead averages four percent of its total budget. CPB is located at 901 E. St. NW, Washington, DC 20004. Tel: (202) 879-9600; Fax: (202) 783-1019.

Cosign
(1) To sign a contract or other document jointly with another person or persons. (2) To endorse another's signature as *guarantor* for the fulfillment of a service, obligation, or performance, as in the case of a loan repayment or a contract with a minor.

Cosigner
Person who signs a contract or other document jointly with another person or persons and thus shares equal responsibility for the fulfillment of a service, obligation, or performance, as in the case of *co-authorship*, a loan guarantee, or as a guardian for a minor.

Cost-per-Thousand (CPM)
A formula used in marketing to work out the cost of delivering an advertisement to each television viewer, radio listener, newspaper or magazine reader, or direct mail recipient. *Example*: The *CPM* of an ad costing $10,000 in a magazine with 50,000 readers is 20¢ ($10,000 ÷ 50,000).

Coterminous
Same as *conterminous*. Two or more contracts or licenses sharing the same termination date. *Collateral contracts* are often coterminous.

COTT
Abbreviation for *Copyright Organisation of Trinidad & Tobago*.

Counterfeit
(1) To make unauthorized copies of a patented, trademarked, or copyrighted product with the intent to pass the imitations off as genuine. (2) A forged or unauthorized replication of a patented, trademarked, or copyrighted product that is represented as genuine, and which is sold without due compensation to the owners of the patent, trademark, or copyright.

Counterpart
(1) A peer, associate, or colleague who has similar functions or characteristics as another. (2) A copy or duplicate of a contract or other legal document. (3) One of two or more parts that go together to form a whole. (4) An equal or equivalent to another.

Country
A market segment or musical genre, which may be further segmented into subgenres such as traditional country, modern or contemporary country, honky tonk, country rock, country & western, bluegrass, etc. See also *Country & Western*, below.

Country & Western (C&W)
Name given to country music in the past, but now more often associated with a particular segment of the country music market and genre. C&W originated from folk music brought to the US by English, Scottish, and Irish settlers, which became Americanized and popularly adapted in the rural areas of the southeastern and western states. Though appealing to mostly white audiences, the genre has influenced, and been influenced by, blues and R&B music, and has also influenced the development of rock and modern pop music. No longer restricted to rural, poor audiences, the genre now enjoys wide popular appeal nationally.

Country of Manufacture
The country in which a product is made, not necessarily the country in which it is published, sold, or distributed. Many countries require recorded product to display the name of the country in which the product was manufactured; in such countries, it is usually also a requirement that album covers, books, and other printed material bear the name of the country in which the material was printed.

Country Music Association (CMA)

A nonprofit trade organization founded in Nashville (1958) to promote country music worldwide. Membership, which is around 9,000, is open to companies and individuals actively involved in country music. CMA produces the annual CMA Awards, *Fan Fair*, and SRO. The organization's headquarters are located at 1 Music Circle North, Nashville, TN 37203. Tel: (615) 244-2840; Fax (615) 726-0314.

Couple

To pair together. The term is frequently used to describe linking one side of a single recording with the other side, as in "coupled with" (*C/W*), or "backed with" (*B/W*), or to make a *compilation* album of recordings by different artists. The term can also refer to pairing two artists together in duet performance.

Coupled With (C/W)

See *C/W* and *couple*.

Coupling

Two performances or tracks linked together, as in a *duet* or the *A* and *B sides* of a single recording. See *C/W* and *couple*.

Covenant

(1) A contract; an agreement; a binding obligation. (2) To enter into a contract; to make a pledge; to make a binding promise to do or not to do a particular thing. (3) An assurance, warranty, or guarantee that something is true or that a circumstance exists or does not exist.

Cover

(1) To record a new version of a song previously recorded and released by another artist. (2) A new version of a song previously recorded and released by another artist. See also *local cover*.

Cover Artwork

The composite graphics, illustrations, line drawings, photographs, and text used on the printed covers of record albums, CDs, CD-ROMs, audiocassettes, music folios, sheet music, books, home videos, etc.

Cover Band

Band whose repertoire focuses on current Top 40 material and/or material previously recorded and released by other acts.

Cover Record

See *cover*, above.

Cowrite

(1) To write a song, script, or book in *collaboration* with another. (2) A song or book that has been written in *collaboration* with one or more other writers.

Cowriter

A person who *collaborates* with one or more other writers to create a song, script, or book.

Cowriting

The act or process of writing a song, script, or book in *collaboration* with another.

CPB

Abbreviation for *Corporation for Public Broadcasting*.

CPI

Abbreviation for *consumer price index*.

CPM

Abbreviation for *cost-per-thousand*.

Crash

(1) A type of cymbal often used to emphasize a beat. (See *crash cymbal*.) (2) To enter an event without buying a ticket or without an invitation. (3) A computer failure or computer program error, resulting in loss of data.

Crash and Burn

To fail spectacularly.

Crash Cymbal

A large cymbal with a relatively shallow cup and upturned edges, made of a special alloy that produces a brilliant crash when struck by a drum stick. Also called *Chinese crash cymbal*.

Crash the Gate

To enter an event without buying a ticket or without an invitation.

Crawl

List of *credits* at the end of a film or television show, which scroll down the screen.

Create

To produce, write, or bring into existence through artistic or imaginative effort (i.e., to create a song).

Created

In *copyright* law, a work is considered to have been created once it has been *fixed* (i.e., recorded or written down in *tangible* form whereby it can be seen, heard, or otherwise perceived, communicated, or transmitted to others).

Creative Control

Same as *artistic control*: The creative direction, choice of producer and material, and/or final judgment as to whether or not an artistic work or performance meets acceptable commercial and aesthetic standards. In a recording contract, creative control may also extend to approval of album artwork, advertising materials, and video production.

Creative Department
Division of a music publishing company, record company, film or record production company, or advertising agency that handles *creative services* for the company.

Creative Director
Person in charge of a *creative department* or who is responsible for the direction of a company's creative services.

Creative Fee
A non-royalty payment to songwriters, copywriters, arrangers, composers, producers, editors, choreographers, designers, and/or other creative personnel employed to create concepts, music, scripts, artwork, or other material for jingles, advertising, marketing, public relations, recording projects, games, film or television productions, translations, adaptations, etc.

Creative Incentive Coalition (CIC)
The Creative Incentive Coalition represents individuals and organizations supporting copyright protection on the Internet and ratification of two new international treaties adopted at the *World Intellectual Property Organization* Diplomatic Conference in Geneva in 1996. These treaties require nations around the world to strengthen copyright laws and would extend copyright protections to cyberspace. The coalition works to educate the public and policy makers on vital issues related to copyright on the internet and on the importance of ratifying the WIPO treaties.

Creative Services
Any combination of functions provided by the *creative department* of music publishers, record companies, ad agencies, production companies, etc., including: (a) management oversight of creative personnel (songwriters, copywriters, copyists, arrangers, composers, producers, editors, designers); (b) *exploitation* of *catalog* and *repertoire*; (c) record, film, demo, jingle, and ad production; (d) design, layout, content, and concept development for marketing, promotion, advertising, *PR*, and artwork, etc.

Creative Work
Term used often in legal documents as a synonym for song, composition, literary production, or other product of the imagination. An intellectually derived artistic work.

Creator
A person who authors, designs, conceives, makes, plans, masterminds, or originates a project or *intellectual work*, such as a song, script, or book.

Credibility
Reputation among critics, peers, or consumers for quality, capability, or good character.

Credit
(1) Acknowledgment and/or approval for an act, an ability, a contribution, or a quality. (2) To offset a debit. (3) To add to an account. (4) To allow, loan, advance, or lend money.

Credit System
System used by *ASCAP* to determine the amount of *performance royalties* earned by members (songwriters and music publishers) from *surveyed performances* of songs and musical compositions during each royalty accounting period. Each surveyed work is *weighted* using a formula based on the type of performance, the length of the performance, and the medium or venue where it was performed. See *credit weighting formula*, below.

Credit Weighting Formula
A system of assigning a measure of relative importance to each variable in a combined group of variables. *Performing-right societies* use weighting formulas to determine the relative value of each *public performance* category in which a musical work is performed in order to calculate performance royalties due songwriters and publishers.

ASCAP payments to members are based on *credits*. Each surveyed work is assigned a number of credits representing the kind of usage and the medium in which it is used. Credits are *weighted* to reflect the value of the performance, ranging from a low of 2% of one credit for some usages of copyrighted arrangements of PD works to 100% of one credit for a full-feature vocal performance on primetime network television.

ASCAP divides performances into several classifications, each of which is subdivided into *weights* (or percentages of one full credit) according to duration, medium, and nature of performance. At the end of each distribution period, the number of ASCAP works surveyed, times the number of credits assigned to each performance, are divided into the gross amount of collections available for distribution (i.e., total collections less administrative costs).

This calculation provides the dollar amount of each credit for the distribution period. The total number of credits received by each member's catalog is then multiplied by the dollar amount of each credit. The resulting amount represents how much performance income each member receives for the distribution period.

For example, suppose $80 million is available for distribution at the end of one quarter, half of which is available for publisher members. And suppose there are 10 million credits earned by all publishers. $40 million ÷ 10 million credits = $4 per credit. A publisher that earned 20,000 credits during the quarter is then due $80,000.

ASCAP also makes *bonus payments* for significant numbers of radio performances. For instance, a song that logs more than 5,000 feature radio performances in any one quarter receives an award that amounts to roughly an additional 44%. For example, if the credit for that quarter is $4, the award would amount to roughly $1.75 times the number of credits received by the work. See also *weighting formula*.

Credits

Written or spoken acknowledgment of work done on a project, such as the production of a record, the authorship of a song, the contributions made to the production of a film, broadcast, or publication. Also see *closing credits*, *opening credits*, *label credits*, *credit system*, and *credit weighting formula*.

Crescendo

A musical term for a gradual, steady increase in the intensity or volume of a musical phrase, passage, or note.

CRIA

Abbreviation for *Canadian Recording Industry Association*.

Critic

Person who specializes in evaluating, appraising, and expressing judgments on the merits and faults of artistic works and performances.

Critique

(1) A review, evaluation, or critical commentary on the merits and faults of literary or artistic talent or works, or of a job performance. (2) To review, analyze, and comment on critically.

Cross-Collateralization

A method music publishers and record companies use to reduce the risks of being unable to recoup advances. It allows royalties earned by one song or recording to be applied against the unrecouped advances still owed for other songs or recordings.

For example, if Smith Music advances songwriter Jones $100 for each of two songs published under separate, cross-collateralized agreements, then Jones owes Smith Music $200 against any royalties earned by either work. If Song A earns Jones $500 in royalties, but song B never earns a penny, Smith Music can deduct the full $200 advanced for both songs from the earnings of Song A, paying Jones a net $300.

If, however, no cross-collateralization is provided in the agreements, Smith Music can only deduct the $100 specifically advanced for song A from

its $500 earnings, and has to write off the $100 advanced for *song B*.

Cross-Collateralize

To recoup an advance for one work or contract against earnings from another work or contract. See *cross-collateralization*, above.

Cross-Registration

The simultaneous registration of a cowritten song with *ASCAP* and *BMI* when the collaborators are affiliated with different *performing-right societies*. Each songwriter's *performance royalties* (as well as performance royalties due their music publishers) are collected by their respective performing-right society.

Crossover

A song or recording that initially sees success in one particular market segment and then "crosses over" to achieve success in one or more other market segments. *Example*: A record that hits the R&B charts then crosses over to hit the Pop charts as well. Also called *multi-format*.

Cross Talk

Audio bleedthrough, or a jumble of two or more unrelated conversations or sounds on a telephone line or recording input. See also *fringing*.

CRT

Abbreviation for *Copyright Royalty Tribunal*.

Cue

(1) Brief musical segment used to introduce or underscore the action or dialogue of a scene. (2) A musical signal or prompt to alert a performer to begin singing, playing, speaking, or dancing. (3) A gesture, word, or sound used to signal the start of a performance, a change of lighting, or some other action connected with a performance. (4) To line up a recording at its beginning for playback.

Cue Music

Music used to introduce a person or event on a radio or television broadcast or live performance.

Cue Send

On a recording studio console, a control device used by the engineer to route audio signals to specific mixing or recording channels, to *monitor* speakers, and/or to *headsets* worn by musicians and vocalists in the studio.

Cue Sheet

A director's or producer's written instructions detailing where, when, and how music is used in a film, television, radio, jingle, or theatrical production. A cue sheet identifies the film, program, or production by name, shows how the song was used (featured, background, theme, etc.) and the duration of each use.

Cue System

In a recording studio, the headphone link between musicians and vocalists so each can hear his or her own performance in context with those of other musicians, vocalists, and previously recorded tracks. The best cue systems provide individually tailored mixes for each headset.

Cume

The cumulative number of people tuning into a broadcast program or station during a given week when a rating company (such as *Arbitron*) is surveying audience share among broadcasters.

Cure

(1) The resolution of a contractual violation, dispute, or complaint. (2) To rectify a contractual failing or violation that has caused one party to a contract to formally complain to the other. (3) To cool phonograph records (see *curing records*).

Cure Period

The period of time allowed by a *complainant* for the other party to cure or rectify a failing, error, or other violation of an agreement before further action is taken. Most contracts and licenses specify the period of time in which one party has to affect a cure after notice is given by the other party.

Curing Records

Same as *cooling records*. During the manufacturing process of vinyl discs, either vinyl or hot liquid styrene is poured into a mold then baked and cured (cooled). Warped discs result from improper curing.

Currency

Any form of money used as a medium of exchange for goods or services. See also *rate of exchange*.

Current

(1) Pertaining to the present time. (2) In vogue, fashionable. (3) Now in progress.

Current Amount Basis

Method of calculating and paying royalties and other copyright income. Payment is made in full at the end of each accounting period for all royalties or other income earned during the period. See also *accrual based accounting*.

Curricula Vitae (CV)

Same as *résumé*. A brief summary of professional qualifications, experience, and accomplishments, as opposed to a *biography*, which is usually fleshed out with more personal anecdotal information to present a profile for publicity purposes.

Customs & Duties

(1) Taxes levied on imported and exported goods. (*aka* tariffs or customs duties). (2) An authorized agency of government that regulates and collects customs duties.

Custom Label

An independent record label whose product is exclusively manufactured, distributed, and marketed by a major record company. See also *distributed label, indie label, independent label, P&D, pressing & distribution*.

Cut

(1) To record (i.e., to cut a record). (2) A verbal cue to halt a performance. (3) A track on a sound recording. (4) A film or audiotape edit.

Cut-In

Typically, a *cut-in* is where a music publisher gives a record company, artist, or producer a percentage of the *mechanical royalties* earned from sales of a particular release, as opposed to a *split*, where the publisher agrees to *copublish* a song with the record company, artist, or producer, giving up a percentage of the copyright. A cut-in on specific types or sources of *ancillary income* may also be given to a film or television producer as an *inducement* to use a song.

Cutouts

(1) Recorded product that is deleted from a record company's inventory and sold at greatly discounted prices (usually far below cost). Cutout merchants buy deleted product in bulk for resale to *rack jobbers* and discount retailers who resell it to consumers at bargain-basement prices. Record manufacturers do not usually pay royalties on cutouts. (2) Brief interruptions in sound signals, as is caused by an electrical short or defective cable linking an amplifier to a speaker.

Cutter

An editor who *synchronizes* recorded music tracks with visual action on film or videotape.

Cutting Edge

State of the art; in the vanguard; ahead of the crowd; most up-to-date.

CV

Abbreviation for *curricula vitae*. Same as *résumé*.

Cyberspace

The terms *cyberspace, information superhighway,*

Internet, and *World Wide Web* interchangeably refer to the electronic access and transmission of information through personal computers.

Cyberspace has no borders. PC users in Prague and Pretoria can access the same data at the same time as someone in Peoria. That means a record company in Peoria can sell its product to consumers in Prague and Pretoria via cyberspace, eliminating the manufacturing process, as well as costs of shipping and cuts by middlemen (distributors, retailers, overseas licensees, etc.). Consumers benefit from being able to acquire music of their choice 24 hours a day, seven days a week.

The rapid development of cyberspace technologies for distributing information and entertainment has caused a scramble among copyright owners to upgrade international standards of copyright protection. The ability to upload, store, and download music affects copyright owners of sound recordings as well as owners of the underlying musical works contained on the recordings.

There are three licensing issues related to the use of music online. First, transmission of the music is a *public performance* and therefore subject to a *performing-right license*. Second, downloading transmitted music constitutes "copying" and is thereby subject to a *mechanical license*. And, third, combining music with visual images for transmission falls within the scope of a *synchronization license*.

While cyberspace presents new marketing opportunities, there are great challenges as well. Though things are very much in flux, and likely to remain so for some time, steps are being taken to solve some of the problems. Copyright owners (through organizations such as *ASCAP, BIEM, BMI, SEAC, CISAC, Harry Fox, et al*) are working to establish clear legal precedents and effective methods for licensing musical works on terms commensurate with the nature of their use. See also *transmission* and *reproduction license*.

D
Music format abbreviation for *dance.*

D.J.
Abbreviation for *disc jockey.*

D.J. Copy
A *promo* record; a recording marked "for promotional use only" and/or "not for sale," etc., which is given to disc jockeys, reviewers, et al in order to get airplay and garner publicity.

Damaged Goods
(1) Product that has been damaged during shipment from manufacturer to customer and is returned for replacement. Many record companies contractually discount artist royalties payable on units sold to compensate for *breakage* and *warpage*, a practice originating when damaged goods were common problems in the shipping and storage of *vinyl* and *shellac* discs. (2) A person whose past conduct has in some way given rise to a reputation that impairs his or her desirability, usefulness, or value as an employee, performer, etc.

Damages
(1) Losses incurred by one party due to negligence or willful actions by another party. (2) Financial compensation ordered to be paid for injuries or losses suffered by one party due to negligence or willful actions by another party.

Dance
Catch-all description of various uptempo music genres and subgenres geared to patrons of *discotheques* and clubs, characterized by heavy emphasis on repetitive bass and drum patterns and electronic sounds.

Dancehall
Also called "dancehall reggae" and *ragga*, a very uptempo, hard-driving dance genre characterized by aggressive rap deliveries and synthesized rhythms married to roots reggae.

DART
Acronym for *Digital Audio Recorders and Tape*, a US *statute* designed to compensate copyright owners for *home taping* with digital recorders. See *Audio Home Recording Act*, *Sound Recording Fund*, and *Musical Works Fund.*

DAT
Acronym for *digital audio tape.*

Data
Information, statistics, facts, figures. The term is typically applied to (1) text, program code, or numbers formatted for computer storage and processing; or (2) raw, unprocessed facts collected for the purpose of processing, analysis, interpretation, and drawing conclusions. See also *database*, *data processing*, *information management*, *information system*, *information services*, and *management information system.*

Data Processing
The collection, storage, and retrieval of *data*, including its analysis, interpretation, and distribution. See also *database*, *information management*, *information system*, *information services*, and *management information system.*

Database
A repository of information that has been collected, cataloged, and systematically organized in order to facilitate fast search and retrieval of specific data as needed. Computer-driven database systems store

vast amounts of information in discrete records (i.e., name of a person) divided into discrete fields (i.e., address, phone number, age, sex, income, etc.), which make it possible to quickly print a list of records sharing common field attributes. Databases in the music business are used to organize data regarding bookkeeping, accounting, royalties, record sales, song catalogs, contracts, licenses, inventory, personnel, contacts, bookings, radio promotion, etc. See also *data, data processing, information management, information system, information services,* and *management information system.*

Day Parting

A method of broadcast programming that divides each day into segments according to the numbers and types of listeners or viewers tuned in. For radio, morning and evening *drive times* generate the most listeners, when people commute to and from work listening to car radios. In television, *prime time* has the largest viewer audience. *Performing-right societies* make use of day-part data when calculating the value of some types of *performance royalties* due copyright owners for music broadcast during certain hours of the day.

dB

Abbreviation and symbol for *decibel.*

dBA

On a *sound-level indicator,* a weighted scale measuring the intensity or loudness of sound compared with the human ear's sensitivity to different frequencies. See *decibel* and *sound-level indicator.*

DBA

Abbreviation for *doing business as.*

DBS

Abbreviation for *direct broadcast satellite.*

DBX

A *noise reduction system* (created by the company of the same name) used in recording, which *compresses* the total frequency of an audio signal. See also *Dolby.*

DCC

Abbreviation for *digital compact cassette.*

DDM

Abbreviation for *direct-to-digital mastering.*

Deal

(1) An agreement, contract, or transaction between two parties. *Examples*: a "record deal" (an artist signing to a label); a "distribution deal" (an agreement for an *indie label*'s product to be distributed by a *major*); a "publishing deal" (a songwriter signing with a music publisher); etc. (2) To negotiate, bargain, compromise, arrive at an agreement or understanding.

Deal Breaker

A contract or license requirement by one party that is unacceptable to the other party and therefore ends negotiations and causes a potential deal to fall through.

Deal Memo

A synopsis of a proposed contract, listing main points of agreement by *headings* and summarized terms of each provision, but omitting the *legalese* and *boilerplate* language to be included in the final document. Also called *heads of agreement.*

Dealer

Retail merchant (i.e., a record store). A person who buys merchandise for resale to others. See also *chain store* and *mom & pop* store.

Dealer Price

The price charged by wholesalers or distributors to retail merchants for the product they resell to consumers. See also *published price to dealers* (PPD) and *base price to dealers* (BPD).

Dealer Spot

A type of *co-op ad*; a radio or television commercial that one or more retailers help pay for in return for mentioning that the product being advertised is available from the retailer(s).

Debit

(1) A charge against an account. (2) A record of a charge or an item of indebtedness. (3) An accounting or bookkeeping entry showing a charge, payment, debit, deduction, or reduction.

Debut

The first performance.

Debut Release

The first commercial recording released by a performer.

Decay

The gradual decrease of sound volume, electric current, or voltage.

Decibel (dB)

A measure or unit of sound volume. Each dB measures the relative power or intensity of an acoustic or electric sound signal. (For a person with normal hearing, 0 dB equals the faintest audible sound and 120 dB is the maximum of toleration.)

Decoding

In recording, a *noise reduction system*, such as *Dolby* or *dbx, compresses* the dynamic range of an audio signal before it reaches the recorder's *head*—a process called *encoding*. During playback, the signal's original dynamic range is restored, or decoded.

Dee-Jay

See *D.J.* and *disc jockey*.

Deems Taylor Award

Award presented by *ASCAP* to publishers and authors of books and articles about music. Named in honor of Joseph Deems Taylor (1885-1966), an American composer, author, and music critic.

Defamation

Making malicious and unjustified statements about someone, injuring the person's reputation. If defamation is expressed orally, it is called *slander*; if it is expressed in fixed or permanent form (written, recorded, pictured), it is called *libel*. In either case, the injured party may be entitled to monetary damages.

Default

(1) Failure to perform a service or an obligation required by contract, or to pay money when due. (2) Failure to answer or defend a lawsuit or to appear in court when ordered.

Default Judgment

A judicial ruling in favor of a *plaintiff* due to a *defendant*'s failure to answer or defend or comply with required legal steps in answering and defending a lawsuit within the allotted time.

Defaulters List

An *AFM* "black list" warning union members not to accept work from the listed individuals and companies who have failed to pay agreed wages, dues, or fees to other union members. Union members who work with defaulters are subject to fines or other disciplinary action.

Defective Title

Title or claim to copyright ownership that is invalid, imperfect, or unsubstantiated because of missing documents, missing signatures, an unresolved civil or criminal action, errors or omissions in the document of assignment or recordation of transfer, or if the title was obtained by unlawful means, including force, fraud, duress, blackmail, bribery, or an illegal consideration. See also *chain of title* and *cloud on the title*.

Defendant

Party accused by another (the *plaintiff* or *complainant*) in a legal dispute.

Deferred Payments

Payments for sales or services that are not made until sometime after the sales took place or after the services were rendered.

Delivery

(1) The formal act of transferring property title or ownership. (2) The fulfillment of a contract obligation, such as turning in a song to a publisher or a master to a record company as and when called for. (3) A shipment of product to a customer. (4) Product that has been shipped to a customer.

Delivery Commitment

(1) An obligation to deliver a specific amount of product (or number of songs or masters) by a certain date. (2) A pledge to fulfill an obligation or perform some act by a certain date.

Demagnetize

To erase previously recorded material from a *magnetic recording tape*.

Demand

(1) A legal requirement or contractual obligation to perform a certain act. (2) To require the performance of some act. (3) To lay a formal legal *claim* to something. (4) The monetary worth of a product or a service on the open market. (5) The desire to acquire, possess, or use a thing or service (i.e., "concert tickets were in great demand").

Demo

(1) Shorthand reference for *demonstration recording*. (2) Shorthand reference for *target demographic* (a specific radio audience or market segment.)

Demo Costs

Expenses related to making a *demo*, which may include studio rental, musicians, singers, arrangers, *cartage*, tapes, copying, etc. In music publishing, demo costs are a matter of negotiation between music publishers and songwriters (i.e., they may either be absorbed by the publisher or charged to the writer as an advance against royalties).

Demo Deal

Also called *development deal*. An agreement between a new artist and a record company whereby the company funds a *demo* session or the recording of a limited number of tracks before committing to a full-scale album recording session. If the artist demonstrates sufficient commercial potential in these "test" sessions, the company offers the artist a recording contract. See also *artist development deal* and *singles deal*.

Demo Reel

A tape containing two or more *demos* showcasing the work of a songwriter, producer, performer, arranger, or artist. Similar to *audition reel*.

Demo Scale

Required minimum payment *scale* for union musicians and singers for *demo* sessions, which is less than the full union session scale payable for recordings intended for commercial release. See also *union scale*.

Demographic

A statistical characteristic of one or more portions of the human population. See *demography*, below.

Demography

A statistical method of research used in marketing to narrowly define segments of the population by studying characteristics of various groups by age, sex, income, education, cultural tastes, spending habits, leisure activities, etc. By gathering statistics on the size, growth, density, and distribution of particular population segments, marketing experts can identify trends, focus marketing techniques, and better predict probabilities of consumer demand for specific types of services or product releases.

Demonstration Recording (Demo)

A recording made as a showcase for a new song or artist, or as a producer's guide for a recording session, but not intended for commercial release.

Denmark Street

Street located in Soho, the principle theater district of London. Prior to the 1980s, many top British record companies and music publishers were located in or around Denmark Street, and the area was known as *Tin Pan Alley* in British music business circles. See also *Tin Pan Alley*, *West End*, and *Soho*.

Deposit

(1) A partial payment made as security before goods are delivered or services are rendered on credit. (2) One of the *formalities* of establishing a claim of copyright ownership under the *Copyright Act of 1976* is that *claimants* must "deposit" two complete copies of the *best edition* of a work in the *Copyright Office* of the *Library of Congress*. See *copyright deposit*.

Depreciation

(1) The loss of a property's monetary value due to age, wear, inflation, or market conditions. (2) In *accounting*, the allowances made for a property's loss of value.

Depressor

(1) A record or song that fails to sell or reach the charts. (2) A deal that falls through. (3) A rejection letter received from a record company, music publisher, etc. (Opposite of *elator*.) Also called *deflator* and *dejector*.

Derivative

Something that evolves, develops, or stems from something else. A style of music or a performance style that evolved from, was adapted from, or copied from another style. *Example: Bluegrass* music is a derivative of British and Celtic *folk music*.

Derivative Recording

A recorded performance of a song constitutes a *derivative work* (see below). When a music publisher's rights to a song expires upon termination of a songwriter's contract, the publisher may continue to participate in *mechanical* income from sales of records produced under *mechanical licenses* that were issued prior to termination.

Derivative Work

Also called *supplementary work*. (1) A song or composition containing essential elements of one or more other songs or compositions and/or new material, such as a medley or a parody. (2) A song or composition that has been rearranged, translated, transformed, adapted, or otherwise altered from its original form. The setting of lyrics to an instrumental would constitute the production of a derivative work, for instance. (3) A secondary use (such as a recording) of an original song. As with *derivative recordings* (see above), when a music publisher's rights to a song expires upon termination of a songwriter's contract, the publisher may continue to participate in royalty income from sales of derivative works produced under *licenses* issued prior to termination.

Designer

(1) Person who creates the graphics, layout, and artwork for album covers, advertisements, posters, logos, etc. (2) Person who designs and carries out building plans for a project or structure, such as a movie set, theater scenery, recording studio's acoustical accessories, etc.

Desk

The *console* or *board* in a recording studio that hosts the sound controls operated by recording engineers.

Desk Drawer Publisher

Also called *vest pocket publisher*, a music publisher that keeps copyrights in a desk drawer, figuratively speaking, rather than dusting them off for active marketing. This type of publisher is entirely passive, or reactive, meaning that it licenses copyrights when requested by users, but makes no effort to sign new writers or promote new uses of the songs.

This situation often arises when a small publishing company's owner retires without selling his or her catalog, but still receives royalty earnings from previous activity. It also happens when a publisher dies and his or her catalog is looked after by an *administrator* who fulfills licensing requests and collects royalties. (The administrator may be a surviving family member, lawyer, accountant, trustee, or hired manager.) Another example is that of an investor who acquires a copyright catalog and is content that the continuing income stream from the previous owner's activities is sufficient to pay back the investment and return a profit.

Development Deal

(1) See *demo deal*, *artist development deal*, and *singles deal*. (2) In film, television, and theater, "putting a work into development" includes the steps of creating a program or bringing a film or play into production (casting, hiring a director, screen or script writing, rehearsals, testing before live audiences, and making necessary changes before going into production or opening on Broadway).

Device

(1) A contrivance, machine, apparatus, appliance, or mechanism. (2) A symbol, emblem, or logo. (3) A means, method, technique, scheme, or strategy.

Diamond Record

In Canada, sales of 1 million records merits a diamond record award. See also *hit*, *silver record*, *gold record*, *platinum record*, and *multi-platinum*.

Digipak

Deluxe method of packaging for compact discs resembling double-album LP jackets. It features a wide spine, like a book, and the CD is secured inside the package by a plastic divider. See also *Eco-Pak* and *jewel box*.

Digital

A *binary* number system consisting of combinations of only two digits (0 and 1), used in computer processing codes and digital sound recordings. In digital audio recording, sound waves are represented and manipulated on *magnetic tape*, and background noises (such as *hiss*, *wow*, and *flutter*) are eliminated. See also *digital recording*.

Digital Audio Recorders and Tape (DART)

Name for royalties collected under the *Audio Home Recording Act*, which is a 1992 amendment to the *Copyright Act of 1976* designed to compensate copyright owners for *home taping* with digital re-

corders. Home taping for personal consumption is legal, but if homemade tapes are sold or traded, *copyright infringement* occurs. The problem for copyright owners is that it is impossible to police millions of consumers in order to prevent abuse of home taping and be compensated for lost revenues.

Congress attempted to address the home taping issue with this act, which puts a levy or tax (referred to by its acronym, *DART*) on the sale of every digital tape recorder and blank digital audiotape. Revenues collected go into a pool that is distributed periodically to copyright owners, songwriters, and performers. DART applies to only *digital* recordings. (*Analog* tape recordings can still be made at home without any method of compensating copyright owners.)

The *Audio Home Recording Act of 1992* provides for a 3% tax on the wholesale price of blank digital audiotapes, a 2% tax on the wholesale price of nonprofessional digital recorders, and a *serial copyright management system* (SCMS) encoded on every digital recorder so that digital copies can't be made of digital recordings.

Taxes collected from sales of digital recorders and blank tapes are distributed two-thirds to copyright owners of the sound recording (record companies) and performers (artists); and one-third to copyright owners of the music (publishers) and songwriters.

Two-thirds of all taxes collected on the sale of digital recorders and blank digital recording tape are placed in the *Sound Recording Fund* for distribution to copyright owners of sound recordings distributed in digital formats, and to the featured artists, and nonfeatured backing vocalists and musicians whose performances are included on digital recordings. Nonfeatured vocalists are allocated 1.375% of revenues placed in this fund; nonfeatured musicians receive 2.725%; featured artists receive 38.36%; and copyright owners of the sound recording (usually the record company) receive 57.54%.

One-third of all taxes collected on the sale of digital recorders and blank digital recording tape are placed in the *Musical Works Fund*, of which 50% goes to the music publisher and 50% to the songwriter. The *Harry Fox Agency* collects the music publishers' share of DART income. *Performing-right societies* collect the songwriters' share, and pay the writers directly.

Revenues collected under DART are paid to copyright owners, writers, and performers in proportion to their respective percentages of all other income collected by the rights organizations. For example, a songwriter whose percentage of income from *BMI* is equal to .0001% of all BMI collections, will receive approximately .0001% of all DART money collected by BMI during the period.

Digital Audio Tape (DAT)

An audiotape capable of storing and playing back digital audio. A DAT is manufactured in *cassette* format that is roughly half the size of a standard *analog* cassette, holds up to two hours of audio per side, and can also be programmed with additional information. Prerecorded DAT cassettes are protected with a copy management system designed to make it impossible to make more than one generation copy. Because of its sound quality, information management, portability, and economy, DAT has largely replaced reel-to-reel tape for making master tapes in recording studios. DATs are also manufactured for use in storing computer data with a storage capacity of approximately 2.5 gigabytes per tape.

Digital Compact Cassette (DCC)

A digitally recorded audiotape manufactured in cassette format with a playing time of 90 minutes. Although it is approximately the same size as a standard cassette, it is not playable on an *analog* cassette player. However, standard analog cassettes can be played on a DCC player (see *backward compatibility*). Prerecorded DCCs are copy-protected to prevent making more than one copy generation. Track selections can be individually programmed for playing order, like a compact disc.

Digital Compact Cassette Player/Recorder

A device for playing and recording *DCCs*. *Analog* audiocassettes may be played on a DCC player, which uses a recording head similar to an analog cassette deck, but DCCs are not playable on analog machines. Many DCC players have display screens to show track titles, playing time, and other encoded information on the tapes.

Digital Delay

A digital *signal-processing* device used in recording and mixing to electronically add or adjust the delay of an audio signal to give the perception of "slap echo" or doubling (so that a vocalist or instrumentalist seems to be performing the part at least twice).

Digital-to-Analog Conversion

The process of converting discrete "off-on" binary *digital* signals to continuously varying electronic or audio *analog* signals, such as when converting sound from a digital master to a standard audiocassette or vinyl record.

Digital-to-Analog Converter

A circuit, switch, or device for converting discrete "off-on" *digital* signals from a digital source into continuously varying electronic or audio *analog* signals. See also *analog-to-digital-converter*.

Digital Recording

(1) A process of recording sound waves and/or visual data with *digital* computer technology. The recorded information is stored as binary code on discs or tapes, which can be later reproduced by digital equipment (i.e., CD, DVD, DCC, or DAT players) or reconverted to *analog* signals for playback on analog equipment (i.e., record players, cassette players). In digital recording, the pressure of sound waves is sampled over 40,000 times a second and converted into precise numerical values, which are retrieved by laser scanning and reconverted during playback to sound waves exactly like those originally recorded. Digital recording eliminates the inevitable distortions and extraneous noises inherent with conventional mechanical-electronic recording methods. (2) A sound or video tape or disc, manufactured for playback on digital equipment, such as a CD player.

Digital Sampling

(1) Process of taking discrete segments from other recorded works and incorporating them into a new work. (2) In the digitizing process, a sound wave is sampled thousands of times a second, and each individual sample is assigned a *binary* code number (combining the numbers 0 and 1), which corresponds to the height of the wave. See also *sample*.

Digitize

To convert sounds, text, pictures, or drawings into *digital* code.

Direct

To exercise control; to lead, conduct, manage, guide, or regulate. See *director*.

Direct Box

A *pickup* device plugged into an electric musical instrument, such as a guitar, which converts mechanical movements into electrical impulses in the reproduction of sound. A direct box routes sound directly to a recorder, rather than having to place a microphone in front of an instrument's amplifier in order to pick it up.

Direct Broadcast Satellite (DBS)

A solar-powered satellite in geostationary orbit that relays telephone, television, telex, and other transmissions from ground stations to small antennae or "satellite dishes" connected to domestic television sets or other receivers.

Direct License

A nonexclusive *performance license* to use music in a movie or television program, which is granted by a music rights owner directly to the broadcaster (i.e., television station or network) that transmits the program. This contrasts with *source licenses* issued by rights owners to producers or owners of works in which the music is used, and with *blanket licenses* issued to broadcasters by rights owners' *performing-right societies*. Music publishers are free to negotiate source licenses and direct licenses directly with broadcasters and owners of television programs as a result of *consent decrees* entered into between the Justice Department, *BMI*, and *ASCAP*. See also *Buffalo Broadcasting Case*.

Direct Mail
A marketing process in which advertising circulars, announcements, and sales solicitations are sent by mail directly to potential customers.

Direct-Metal Mastering (DMM)
A process used to prepare master recordings for compact disc manufacturing. In the direct metal mastering process, microscopic pits are embossed on copper layered over a glass base, then galvanized to prepare stampers for manufacturing. See also *compact disc mastering*, *premastering*, and *glass mastering*.

Direct Response Ad
A commercial advertisement or announcement, which calls for a direct action on the consumer's part, such as phoning an 800 number, returning an order coupon, or going to a store and purchasing a particular product (as opposed to an *institutional ad*, which is used to reinforce or build a company's image and keep its name before the public).

Direct-to-Digital Mastering (DDM)
Process of making a *glass master* directly from a DAT master tape, rather than first transferring the master to a *U-Matic* or 1630 tape.

Director
(1) A person with supervisory control and management authority over the operations and business affairs of an institution or a corporation. See *board of directors*. (2) Person with supervisory control and management authority over the creative elements of a theatrical, film, video, or television production. (3) The conductor of a band, an orchestra, or a chorus.

Directory
(1) An alphabetical listing of companies together with names of personnel or contacts, addresses, telephone and fax numbers, etc., usually grouped by classifications within a trade, such as recording studios, distributors, music publishers, radio stations, etc. (Also called a *trade directory*.) (2) A telephone book. (3) In computing, a listing of files contained in a storage device, such as a hard drive or floppy disk.

Direct-to-Disc
A recording process whereby music is simultaneously performed, mixed, and cut directly onto a *master lacquer*. Direct-to-disc recording produces superior sound quality and greater dynamic range compared with recording onto magnetic tape. However, it requires perfection in the performance and mixing; there can be no overdubbing, edits, splices, etc. Discs containing inferior performances or mistakes must be scrapped. Moreover, only a few thousand discs can be pressed from each master lacquer, so this process is not feasible for recordings intended for mass production.

Disability
A triggering event for *suspension* of a contract due to the inability of a service provider (i.e., an artist, a producer, a songwriter, etc.) to perform because of a legal, physical, or mental condition.

Disc
Also called *disk*. A flat, round object used for recording, storing, and playing back data. Originally. the term disc was synonymous with phonograph record, but with emerging technology it now also applies to a variety of both audio and video software formats as well as computer-driven data software. See also *compact disc*, *CD-ROM*, *CD-I*, *CD-WORM*, *videodisc*, *laser disc*, *phonograph record*, *vinyl*, *shellac*, *platter*.

Disc Cutting
See *disc mastering*.

Disc Jockey (D.J.)
Person who emcees, presents, and announces a program of recorded music, which may either be broadcast (i.e., on radio), or presented in front of a live audience (i.e., at a *discotheque*).

Disc Mastering
Process of converting sound from a master tape to the grooves of a master *lacquer*-coated aluminum disc used in the manufacturing of vinyl phonograph records. Master tapes are "tuned" by a mastering engineer using a disc-mastering *console* to adjust equalization, sound and tone levels, etc. As the master tape is played, a *stylus* cuts the spiral grooves into the *master lacquer* disc. A separate *lacquer* is cut for each side of the record, and then sent to the pressing plant where the vinyl discs are manufactured.

Discharge
(1) To perform obligations required by contract. (2) To comply with the demands or terms of a contract, court order, or obligation. (3) To free one party from obligation to another. (4) To set aside, nullify, or

void a contract, court order, debt, or obligation. (5) To fire or remove someone from a job. (6) An official document certifying annulment of a contract or dismissal of a court order.

Disclaimer

A clause in a contract, license, sale agreement, etc., wherein one party denies responsibility for something, or connection with something, or renounces any rights or claims to something.

Disco

(1) An uptempo *dance* music format characterized by repetitive bass and drum patterns and electronic sounds. (2) Abbreviated reference for *discotheque*.

Discography

(1) The complete catalog listing of recordings made by a recording artist, producer, musician, or record company. (2) The complete catalog listing of recorded works by a songwriter or composer. (3) A catalog listing of a collection or library of recorded works.

Discotheque

A nightclub or party where recorded or live *disco* music is featured for dancing.

Discount

A price reduction; a deduction or allowance. Discounts are frequently offered as sales incentives by record companies to distributors, or by distributors to retailers, or by retailers to consumers. Typical record discount incentives include two-fors (two for the price of one), reductions in price if credit accounts are paid in full within a stated period of time, or what amounts to discounts by adding bonus records (buy nine, get a tenth one free, etc.).

Disk

Alternative spelling for *disc*, usually applied to computer media, such as *floppy disks*.

Diskette

A plastic *disk* coated with magnetic material to record and store data for computer access. The disk itself is protected by a hard jacket, which is inserted into the computer's *drive* system. Also called *floppy disk*.

Display

(1) A showcase, a rack, or an area set aside in retail or exposition space with special advertising materials to call consumers' attention to a product. (See also *point-of-purchase*.) (2) A screen on a computer monitor that gives visual access to information. (3) To show a copy of a work, whether directly (as with a theatrical performance of a motion picture) or indirectly (as with a television broadcast).

Distortion

The alteration of a sound signal's waveform that changes its quality, fidelity, reception, or reproduction. See also *harmonic distortion* and *intermodulation distortion*.

Distribute

(1) To deliver or supply product to retailers, and, ultimately, to consumers. (2) To make royalty payments. (3) To allocate, apportion, share out.

Distribution

(1) The process of supplying product to retailers. (2) The method or system by which a product is channeled from the manufacturer to the consumer. (3) The payment of royalties, bills, salaries.

Distribution Deal

An agreement between an *indie* label or production company with a major label whereby the latter *distributes* the former's product to retailers. The indie label is responsible for manufacturing, packaging, and delivering finished product to the *distributor*. In distribution deals where the indie does all its own marketing and promotion, the distributor typically retains 20% to 30% of the product's wholesale selling price. When the distributor provides marketing services, it either charges direct costs of advertising and promotion back to the indie label, deducts the expenses from the indie's share of sales revenue, or retains a higher royalty on sales to cover marketing costs. See also *label deal*, *production company*, and *pressing & distribution (P&D) deal*.

Distributor

A company that distributes product to retailers. This can be an *independent distributor* handling product for indie labels, or a *major* record company that distributes its own product and that of others through its *branch* system. (See also *branch operation*, *distribution deal*, *rack jobber*, *music jobber*, *selling agent*, and *pressing & distribution [P&D] deal*.)

Distributor Free Goods

Terminology used by some record companies as a loophole to avoid paying royalties on product sold to distributors at a discount. This practice essentially "gives" the distributor 15 "free records" for every eighty-five units purchased. In reality, the company is giving the distributor a 15% discount on the purchase of one hundred units. But, since the distributor only "buys" 85 units, the company doesn't have to pay royalties on the 15 so-called "free" copies. See also *free goods* and *special programs*.

Ditty

A catchy tune, jingle, rhyme, musical sales pitch, etc.

Divisibility

A right or claim capable of being divided or apportioned. The issue of divisibility can be confusing where it relates to a copyright. Copyright bestows five types of rights to the copyright owner (the *bundle of rights*): (1) the right to *reproduce* copies (sheet music, phonorecords, etc.); (2) to *distribute* copies to the public by sale, rental, lease, or lending; (3) to prepare *derivative* works (adaptations, arrangements, dramatizations, etc.); (4) to *perform* the work publicly; and (5) to *display* the work publicly. These rights are distinct, so that a copyright is divisible, meaning songwriters can theoretically assign *mechanical rights* to one publisher, *print rights* to another publisher, *performance rights* to a third publisher, and *synchronization rights* to yet a fourth publisher.

In practice, divisibility is rarely an issue, and copyright assignments normally are made involving the entire bundle of rights. In any event, though various rights can be licensed separately, and copyright ownership can be shared among two or more parties, a copyright always remains *undivided*, meaning that all rights ultimately continue to vest in the work itself. See also *undivided copyright* and *undivided interest*.

D.J.

A *disc jockey*.

D.J. Copy

A *promo* record; a recording marked "for promotional use only" and/or "not for sale," etc., which is given to disc jockeys, reviewers, et al in order to get airplay and garner publicity.

DMM

Abbreviation for *Direct-Metal Mastering*.

Docudrama

A dramatized television play or movie based on real personalities, historical or current events, or other factual stories.

Documentary

An informational film or television presentation dealing with biographical, historical, political, social, or newsworthy material, usually containing editorial commentary, film clips of actual events, and interviews with experts on the subject and/or with personalities involved.

Dog

In marketing, a product that has either fallen on its face at the outset, or has had its day, and on which there is no point in expending further time or money.

Dog Bone

A small adhesive silver label used to seal shut *jewel boxes* before shrink-wrapping. So-called because of its shape.

Doing Business As (DBA)

Phrase inserted between the real name of a person or company and the *trade name* or *fictitious name* under which the person or company operates for business or professional purposes. *Example*: Joe Smith *dba* Smith Music Publishing Company.

Dolby

A *noise reduction system* (named after its creator, Ray Dolby) used in recording to reduce or eliminate unwanted audio signals, such as high-frequency *hiss*. The Dolby A system *compresses* the dynamic range within each frequency band. The Dolby B system compresses the dynamic range of high frequencies only. See also *dbx*.

Domestic

Pertaining to one's own country. For instance, an American music publisher's domestic revenue comes from licensing copyrights within the United States, as opposed to foreign income arising from overseas licensing.

Dominant

The 5th note (or degree) of a major or minor *scale*. For instance, in the C major scale, the dominant note is G, and the dominant chord is the G major chord (G, B, and D). See also *tonic*.

Donut

An advertising jingle with a *voice-over* against an instrumental section sandwiched between vocals at the beginning and end.

Dormant

A company, product, song, or catalog that is *inactive*, but which may have the potential of being *activated*.

Double

To play a second instrument during a performance or recording, or to play a second part on a recording over another, previously recorded part. See also *double track*.

Double Album

An album containing two discs or tapes.

Double Scale

Payment to a union musician or vocalist at the rate

of twice the normal *union scale*. Typically, double scale is paid for recording session *leaders*, or for musicians who *double track* instruments. Double scale may also be required by session musicians who can command higher fees by virtue of experience, talent, and demand for their services. See also *union scale*.

Double Track

To record a second instrument or second part on a separately recorded track in accompaniment with another, previously recorded instrument or part. Also, to record a second vocal part on a separately recorded track in accompaniment with another, previously recorded vocal part.

Dove Awards

In the *Christian* music genre and market, the equivalent to a *Grammy*. See *Gospel Music Association (GMA)*.

Downbeat Magazine

A magazine catering to jazz aficionados, located at 180 W Park Ave., Suite 105, Elmhurst, IL 60126. Tel: (708) 941-2030; Fax: (708) 941-3210.

Downbeat

(1) The first beat of a musical measure. (2) The gesture made by an orchestra leader or conductor to signal the first beat of a measure. (3) A sad musical mood characterized by a slow tempo, minor key, and/or pessimistic lyrics.

Download

(1) To transfer computer programs or data from one format or device to another. (2) Data or a program that has been transferred from one source of storage to another (i.e., "a copy of the contract was downloaded from a computer hard drive to a floppy disk").

Downtime

Period of time when a studio is not in use, particularly when equipment is being serviced or replaced.

Drama

(1) A theatrical play performed on stage or produced for television, radio, or the cinema. (2) A narrative work using actors to perform the dialogue and action of the characters.

Dramatic Adaptation License

Permission to dramatize the lyrics of a musical work as the basis for the storyline of a movie, television program, or play. Dramatizations that also include a performance of the adapted musical work require separate *dramatic performance licenses*, and, if performed in a movie or television program, *synchronization licenses* as well.

Dramatic Music

Music composed for, or used specifically with, the production of an opera, operetta, musical play, or ballet, without which the performance would be incomplete or meaningless. See also *grand rights* and *dramatico-musical performance*.

Dramatic Performance

The staging, broadcast, or film production of a story, dialogue, drama, play, act, or scene, with actors, scenery, props, costumes. See also *dramatico-musical performance*.

Dramatic Performance License

Permission to use a copyrighted musical work as an integral part of a theatrical production (movies, television, musical plays) where the music forms part of the story, furthering the plot, dialogue, or storyline. Not to be confused with a *grand performance license*.

Dramatic Rights

Copyright in *dramatico-musical* works created for and performed on the *living stage*, frequently called "grand rights." (Rights to *nondramatic* music works are referred to as *small rights*.) See *grand rights*.

Dramatic Work

(1) A theatrical play performed on stage or produced for television, radio, or the cinema. (2) A narrative work using actors to perform the dialogue and action of the characters.

Dramatico Musical

A play set to music or accompanied by music written specifically for the production, and in which the music furthers the plot or materially enhances the production. See *dramatico-musical performance*, below.

Dramatico-Musical Performance

The staging, recording, broadcast, or film production of a story, dialogue, drama, play, act, or scene, which is set to music or accompanied by music written specifically for the production, and in which the music furthers the plot or materially enhances the production.

A song can be taken out of context from a musical play and rendered as a dramatic performance with scenery, costumes, and an acting out of the storyline. This can apply to a song that wasn't specifically created as a dramatic work, but is dramatized when performed. For instance, a theatrical troupe might dramatize the Dolly Parton/Whitney Houston hit *I Will Always Love You*. Or, a dramatist might take the song *Memories* from "Cats" and write a new script so that it is performed in a dramatization that has nothing to do with the original play itself.

Controversies often arise as to whether a musical performance is dramatic or not. Sometimes a copyright owner contends it does, the performer disagrees, and a judge has to decide. A song performed with costumes, scenery, and "acting out" of the lyrics doesn't necessarily constitute a "dramatic performance" in the strictest sense. But the song is usually considered a dramatic performance when it is integrated into a plot or action or storyline and the overall production is diminished by eliminating the song. This also applies to songs not specifically created for the *living stage* but incorporated later into dramatic productions.

Dramatico-Musical Work

A song, score, or composition written as part of a *dramatic work*, which enhances the production, furthers the storyline, or in some way is essential to the work as a whole, and without which the overall production is diminished or incomplete. See also *grand rights* and *dramatico-musical performance*.

Dramatists' Guild

A trade association established in 1919 comprising composers, lyricists, and playwrights professionally active in musical theater. Though the guild represents, protects, and promotes interests of its 7,500 members, it is not a labor union. Most composers and lyricists active in musical theater belong to the *Dramatists' Guild*, which sets minimum benchmark terms for contracts with theatrical producers under its Approved Production Contract (APC). The guild is headquartered at 234 West 44th Street, New York, NY 10036. Tel: (212) 398-9366.

Dramatization

(1) A work, such as a novel, that is adapted for dramatic presentation. (2) The acting out of a storyline, song, or event.

Draw

(1) To receive regularized payments from a fund or account set aside for a specific purpose, such as a weekly draw for expenses, or a royalty advance that is paid in installments. (2) To write or draft a legal document, such as a contract. (3) To attract an audience for a performance or customers for a product.

Dream Pop

A British music genre surfacing as a variant of *ambient music*, characterized by layers of surrealistic, white-noise guitars and "dreamy" vocals.

Drive

A computer hardware device, such as a *hard drive*, that writes, stores, and reads data; a computer hardware device that reads data from external storage media, such as *floppy disks* or *CD-ROMs*.

Drive Time

The radio audience peak times of early morning and late afternoon, when commuters listen to car radios as they drive to and from work. See also *prime time*.

Droit Moral

French for *moral rights*, a concept incorporated into the copyright laws of several European countries. Droit moral essentially gives the author of a work creative veto over any changes or alterations to the work by others. For instance, a songwriter would be able to prevent his or her music publisher from authorizing a translation, adaptation, synchronization, or other usage of a song (in a commercial, for instance) if the songwriter felt the changes or usage harmed the work's integrity.

Dropship

To fill an order for product by shipping it from an address different from the one to which the order was placed. *Example*: Orders are placed to a record company who then instructs its manufacturer to ship product to the customer directly from the factory.

Drum and Bass

A variant of the *jungle* genre of electronic dance music emerging from Bristol, England in the 1990s.

Dub

(1) To copy recorded material from one medium to another. (2) A copy made from a master recording. (3) To add new recorded material to the original (i.e., to dub a lead vocal onto a rhythm track, or a music soundtrack in *synchronization* with a film). (4) Subgenre of Jamaican *reggae*, with psychedelic to Afro-Caribbean influences. Characterized by sparse rhythm tracks with sound effects and various instruments dropping in and out of the track at random.

Due Diligence

The process by which one party to a deal researches the claims of the other party before signing the final agreement. For instance, after terms of a copyright or catalog purchase have been agreed in principle, the prospective buyer undertakes due diligence to determine whether the claims of the seller are accurate with regards to two major aspects of the catalog: (1) financials and (2) legalities.

The seller's books, bank statements, receipts, and records are examined in order to compare actual royalty receipts and payments with the seller's claims. The audit also tests claims regarding advances owed by songwriters and third parties, as well as balances on advances still owed by the seller to subpublishers and other licensees. All *pipeline* monies owed *by*, and owed *to* the seller must be substantiated.

While accountants pore over the financials, lawyers pursue the legal aspects of a potential copyright purchase (i.e., copyright registrations, contracts, and licenses), to determine validity, enforceability, and obligations, financial or otherwise. A *copyright search* may be made in the Library of Congress, and contracts and major licenses are investigated to insure rights claimed in the *prospectus* are accurate and have not in any way been diminished by failure on the part of the seller. In addition, court records are normally searched for undisclosed loans, mortgages, or liens existing on any of the copyrights, and any litigation that is threatened, pending, or underway. Any of these things could impose unwanted liabilities on the buyer, and affect the legality of any sale. Discrepancies turned up during due diligence audits either result in the terms of a deal being adjusted, or the deal being aborted. See also *chain of title* and *title search*.

Duet
A song, recording, or musical performance featuring two lead vocalists or lead instrumentalists.

Duopoly
A situation where market ownership, control, or power is in the hands of two persons or groups (as opposed to a *monopoly*, where one party controls everything).

Dupe
Abbreviated reference for *duplicate*. (See also *dub*.)

Duplicate
(1) To make a copy. (2) An exact copy.

Duplication
(1) An exact copy. (2) A repeat of a previous occurrence.

Duration
(1) The period, term, lifetime, or span of time in which a contract or license is in effect. (2) The period of time (or lifetime) of statutory protection in effect for a copyright or patent. (3) The length, playing time, or running time of a performance, recording, film, or broadcast.

DVD
Abbreviation for digital video disc or digital versatile disc.

E
Music format abbreviation for *ethnic*.

Earnest Money
A nonreturnable cash payment made by a purchaser, licensee, or assignee to a seller, licensor, or assignor upon agreeing in principle to a transaction, but before the final contract, license, or assignment is executed. As with a *commitment fee*, the payment of earnest money locks up a deal, option, or obligation.

Easy Listening
(1) A musical style embracing "soft" arrangements of melodic material. (2) a radio station programming format focusing on Easy Listening music.

EAU
The *performing-right society* in Estonia.

EC
Abbreviation for *European Community*.

Echo
The repetition of a sound wave, reflected back to its original source at least 1/10th of a second later so that the reflected sound is audibly distinguished as separate from the original. See also *reverb*.

Echo Chamber
A small, reverberant room or enclosure in a recording or broadcasting studio, acoustically constructed to create echo effects.

Echo Song
A song characterized by the title being repeated somewhere in every line of the lyrics.

Eco-Pak
A deluxe method of packaging for compact discs, resembling double-album LP jackets. It features a wide spine, like a book, and the CD is secured inside the package using a small slit. See also *Digipak and jewel box*.

Edison, Thomas (1847-1931)
American inventor credited with more than a thousand patented inventions, including the microphone (1877), the *phonograph* (1877), and incandescent lamp (1879). See also *Berliner, Emile* and *Gramophone*.

Educational Edition
A musical arrangement, or collection of arrangements, for bands, orchestras, choral groups, or individual instruments, published primarily for students or learners. See also *method book*.

Educational Television (ETV)
Noncommercial television programming focusing on documentaries, interviews, panel discussions, etc., as well as entertainment of an educational nature. Educational television of instructional material may be transmitted by *closed-circuit* video systems, but the term more often applies to ETV, or *public television*, which is broadcast over conventional television airwaves and rebroadcast by cable and satellite delivery systems. Local educational stations formed a national network (*Public Broadcasting Service*, or *PBS*) in 1967. Also see *NET*, *public television*, and *compulsory licensing*.

EEC
Abbreviation for *European Economic Community*.

Effective Date
(1) The date when a contract, license, court order,

or other legal undertaking becomes binding. (2) The date on which a statute is scheduled to become law.

Eight by Ten (8x10)
Standard dimensions, in inches, of glossy publicity photos and *head shots*.

Electrical Transcription
The recording of music specifically for broadcast or *public performance*, but not for sale to the public. Examples include production of recorded programs for radio *syndication*, radio advertisements, *in-flight entertainment* on airlines, and *background music* used in commercial establishments.

Electrical Transcription License
A license permitting the recording of music specifically for broadcast or *public performance*, but not for sale to the public. Transcription licenses combine aspects of *performance licenses* as well as *mechanical licenses*, because they involve (a) the public performance of music, and (b) the mechanical reproduction of recorded music.

However, most transcription licenses do not include the right to publicly perform the music, only the right to record it for the purpose of performing or rebroadcast. And an electrical transcription license differs from a mechanical license in that the latter permits the making of copies of a recording for sale to the public, whereas the former permits making copies of the recording only for public performance, *not* for sale. Unlike mechanical licenses, electrical transcription licenses are not subject to the *compulsory licensing* provision of the *Copyright Act*. Each license must be negotiated directly between the *user* and the publisher or the publisher's agent.

Electrical Transmission and Reproduction License
Also called *transmission and reproduction license*. Any type of license granting permission for the online transmission and *interactive* reproduction of copyrighted musical works, as through *cyberspace*. Though such licenses do not yet have specific names that are accepted within the music industry, there are three licensing issues related to the use of music online. First, transmission of the music is a *public performance* and therefore subject to a *performing-right license*. Second, downloading transmitted music constitutes "copying" and is thereby subject to a *mechanical license*. And, third, combining music with visual images for transmission falls within the scope of a *synchronization license*. A permission for "electrical transmission and reproduction," by whatever name, may combine aspects of all three licenses.

Electromagnetic Recording
In analog recording onto audio tape, amplified sound waves are converted into electrical impulses, and then impressed onto a magnetized tape by an electromagnetic recording head. An electromagnetic playback head then converts the tape's magnetic fields into electrical impulses, which are then amplified and reconverted into audible sound waves.

Electronic Bulletin Board Service (BBS)
An online computer network, generally catering to users who share specific interests. Using modems, BBS subscribers or patrons dial into the network in order to exchange e-mail, post information, or download information or software programs. See also *transmission and reproduction license*.

Electronic Game
A software program or computer-programmed device manufactured and marketed in various formats ranging form floppy disks, compact discs, cartridges, self-contained hand-held units, to stand-alone *arcade*-type machines, etc. Characterized by synchronized sound effects, graphics, and music, electronic games challenge players' skills on theme-oriented subjects (i.e., action, adventure, fantasy, space, sports, flight simulators, war games, etc.), and on more traditional games, such as chess, poker, bridge, blackjack, roulette, etc. When music is used, a variety of copyright issues come into play, and, depending on whether or not the music is *commissioned* as *a work made for hire*, or whether existing material is used, the manufacturer must negotiate *mechanical licenses*, *performing-right licenses*, and/or *synchronization licenses*, etc., with copyright owners. See also *video game*.

Electronic Music
Music created, produced, modified, manipulated, or altered by electronic devices, such as *synthesizers*, *sequencers*, *MIDI* (*Musical Instrument Digital Interface*) etc. In addition to purely electronic music, contemporary producers, artists, and composers frequently use various electronic techniques, such as *filtering*, *frequency shifting*, and *time delay*, combined with traditional instruments, to create new works in all genres.

Electronic Publishing
The publishing, distribution, or dissemination of information and data via linked or networked computer delivery systems or other electronic media, including CD-ROMs, floppy disks, etc., as opposed to traditionally printed material. The term also applies to preparing, designing, and editing material for publication using desktop publishing software rather than traditional methods of typesetting.

Electronica

An electronic dance music genre emerging in the mid- to late 1990s, characterized by a blending of other dance-music styles such as *trip-hop*, *jungle*, *techno*, and *drum 'n' bass*.

Electroplating

Process used in the preparation of master audio discs whereby the disc is placed in a bath containing a salt solution of the plating metal (i.e., zinc, nickel, chromium, cadmium, copper, silver, etc.), and an electrical current is then passed through the solution to coat the disc's surface with the metal. See *plating*, *matrixing*, *master lacquer*, *metal stamper*, and *mother*.

Elevator Music

Slang term for *piped music* ("the kind of music you hear in elevators"). See *background music*.

Emcee

Abbreviated reference for *master of ceremonies*.

Emmy

An annual award presented by the *Academy of Television Arts and Sciences* for outstanding technical and creative achievement in television. The name for the award is derived from the nickname for image orthicon ("immy"), a television camera tube.

Emolument

A fee, royalty, or salary paid to compensate work done or services rendered.

Employee For Hire

An employee is someone who works for another (the employer) on agreed terms, including the amount of compensation, financial or otherwise. In the music business, the term "employee for hire" often applies to creative personnel, such as songwriters, arrangers, producers, etc., whose work during the term of agreement belongs to the employer, including the copyright therein. Many exclusive songwriter contracts, for instance, are employee-for-hire agreements whereby the music publisher owns the copyrights to all works created by the songwriter "within the scope of his or her employment." Officially, this means there must be a continuing business relationship during the creative process in which the employer-publisher guides, supervises, and oversees the writer and/or provides facilities, equipment, and materials. See also *work made for hire*.

Employers Pension Fund (EP)

Under the *Phonograph Record Labor Agreement*, employers of union musicians for recording sessions are required to pay up to 10% of the gross scale wages paid for each session into this fund, which provides pension benefits to participating members.

Encoding

(1) Process of converting information into *binary* code, used to program computer operations and software applications. (2) In recording, a *noise reduction system*, such as *Dolby* or *dbx compresses* the dynamic range of an audio signal before it reaches the recorder's *head* (a process called encoding). During playback, the dynamic range is restored, or *decoded*.

End Cap

In retail merchandising, a display rack or shelf at the end of a store aisle; a prime store location for stocking product.

Endorsement

(1) A public recommendation, testimonial, commendation, or expression of approval for a product, cause, political candidate, or company. Endorsements are significant sources of *ancillary* income for high-profile entertainers and athletes who promote products by appearing in advertisements or allowing their names and likenesses to appear on product packaging. (2) A signature on a legal document that binds the signer to the terms therein, or transfers property rights or ownership from one party to another. (3) A signature on a financial instrument that validates the transfer of funds from one party to another. (4) An amendment or attachment to a contract or license, which changes the terms of the original document.

End-User

The consumer for whom a product is made. For instance, a recording is first sold to a distributor, then to a retailer, and, finally, to the public, the product's end-users. In the case of a music publisher, however, the end-user may be said to be the *licensee*. For example, the publisher markets songs to record companies, film producers, broadcasters, etc., who become the end-users in the publisher's marketing chain. See also *user*.

Enfranchise

To license, to grant permission, a right or a privilege. Also called *franchise*.

Engineer

(1) A sound technician charged with recording audio performances or *mixing* recorded performances. (2) A sound technician charged with maintaining, manipulating, and mixing sound delivery systems in order to provide quality sound reproduction for a live performance or broadcast. (3) To record and/or mix audio performances. (4) To capture or ma-

nipulate recorded sound onto memory systems such as tape recorders from which quality reproductions can be made.

Engineer-Producer

A record producer who also engineers his/her own recording sessions.

English Block

Though the distinction has blurred somewhat in recent years, Western Europe has traditionally been thought of as two distinct blocks of countries from a cultural and marketing perspective when it comes to licensing creative works. The English Block consists of countries where English-language music tended to be successful without the necessity of lyric translations. Aside from Great Britain and Ireland, this block includes Scandinavia (Denmark, Sweden, Norway) and the Netherlands. Music licensed in the *Continental Block*, on the other hand, tended to need translations into local languages. This block consists of the *GAS* territories (Germany, Austria, Switzerland), France, Belgium, Italy, Spain, and Portugal.

Ensemble

(1) A small band, combo, unit, or group of musicians and/or singers. (2) A troupe, cast, or company of dancers and/or or actors. (3) A musical work composed for, or arranged for, two or more vocalists or instrumentalists.

Entire Agreement

A legal *boilerplate* term included in the *integration clause* of a written contract to express the fact that the document represents the full scope of the terms, obligations, and conditions agreed to by the parties. The statement "This contract represents the entire agreement between the parties" virtually means that any side agreements or other understandings between the parties have been merged or integrated into the written agreement and any pre-existing documents to the contrary will not be admissible as evidence that modifies or alters the terms of the contract.

Environmental Music

A type of *background music*, generally of the *easy listening* genre, offered to business clients by services such as *Muzak*.

EP

(1) Abbreviation for *extended play*. (2) Abbreviation for *employers pension fund*.

EP Form

Under the *Copyright Act of 1909*, copyright *claimants* for *published* musical works were required to register their claims with *Copyright Office* by submitting two copies of the *best edition* of the work along with an EP Form. (Copyright claims for *unpublished* works were registered by submitting one copy of the work and an *EU Form*.) Since January 1, 1978, when the *Copyright Act of 1976* took effect, copyright claimants for musical works may register either published or unpublished works using a *PA Form*; EP and EU Forms are now obsolete.

EQ

Abbreviation for *equalization, equalize,* and *equalizer*.

Equalization (EQ)

In recording, a process used to adjust and control the amplitude of selected audio frequencies and frequency ranges, and to compensate for any distortion caused by an imbalance in the amplification of frequencies.

Equalize (EQ)

In recording, to use an *equalizer*, to apply *equalization* to selected sound wave frequencies.

Equalizer (EQ)

In recording and playback, a device used to control the amplitude of selected sound wave frequencies. An equalizer is an auxiliary device to equalization controls on a mixing console. By controlling the *timbre* of a sound, engineers can change the sound of an instrument, enhance separation between instruments, and improve the blending of tracks during mixdowns. EQ sound frequencies are commonly divided into separate bands a third of an octave apart. An equalizer enables adjustment of amplification levels for each band with a sliding contact in order to bring the frequencies into balance and eliminate unwanted noise or distortion. See also *graphic equalizer* and *parametric equalizer*.

Equitable

A matter of fairness or natural justice, which may be recognized as such in court, though there is not necessarily a clear legal precedent, remedy, or law applicable in the specific instance.

Equity

(1) Abbreviated reference for *Actors Equity Association*. (2) In law, a claim that is "fair and *equitable*." (3) A proportion of unencumbered ownership (i.e., the residual worth of *market value* less debt owed). *Example*: If a company finances the purchase of a copyright catalog at a price of $100,000, and, after making several installment payments, still owes $25,000, the company's equity in the catalog is $75,000. If, however, the market value of the catalog has risen to $125,000 at the

time $25,000 is still owing, the company's equity in the catalog has increased to $100,000.

Errors & Omissions

Two types of mistakes that cause damage to a client, customer, or party to a contract. In this context, an "error" is an active mistake, miscalculation, or inaccurate assertion, while an "omission" is an act of neglect, failure to disclose or declare pertinent information, or forgetfulness. In contracts, typically, the party guilty of an error or omission may be given an opportunity to *cure* the mistake upon written notice by the other party. A contract may be *amended* to correct errors and omissions. Errors & Omissions insurance is available to lawyers, accountants, and other professional service providers, to offset damages caused to clients by such mistakes.

Escalation Clause

See *escalator clause*, below.

Escalator Clause

Also called *escalation clause*. A contractual provision for increasing the amount of an advance, royalty rate, benefits, prices, or other forms of compensation or obligations in the event certain conditions occur, such as the exercise of an option, the achievement of a specific number of unit sales, the attainment of specific chart placings, the delivery of a specific number of songs or masters, etc. See also *minimum/maximum royalty formula*.

Escrow

The placement of fees or royalties due one party by another into the custody of a *third party* until certain conditions are met. For example, in a dispute over copyright ownership of a song by two music publishers, a record company may deposit *mechanical royalties* in escrow until it receives official notification as to which publisher is entitled to the royalties.

Estate

A person's entire possessions, assets, debts, rights, entitlements, and obligations, particularly at the time of death, and which are inherited by or left to the deceased's heirs or *statutory beneficiaries*.

Estoppel

A legal barrier against a retraction, allegation, or denial in contradiction of what a party has previously sworn as true.

Ethnic Music

A style of music common to, associated with, or popular among a particular group of people who share distinctive racial, national, religious, linguistic, or cultural characteristics.

ETV

Abbreviation for *Educational Television*. See also *Public Television* and *Public Broadcasting Service* (PBS).

Evaluate

(1) To assess, appraise, critique, or review a creative work or performance. (2) To appraise or assess financial worth through analytical examination of financial records.

Evaluation

(1) An assessment, an appraisal, a critique, or a review of commercial potential, artistic ability, creative merit, or job performance. (2) An appraisal of financial worth based upon analytical examination of financial records.

EU

Abbreviation for *European Union*.

EU Form

Under the *Copyright Act of 1909*, copyright *claimants* for *unpublished* musical works were required to register their claims with *Copyright Office* by submitting one copy of the work along with an EU Form. (Copyright claims for *published* works were registered by submitting two copies of the *best edition* of the work with an *EP Form*.) Since January 1, 1978, when the *Copyright Act of 1976* Act took effect, copyright claimants for musical works may register either published or unpublished works using a *PA Form*; EP and EU Forms are now obsolete.

European Community (EC)

See *European Union (EU)*.

European Economic Community (EEC)

See *European Union (EU)*.

European Union (EU)

Formerly known as the *European Community*, *European Economic Community*, and *Common Market*, the name European Union was adopted with the ratification of the Maastricht Treaty in 1993 by the member nations, which now include Belgium, Britain, Denmark, France, Germany, Greece, Ireland, Italy, Luxembourg, the Netherlands, Portugal, and Spain. The purpose of the Union is to develop and govern common policies for the member countries on foreign affairs, security matters, labor relations, trade, criminal and civil justice, environmental and safety concerns, etc. Governing bodies include the Council of the European Union, the European Commission, the Court of Justice, and the

European Parliament, which is elected by voters in the various EU countries.

The EU's goal is to integrate the economies of Western Europe, eliminate internal tariff and customs barriers, and develop common price levels, a unified monetary system, and a common currency. The EU has affected the music business by bringing the statutory copyright laws of various member countries into line with each other, making possible *central licensing*, and eliminating export and import duties on recorded product shipped across national borders within the Union.

Evergreen

A perennial hit. Songs that achieve hit status and are then covered, or re-recorded, by other artists over time become the backbone of a music publisher's catalog. These are the songs heard everywhere: on elevators, in department stores, etc. They become instantly recognizable, and are known as evergreens, because they are "good for all seasons." Also known as a *standard*.

Exchange Rate

The value of one unit of currency from one country measured against one unit of currency from another country.

Exclusion

A negotiable contractual provision that prohibits one party from engaging in a specific activity. For instance, in a songwriter's agreement with a music publisher, a writer may insist on provisions that prohibit the publisher from making certain uses of a copyright or authorizing others to do so. Depending upon the songwriter's negotiating clout, some exclusions may be absolute; others may merely require the publisher to first consult with and obtain permission from the writer before specific usages are made or authorized. Examples include: (a) *First use mechanical licensing.* (Since the copyright owner controls the first use of a new song, a writer who is also a recording artist may want to maintain the right of approval over who the publisher chooses to grant a mechanical license to for first use. The writer/artist may intend the song to be released first by himself/herself.); (b) *Reduced royalty rates* (the writer may successfully negotiate to prohibit the publisher from issuing mechanical licenses at rates less than the current *statutory mechanical rate* to any company affiliated or financially connected with the publisher, as well as granting lower royalty rates or licensing fees to other users connected in any way with the publisher. In other words, any usage authorized by the publisher to a parent, subsidiary, or affiliated company must be made *at arm's length*, so as not to favor the publisher, parent company, affiliates, or subsidiaries at the writer's expense; (c)

Altering, changing, editing, adapting: though publishers usually insist on the right to change, adapt, arrange, translate, or otherwise alter all works assigned by a writer, more established writers may negotiate the right to be consulted first, to approve or disapprove any changes, and to not have any royalty share diminished by the addition of other songwriters who make such changes. A songwriter may also insist on the right to be allowed first to make any changes proposed by the publisher, allowing third-parties to attempt the changes only in the event the writer declines to do so, or in the event the writer's efforts fail to meet the publisher's objectives; (d) *Specific types of licenses*: some songwriters may insist on right of approval before the publisher can license the works in commercials, films, or other usages. Many writers are particularly concerned about the "trivializing" of their output through uses in commercials, parodies, sampling, etc. Others may be offended by the use of their material in X-rated movies, political campaigns, or for the promotion of certain products, such as tobacco or alcohol.

Exclusive

The undivided rights to a party's services and the product created thereby; the sole rights to market a product; complete, undivided rights and privileges not shared with others. For example, in an *exclusive songwriter contract* (or *term contract*), the songwriter assigns to the music publisher either permanent copyright ownership or temporary exclusive rights to the copyrights of *all* songs written by the writer during the term covered by the agreement. In an exclusive recording agreement, the record company has sole rights to all recorded works by the artist during the term of agreement. In an exclusive distribution agreement between a *major label distributor* and an *indie label*, the distributor has sole marketing and selling rights to all product created and manufactured by the indie during the term covered by the agreement. In an exclusive foreign *subpublishing* agreement, the subpublisher has exclusive rights during the term of agreement to all copyrights covered by the agreement in the specified territory.

Although exclusive contracts and licenses bestow rights and privileges on one party, they normally also carry obligations, such as timely payment of specified advances, royalties, etc., and, perhaps, other requirements, such as *release commitments*, etc. Since the party granting exclusivity cannot assign rights to its product to any other party during the term of agreement, the *assignor's* very livelihood may depend upon the other party's fulfillment of its obligations.

Exclusivity

The legally binding assignment of exclusive rights from one party to another. For instance, a songwriter bound by an exclusive songwriter's agreement may not use his/her craft for, or assign any of his/her works to, any other music publisher during the term of agreement. And, a copyright confers upon its owner the authority to exclude anyone else from using, copying, appropriating, or interfering with the copyrighted work.

Execute

To do, accomplish, carry out, sign an agreement, perform, render.

Execution

An accomplishment, fulfillment, contract signing, performance, rendering.

Executive Producer

Person or company that funds and/or maintains oversight over a record, television, or film production. The executive producer usually employs a *line producer* who directs the production itself. The executive producer is ultimately responsible for administering the business affairs of the production (contracts, licenses, budgeting, payments, scheduling, booking studios and creative personnel, etc.).

Executor

A person appointed to govern or manage the affairs of an *estate*.

Executory Provision

Contractual requirement that a party perform specified acts or fulfill specified obligations following *termination* of the agreement.

Expander

A signal processing device used in recording and playback to increase dynamic range. Also called a *gate*, it can turn off (or on) an audio signal at a predetermined threshold in order to eliminate unwanted noise and *leakage*.

Expectancy, Rule of

Under the *Copyright Act of 1909*, creative works were given *statutory* copyright protection for an initial period of 28 years, which could be renewed for an additional 28 years. A copyright owner could assign (give, sell, transfer) the copyright to another party during the original term, just as any other type of property right could be transferred. However, a copyright owner had no rights per se in the work beyond the original term unless and until those rights were renewed for a renewal term. Therefore, the copyright owner had only an "expectancy" of continuing rights beyond the original copyright term, contingent upon renewal. In order, then, to assign those future rights before they existed, the copyright owner could only make an assignment of *renewal expectancy*.

Assuming the copyright owner made such an assignment, and was still living at the expiration of the original copyright term, the original owner was bound by the terms of the assignment. The rights vested in the copyright upon the renewal date would then become the property of the *assignee*. If, however, the copyright owner died before expiration of the original term, the rights vested upon renewal belong to the *statutory beneficiaries* of the deceased's estate.

If, for example, a music publisher wished to obtain renewal rights from a songwriter, the publisher would have to also obtain the renewal expectancies of the writer's statutory beneficiaries (normally, the spouse and children) at the same time. Even this was not foolproof, because, if the writer *and* the spouse and children had died by the time of renewal, the expectancies would pass to the *their* statutory beneficiaries. The issue could be further complicated by the writer having additional children or re-marrying after the publisher had received assignments of renewal expectancy from the original statutory beneficiaries.

The *rule of expectancy* applies only to songs in their original terms of copyright as of the effective date of the Copyright Act of 1976 (January 1, 1978). Works created after that date are provided with one term of copyright protection, and there are no renewals.

Expiration

The process of termination or ending. *Example*: Upon expiration of a contract, the *assignee* relinquishes all rights granted by the *assignor*, subject to any *retention* or *renewal options* specified in the agreement.

Expiration Date

(1) The day specified in a contract or license on which the agreement terminates, upon which day the *assignee* relinquishes all rights granted by the *assignor*, subject to any *retention* or *renewal options* specified in the agreement. (2) The last day on which a contractual option can be exercised.

Expire

To end or terminate. For instance, all rights assigned by one party to another *terminate* and *revert* to the assignor upon *termination* of the agreement in which those rights were assigned, subject to any *retention* or *renewal* provisions of the agreement.

Exploit

To market and promote song copyrights and recorded releases specifically, or to market and promote catalogs or the careers of songwriters and artists generally.

Exploitation
The process of marketing and promoting songs, records, copyright catalogs, and careers.

Export
(1) To ship finished product overseas for sale (as opposed to licensing the rights to an overseas manufacturer that will make and sell the product in its own territory). (2) To transfer data from one computer file to another.

Exposure
(1) The process or act of gaining public recognition through personal appearances, interviews, advertising, promotion, airplay, performances, and/or publicity in the mass media. (2) Proximity to something that influences, educates, or enlightens (i.e., a songwriter's style may be influenced by exposure to another writer's works). (3) A film negative or plate that has been developed.

Express
(1) To state, make clear, explicitly declare, put into exact words. (2) Something, such as a condition, promise, prohibition, obligation, authorization, empowerment, transfer, or relinquishment, that is clearly stated, explicitly declared, or put into exact words, so as not to be left to implication or open to interpretation.

Express Authority
See *express*. A clearly defined grant of *agency* or authority given to an agent, representative, or employee. See also *apparent authority*.

Express Condition
A contractual provision or condition of agreement that is clearly stated and defined, rather than being implied or left open to interpretation.

Express Contract
A clearly written contract whose terms are explicitly defined, stated, and agreed to by the parties involved. See also *implied contract*.

Expression
(1) Artistically, the term refers to the way in which a musical work is performed or in which an actor interprets a role or in which an artist conveys his/her perception of his/her subject. In this context, expression consists of nuances, subtleties, dynamics, and moods, which are difficult to verbalize or impart using conventional terms. (2) An idiom, a phrase, a term, or jargon peculiar to a situation, generation, condition, person, group, technology, trade, or profession. (3) An utterance, assertion, declaration, or verbalization.

Extended Play (EP)
A seven-inch 45-rpm vinyl disc containing four tracks (2 tracks per side), as opposed to a conventional 45 rpm *single* containing one track per side. Largely obsolete, EPs traditionally were packaged in cardboard jackets (as opposed to paper sleeves used for singles), which resembled album covers used for 33-1/3 rpm *LP* releases, and which contained *artwork* on one side and *liner notes* on the reverse.

Extended Use
The use of a broadcast commercial beyond an initial 13-week period. Under agreements between *AFTRA* and producers of commercials, AFTRA members whose performances are recorded in broadcast commercials must be paid additional fees for extended broadcast usages of the commercials.

Extension
(1) A continuation of an agreement beyond the original termination date (not the same as a *renewal*). (2) A grant of extra time to fulfill a promised obligation (such as a debt repayment), or complete a project, or consider an option. See also *renewal* and *retention*.

Extra
An actor or performer used in minor roles, such as walk-ons or crowd scenes.

F
Music format abbreviation for *folk*.

Fabricate
To assemble, put together, make, or manufacture a product.

Fabrication
The process of making or manufacturing a product. The term in the music business usually refers to the printing, labeling, assembly, and binding of album jackets, folios, *jewel boxes*, cassette cases, and other types of packaging.

Fade
An audio control technique by which sound is gradually decreased or increased.

Fade In
The introduction of sound from the point of inaudibility to the desired level of perception.

Fade Out
A means by which sound is gradually decreased until it is inaudible; a technique used to end a recorded performance by phasing out the sound instead of coming to an arranged ending.

Fader
The control device on a recording studio *console*, audio mixer, recorder, or playback system by which sound levels are changed. Also called *slider*.

FAI
Abbreviation for *Fox Agency International*.

Fair Market Value
The price mutually agreed between seller and buyer when both parties are rational and reasonably informed of all facts pertaining to the asset or service being sold. See also *market value* and *book value*.

Fair Use
A concept incorporated into copyright law, which permits the reproduction of small amounts of copyrighted material for the purposes of critical review, parody, scholarship, news reporting, etc. The amount of copying must have no practical effect on the market for, or value of the original work, and must be used only for purposes of teaching, illustration, comment, criticism, quotation, or summary. One defense against a charge of copyright *infringement* is the principle of fair use.

Fake Book
A collection of songs (presented with the melody line, lyrics, and chord symbols, instead of full-scale arrangements) used by musicians and singers who improvise their own arrangements. Historically, fake books were compiled and sold illegally (without proper licensing and payment of copyright royalties), but, seeing the commercial popularity of such publications, many music publishers now make available legitimate fake books for performers.

Fan
Derived from the word fanatic, an enthusiastic follower or *aficionado* of, for instance, a particular artist or musical style.

Fan Club
An organization of fans devoted to a particular artist or musical style.

Fan Fair

Event presented annually in Nashville by the *Country Music Association (CMA)* and the *Grand Ole Opry*. Founded in 1972 as an opportunity for fans to meet their favorite country music artists, the week-long fair is held at the Tennessee State Fairgrounds. Features include live performances by more than 100 acts and booths where fans can get autographs and pose for photographs with various artists.

Fanzine

A magazine focusing on the activities of, and marketed to fans of, a particular artist or musical style.

Father

A negative *metal master* used in conjunction with a *mother* (positive metal master) to *press* phonorecords.

Favored Nations Clause

Also called *most favored nations clause*. A contract or licensing provision stipulating that a *licensor* or *assignor* will automatically be extended the benefits of any better terms, conditions, advantages, or compensation granted to a *third party* in a similar agreement. *Example*: Where a music publisher licenses the use of a song in a commercial video release, this clause insures that if, during the term of the license, the distributor agrees to pay any other publisher a higher *fixing fee* and/or royalty rate to use another song in similar fashion in the same video, then that higher fee and/or royalty rate shall also apply to the composition in question, and that higher fee and/or royalty rate shall be retroactive to the date of the license. In such event, the distributor shall immediately pay the publisher the difference between the original fee and/or royalty with regards to past sales, and the distributor must continue to pay the publisher at the higher royalty rate for all copies distributed thereafter.

FCC

Abbreviation for *Federal Communications Commission*.

Feature

To showcase, highlight, publicize, display, or promote with special attention.

Feature Film

A movie made as a main film presentation for theater showings, as opposed to *shorts*, newsreels, documentaries, travelogues, etc. Also called a "feature-length film."

Feature Story

A news or human interest story or an article given prominent space in a newspaper or periodical.

Feature Work

(1) A musical composition or song performed for the primary focus of audience attention on a television program (musicians, vocalists and/or choreographed dancers are on camera). (2) A musical composition or song performed or played on a radio program in its entirety without interruption.

Federal Communications Commission (FCC)

An agency of the United States Government created in 1934 to regulate interstate and foreign radio and wire communications, and whose oversight has expanded with newer technologies to include all transmissions, such as television, cable television, and satellite broadcasting. The FCC assigns station *call letters*, broadcast frequencies, and operating power, and has authority to grant, revoke, renew, and modify broadcasting licenses.

Fee

A fixed sum of money charged for professional services (i.e., legal or accounting fees, etc.), or as an upfront charge for a license, privilege, or permission. See also *flat fee* and *commitment fee*.

Fee Structure

A *sliding scale* of fixed fees. For example, a music publisher might charge a film producer a specific *synchronization fee* if one song from the publisher's catalog is used in a movie, but the fee per song is reduced by, say, 10% if two songs are used, and by 15% per song if three songs are licensed.

Feedback

(1) Information received in response to a marketing campaign, idea, suggestion, or test of a new product, which is used to evaluate the commercial acceptance of a product or the validity of an idea. (2) An unwanted audio noise caused by the return of sound from one amplified output source through the input source of another amplified instrument or microphone.

Ferric

One of three basic types of cassette tape (the others being *metal* and *chrome*). Ferric tape is the most common, but metal and chrome offer higher playback quality. However, chrome and metal each require cassette players that are *calibrated* to play them, because of their higher *bias* and *EQ* requirements. In addition to being more expensive than ferric, chrome and metal cassettes are abrasive, which causes wear on the recording and playback *heads*.

Audiocassettes are graded according to dynamic range, *signal-to-noise ratio*, and *frequency response*.

Types 0 and 1, called *normal* bias, use ferric tape and are subject to more *hiss*. Type 0 is subject to more *hiss* and has a rather limited high-frequency response. Type 1 offers better bass and midlevel frequency response than type 0. *High bias* tapes (types 2 and 3 *chrome* and type 4 *metal*) provide the best frequency responses, wider dynamic ranges, and lower hiss. See also *chrome cassette, metal cassette, bias,* and *high bias.*

Fiber Optics

A technology used to transmit data and communications as light through fibers or thin rods of glass, plastic threads, or other type of transparent material. Both long-haul communications networks and local area networks (*LANs*) are using fiber-optic laser systems, because of their capacity to carry significantly more signals with greater clarity than older electrical systems. And, fiber systems can be maintained over longer distances before signal repeaters are required for signal regeneration.

Fictitious Name

A *trade name* adopted or assumed for business purposes; a *stage name* adopted or assumed for professional purposes. A *pen name, pseudonym,* or *nom de plume.* See also *doing business as (DBA)* and *name rights.*

Fictitious Name Certificate

An official certification by a government agency that a business's *fictitious name* is properly registered as a matter of public record, so that customers, clients, creditors, and others can determine the true identity of the parties conducting the business.

Fiduciary

A person or institution appointed to manage another person's assets, estate, and/or financial matters. *Examples*: attorney, administrator, guardian, executor, receiver, trustee, or conservator.

Fiduciary Relationship

See *fiduciary* and *fiduciary responsibility*. A fiduciary relationship obligates the person acting in a fiduciary capacity to conduct the affairs or handle the property of the other person with good faith, integrity, loyalty, prudence, discretion, and responsibility. The relationship necessarily requires the client, ward, or beneficiary to place full faith, trust, and confidence in the fiduciary.

Fiduciary Responsibility

Also called "fiduciary duty" and "fiduciary capacity." A fiduciary is under a legal and moral obligation to conduct the affairs or handle the property of the other person with good faith, integrity, loyalty, prudence, discretion, and responsibility. All states have laws governing fiduciary responsibilities, including a prohibition against investing or misappropriating money entrusted under the relationship for personal gain. Fiduciaries are also expected to follow the "prudent-man-rule" (i.e., to handle assets and money prudently, seeking to preserve capital and avoiding speculation).

Filing

(1) A legal document submitted for, or entered into the public record. (2) The initial stage of a lawsuit whereby a *complaint* or answer to a complaint is lodged with a court. (3) A formal application, appeal, request, pleading, or petition. (5) The process of storing documents, correspondence, or other items in systematic order for quick reference and access.

Filipino Society of Composers, Authors, and Publishers (FILSCAP)

The *performing-right society* in the Philippines.

Film

(1) A movie, a motion picture. (2) To photograph; to videotape; to shoot a scene; to make a motion picture.

Film Clip

A brief segment or extract taken from a complete film or videotape performance or visual production, used for promotional purposes, review, commentary, or news reporting, etc.

Film Director

Person with supervisory control and management authority over the creative elements of a theatrical or non-theatrical film.

Film Score

Music composed or arranged as a backdrop for a film or movie, including opening and closing themes, *segueways*, incidentals, and orchestrated effects used to enhance the moods of various scenes.

FILSCAP

Acronym for *Filipino Society of Composers, Authors, and Publishers*.

Filter

One of several types of electronic audio devices used to allow certain frequencies through desired channels while rejecting unwanted signals, vibrations, or frequencies. Filters are classified by the characteristics of their frequency response (i.e., low-pass, high-pass, band-pass, and band-stop). As a *signal-processing* device used in recording and mixing, filters can exclude *hiss*, rumble, and other extraneous noises without affecting the music.

Filtering

The process of using a *filter* to manipulate sound frequencies.

FIM

Abbreviation for *International Federation of Musicians*. An umbrella labor organization comprising musicians unions from various countries, including the *AFM*. FIM has nongovernmental organization (NGO) status in *WIPO* and the International Labor Office of the United Nations. FIM negotiates directly with *IFPI* regarding distribution of broadcasting royalties to their respective members. (FIM royalties go to performers; IFPI royalties are allocated to producers.)

Final Take

(1) The last *take* of a recording, videotaping, or filming session, or the take selected from several alternatives as the one to use. (2) The ultimate amount of money collected; the *gate*; the total receipts from ticket sales or product sales.

Finale

(1) The closing number or performance or act. (2) The last of several movements in a work such as a symphony, suite, concerto, etc. (3) The end; a denouement.

Find

In law, to make a judgment on a matter after deliberation of evidence presented; to decide on and declare a verdict or judgment.

Finder

(1) A person who links entrepreneurs or others needing money for a venture or project with investors or lenders. (2) A deal-packager or deal-maker. (3) A person who locates prospective acquisition targets for companies or investors seeking to buy or merge with other companies; an *intermediary*. (4) A *talent scout*.

Finder's Fee

The *fee* paid to a *finder* or deal-maker who successfully brings together investors or lenders with people looking for financial backing, or who locates assets or companies for acquisition or merger, or who otherwise acts as an *intermediary* in a *transaction*. Typically, finders' fees are based on a percentage of the value of the deal (i.e., 2% to 5% of money raised).

Finding

In law, a legal decision or verdict arrived at by a jury or court after consideration of the facts presented.

Fine Arts

Same as *beaux arts*. Those art forms used as creative expressions of beauty or aesthetics, rather than for practical application. Examples include music, poetry, painting, sculpture, etc.

First Amendment

The first of ten amendments to the United States Constitution known as the Bill of Rights. The First Amendment is the bedrock of creative freedom, and is often used as a legal defense against attempts to curb what many consider to be pornography and obscenity in song lyrics or literature, etc. Specifically, the First Amendment declares: "Congress shall make no law . . . abridging the freedom of speech, or of the press; or the right of the people peaceably to assemble, and to petition the government for a redress of grievances."

First Call Musician

A musician whose expertise is such that producers and *contractors* are willing to pay *double scale* or more in order to obtain their services for recording sessions and other types of performances.

First Chair

The leader of an orchestral section (such as the trumpet section or string section) and/or those musicians belonging to a particular instrumental section who play the lead parts of arrangements written for those instruments.

First Desk

Another name for *first chair*.

First Refusal

A right given to one party to exercise an option, distribute a product, license a copyright, sign an artist, or purchase an asset, etc., by matching a price or other terms offered by any other party. Also called *last refusal*.

First Sale

Copyright owners are paid on the "first sale" of products embodying their copyrights (i.e., CDs, audiocassettes). Purchasers then own the physical product, though not the copyright. But, as owner of the physical product, a purchaser can resell the product without additional payment to the copyright owner. For instance, a consumer can sell his/her CD collection without having to compensate the music publishers or recording artists. The concept of First Sale is the legal basis video stores use to buy videos that they in turn rent out and ultimately resell as used videos. Many record stores also buy and sell used CDs on the same legal grounding.

First Use

The concept of "first use" is that a music copyright

owner can prevent anyone from releasing a recorded version of a song that has not yet been recorded and released. Once a recording has been authorized for release, however, the copyright owner can no longer prevent anyone from making similar use of the song as long as a *mechanical license* is obtained under the *compulsory mechanical licensing* provision of the *Copyright Act*.

Fix

To make permanent. Any original creative work is automatically copyrighted once it has been "fixed in any tangible medium of expression." A "tangible medium" is any format "now known or later developed" from which a song, performance, or other artistic work "can be perceived, reproduced, or otherwise communicated, either directly or with the aid of a machine or device." *Example*: A song is "fixed" sufficiently for copyright protection the moment the writer jots down the lyrics on a piece of paper with musical notations, or records a rough demo on a cassette recorder.

Fixation

A tangible medium of expression, such as a recording, by which a creative work is *fixed* so that the work "can be perceived, reproduced, or otherwise communicated, either directly or with the aid of a machine or device."

Fixed

A creative work that has been recorded, written down, or otherwise put into any format by which it can be "perceived, reproduced, or communicated, either directly or with the aid of a machine or device."

Fixing Fee

A one-off *fee* paid to copyright owners for use of a work in a *synchronization*. Also called a *synchronization fee*.

Flack

Slang for *publicist* or *press agent*.

Flash

Excess vinyl trimmed from the edges of phonograph records during the *pressing* process.

Flash and Trash

Slang reference to decisions by some television news producers to feature stories on sex and violence in order to boost viewer ratings during audience survey periods. Also, a derogatory term for recording artists whose works seem to glorify sex or violence.

Flash in the Pan

One who achieves a degree of sudden success, then fails to perpetuate that success or build upon it as expected or hoped. See also *one-hit wonder*.

Flat

(1) In recording or performing, a "flat" sound is one that isn't altered or enhanced by such effects as echo, reverb, tonal modulation, etc. (2) In music, a voice or an instrument is "flat" if its pitch is lower than desired. (3) In music, a "flat note" is one that is intentionally lowered by at least one-half step (i.e., B-flat). See also *blue note*. (3) In marketing, a product is "flat" when sales are weak or consumer response is negligible.

Flat Fee

A one-time fee, usually paid up front, for the privilege of obtaining a license or the retention of professional services, as opposed to royalties, wages, or other forms of continuing compensation.

Flat Rate

An all-inclusive charge for goods or services. For instance, a recording studio may charge a flat daily rate regardless of how many hours are actually used by a client, or an arranger will charge a flat rate regardless of how long it takes to complete the arrangement.

Flier

See *flyer*.

Flip

(1) To turn a record over and play the other side. (2) The reverse side of a record (the flip side or *B side*).

Float

Profit from monies deposited in interest-bearing accounts between the time of collection and the date they must be paid out in royalties to songwriters, artists, producers, copublishers, licensees, etc.

Floor

A royalty base rate, or stated minimum level of compensation (as opposed to *ceiling*, which is a maximum amount). See also *cap*.

Floor Show

A nightclub act; an entertainment presented in a nightclub or cabaret (as opposed to being staged in a theater).

Flop

A failure in terms of product sales, critical review, commercial acceptance, or audience appreciation.

Flop Sweat

Slang for the worry felt by investors, artists, producers, et al when it appears likely their production, film, release, or play will not succeed.

Floppy Disk

A plastic magnetic disk inside a hard jacket, used to store, read, and write data for computers. Also called *diskette*.

Flow-Through Clause

A contractual provision in a deal between a record company and a record production company guaranteeing that the production company's artist will fulfill all recording obligations directly for the record company in the event the production company is unable or unwilling to render its obligations under the agreement. In a typical production deal, an artist is signed directly to a producer who contracts with a record company to deliver finished masters by the artist. A flow-through clause protects the record company's investment if the producer defaults, has a falling out with the artist, or goes out of business. If a flow-through clause is exercised, the artist's obligations are transferred to the record company. Generally, when the production agreement is signed, the artist simultaneously signs a *side letter* or *inducement letter* agreeing to be bound by the terms of the agreement in the event the flow-through clause is exercised. Among the events that trigger a typical flow-through clause are: bankruptcy or insolvency of the production company; breach of the production agreement by the production company; and any breach by the production company of its agreement with the artist that adversely affects the record company's rights. If the production company defaults on the contract with the artist, the record company must cure the default when it exercises its flow-through rights. Flow-through clauses are also written into contracts between record companies and *loan-out corporations* when the artist is signed directly to the loan-out entity.

Flutter

A rapid oscillation, wavering, or pulsing of pitch in audio signals, caused by mechanical speed variations of recording or playback equipment. See also *wow*.

Flyer

Also called *flier*. A printed sheet, pamphlet, or circular containing an advertisement or notice, distributed as inserts with product, posted in public places, or handed out.

FM

Abbreviation for *frequency modulation*, the broadcast airwave band used by FM radio stations. Approximately 7,750 radio stations broadcast on FM in the United States, compared with around 5,250 *AM* stations. Roughly 1,900 FM stations are *noncommercial*, relying on financial support from educational institutions, local governments, nonprofit civic organizations, listener contributions, and federal funding via *National Public Radio*. See also *frequency modulation*, *AM*, *and amplitude modulation*.

F.O.B.

Abbreviation for *free on board*.

Focus

(1) To concentrate or direct one's attention on a specific objective, object, or task. (2) To narrow a broad scheme, plan, or objective into a sharply defined area of concentration (such as marketing a product to a specifically targeted population segment, rather than attempting a mass marketing campaign). (3) To devote one's self to work in a particular style, genre, or field. (4) An area of concentration. (5) In photography, to adjust the lens of a camera in order to produce a sharp image.

Folio

Also called *songbook*. A large, softbound book format for printed music, usually consisting of large sheets of paper each folded once in the middle to make two to four pages.

Folk Music

(1) Music originating from traditional ethnic or regional cultures, usually passed down with variations from one generation to another in oral, rather than written, form. See also *traditional*. (2) Contemporary music composed and performed in a folk style.

Folk Rock

A contemporary musical genre blending traditional *folk music* with rock & roll influences.

Folkie

A folk singer, folk musician, or folk music aficionado.

Follow Up

A recording released subsequent to another by the same artist, particularly when the first recording was successful enough to provide a degree of built-in marketing momentum for the artist.

Follow-Up Call

Telephone call made to the recipient of a *submission* (i.e., of a promo recording sent to a radio station or reviewer; of a press release sent to a newspaper or magazine; of a demo sent to a music publisher or record company, etc.) Follow-up calls are ideally a form of *schmoozing*, rather than trying to apply hard sell tactics. The purpose of such a call is ostensibly to see if the recipient received the submission and to gauge reaction to it. More subtly, the call is to remind the recipient of the submission in hopes it will be given careful consideration.

Follow-Up Rights

An *option* or right of *first refusal* to license, enter into a contract, or otherwise acquire the rights to publish, distribute, market, manufacture, sell, print, or release (as the case may be) a *follow-up* work, such as a recording. Variations of follow-up rights apply to many types of contracts and licenses. For instance, in an agreement between a record company and an independent producer to produce an artist, the producer may be given the right to produce follow up records if certain sales levels are reached. Or, in a singles deal between a record company and independent producer, the company will reserve follow-up rights to release subsequent recordings by the artist in question.

Footage

Film or videotape, or a grouping of scenes photographed on film or videotape.

Force Majeure

A contractual provision allowing a contract to be extended by the same number of days during which the company was unable to benefit from the contract due to any event, or effect of any event, that could not be reasonably anticipated or controlled. Examples of force majeure events include any *act of God* (earthquake, flood, violent storm), fires, strikes, riots, war, government decrees, shortages, breakdowns, or failures of delivery of supplies, materials, labor, or equipment, etc.

Foreground

(1) In the *synchronization* of music with film, a "foreground use" or *foreground rendition* (of music) is one where the music is part of the subject matter, such as in a scene where musicians and/or singers perform on camera. See also *visual vocal*. (2) A type of service provided by companies such as *Muzak* where the music transmitted is intended to create a noticeable environment, as opposed to *background music*, which is intended for a more subconscious or subliminal atmosphere. (3) The primary object of focus in a photograph or in a filmed or videotaped scene.

Foreground Rendition

Also called "foreground use." See *foreground*, above.

Foreign Collections

The receipt of income arising from overseas copyright sales and usages. Revenues generated overseas are typically collected from overseas *users* by *licensees* (such as *subpublishers* and foreign record manufacturers) and rights-agencies (such as *performing-right* and *mechanical-right societies*) and forwarded to *domestic* copyright owners (record companies and music publishers or their domestic rights agencies, such as *Harry Fox*, *BMI*, *ASCAP*, etc.), who then must account to artists, songwriters, and producers, etc. for their respective shares.

Foreign Department

Same as *international department*; a division of a record company or music publishing company that deals with overseas licensing, marketing, and collections.

Foreign Language Edition

Printed material, such as a book or periodical, translated into a foreign language for publication overseas.

Foreign Language Version

A song with original lyrics translated into a foreign language; a recording with vocal overdubs in a foreign language; a film or television program released overseas with foreign language subtitles or voice overdubs.

Foreign Licensee

An overseas company who *licenses* rights to copyrighted works (such as recordings or songs) in order to publish, manufacture, market, distribute, and sell the works in the *licensed territory*.

Foreign Rights

A license to reproduce, perform, and sell copyrighted material in an overseas territory, as opposed to the *export* of finished product for sale in a foreign country.

Form CA

A form for registering amended copyright claim information with the *Copyright Office*. Under the *Copyright Act of 1976*, Form CA is used for filing corrections or additional information about works previously registered.

Form EP

Under the *Copyright Act of 1909*, copyright *claimants* for *published* musical works were required to register their claims with the *Copyright Office* by submitting two copies of the *best edition* of the work along with an EP Form. (Copyright claims for *unpublished* works were registered by submitting one copy of the work and an *EU Form*.) Since January 1, 1978, when the *Copyright Act of 1976* took effect, copyright claimants for musical works may register either published or unpublished works using a *PA Form*; EP and EU Forms are now obsolete.

Form EU

Under the *Copyright Act of 1909*, copyright *claimants* for *unpublished* musical works were required to register their claims with *Copyright Office* by submitting one copy of the work along with an EU Form. (Copyright claims for *published* works were registered by submitting two copies of the *best edition* of the work with an *EP Form*.) Since January 1, 1978, when the *Copyright Act of 1976* Act took effect, copyright claimants for musical works may register either published or unpublished works using a *PA Form*; EP and EU Forms are now obsolete.

Form GATT

A form for restoring United States *copyright protection* to foreign copyrights that fell into *public domain* prior to the US joining the *Berne Convention*. Under the *Copyright Act of 1909*, the term of copyright protection in the United States was limited to 56 years maximum (a 28-year term plus a 28-year renewal). Many foreign copyrights thus fell into public domain in the United States, either because renewal *formalities* weren't taken properly or because 56 years lapsed, even though the works were still under copyright protection in their countries of origin. Since the United States joined the Berne Convention in 1989, copyright owners of songs originating in countries that are *signatories* to the Berne Convention (or which are members of the *World Trade Organization*) can have copyright protection restored to works that fell into the public domain, as long as those works are still in copyright in their countries of origin. Copyright restoration is accomplished by filing a *GATT form* with the *US Copyright Office*.

Form N

Under the *Copyright Act of 1909* as amended in 1972 (but superseded by the *Copyright Act of 1976*) copyright *claimants* for sound recordings were required to file Form N with the Copyright Office. Under the 1976 Act, copyright claimants for sound recordings now use *Form SR*; Form N is now obsolete.

Form PA

A form for registering copyright claim information with the Copyright Office. Under the *Copyright Act of 1976*, Form PA is used for registering both *published* and *unpublished* songs.

Form R

Under the *Copyright Act of 1909*, statutory copyright protection was given for an initial term of 28 years with the right to renew copyright protection for an additional 28 years. A claim for *copyright renewal* was made using Form R, which is now obsolete since the *Copyright Act of 1976*, now in effect, grants statutory copyright protection for one term only (currently life of author plus 50 years, though legislation was being considered in 1998 to extend protection to life of author plus 70 years), with no renewal options.

Form SR

A form for registering copyright claim information with the Copyright Office. Under the *Copyright Act of 1976*, Form SR is used for registering both *published* and *unpublished* sound recordings. (Claimants who wish to register a recorded performance *and* the songs rendered on the recording may register both claims with this one form—rather than separately filing an SR form for the recording and a *PA form* for the song.)

Form TX

A form for registering copyright claim information with the Copyright Office. Under the *Copyright Act of 1976*, Form TX is used for registering nondramatic literary works.

Form U

Under the *Copyright Act of 1909*, song copyright owners filed Form U with the Copyright Office once a song had been commercially recorded and released, so that anyone else wishing to record the work would be subject to the *compulsory mechanical licensing* provisions of the Copyright Act. Under the *Copyright Act of 1976*, there is no requirement for copyright owners to file Form U.

Form VA

A form for registering copyright claim information with the Copyright Office. Under the *Copyright Act of 1976*, Form VA is used for registering visual arts (photos, models, prints, posters, album covers, designs, advertisements, etc.).

Formalities

Term used for procedures required to establish a valid copyright claim. Under the *Copyright Act of 1976*, copyright claimants in the United States were required to affix a *copyright notice* on all copies of published works, *deposit* two copies of the *best edition* of the work, and *register* the claim to copyright with the *Copyright Office*. But, with the *Berne Convention Implementation Act of 1988*, these formalities are no longer required for establishing a copyright claim to works published on or after March 1, 1989. However, voluntary compliance with these formalities is strongly recommended, because they aid in validating a claim in the event of *infringement*, and, unless the formalities have been undertaken, the copyright claimant may not be eligible for all statutory civil remedies and damage awards that are otherwise available.

Format

(1) The physical form of a manufactured or printed product containing copyrighted material (i.e., compact disc, audiocassette, 45 rpm vinyl record, *piano copy*, etc.). (2) The physical layout of a publication (i.e. tabloid, magazine, paperback, hard cover, folio, etc.). (3) To prepare a computer disk for the storage of data. (4) To arrange data or a display. (5) A radio station programming process to target specific market segments (i.e., an *adult contemporary* format) with selected music appealing to that market. (6) To program a radio station for specific audiences. (7) The type of programming focused on by a radio station (i.e., "news and talk," "quiet storm," urban contemporary, etc.). See below.

Format Abbreviations

The following are commonly used abbreviations to denote the style of music programmed by a radio station or reviewed in a periodical.

AAA - Adult Album Alternative
AC - Adult Contemporary
B - Blues
BG - Bluegrass
C - Country
CH - Christian
CHR - Contemporary Hit Radio (Top 40)
CL - Classical
D - Dance
E - Ethnic
F - Folk
G - Gospel
I - Industrial
J - Jazz
M - Metal
NA - New Age
NAC - New Adult Contemporary
QS - Quiet Storm
R - Rock
RA - Rap
R&B - Rhythm & Blues
R&R - Rock & Roll
RG - Reggae
SW - Spoken Word
UC - Urban Contemporary
WB - World Beat

Forms

(1) Musical arrangements, structures, patterns, or stylistic organization. (2) Generic documents containing blanks to insert applicable details or information. See also *clearance form*, *Form CA*, *Form EP*, *Form EU*, *Form N*, *Form PA*, *Form SR*, *Form R*, *Form TX*, *Form U*, and *Form VA*.

Forty-five

Reference to a phonograph record format configured to play at 45 *rpm*, usually manufactured on seven-inch vinyl discs. See also *single* and *extended play* (*EP*).

Four A's, The

Abbreviation for *The Associated Actors and Artists of America*, a cooperative alliance of six show business unions affiliated with the *AFL-CIO*: *Actors Equity Association* (*AEA*), *American Federation of Television and Radio Artists* (*AFTRA*), *American Guild of Music Artists* (*AGMA*), *American Guild of Variety Artists* (*AGVA*), *Screen Actors Guild* (*SAG*), and *Screen Extras Guild* (*SEG*).

Four-Color Printing

In printing, the four-color process replicates an original photograph, design, layout, or artwork in complete color by converting the original into four *halftones* separating or filtering the primary colors (red, yellow, and blue, plus black), which are then printed over each other to reproduce the original colors.

Four Walling

Term used when a concert promoter or theatrical producer rents a venue for a performance and must independently supply stage, sound, and lighting crews, as well as security, ushers and box office personnel, since the landlord furnishes only the facility (four walls and a roof).

Fox

Abbreviated reference for the *Harry Fox Agency*.

Fox Agency, the

Abbreviated reference for the *Harry Fox Agency*.

Fox Agency International (FAI)

A subsidiary of the *Harry Fox Agency* with regional headquarters in Singapore for the purpose of *mechanical licensing* and mechanical royalty collections in Southeast Asia. FAI represents the repertoire of over 4,000 US music publishers and several European *mechanical-right societies*, and has additional offices in Taiwan and other Pacific Rim countries. See also *MOU*.

Franchise

(1) To license, to grant permission, a right or a privilege. Also called *enfranchise*. (2) A license granting the right to sell the *licensor*'s products or services using the licensor's *trade name*, *logo*, or *trademark*.

Franchised Agent

A talent or booking agency approved by the *AFM*, *AFTRA*, etc. for professional representation of union members.

Franchisee

A *licensee*; a person or company licensed to use, make, or sell a product or copyright under the *licensor*'s *trade name*, *trademark*, or *logo*.

Free Copies

A number of manufactured or printed copies (i.e., sheet music, compact discs, cassettes, etc.) supplied without charge to a *licensor* by a *licensee*, or by a company (i.e, a record company or music publisher, etc.) to the creator of an original work (i.e., songwriter, recording artist, producer, etc.). Publishing, *subpublishing*, recording, and distribution contracts generally define the number of free copies that must be supplied, and typically provide that additional copies may be made available at a discount from the retail price. See also *free goods, free records, distributor free goods,* and *freebie.*

Free Goods

(1) Product intended for promotion, publicity, and marketing purposes, which is not sold and for which no royalties are payable (to artists, producers, licensors, music publishers, etc.). (2) Bonus product given to consumers, retailers, and/or wholesalers as inducements to purchase additional product. For example, record clubs give away free records as inducements to attract new members. Although most record company contracts with artists specify that royalties won't be paid on "free goods," a 50% royalty is sometimes paid on free goods issued by record clubs. However, some record companies issue what are called *distributor free goods* for which no royalties are paid at all. This practice essentially "gives" the distributor, say, 15 "free records" for every 85 units purchased. In reality, the company is giving the distributor a 15% discount on the purchase of one hundred units. But, since the distributor only "buys" 85 units, the company doesn't have to pay royalties on the 15 so-called "free" copies. (3) See also *special programs, free copies,* and *freebie.*

Free on Board (F.O.B.)

A price for product based on the point at which the purchaser takes delivery. From the delivery point, the purchaser assumes all further risks and costs of storage, shipment, reshipment, and delivery to customers.

Free Records

See *free copies, free goods, distributor free goods,* and *freebie.*

Free Speech

See *First Amendment.*

Free Television

"Free television" refers to programs viewers can get without charge, broadcast over media licensed by *performing-right societies*. In the main, free television includes the networks (ABC, CBS, Fox, NBC, and their local affiliates), independent local stations, and syndicated programs broadcast by local stations. Contrasts with television programming distributed by cable and satellite to paying subscribers only.

Free Television License

A television *synchronization license* for music used in *free television*. The license itself isn't actually free in the sense that the copyright owner doesn't get paid for the usage. The term simply means that, once having been granted the license, the producer can sell or license the program to any network, syndicator, or television station during the license term without additional payment to the copyright owner, as long as the ensuing broadcasts are carried free to viewers (not cable or satellite subscription services or *pay-per-view*). In other words, the term applies to "free television," which is not the same thing as a "free license." See *television synchronization license.*

Freebie

An item, such as a tee-shirt or concert ticket, provided fee of charge, usually as an inducement to purchase another item, or as a means of promoting and marketing a product or performer's career. See also *free copies, free goods, distributor free goods,* and *free records.*

Freelance

To do work, especially creative work, for others on a non-exclusive, short-term basis. *Example*: A freelance recording engineer might work on specific projects for several different studios or producers without a formal employer/employee relationship with any of them.

Freelancer

A person who does *freelance* work for different short-term employers, as opposed to being employed exclusively by one company or person.

Frequency

One of three physical characteristics of sound (the others being *amplitude* and harmonic constitution). Frequency corresponds to *pitch*, one of the perceptual characteristics of sound.

In measuring wave motions (of sound, radio signals, electricity, etc.), a frequency is the number of complete *oscillations* or wave crests reaching a given point in a second. One cycle per second equals one hertz (Hz). Radio waves and the *frequency response* limits of audio amplifiers and other audio components are often measured in kilohertz (kHz), or thousands of cycles per second, megahertz (MHz), or millions of cycles per second, and gigahertz (GHz), or billions of cycles per second. (Radio waves are also sometimes characterized by their wavelengths rather than their frequencies.)

Every broadcasting station is allocated one of two types of modulated frequency to carry information: *amplitude modulation* (*AM*) or *frequency modulation* (*FM*). AM broadcasts are made on short-, medium-, and long-waves; ultra-high-frequency (*UHF*) and very-high-frequency waves (*VHF*) are used for FM and television broadcasts. In FM, the frequency of the carrier is made to fluctuate: in AM, the strength of the carrier is made to fluctuate in time with the audio signal. See also *sound, FM, AM, frequency modulation,* and *amplitude modulation.*

Frequency Modulation (FM)
A system of modulating carrier waves for FM radio transmissions, whereby the frequency of the carrier is made to fluctuate. (In AM broadcasting, the strength of the carrier is made to fluctuate in time with the audio signal.) FM transmissions are not sensitive to atmospheric interference and electrical disturbances that cause static in AM radio broadcasting. In addition, FM broadcasting stations can be operated in very-high-frequency bands that are much wider than the standard broadcast AM bands, allowing for a greater number of broadcasting stations in a given area without mutual interference. The superior reception of FM, and the ability to broadcast in stereo, together with comparatively inexpensive broadcasting equipment, have resulted in the rapid growth of FM stations and radio audiences at the expense of AM broadcasting. See also *FM, AM, frequency,* and *amplitude modulation.*

Frequency Response
(1) The capacity of a loudspeaker or other device to reproduce audio frequencies accurately. (2) A display device, such as a graph, used to measure the capacity of an audio amplifier to handle the frequencies applied to it.

Frequency Shifting
In music software synthesis, the manipulation of sound waves to alter pitch.

Fringe Area
A zone beyond the optimum range of a television or radio station's broadcast signals where reception becomes weak and distorted.

Fringe Benefit
A benefit or method of compensation that is in addition to, but not part of, an employee's salary or commission. *Examples*: use of a company car, insurance coverage, stock options, etc. Also called a *perquisite* or *perk,* for short.

Fringe Market
A market for product that is out of the mainstream. See also *niche market.*

Fringing
(1) A spillover of an audio signal recorded on one *magnetic tape* track onto another track. (2) A jumble of two or more unrelated conversations or sounds on a telephone line or recording input. Also called *cross talk.*

Front
To lead a band, to head up an organization, to take the spotlight.

Front-End Loaded
A deal where a company makes a firm commitment to take two or more albums (as opposed to options for the additional albums). The initial advance also includes partial payment for the second album. For example, a three-album front-end loaded deal at $300,000 per album might call for an up-front advance of $450,000 covering $300,000 for the first album and 50% of the advance for the second album.

Front-End Money
Money earned by a record or film before release from advance sales, licensing, commercial advertising *tie-ins, ancillary* rights, etc.

Front Line
(1) Artists or product with proven commercial acceptance, which provide the bulk of a company's sales. (2) Featured performers, as opposed to opening acts or backup musicians and vocalists. (3) The lead, melodic section of a band versus rhythm instruments.

Front Money
(1) An advance against royalties or other monies, paid before delivery of contracted goods or services. (2) Funds required for investment before a project, production, venture or enterprise can be undertaken.

Frozen Account
(1) A credit sales account that is delinquent or in which a customer's financial situation has deteriorated, so that the vendor won't issue further delivery of product on credit unless the customer either pays off or pays down sums owed, or makes a deposit. (2) A royalty account from which no payments are made until a dispute is settled. See also *escrow.*

Frozen Asset

An asset, such as a copyright catalog or product inventory that may not be sold or otherwise disposed of until a dispute or situation is settled.

Frozen Collateral

Collateral, such as a deposit or property, that a creditor cannot seize to satisfy repayment of a debt, because the debtor has been given judicial protection and/or because of a legal dispute over the true ownership of the asset that was pledged as collateral.

Frozen Funds

A financial account that can not be touched, and from which no withdrawals or payments may be made, until a dispute or legal question is settled.

Full-Court Press

Slang phrase borrowed from the basketball term, which refers to a concentrated, coordinated defensive strategy applying intensive pressure on the opponent, and which typically means to pull out all stops in a marketing campaign, to break a record, to put an artist over the top, to win a contract negotiation, to clinch a deal, etc.

Full Price Unit

A recording sold through *normal retail channels* at normal retail price (i.e., excluding *budget*-line and *midline* product, record club sales, export sales, special-market *premium* records, *military sales*, etc.).

Full Protection Matrixing

Service offered by a *pressing plant* whereby permanent *metal molds* or *parts* are made of *masters*, *mothers*, and *stampers*, which can be stored for up to 20 years.

Full-Service Agency

A large, national talent agency authorized to represent performers in booking personal appearances and other types of employment. Their function is much like that of an employment agency, finding work, negotiating terms of engagements, administering the flow of contracts. While a small, specialized agency may be restricted to handling personal appearances, a full-service agency might also represent a client in every conceivable area of employment, including commercials, endorsements, and ancillary activities (such as a recording artist branching into acting or writing books, etc.). Talent agencies are compensated with *commissions* based on a percentage of the fees received from employment they generate.

Full-Service Publisher

A fully-staffed music publishing operation involved in all areas of publishing. Full-service publishers may act as *banker-publishers* in some cases, *administrative* publishers in other cases, but they also sign and nurture songwriting talent, develop artists, finance demos, videos, and recording sessions, purchase catalogs, pay advances for new works from well-known writers, sub-license catalogs from overseas publishers, market material to recording artists, and promote songs in all media. While larger operations of this type do their own collections, administration, and licensing, etc., smaller ones may make contract arrangements with service firms to handle specific functions.

Full-Track Mono

A *magnetic tape* recorded across the entire width of the tape, so that one audio channel only is available to play back.

Fund

See *recording fund* and *all-in advance*.

Funding

(1) Money earmarked to finance a specific project, event, or enterprise. (2) The act of financially sponsoring or backing a specific project, event, or enterprise.

Future Rights

(1) Rights to acquire or license copyrights not yet created or delivered. For instance, in an exclusive songwriter's contract, the music publisher is generally given future rights to any songs the writer creates between the effective date of the contract and its termination date. (2) An option to acquire the rights to a product or copyright either after a current license or contract ends, or the rights to product or copyright usages derived from current commercial activity arising from the product or copyright. See also *follow-up rights* and *rule of expectancy*.

G
Music format abbreviation for *gospel*.

Gaffer
Chief electrician on the set of a film, video, or television production.

Galley
In printing, a tray used to set type. Also an abbreviated reference for *galley proof*.

Galley Proof
In printing, a *proof* or sample printing of a type-set page or manuscript, used for editing and correcting typos before final printing is authorized.

Games
See *electronic game*, *video game*, and *management game*.

Gang Run
In printing, the coordination, arrangement, or assembly of several pages onto one printing plate to allow for simultaneous production of two or more print jobs. Big printing companies frequently do large, full-color print-runs for major clients, and are thus geared up to run smaller orders on their presses at the end of the original job in a "gang run." In such cases, the printer might offer a client needing a small run anywhere from 50% to 75% off the full-color printing rate, since the set-up costs are already paid.

Gangsta Rap
Rap genre associated with West Coast hip-hop, characterized by macho boasting, gang-oriented in-your-face attitude, and street language.

Garage Band
Young three- to four-piece band that plays straight-ahead, unsophisticated, guitar-driven music.

GAS
Acronym for *Germany*, *Austria*, and *Switzerland*, when grouped together as one *territory* for licensing purposes.

Gate
(1) The total amount of money collected from ticket sales and admission to a concert or other event. Also called the *take* or *box office receipts*. (2) A signal processing device used in recording and playback to increase dynamic range. Also called an *expander*, it can turn off (or on) an audio channel at a predetermined threshold in order to eliminate unwanted noise and *leakage*.

Gatefold
A cover or page (of an album, magazine, folio, etc.) that opens or folds out, usually to double the size of the page.

Gatekeeper
Slang for someone, such as a personal assistant or receptionist, who screens calls and visitors, and who shields an employer from unwanted intrusions.

GATT
Acronym for *General Agreement on Tariffs and Trade*.

GATT Form
A form for restoring United States *copyright protection* to foreign copyrights that fell into *public domain* prior to the US joining the *Berne Convention*. Under the *Copyright Act of 1909*, the term of copyright protection in the United States was lim-

ited to 56 years maximum (a 28-year term plus a 28-year renewal). Many foreign copyrights thus fell into public domain in the United States, either because renewal *formalities* weren't taken properly or because 56 years lapsed, even though the works were still under copyright protection in their countries of origin. Since the United States joined the Berne Convention in 1989, copyright owners of songs originating in countries that are *signatories* to the Berne Convention (or which are members of the *World Trade Organization*) can have copyright protection restored to works that fell into the public domain, as long as those works are still in copyright in their countries of origin. Copyright restoration is accomplished by filing a *GATT form* with the *US Copyright Office*.

Gavin Report

Weekly *trade publication* or *tip sheet*, offering reviews of new releases, charts, and playlist surveys from radio stations focusing on *alternative*, *CHR*, *AOR*, *AC*, *jazz*, *country*, *rock*, *R&B*, *New Age*, etc. Located at 140 Second Street, San Francisco, CA 94105. Tel: (415) 495-2580.

GEMA

The *mechanical-* and *performing-right society* in Germany, which also covers Bulgaria, the Czech Republic, Slovakia, Poland, Romania, Turkey, and Yugoslavia.

General Agreement on Tariffs and Trade (GATT)

A 1947 multilateral treaty dealing with international trade, under which member countries meet periodically to address barriers to the flow of commerce between nations. GATT decisions affect the music business in various important ways. The question of duties and excise levied on exports and imports apply to finished product sold overseas, but, perhaps more importantly, reciprocal copyright protection for intellectual properties, such as music and sound recordings, goes to the heart of the music industry. Therefore, GATT decisions often can and do have significant impact on the international value of copyright properties. See also *Trade Related Aspects of Intellectual Properties* (TRIPS).

General Partnership

A venture formed between two or more parties, who may be individuals, companies, corporations, other partnerships, or any combination thereof.

All partners share profits, assets, liabilities, and responsibilities. Assets belong to partners collectively. Each general partner has authority to enter into contracts on behalf of the partnership. Each partner is accountable for actions by any other partner, and is responsible for the partnership's debts and losses.

A general partnership itself pays no taxes. Part-
ners must individually account for their shares of profits or losses on their personal tax returns.

When a general partnership is disbanded, assets are liquidated and proceeds are used to (1) pay creditors, (2) repay loans to the partnership by any of the partners, and (3) compensate partners who have contributed funds or assets. Money left over is distributed between partners in proportion to their shares in the business. See also *limited partnership*.

Generate

To produce, create, make, originate.

Generation

(1) A creation or production. (2) A span of time, an era, an age group. (3) A stage, step, or sequence, as in "a third-generation tape copy" (i.e., a copy of a copy of the original master tape).

Generation X

People born after 1965, who have proven difficult for marketers to define as a group in that they are spread across numerous socio-economic sectors and seem to evidence few distinct trends as consumers.

Geneva Phonograms Agreement

An international treaty drafted in 1971, which took effect in the United States in 1974, extending copyright protection in all other member countries to sound recordings originating in any member nation. The treaty members agreed to prohibit unauthorized copying, manufacturing, importation, and distribution of recordings in an effort to stem record *piracy* and *bootlegging*. The convention augments the broad protections guaranteed by the *Rome Convention*, and has been signed thus far by 43 countries.

Genre

A type, category, or classification of creative style, form, content, or performance. *Examples*: a *blues* guitarist, *folk* song, *heavy metal* band, etc.

Gentlemen's Agreement

An oral, verbal, or unwritten agreement undertaken on the basis that the participants will each uphold their end of the deal as pledged.

Get the Hook

To replace a performer who performs badly; to fire or give someone the boot.

Ghostwriter

A person hired to write music, books, articles, etc. under the name of his/her employer.

Gig

Slang for a performance or booking.

Glass Master

A process used to prepare master recordings for compact disc manufacturing. In the glass mastering process, a polished glass master disc containing a layer of photo sensitive material is exposed to a laser beam controlled by digital information encoded on the *U-Matic* master tape. The exposure creates approximately 3 billion microscopic pits on the disc surface. These pits represent audio information in binary code, to be read by a CD player.

The glass master is next coated with a metal layer to make the pit surface electroconductive. An electroforming process then takes place to make negative and positive metal masters (*fathers* and *mothers*, respectively). The metal masters are used to produce the finished compact discs, serving much the same purpose as *stampers* in the process of *pressing* vinyl records. See also *compact disc mastering*, *premastering*, and *direct-metal mastering*.

Glissando

A rapid slurring or sliding of musical notes to produce an up or down transition from one note to another.

GMA

Abbreviation for *Gospel Music Association*.

Gofer

Slang for an aide or assistant who is on call to run errands, carry messages, and "go for" whatever is needed by his/her employer.

Gold Album

A phonorecord album that is certified by the *RIAA* to have sold 500,000 units. Music industry associations in various countries set the number of units that must be sold in order to achieve gold or *platinum* status. For instance, in the United Kingdom 100,000 units sold warrants a gold record award; 25,000 sales are needed for such an award in Norway. For a listing of sales requirements needed to obtain gold and platinum status in various countries, see *hit*. See also *silver record*, *platinum record*, *multi-platinum record*, and *diamond record*.

Gold Single

A *single* recording that is certified by the *RIAA* to have sold 500,000 units. Historically, one million sales of a commercially released single recording earned a *gold record* award in the United States. In recent years, however, sales of singles have declined in favor of album purchases, so a single now needs only 500,000 units sold to be certified gold. One million certified singles sales now merits an RIAA *platinum* award. For a listing of sales requirements needed to obtain gold and platinum status in various countries, see *hit*. See also *gold album*, *silver record*, *platinum record*, *multi-platinum record*, and *diamond record*.

Goodwill

The appraised worth of a company over and above its *tangible* assets. Goodwill is attributable to the company's reputation established over the years, and the market base of loyal customers for its product. Goodwill is a subjective value and thus does not appear on a company's financial statements, except when the listed assets include the purchase of another business at a price greater than *book value*.

Gospel Music

A religious musical genre developed out of late 19th century American evangelical and Pentecostal movements, popular Sunday school hymns, and camp meeting spirituals. Characterized by simple folk melodies, harmonizing, and rhythmic performances, with texts focusing on salvation, consolation, and conversion, the genre was predominantly white until around 1930 when black gospel music emerged as a distinctive variant. Though white and black gospel remain distinct genres, there is a shared repertoire and free exchange of stylistic ideas. The gospel music category and market segment today often includes *spiritual*, *inspirational*, *contemporary Christian*, and other religious music.

Gospel Music Association (GMA)

A nonprofit trade organization based in Nashville. GMA was founded in 1964 to promote *gospel music* worldwide. Membership is open to companies and individuals actively involved in gospel music, who are eligible to receive educational and resource materials developed by the organization. GMA stages the annual Gospel Music Week and produces the *Dove Awards*. The organization's headquarters are located at 7 Music Circle North, Nashville, TN 37203. Tel: (615) 242-0303.

Governing Law

The law in effect at the time and place of an action or dispute; the laws of a *jurisdiction* in which the terms of a contract or license apply.

Gramophone

Originally, a trademarked name for a device (patented in 1884 by *Emile Berliner*) that played sounds recorded onto discs. It is considered to be the first *record player*, though *Thomas Edison*'s *phonograph* (patented in 1877) also played sounds, recorded onto cylinders. The terms phonograph and gramophone are used interchangeably today as generic references to records and record players, though the word phonograph is more often used in the United States, while the word gramophone is more often used in Great Britain. Both terms are derived from the Greek words for "sound" or "voice" (*phone*) and "to write" (*graphein*) or "something written" (*gramma*), because sounds are "written" (recorded) onto devices from which they can be "read" (played) back.

Grammy

An award (in statuette form) presented annually by the *National Academy of Recording Arts and Sciences (NARAS)* for excellence in the recording industry. Grammy Awards are awarded in numerous performance-based and technical categories, including Best Record, Album, Song, Pop Vocalist (Female and Male), Pop Duo or Group, Traditional Pop Vocalist, Rock Vocalist (Female and Male), Rock Duo or Group, Rock Instrumental, Hard Rock, Metal, R&B Vocalist (Female and Male), R&B Duo or Group, R&B Song, Traditional Blues, Contemporary Blues, Rap Solo, Rap Duo or Group, New Age, Contemporary Jazz (Instrumental), Jazz Vocalist (Female and Male), Jazz Instrumentalist, Large Jazz Ensemble, Country Vocalist (Female and Male), Country Duo or Group, Country Instrumentalist, Country Song, Rock/Contemporary Gospel, Pop Gospel, Southern Gospel, Traditional Soul Gospel, Contemporary Soul Gospel, Gospel Choir or Chorus, Latin Pop, Tropical Latin, Mexican-American Album, Traditional Folk, Contemporary Folk, Best Polka, Reggae, For Children, Comedy, Spoken Word or Nonmusical, Musical Show Album, Instrumental Composition, Instrumental Composition Written for a Motion Picture or for Television, Instrumental Arrangement, Music Video-Short Form, Music Video-Long Form, Historical Album, Classical Album, Orchestral Performance, Opera, Classical Soloist with Orchestra, Classical Soloist Without Orchestra, Chamber Music, Classical Vocal Performance, Classical Choral, Contemporary Classical Composition, Producer (Non-Classical), Producer (Classical), Engineer (Non-Classical), Engineer (Classical), Album Cover Artwork & Design, Liner Notes, etc.

Grammy in the Schools

Sponsored annually by *NARAS* as an introduction to the music business and as a mentoring experience for high school students across the country. The day begins with panels on various aspects of the business followed by career workshops that provide insiders' tips on what it takes to achieve a successful career in the industry. Panels and workshops are led by volunteer experts from all areas of the industry (performers, producers, music publishers, managers, songwriters, engineers, etc.) The day's events conclude with a concert by upcoming recording artists.

Grand March

An opening or closing ceremonial march, particularly at a formal ball, in which all participants in the occasion take part.

Grand Musical Play

Term formerly used interchangeably with *grand opera* and now largely replaced by *dramatico-musical work*.

Grand Ole Opry

The longest-running, continuously aired radio program in America (via WSM in Nashville). Since the program started broadcasting in 1925, the history of Country music has been inextricably linked with the Opry. Located at 2804 Opryland Dr., Nashville, TN 37214. Tel: (615) 889-3060; Fax: (615) 871-5971. See also *Ryman Auditorium*.

Grand Opera

A term often interchangeably used to describe (1) an opera in which the entire *libretto* is sung, rather than having at least some of the dialogue spoken; (2) a "serious" or melodramatic drama in operatic form, as opposed to an *operetta*; or (3) a melodramatic operatic work based on an epic or historical theme, performed with a large orchestra and chorus in 4 or 5 acts.

Grand Performance

The performance of a *dramatico-musical* work (opera, operettas, ballet, musical plays, etc.). See also *grand rights*.

Grand Performance License

Permission to perform all aspects included in the *grand right* of a *dramatico-musical* work (i.e., *literary content* as well as music, choreography, etc.). Not to be confused with a *dramatic performance license*.

Grand Right

Copyright in *dramatico-musical* works created for and performed on the *living stage*. (Copyright in *nondramatic* musical works is referred to as *small rights*.) Grand right encompasses the work in its entirety: i.e., the *literary content* of a musical play, opera, operetta, or ballet combined with the music as a copyrightable whole, or single work, all covered under a single grand right. No single element of the work has a grand right in and of itself; every element is essential to the whole.

For a song to be included in a grand right, it must be woven into the storyline as an integral element of the plot. It must further the action and be every bit as essential as the dialogue, either lyrically (as in operas, operettas, and musicals), or instrumentally (as in ballet).

Grand rights are administered differently than *mechanical*, *performance*, *print*, *transcription*, and *synchronization rights*, which are collectively called small rights. For instance, *mechanical-* and *performing-right societies* do not license grand rights. But music incorporated into a grand right can be extracted and licensed as a small right. For example, the song "Don't Cry for Me, Argentina" from the musical *Evita* has been licensed for records (mechanical rights), played on radio (performance rights), and sold as sheet music (print rights).

The *dramatic performance* of a song does not necessarily fall within the scope of a grand right. A song can be taken out of context from a musical play and rendered as a dramatic performance with scenery, costumes, and an acting out of the storyline. This can apply to a song that wasn't specifically created as a dramatic work, but is dramatized when performed. For instance, a theatrical troupe might dramatize the Dolly Parton/Whitney Houston hit "I Will Always Love You." Or, a dramatist might take the song "Memories" from *Cats* and write a new script so that it is performed in a dramatization that has nothing to do with the original play itself.

A song can also be taken out of context from a musical play and performed as a *nondramatic* small right—the performance of a song *as* a song. For instance, the song "Memories" from *Cats* is covered under a performing-right *blanket license* as a nondramatic performance when Peter Pianoman plays it in a Holiday Inn lounge, or WZIT-FM plays a recorded version by Barry Manilow.

Venue does not dictate whether or not a performance falls within the scope of grand rights. Grand rights could cover a musical play performed in a nightclub. But grand rights do not apply to live, stand-alone performances in the course of a *revue*, concert, or club act. A Broadway revue of songs loosely connected by a theme, but not individually essential to a central storyline, would constitute small rights.

Nor does a grand right necessarily apply to music in every type of dramatic production. *Incidental music* used for opening and closing themes and background ambiance is outside the scope of grand rights when it occurs in *non-musical plays* and *plays with music* (productions where music is incidental to the story, because it enhances the performance, but is not essential).

Grant

(1) To allow, confer, permit, or license the use of a property, title, or right. (2) A permission, privilege, or license. (3) To transfer rights or title or property ownership by deed. (4) A right, title, or property transferred by deed. (5) To give or bestow funds for a specified purpose. (6) The funds so given.

Grant of Rights

Provision in a contract defining the nature and scope of rights being transferred from one party to the other.

Graphic Arts

The techniques associated with designing, creating, and reproducing visual images from blocks, plates, or type, as in engraving and lithography. When used in the context of *fine arts*, the term generally refers to the use of line or tone in artwork rather than color. When used in the context of *graphics*, the term generally refers either to (1) the entire field of commercial printing, including text layout and illustrations, or to (2) computer science, where data is visually represented, manipulated, and displayed.

Graphic Designer

Person who creates the graphics, layout, and artwork for album covers, advertisements, posters, logos, etc.

Graphic Equalizer

In recording and playback, a device used to control sound wave frequencies or tones in order to offset, cancel, balance out, or compensate for audio distortion caused by unequal amplification of different sound wave frequencies. Sound frequency signals are divided into separate bands a third of an octave apart. An *equalizer* adjusts levels of amplification for each band with a sliding contact in order to bring the frequencies into balance and eliminate unwanted noise or distortion. In recording, a graphic equalizer controls many frequencies simultaneously, in contrast with a *parametric equalizer*, which is used to isolate specific tones.

Graphics

(1) In *graphic arts*, the visual design and manipulation of data for typesetting, printing, and pictorial representations. (2) In computer science, the computer-driven visual representation and manipulation of data, and the process by which a computer displays data.

Gratis

The giving of something without charge.

Great White Way

Nickname given to *Broadway*, because of the vast array of flashing electric lights, signs, billboards, and theater marquees.

Greatest Hits Compilation

An album collection of songs or recordings by one or more artists containing the top-selling songs or recordings by that artist or those artists.

Green Card

A United States certification that allows a non-US citizen to remain and work in the United States for a certain period of time, subject to review and renewal. See also *work permit*.

Greenlight

To approve a deal or authorize a budget, production or project.

Greeting Cards

Greeting cards (for Christmas, birthdays, etc.) are sometimes published containing lyrics from popular songs, and, since the development of the microchip, with the capability to play a brief musical recording when the card is opened up. Both the use of copyrighted lyrics and music require greeting card manufacturers to obtain licenses from music publishers or copyright owners.

Royalties for lyrics reprinted on greeting cards may be based on either the wholesale or retail price of the card. However, the policy of some greeting card companies is to pay a set fee based on the number of cards printed (such as $1,000 for 50,000 cards).

Typical royalties range from 5% of wholesale to 5% of retail, which translates to approximately 2¢ upwards per card. The size of the royalty or fee (or advance) depends upon the number of lines used, whether lyrics are used on the face as well as the inside of the card, the territory granted, etc. Most licenses are limited to 1 to 3 years, or to a specific number of cards.

Publishers generally retain the right to approve the design of the card in order to protect the integrity of the lyric in so far as it is used. And, of course, proper copyright notice should be printed on the card.

Mechanical licenses are also needed for greeting cards that use microchips to play copyrighted music.

Grievance Procedure

A pre-agreed or pre-arranged process (in a contract or labor agreement, for instance), by which one party may bring a complaint against another and seek redress. See also *arbitration*.

Groove

An undulating, spiral cut made into a phonograph record, from which a *stylus*, or needle, picks up vibrations as the record rotates on a turntable, so that the vibrations can be converted into electrical signals, amplified, and converted to sound. From the fact that any sound must come first from a record's groove, various music business slang terms have arisen. For instance, a recording is said to be "in the groove" if it is good.

Gross

The total sum earned or received, without, or before, or not including, deductions, expenses, taxes, etc. (as opposed to *net*, which is the sum leftover after deductions, expenses, taxes, etc.).

Gross Sales

The total value of sales (at full invoice prices), with-out reductions or other adjustments factored in from customer discounts, returns, or allowances. See also *net sales*.

Group

A band, an *ensemble*, a *troupe*, or assembly of performers.

Grunge

A fashion or cultural movement emerging from Seattle and becoming popular among some *Generation X*-ers, characterized by *alternative* rock music and oversized, thrift-shop style clothing.

Guarantee

A pledge or an assurance that a condition will be fulfilled. In music business contracts and licenses, an *advance* is in essence a guarantee that the party acquiring certain rights will generate sufficient sales activity from using those rights to provide the other party with at least enough income to equal the amount of the advance. Other types of guarantees include a pledge to release a certain number of recordings, to deliver a specified number of songs or masters, to produce a stated number of recordings, etc. See also *warranty* and *performance obligation*.

Guaranteed Release

Provision in a recording contract requiring the company to release product by the artist within a specified time frame. If the company fails to release product within that period, the artist can put the company on notice to *cure* the inaction. The artist can then *terminate* the contract if the company fails to act within the cure period. See also *release commitment*, *minimum release obligation*, and *performance obligation*.

Guarantor

One that *guarantees* something; one who makes a *guaranty*.

Guaranty

A *guarantee*: an undertaking, a security, a pledge, or a promise to answer for the performance of a duty, payment of a debt, protect a right or claim, or cure a *default*.

Guild

A union, trade organization, or association of people professionally engaged in a craft or industry, whose purpose is to promote and protect the interests of its members.

Guitar-Vocal

A *sheet music* publication of a song arranged for vocalist with guitar accompaniment.

H&W Fund

Abbreviation for Health and Welfare Fund. Under the *Phonograph Record Labor Agreement*, employers of union musicians for recording sessions are required to pay certain amounts into this fund, which provides health insurance for participating members. Certain eligibility requirements apply before a member can be covered.

Hack

Slang term for a writer who works for hire on routine, commercial assignments, such as jingles, press releases, advertising copy, etc. The term is somewhat derogatory given its roots, which include *hackney* (a carriage, taxi, or horse rented out indiscriminately to anyone willing to pay) and *hackneyed* (tired, uninspired, banal). *Examples*: a hack writer, a hack piece.

Half-Track Mono

Magnetic tape recorded on half the width of the tape in *monaural* (one audio channel only); the tape can be reversed to record one audio channel on the remaining half track.

Half-Track Stereo

Sound signals recorded on two *stereo* channels across the full width of a *magnetic tape* in one direction only.

Halftone

(1) In music, a half-step or *semitone*, the smallest interval in a European musical scale between any one note and the next, whether up or down on the scale. See *semitone*. (2) In printing, a process by which photographs and other illustrations are screened into areas of dots representing the intensities of the original color, shade, or tone. The darker the area, the closer dots are together; the lighter an area, the more space there is between the dots.

Hall Fee

A fee charged by proprietors of venues for handling sales of *merchandising tie-ins* (T-shirts, programs, posters, etc.) for featured performers. Performers (or their licensed merchandising companies) usually supply the venues with merchandise and the venues themselves display and sell it using their own personnel. At the close of a performance, the venue returns unsold merchandise and turns over the proceeds minus their hall fee, which typically ranges between 30% and 40% of gross sales.

Hard Asset

Something of value that has physical properties, and which can be valued monetarily. Also called *tangible asset*.

Hard Copy

A print-out of textual or graphic information stored in a computer.

Hard Disk

A sealed high-capacity data storage device for computers. Also called a "hard drive."

Hard Rock

An energetic, driving form of *rock music*. See also *heavy metal*.

Hardcore

(1) A pure, fundamental, basic, undiluted form of something (i.e. hardcore blues music). (2) A subgenre of *techno* music, representing the more aggressive, physical, thrash-driving element versus the more laid-back, cerebral style of *ambient*-oriented techno. (3) An intensely loyal follower or confirmed believer (a devoted *fan*, an *aficionado*).

Hardware

A device or machine, such as a computer or CD player, which uses *software* (i.e., CD-ROMs, CDs) to perform the functions for which it is designed (i.e., data-processing or sound playback).

Harmonic

A tone or an overtone produced by the vibrations of a pitch, at a frequency that is a multiple of the fundamental tone.

Harmonic Distortion

Multiples of an audio signal produced by recording equipment in addition to the original input signal. See also *specifications* and *intermodulation distortion*.

Harmonizer

An audio device that processes sound signals to alter a pitch or add delay without changing the tempo of the recorded performance.

Harry Fox Agency, Inc. (HFA)

The dominant *mechanical-right licensing society* in the United States, the Harry Fox Agency (HFA) was founded in 1927 by the *National Music Publishers Association* (NMPA). In 1995, HFA issued over 162,000 licenses and collected nearly $400 million on behalf of its 14,000 music publisher clients. Fox maintains reciprocal agreements with major mechanical-right societies in other countries to license clients' copyrights overseas and to collect mechanical royalties in the United States on behalf of overseas copyright owners. Besides routine licensing, HFA is active in identifying and prosecuting record *pirates* and protecting clients' rights under copyright laws.

Fox bolsters its in-house auditing staff with the services of two outside auditing firms. Every record company is subject to audit by Fox. Each major record company is audited at least once every two years; smaller companies are audited at least once every one to three years, depending on need. Fox's affiliated publishers frequently receive checks representing under-payments the agency has recovered. Audits by Fox resulted in distributions of more than $12 million to publishers in 1994.

The Harry Fox Agency charges publisher-clients a *commission* of 4.5% of gross mechanical royalties collected. When collections run ahead of pro-

jections, as they consistently have in recent years, Fox voluntarily reduces its commission fee. In 1994, for instance, the commission was reduced to 3.5%, and in 1995 the fee was further reduced to 2.75%.

Fox also advises clients, and/or negotiates on their behalf, regarding appropriate fees to charge users for synchronization and jingle licensing. For *synchronization* licenses, HFA charges 5% of fees collected or $2,200, whichever is less. This fee is also reduced when collections outpace budgeted overhead needs. Thus, in 1995, the commission fee for synchronization licensing was reduced to 3%. See also *Fox Agency International*.

Hat Act

A male contemporary *country music* singer typified by George Strait, Garth Brooks, Alan Jackson, Clint Black et al.

HDS

The *performing-right society* in Croatia.

HDTV

Abbreviation for *high-definition television*.

Head

(1) In recording, the magnetic piece on a tape recorder against which a recording tape passes and receives/reads data. (2) The starting end of a reel of recording tape or film. (3) The skin stretched across the top or bottom of a drum. (4) The top of a page. (5) A headline or heading.

Head Alignment

An adjustment or *calibration* of recording and playback heads on a tape recorder so that they are in proper position relative to each other. When tape heads aren't properly aligned, tracks on the tape are out of phase with each other; loss of audio information may also occur.

Head Arrangement

Musical arrangements worked out through on-the-spot improvisation, rather than being scored or written down by an arranger.

Head Crash

A failure of the *head*(s) of a tape recorder, disk drive, or CD player, etc. to read, store, or write data, frequently caused by dust particles. In some cases, a head crash can damage the tape or disk, resulting in the permanent loss of data.

Head Set

Same as *earphones*.

Head Shot

A black & white 8 x 10-inch glossy photo of a performer (usually face-on, from the neck up) used for publicity and auditions.

Heading
In a book, contract, advertisement, or on a page, a topical headline briefly summarizing the section which follows.

Headline
(1) A *heading*. (2) To star in a performance or take the featured role. (3) To heavily promote or publicize.

Headliner
A star performer; an act that is given top *billing*.

Heads
(1) See *head*. (2) A notation on a box containing a recording tape or film, indicating that the tape or film is wound normally on the reel, with the start of the tape at the head. Also called *tail in*.

Heads of Agreement
A synopsis of a proposed contract, listing main points of agreement by *headings* and summarized terms of each provision, but omitting the *legalese* and *boilerplate* language to be included in the final document. Also called *deal memo*.

Heatseekers Chart
A chart published each week in *Billboard* magazine listing the top fifty selling album titles by new and developing artists (defined as those artists who have never appeared in the top 100 of *Billboard*'s Top 200.)

Heavy Metal
Highly energetic and loudly amplified electronic *rock music* emphasizing guitars and a driving beat.

Heavy Rotation
In radio programming, *rotation* is a term used to describe how many times a recording is featured (aired) on a current *playlist* each week. Recordings that receive the most airplay are categorized as having *heavy rotation* (30+ plays), followed by those with *medium rotation* (15 to 29 plays), and then those with *light rotation* (less than 15 plays).

Heir
Someone who is designated by law (a *statutory beneficiary*) or will as entitled to inherit the estate of another, or a specified portion thereof.

HFA
Abbreviation for the *Harry Fox Agency*.

Hi-Fi
Abbreviation for *high-fidelity*.

Hi-Fi System
See *high fidelity*.

High Bias
Bias is the adjustment of the strength of a magnetic field applied during the recording process to a *magnetic tape*. High-frequency voltage combined with an audio signal reduces distortion in tape recording. Audiocassettes are graded according to dynamic range, *signal-to-noise ratio*, and *frequency response*. Types 0 and 1, called *normal bias*, use *ferric* tape and are subject to more *hiss*. High bias tapes (types 2 and 3 chrome and type 4 *metal*) provide the best frequency responses, wider dynamic ranges, and lower hiss. See also *ferric*, *chrome cassette*, *metal cassette*, *bias*, and *normal bias*.

High-Definition Television (HDTV)
Various new technologies developed to produce higher quality video images than the standard television technology. Japanese companies pioneered HDTV with an analog system that scans 1,125 horizontal lines; a European analog system (HD-MAC) uses 1,250 lines. However, an American system coming online will offer digital images.

High-Fidelity
(1) The highly accurate or faithful reproduction of sound. (2) The equipment used to faithfully reproduce sound. (3) Technique of recording, broadcasting, and reproducing sound that accurately matches the original sound's characteristics, as free as possible of distortion and extraneous noises, and covering the full frequency range of normal human hearing (20 Hz to 20 KHz). (4) A *hi-fi* system includes the following components: amplifier, control unit, turntable, tone arm, cassette deck, CD player, FM-AM radio tuner, and two or more loudspeakers.

High-Speed Duplication
A method of copying audio and videotapes by running both the master and the blank tape onto which the master is copied at speeds ranging from 8 to 64 *ips* faster than *real time*. High-speed duplication at a ratio of 8 to 1 produces copies that are not noticeably different in quality than real-time reproductions. But, at the fastest duplication speeds, higher frequencies tend to be lost and tape *hiss* is more apparent. Therefore, most mass-produced cassettes are duplicated at a ratio of 32:1 or less.

Hip-Hop
A genre of contemporary R&B music characterized by distinctive funk rhythms and dance beats; often

used to accompany Rap performances. Originated in the late 1970s among East Coast African-American and Hispanic performers, the genre gained widespread popular appeal during 1980s and 1990s.

Hiss

Unwanted high-frequency noise picked up on an *analog* audiotape during the recording process. Engineers often use one of several *Dolby* devices to suppress hiss, and *digital* recording systems eliminate hiss altogether.

Hit

A record, song, film, play, or book that "hits it big," "hits the charts," or "hits the jackpot" by achieving widespread popularity and sales. Although music is published and sold in virtually all media, most consumers purchase it in recorded form, so a "hit" is normally determined by the number of recordings sold. However, there is no threshold number of unit sales accepted as a universal definition of a hit.

It could be said that a hit is defined by who's counting. Some musical genres have larger market potential than others, and some markets are larger than others. Sales of any one recording must be measured against sales of similar types of recordings released in similar circumstances. The comparison must be between apples and apples, not apples and oranges.

Bluegrass music, for instance, appeals to a rather small niche market. Therefore, 50,000 sales of a Bluegrass album is a notable achievement. And 50,000 sales of a new artist's debut release on a small *indie* label might also be noteworthy. But, 50,000 sales of a heavily promoted Pop album by a big-name act on a major label might mean failure; yet, 50,000 albums sold in a small market like Norway, where it only takes 25,000 sales to earn a *gold record*, is a great success.

There are, however, certain yardsticks by which a record is acclaimed a hit. Music trade groups in most countries have established sales levels a record must obtain to be officially awarded hit status as either a *gold record*, *platinum record*, *multi-platinum record*, *diamond record*, or *silver record*. Below is a listing of unit sales-level eligibility for these awards in various countries:

	Gold	Platinum
Argentina	30,000	60,000
Australia	35,000	70,000
Belgium	15,000	30,000
Brazil	100,000	250,000
Canada	50,000	100,000
Chile	15,000	25,000
Colombia	30,000	50,000
Denmark	40,000	100,000
Finland	20,000	40,000
France	100,000	300,000
Germany	250,000	500,000
Greece	30,000	60,000
Hong Kong	10,000	20,000
Italy	100,000	200,000
Japan	200,000	400,000
Malaysia	25,000	50,000
Mexico	100,000	250,000
Netherlands	50,000	100,000
Norway	25,000	50,000
Philippines	20,000	50,000
Portugal	20,000	40,000
Singapore	7,500	15,000
South Africa	25,000	50,000
Spain	50,000	100,000
Sweden	50,000	100,000
Taiwan	50,000	100,000
UK	100,000	300,000
USA	500,000	1 million

Diamond = 1 million+ sales in Canada
Silver = 60,000 sales in UK
Multi-Platinum = 2 million+ sales in USA

Hit Parade

A chart or list ranking the currently most popular songs or recordings.

Hit Parader

Consumer magazine featuring lyrics and articles about current hit recordings, located at: 210 Route 4 East, Suite 401, Paramus, NJ 07652. Tel: (201) 843-4004; Fax: (201) 843-8636.

Hit the Charts

To sell enough recordings and/or garner sufficient airplay to be ranked on a *chart* or *hit parade*.

Hit the Road

To set off on a tour.

Hit the Streets

(1) The commercial release of a product; the issue of a publication. See *street date*. (2) To become public (as in "when the news hit the streets...").

Hold

An agreement by a music publisher not to exploit or license a song to others when a record company, producer, or recording artist plans to record it.

Under the *compulsory mechanical licensing provision* of the *Copyright Act*, publishers cannot prevent anyone from recording and releasing a song once it has already been released. Therefore, a publisher cannot place a hold on a song that has already been released. The best a publisher can do for a record company or producer wanting to record a previously released song is to promise not to actively plug it to other labels for a period of time. But, for new, unreleased songs, the publisher has complete discretion over whether or not to issue a mechanical license.

A publisher granting a hold is promising not to plug the song to others, nor issue a mechanical license to anyone else, until such time as either: (a) the label decides not to use the song; (b) the record is released; or (c) the time period for the hold lapses without a definite decision by the label.

Film producers also ask for holds when considering a song for a production, and often are willing to pay an option fee for the privilege, which is not returnable if the song isn't used. However, it is not normal practice for record companies to pay for the privilege of putting holds on songs. There is no real onus on a label to follow through with actually recording a song for which a hold is granted, much less to release it as an *A side*, or even to release it at all. See also *hold back license*.

Hold Back

(1) To suspend an action, restrain someone from doing something, or refrain from doing something. (2) To withhold payment or a portion of a payment, such as when putting money into a reserve or *contingency* fund, or placing funds in escrow pending settlement of a dispute. See also *reserve fund* and *liquidation of reserves*.

Hold Back License

A license to use a song in a motion picture where the film producer is willing to pay a premium to induce the copyright owner not to license the song for any other purpose for a stated period of time.

Hold Harmless

(1) To protect or insure a party against damages, losses, or liabilities arising from the actions or inactions of another. (2) To compensate a party for damages, losses, or injuries suffered because of the actions or inactions of another. See also *indemnify*.

Holding Company

A company that owns or controls partial or complete interest in another company or other companies. A holding company exists primarily to invest in and exercise control over other companies. The holding company's earnings are entirely derived from earnings of those companies it controls. See also *copyright holding company*.

Hollywood Reporter

A trade magazine catering primarily to the film and television industries, but also covering music industry news where the interests of the industries intersect. Located at 5055 Wilshire Blvd., Suite 600, Los Angeles, CA 90036. Tel: (213) 525-2000; Fax: (213) 525-2377.

Hologram

See *holograph* and *holography*.

Holograph

(1) Also called *hologram*, a three-dimensional image produced through the process of *holography*. (2) A letter or other document in the handwriting of the person who signed it.

Holography

A process by which three-dimensional images are produced using a split laser beam to create a pattern of interference in the recording of an object on a photographic plate or film and then illuminating that pattern with a laser or an ordinary light.

Home Studio

A small recording studio set up in a home, typically used for demo recordings, but sometimes sufficiently equipped to produce master recordings as well. Home studios are normally operated by and for the benefit of the owner and are not open for commercial rental, especially since commercial use may not be permitted under local zoning ordinances.

Home Taping

Making tape recorded copies for personal use of records, CDs, and other recorded product purchased commercially by the person making the copies. Home taping is permissible under copyright law when done by the owner of the product that is copied and when the copies are intended solely for personal use (*home use*) in alternative playback devices, such as an automobile tape deck or a Walkman-type personal cassette player. Home taping is not permissible when the copies are sold or given away to others, though it is difficult to police such activity. See also *Audio Home Recording Act* and *DART*.

Home Use

See home taping.

Home Video

Feature films and other types of *audiovisual works* released in *videocassette* and *videodisk* formats for consumer rental or purchase. See *videogram*.

Hook

(1) A chorus, refrain, lyrical phrase, or melodic section of a song intended to "hook" the listener's attention. (2) In advertising, a catchy slogan or jingle refrain intended to "hook" potential customers' interest.

House

(1) A contemporary electronic dance music genre originating in Chicago during the 1980s. Characterized by 120 *bpm* electronic drum tracks, se-

quenced keyboards and bass. (2) A publisher. (3) A business. See also *in-house*.

House Agency

A company's *in-house* or subsidiary advertising department, travel agency, or booking agency, used as an alternative to using the services of an unaffiliated agency for advertising purposes, making travel arrangements, or booking talent signed to the company.

House Producer

A producer who is employed as a full-time staff member at a record company, music publisher, or production company, as opposed to an independent or *freelance* producer hired for specific projects.

Hype

(1) To excessively publicize and promote a product with extravagant or inflated claims. (2) Exaggerated publicity and misleading promotional claims.

Hyphenate

To provide more than one service, as in a singer-songwriter, engineer-producer, etc.

I

Music format abbreviation for *industrial.*

I.D.

Abbreviation for identification. In broadcasting, the FCC requires radio and television stations to announce their call letters and frequency assignments at regular intervals ("to make a *station I.D.*").

IFPI

Abbreviation for *International Federation of Phonographic Industries.*

IIPA

Abbreviation for *International Intellectual Property Alliance.*

Illegal Copying

The unauthorized duplication by any method of copyrighted material. There are exceptions where copyrighted material can be copied without permission, most notably *home taping* and in cases where the principle of *fair use* applies.

Illustration

Images or artwork, such as graphs, charts, drawings, photos, or other visual material used to clarify, explain, highlight, or emphasize written text.

Illustrator

An artist or a graphics designer who creates *illustrations.*

ILMC

Abbreviation for *International Live Music Conference.*

Image

(1) A reproduction or copy of visual material, transferred from one medium to another. (2) A represen-
tation, such as a photo or drawing, of a person or an object. (3) A quality, trait, set of values, or characteristic projected to the public, and/or as perceived by the public, and/or as interpreted by the mass media.

Image Processing

See *imaging*, below.

Imaging

(1) The process of making or producing a copy or likeness of something by transferring it from one medium to another. (2) The process of digitally creating, manipulating, storing, or translating visual materials. (3) The transmission of digitized images from one computer to another computer, which reconverts the digitized data into visual material duplicating the original. (4) The process of describing, visualizing, imagining, or evoking mental pictures.

IMF

Abbreviation for *International Managers Forum.*

Immaterial

A matter that doesn't affect a situation; something that is not essential.

Impedance

The measure of a circuit's opposition to current flow. See also *output impedance.*

Implied Agency

See *implied authority*, below.

Implied Authority

Same as *apparent authority*: The power of *agency*, or the accepted authorization, to represent and act for or on behalf of another, which is not expressly granted but which is recognized as clearly evident and obvious from a record of established precedents wherein one party has allowed another to so act on his/her behalf. See also express authority.

Implied License

A license neither written nor orally given, but which may be reasonably understood to have been given because the copyright owner's conduct implies approval of the usage. See implied contract, below, and *license by operation of law.*

Implied Contract

An unwritten contract either (1) recognized in law or (2) imposed by law. In the first case, called a "contract implied in fact," the law upholds the fact that a contract exists between the parties by virtue of the circumstances, and of the relationship between the parties as established by their conduct and acts. In the second case, called a "contract implied in law," the law imposes what may be termed a "quasi contract" or "constructive contract" on the parties in order to prevent unjust enrichment of one party at the other's expense. See also *express contract.*

Import

(1) To bring in product manufactured overseas for sale in the importer's country. (The *Copyright Act* prohibits importation of records containing copyrighted musical works owned by Americans without specific permission of US copyright owners. See *import license*, below.) (2) To bring something in from an outside source. (3) To transfer data from one computer file to another. (4) Something of significance or the meaning of something.

Import License

The *Copyright Act of 1976* (Section 602) prohibits importation of records containing copyrighted musical works owned by Americans without specific permission of US copyright owners, even though the works were properly licensed to overseas manufacturers. Copyright owners who wish to authorize importation of their works from overseas may grant import licenses to importers and/or others involved in importing their works. An import license is usually a variation of a *mechanical license*, and can be issued at the copyright owner's request by a *mechanical-right society*, such as *Harry Fox.*

Importance of Copyright

When negotiating copyright licensing terms, the importance of the copyright and the *nature* of its proposed usage affects, among other things, the size of the fee and/or royalty the copyright owner can demand from the user. The importance of the copyright itself may also affect the copyright owner's willingness to even license the work for some types of usages. For instance, some song copyright owners may be unwilling to license *standards* or *evergreens* for advertising certain types of products, such as alcohol, tobacco, or political campaigns.

Whether the copyright pertains to a song, sound recording, or other creative work, its commercial history should always be a factor in determining the size of a licensing fee and types of licenses granted. For example, a song that has become a major hit likely will be sought after for many types of usages in years to come, and shouldn't be devalued by accepting the same licensing fees applicable for a song that has never sold a single record; the copyright owner should also be careful about granting exclusive licenses that limit future licensing and income opportunities.

Importance of Use

When negotiating copyright licensing terms, the *nature of the usage* affects, among other things, the size of the fee and/or royalty the copyright owner can demand from the user. For instance, the more essential a song is to a user's project, the more the user should be expected to pay. When numerous other songs can easily be substituted, the user can opt to license one from whichever copyright owner is willing to accept the least expensive terms.

IMPRIMATUR

Acronym for Intellectual Multimedia Property Rights Model & Terminology for Universal Reference. This is a project being undertaken by the *European Commission* (EC) to coordinate various other projects working in the area of intellectual properties in order to standardize copyright identification and protection methods in the digital age. Located at Marlborough Court, 14-18 Holborn, London EC1N 2LE, England.

IMRO

Abbreviation for *Irish Music Rights Organization.*

In-Cassette Duplication

Process used in *real-time* cassette tape duplication. Blank tapes are already loaded into cassette shells, as opposed to the *bin-loop* system commonly used in high-speed duplication, where the music is recorded first, then loaded into individual cassette shells.

In Profit

A project, venture, or company that has earned back start-up costs and is generating sufficient income to cover operating expenses and provide a return on investment.

In the Black

A condition in which a project, venture, or company is *in profit.*

In the Can

(1) Material that is shelved, not used; or (2) material that has gone through all production stages but is not yet released or published.

In the Pipeline

Something already in progress, on the way, soon to come about. *Example*: Royalties are "in the pipeline" when they are due to be paid at the next accounting, but have not yet been received. See also *pipeline*.

In the Red

Opposite of *in the black*: a project, venture, or company that has not earned back start-up costs nor generated sufficient income to cover operating expenses or provide a return on investment.

Inc.

Abbreviation for *incorporated*.

Inches Per Second (IPS)

On a tape recorder, the measurement of speed at which a tape passes across the magnetic playback and recording *heads*. For instance, 15 inches of tape passes across the head every second when the tape is playing at 15 ips.

Incidental Music

(1) Music used for background atmosphere and segues in plays, films, or television or radio programs. (2) Music performed on television or radio that is not contained in a specific program (i.e., music used as backdrop to commercials, PSAs, station IDs, etc.).

Incidental Music Performance Royalty

A performance royalty paid by local television stations who opt for *per program performance licenses* for each *incidental music* usage in commercials, PSAs, *station IDs*, etc.

Income Averaging

An accounting technique used by individuals (such as royalty earners) whose income varies widely from year to year. The aggregate sum received over a specified number of these years is divided by the number of years in the period to arrive at an average per annum income. Prior to the 1986 tax reform, this technique was principally used to reduce annual income tax assessments on royalty earnings.

Incorporate

(1) To form or register a company as a legal *corporation*. (2) To merge, combine, or unite something with some other existing work, organization, or entity. (3) To give something substance or material form.

Incorporated

(1) A company or business registered as a legal *corporation*, by which means the owners are given *limited liability*. (2) Something that has been merged, combined, or united with another existing thing to form one whole (i.e., lyrics incorporated with a melody to form a song).

Indemnify

(1) To protect or insure a party against damages, losses, or liabilities arising from the actions or inactions of another. (2) To compensate a party for damages, losses, or injuries suffered because of the actions or inactions of another. (3) To exempt a party from liability. See also *hold harmless*.

Indemnities

(1) Compensation made to one party for damages, losses, or injuries suffered as a result of actions or inactions of another. (2) A bond, deposit, or pledge of security to *indemnify* one party against damage, loss, or injury. (3) Exemptions from liability, damages, or losses.

Independent Distributor

A company that is unaffiliated with a major, national distributor, and which buys product from numerous suppliers, producers, and/or manufacturers for resale to retailers, usually within a regional area rather than nationwide. Most recorded product is distributed by one of the *majors* through their *branch operations*. However, several local, regional, and national independent distributors service *one-stops*, *rack jobbers*, and *retailers* with product from *indie labels*. Many independent distributors function like the branch operations of the majors, employing promotion personnel along with *route people* or *salespeople* to service accounts. See also *National Association of Independent Record Distributors* (*NAIRD*) and *AFIM*.

Independent Label

A record company that is not affiliated with a major distributor through ownership or control, and whose product usually is distributed through a network of regional, independent distributors, or under terms of a *distribution deal* or *P&D* agreement with a major label or national distributor. However, many independent labels rely on alliances with major labels for financing, manufacturing services, marketing, and national distribution.

Independent Producer

A producer of film or music whose services are not exclusively conducted for any one organization, and who is not directly affiliated with, or employed full-time by any one company. Prior to the 1960s, record production was mostly a function of uncredited "house producers" working in A&R department staffs at record labels. The hiring of outside, or independent producers, evolved from the assertion of *creative control* by more successful recording artists in the 1960s.

Independent producers generally work in one of two ways: (1) as a *freelancer*, producing artists on an assigned contractor basis for different record companies, or (2) signing artists directly and financing and producing sessions on spec, with the aim of leasing or selling the finished masters to a record company for distribution and marketing. As a contractor, or freelancer, the indie producer negotiates an advance, royalty, and recording budget with a record label or artist, and assumes responsibility for delivering a commercially acceptable master recording. When a producer works on spec, he or she operates as an entrepreneur, finding and signing the artist, funding the session, producing the recording, and shopping the finished master to a record label for manufacturing, marketing, and distribution.

Independent Promotion Representative

Person who promotes commercially released recordings for a variety of clients on a *freelance* basis, and who is not employed by any one company to promote its product exclusively. Indie promoters may be hired to work a specific record in a specific territory for a specific period of time. They may work on retainer, or be paid by the number of adds they achieve, or be paid by the actual airplay results reported by *BDS*, or a combination thereof. While radio promotion remains their primary focus, they are also used to promote video airplay on television, in-store play and *POP* displays, and to coordinate promotional activities with local appearances by artists in their territories. See also *indie promotion*.

Independent Publisher

A music publishing company that is unaffiliated with a major international operation. An independent publisher might range in size from one-person operations to multi-million dollar, full-service companies.

Index Department

Division of a copyright service organization or rights society (such as *BMI*, *ASCAP*, *Harry Fox Agency*, etc.), which maintains cross-referenced records of copyright repertoire, including titles, authors, composers, copyright ownership details (divisions of rights, royalty distribution percentages, chains of title, dates of creation), individual licenses issued, etc. See also *POLI* and *SIR*.

Indian Performing-Right Society (IPRS)

The *performing-right society* in India.

Indie

Abbreviated reference for "independent," as in indie distributor, indie record label, indie producer, independent television station (unaffiliated with a network), etc.

Indie Label

See *independent label*.

Indie Promotion

One of three layers of record promotion. An indie promotion person is hired to promote a specific release. (A local promotion person generally covers a specific region or territory on all types of product released by a record company, and a *national promotion* person usually concentrates on a specific genre or market segment, such as R&B.)

Indie Publisher

See *independent publisher*.

Indie Rock

Contemporary rock music, derivative of the *punk* rock movement, released by "do-it-yourself" indie labels, many of which ultimately graduated to distribution alliances with major labels.

Inducement

(1) An incentive or enticement offered in order to get someone to do something. A *consideration*. An essential element of a valid and enforceable contract is the inducement, or consideration of agreement (i.e., something given in exchange for performance or the promise to perform). *Examples*: a contract signing bonus, a royalty advance, etc. (2) In legal proceedings, an introductory statement highlighting the claims made by one party in a case.

Inducement Letter

Also called a *side letter*. When a recording artist is under contract to a *production company* or a *loan-out corporation* that enters into a contract with a record company to provide the artist's services, the artist simultaneously signs a side letter or inducement letter agreeing to be bound by the terms of the agreement in the event a *flow-through clause* is exercised. (A flow-through clause in a deal between a record company and a record production company or a loan-out company guarantees the artist will fulfill all recording obligations directly for the record company in the event the production or loan-out company is unable or unwilling to render its obligations under the agreement.) A flow-through clause protects the record company's investment if the producer or loan-out defaults, has a falling out with the artist, or goes out of business. If a flow-through clause is exercised, the artist's obligations are transferred to the record company. Among the events that trigger a typical flow-through clause are: bankruptcy or insolvency of the production or loan-out company; breach of the production agreement by the production or loan-out company; and any breach by the production or loan-out company of its agreement with the artist that adversely affects the record company's rights. If the production or loan-out company defaults on the contract with the artist, the record company must cure the default when it exercises its flow-through rights.

Industrial Music

Music genre associated with style of acts initially released by indie British labels, characterized by neo-punk aggressiveness, extreme lyrics, and experimental sounds.

Industrial Show

A privately produced exhibition staged by a large corporation or trade association to introduce new products and sales promotions, etc. Industrial shows frequently include entertainment for attendees, which provides booking opportunities for name entertainers and musicians.

Industry

A trade or business as a group, as in "the music industry" or "the film industry." The term is often used by those within a certain field as a slang reference to the world in which they and others in their profession operate.

Industry Norm

A standard, custom, or practice that has evolved within a particular industry. See also *trade practice*.

Indy

See *indie*.

In-Flight Entertainment

See in-flight programming, below.

In-Flight Programming

Also called *in-flight entertainment* and *airline music*. Airlines provide music for passengers to listen to on *headsets*. The nature of the usage more closely resembles syndicated radio programs than *background music*, because it is intended for entertainment rather than mood enhancement. Therefore, *transcription licenses* issued for airline music programming are similar to those issued to radio syndicators, as opposed to background music services. The transcription license is akin to a *mechanical license* that authorizes the packager to duplicate the work, and is issued by the music publisher or the publisher's *mechanical-right society*. Rights to perform songs on the transcribed program are obtained from *performing-right societies*.

Information Management

A system or process by which a company or an organization produces, organizes, stores, and distributes information, such as market research, sales, billings, inventory, personnel records, customer accounts, royalty receipts and payments, etc. See also *data*, *data processing*, *database*, *information services*, *information system*, and *management information system*.

Information Services (IS)

The department or division of a company or an organization in charge of *data processing* and *management information systems*, and which provides access to information as needed by management, employees, clients, customers, et al.

Information System

The software, hardware, and personnel used in producing, collecting, organizing, and distributing information for a company or an organization. See also *data*, *data processing*, *database*, *information management*, *information system*, and *management information system*.

Infringement

A trespass or unlawful encroachment on, or violation of, the rights of another. See *copyright infringement*.

In-House

Any process or function a company performs internally, using its own staff and facilities. For instance, a record label might produce its own album cover artwork "in-house," as opposed to contracting design functions to outside specialists.

Injection Method

Also called "injection molding." One of two methods used to press phonograph records (the other process is called the *compression method*). The injection method uses a plastic called *polystyrene*, which is harder and more brittle than the *polyvinyl chloride* (PVC) used in the compression method. The polystyrene is melted so that it flows like liquid, then injected into the mold where it cools and hardens. Though the injection method is faster and cheaper than the compression method, the records tend to wear out quicker and are more susceptible to surface noise during playback.

Injunction

A court order either (1) requiring a specific action or conduct or (2) prohibiting some action or conduct. The purpose of an injunction is to protect the person or property of a *plaintiff* from irreparable injury allegedly caused directly or indirectly by a *defendant*.

Inlay Card

Also called a *tray card* or *backing card*. A card cut to be inserted in a *jewel box* with a *booklet* and *compact disc*. It contains printed material corresponding to the backside of an album cover (i.e., song titles, *bar code*, etc.), and shows through the back of the transparent jewel box.

Input

(1) Information, data, commentary, feedback, opinion. (2) To put information or data into a system for processing or for transmission. (3) To give ad-

vice, comment, feedback, opinion. (4) Fuel, funds, information, or other material necessary for production, power, creation, manufacturing, or processing. (5) A device or position where information or data is put into a system. See also *output*.

Insert

(1) A flyer, circular, advertisement, announcement, photo, sheet of lyrics, or other information inserted inside or between the covers of an album or a publication. (2) A photo, drawing, chart, graph, or other illustration incorporated or intended for incorporation with text or printed material.

Inset

(1) A small illustration, photo, chart, or bordered block of text set within a larger one. (2) An *insert*.

Inside Out

An obsolete mode of phonograph record playback using a turntable and tonearm with the stylus placed on the grooves nearest the center of the record; as the disc turns, the stylus moves along the grooves towards the outer edge or rim of the disc, rather than from the outside towards the center.

Insolvency

The lack of sufficient income to meet debts, liabilities, and operating costs.

Inspection

(1) An *audit*; the examination of financial records and accounts in order to check for accuracy. (2) An examination of product or materials for manufacturing flaws, inventory count, shipping damages, etc.

Institutional Ad

A commercial advertisement or announcement used to reinforce or build a company's image and keep its name before the public (as opposed to a direct response ad, which calls for a direct action on the consumer's part, such as phoning an 800 number, returning an order coupon, or going to a store and purchasing a particular product).

In-Store Play

The playing of recorded product over speakers located in a record shop, boutique, or music department of a variety store. In-store play is intended to pique the interest of customers in the product being played, and is a form of *point-of-purchase* merchandising.

Instrumental

Music composed without lyrics, or music performed without vocals, using instruments rather than singers to carry the melody.

Instrumental Folio

A collection of musical arrangements for solo instruments, or of orchestrations for groups of instrumentalists, published in a large, softbound book format. See also *folio*.

Instrumental Rendition

The use of a song in a motion picture or television program without a vocal performance of the song's lyrics. An instrumental rendition does not necessarily mean the synchronization fee should be less than that required for a *vocal rendition*.

Insurance

A contract, called a "policy," by which the insuring party agrees to compensate or indemnify the insured party against losses, damages, or liability arising from certain covered contingencies, such as disability, loss of life or property, etc. Insurance is a significant issue for some types of businesses, and the costs and necessary coverages vary widely. A recording studio, for instance, requires much more extensive (and expensive) coverage than that needed by a small music publishing operation. But to some degree, adequate insurance is needed to cover losses of equipment, furnishings, data, inventory, company vehicles, etc. See also *key man insurance*.

Intangible

Something, such as a thought or idea, that cannot be perceived by the senses (sight, hearing, touch, smell). See also *intangible asset*, *intellectual property*, and *tangible asset*.

Intangible Asset

An asset, such as *goodwill* or a *copyright*, having no physical properties. Intangible assets are more difficult to value accurately than *tangible* properties, since there is no easily definable replacement value or verifiable cost of raw material. The real value of an intangible asset may, therefore, be significantly different from the dollar amount listed on a corporate balance sheet. See also *copyright asset*, *intellectual property*, and *tangible asset*.

Integration Clause

A legal *boilerplate* provision included in a written contract to express the fact that the document represents the full scope of the terms, obligations, and conditions agreed to by the parties. The statement "This contract represents the *entire agreement* between the parties" virtually means that any side agreements or other understandings between the parties have been merged or integrated into the written agreement and any pre-existing documents to the contrary will not be admissible as evidence that modifies or alters the terms of the contract.

Intellectual Property

A creation of original thought translated into *tangible* modes of expression or communication, such as sound recordings, sheet music, books, etc. When fixed in tangible form, an intellectual property may be protected by *copyright* or *patent*. See also *intangible asset*.

Interactive Media

Any medium in which responses are given to commands. *Examples*: video games, database and word processing programs, interactive television. *Multimedia* products combine various technologies into an interactive format containing data that can be manipulated, changed, or added to by the user. For example, music, text, photographs, drawings, recorded voice-overs, and movies may be combined on a *CD-ROM* or an interactive compact disc (*CD-I*), which users can manipulate on home computers by changing the sequence, altering the sound, and blending music or spoken word with visual images, etc., to produce material tailored to specific tastes or needs.

Interactive TV

A television entertainment or educational format wherein the broadcast signal activates an electronic device in the viewer's home, which the viewer uses to manipulate images on the screen or to filter the type of data received.

Interactive Video (IV)

A *multimedia* combination of text, sound, pictures, and moving images stored on media such as *CD-ROM*. Users interact with the discs by selecting, controlling, and manipulating the information as desired or by responding as instructed.

Interest

(1) A legal share of ownership, right, or claim. (2) A percentage of a loan amount charged to the debtor by the lender. (3) A percentage of an amount of money on deposit, such as in a savings account, which is earned by leaving the money on deposit. (4) A concern, curiosity, or desire to be involved in some activity or project.

Interface

The connection or meeting point between two or more distinct systems, groups, or entities, where communication and/or functional coordination is established. *Examples*: A keyboard is an interface between a the user and computer; special software creates an interface between a computer and a printer.

Intermediary

A go-between, broker, finder, arbiter, agent. A person who transacts, negotiates, arbitrates, or conducts business on another's behalf, or between two or more parties.

Intermodulation Distortion

The effect of an interaction between two or more audio signals. See also harmonic distortion and specifications.

Intern

A graduate or student (usually a volunteer), who studies a craft or profession under the supervision of a professional in order to gain hands-on experience and practical training.

International Confederation of Societies of Authors & Composers (CISAC)

A Paris-based organization of "creators societies" (mechanical- and performing-right societies) from over 60 countries that meets every 2 years to govern matters of international and reciprocal concern to the member societies, and to address copyright issues arising from new technologies.

International Department

Same as *foreign department*; a division of a record company or music publishing company that deals with overseas licensing, marketing, and collections.

International Federation of Musicians (FIM)

An umbrella labor organization comprising musicians unions from various countries, including the *AFM*. FIM has nongovernmental organization (NGO) status in *WIPO* and the International Labor Office of the United Nations. FIM negotiates directly with IFPI regarding distribution of broadcasting royalties to their respective members. (FIM royalties go to performers; *IFPI* royalties are allocated to producers.)

International Federation of Phonographic Industries (IFPI)

International trade association of over 1,250 recording industry companies and recording industry trade groups in over 50 countries. The IFPI's secretariat is based in London, where it publishes yearly statistical data on sales of recorded music worldwide, information on record *piracy*, lobbies for international copyright reform and cooperation, and coordinates negotiations with *BIEM* on *mechanical licensing* terms and *mechanical royalties*. IFPI also negotiates the distribution of broadcasting royalties with *FIM* (*International Federation of Musicians*). IFPI's share of broadcasting royalties is distributed to producers; FIM's share goes to performers. IFPI is located at 54 Regent St., London W1R 5PJ, England.

International Intellectual Property Alliance (IIPA)

Coalition formed in 1984 to represent US copyright industries in international efforts to promote and protect copyrighted works, including music, recordings, films, video, software, books, journals, etc. The Alliance consists of seven trade organizations (Association of American Publishers, American Film Marketing Association, Business Software Alliance, Interactive Digital Software Alliance, Motion Picture Association of America, *National Music Publishers Association*, and *Recording Industry Association of America*) representing over 1,350 US companies that produce and distribute copyrighted works.

International Live Music Conference (ILMC)

An annual conference in London of booking agents and concert promoters. Begun in 1988, ILMC is by invitation only, and has attendance from agents, promoters, and personal managers from over 35 countries. Applications for membership and conference invitations may be made by contacting the ILMC at 2-12 Pentonville Rd., London NN1 9PL. Telephone (0171) 833-8998; Fax: (0171) 833-5992.

International Managers Forum (IMF)

A London-based organization founded in 1992 as a forum for discussion and action on issues of concern to managers of recording artists and producers. IMF currently has representative offices in seven countries. In the United States, IMF's contact address is 350 East 30th St., Suite 4D, New York, NY 10016. Tel: (212) 213-8787; Fax: (212) 213-9797.

International Musician

Monthly magazine published by the *American Federation of Musicians* (AFM) for distribution to members. Included with articles and interviews of interest to professional musicians are monthly updates of AFM defaulters, the *blacklist* of nonpaying or slow-playing employers that members are prohibited from working with.

International Record and Music Publishing Market

See *MIDEM*.

International Reply Coupon (IRC)

A coupon purchased at the post office, which can be redeemed at an overseas post office to purchase postage equivalent to US dollar amount on the coupon. Used when submitting material to foreign record companies, music publishers, etc. when the sender wishes the material to be returned.

International Standard Book Number (ISBN)

A universally recognized copyright identification tool for book sellers, libraries, publishers, and authors. A unique identifying number is assigned to each book published, which then appears on the same page as the copyright information, so that the publisher and copyright owner can readily be located. See also *International Standard Recording Code (ISRC), International Standard Music Number (ISMN), Interna-*

tional Standard Serial Number (ISSN), and *International Standard Work Code (ISWC)*

International Standard Music Number (ISMN)

Similar to an *ISBN* (see above), the *International Standard Music Number* was adopted in 1995 by the ISO to provide a standardized procedure for identifying printed editions of musical works. The administration of both ISBN and ISMN systems is provided by the International Standard Book/Music Number Agency located at Potsdamer Strasse 33, Postfach 1407, D-10785 Berlin, Germany. See also *Common Information System (CIS), International Standard Recording Code (ISRC), International Standard Book Number (ISBN), International Standard Serial Number (ISSN),* and *International Standard Work Code (ISWC).*

International Standard Recording Code (ISRC)

A universally recognized copyright identification tool for sound recordings. A unique identifying number is assigned to each commercially released sound recording, which is then used to locate or identify the copyright owner, rather than relying on secondary information, such as names of artists and record companies. ISRC numbers are usually encoded digitally on a recording for purposes of copyright control, as opposed to being printed on the label in eye-readable form. The ISRC system is administered by *IFPI*. See also *Common Information System (CIS), International Standard Book Number (ISBN), International Standard Music Number (ISMN), International Standard Serial Number (ISSN),* and *International Standard Work Code (ISWC).*

International Standard Serial Number (ISSN)

A universally recognized copyright identification tool for serial publications, regardless of medium, that are issued in separate editions indefinitely (i.e., magazines, as opposed to a finite number of volumes, such as a set of encyclopedias). The ISSN system complements the ISBN system used for books, and is administered by the International Serials Data System, located at ISSN International Centre, 20 rue Bachaumont, 75002 Paris, France. See also *International Standard Book Number (ISBN), International Standard Music Number (ISMN), International Standard Recording Code (ISRC),* and *International Standard Work Code (ISWC).*

International Standard Work Code (ISWC)

A universally recognized copyright identification tool for songs. Upon registration of a song with a *performing-right society*, the society issues an ISWC number that is unique to the song. The number provides a method for identifying music copyright owners in order to ensure fast, accurate, and efficient distribution of royalties earned by songs throughout the world. The ISWC is a nine-digit number sandwiched between the letter T and a single check digit, which confirms a work has been correctly numbered. *Example*: ISWC T-034.275.981-1.

The ISWC works like the ISBN number given to each book that is published. The ISWC number identifies the song itself, rather than relying on secondary identifiers, such as names of songwriters and publishers. (Sound recordings are assigned ISRC [*International Standard Recording Code*] numbers to identify recordings, so that copyright owners can be quickly identified, rather than relying on secondary information, such as names of artists and record companies.)

The society with which a work is first registered assigns the ISWC and links the number to the international *WorksNet* database in New York. Then, any rights agency or society anywhere in the world can identify the work by plugging the ISWC number into the database, thereby locating the proper copyright owner.

The use of ISWC numbers is intended to slash administrative costs for mechanical- and performing-right societies, while increasing copyright protection for copyright owners. Any society in any country can access the WorksNet database in order to unlock ownership information and ensure royalties are distributed in timely and accurate fashion. See also *Common Information System (CIS)*, *International Standard Book Number (ISBN)*, *International Standard Music Number (ISMN)*, *International Standard Serial Number (ISSN)*, *International Standard Recording Code (ISRC)*, *black box*, and *Warsaw Rule*.

Internet

A *Wide Area Network* (*WAN*) connecting thousands of computer-linked networks throughout the world to enable the exchange of data. The term is sometimes used interchangeably with *cyberspace, information superhighway*, and *World Wide Web* in reference to the electronic access and transmission of information through personal computers. The convenience of digital transmission via computer links may make online services the preferred mode of music distribution in the not-too-distant future.

Already, commercial Internet service providers like CompuServe and America Online reach an estimated 14 million subscribers throughout the United States. In addition, some 60,000 bulletin board operators link between fifteen and 20 million PC users nationwide. But cyberspace has no borders. computer users in Prague and Pretoria can access the same data, at the same time, as someone in Peoria. That means a record company in Peoria can sell its product to consumers in Prague and Pretoria via cyberspace, eliminating the manufacturing process, as well as costs of shipping and cuts by middlemen (distributors, retailers, overseas licensees, etc.). Consumers benefit from being able to find music of their choice 24 hours a day, seven days a week. They don't have to wait until stores open, fight traffic and find a parking space, or face disappointment when product is out of stock.

The rapid development of Internet technologies for distributing information and entertainment has caused a scramble among copyright owners to upgrade international standards of copyright protection. The ability to upload, store, and download music affects copyright owners of sound recordings as well as owners of the underlying musical works contained on the recordings.

There are three licensing issues related to the use of music online. First, transmission of the music is a *public performance* and therefore subject to a *performing-right license*. Second, downloading transmitted music constitutes "copying" and is thereby subject to a *mechanical license*. And, third, combining music with visual images for transmission falls within the scope of a *synchronization license*.

While cyberspace presents new marketing opportunities, there are great challenges as well. Though things are very much in flux, and likely to remain so for some time, steps are being taken to solve some of the problems. Copyright owners (through organizations such as ASCAP, BIEM, BMI, SEAC, CISAC, Harry Fox, et al) are working to establish clear legal precedents and effective methods for licensing musical works on terms commensurate with the nature of their use. See also transmission and reproduction license.

Internet Underground Music Archive (IUMA)

A web site that makes available music by unsigned acts on the internet. IUMA charges acts a fee to publish their works, along with photos, videos, lyrics, and bios, thus by-passing traditional channels of marketing and distribution.

Internship

See *intern*. A program of hands-on, real-world training in a craft or profession whereby the intern learns by working, often as a volunteer, under professional supervision.

Intestate

Legal term for an estate belonging to one who dies without a will.

Intestate Succession

The inheritance of a copyright or other property right by operation of state law when the deceased left no will. See also *statutory beneficiary*.

Intro

Abbreviated reference for *introduction*.

Introduction

(1) A brief segment at the beginning of a musical work that hints at or sets up the body of the work to follow. (2) A preface, foreword, summary, or other brief exposition of a text or collection of materials, such as a book, which follows.

Inventory

(1) A quantity of product, merchandise, or materials on hand, in stock, or stored for ready access. (2) An itemized list or report of product, merchandise, or materials on hand, in stock, or stored for ready access. (3) To make a list, report, or record of product, merchandise, or materials on hand, in stock, or stored for ready access. (4) A detailed evaluation of abilities, assets, or resources in one's possession.

Inventory Control

The management of *inventory*, including stock taking, security, insurance, storage, accounting, valuation, and replacement.

Invoice

(1) An itemized list of charges due for product shipped, services rendered, or goods sold on credit. (2) A bill for monies due for goods shipped or services rendered. (3) To issue an itemized bill with a request for payment.

IPRS

Abbreviation for *Indian Performing-Right Society*.

IPS

Abbreviation for *inches per second*.

IRC

Abbreviation for *International Reply Coupon*.

Irish Music Rights Organization (IMRO)

The *performing-right society* in Ireland.

IS

Abbreviation for *information services*.

ISBN

Abbreviation for *International Standard Book Number*.

ISMN

Abbreviation for *International Standard Music Number*.

ISRC

Abbreviation for *International Standard Recording Code*.

ISSN

Abbreviation for *International Standard Serial Number*.

Issue

(1) To publish, release, or distribute. *Examples*: Issue a *press release*; issue a record. (2) An edition or single volume of a periodical ("the June issue" of a magazine). (3) A matter of concern or dispute. (5) The crux of a matter, or the central point.

ISWC

Abbreviation for *International Standard Work Code*.

Itemize

To list in detail; to summarize with particulars.

Iteration

A repeated section of a recording or computer program. See *sequencer* and *loop*.

IUMA

Abbreviation for Internet Underground Music Archive.

IV

Abbreviation for *interactive video*.

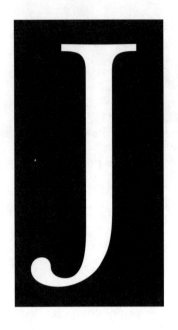

J

Music format abbreviation for *jazz*.

Jam

To improvise or ad lib a performance; to play spontaneously, without written or formal arrangements.

Jam Band

Term applied to type of bands in the mid-1990s playing heavily improvised neo-psychedelic music.

Jam Session

(1) A collective performance by a group of musicians ad libbing, improvising, and playing without written or formal musical arrangements. (2) A group of musicians putting on an impromptu performance of ad libs and improvisations. (3) A free-form, impromptu discussion, as opposed to a formal meeting that addresses items on an agenda.

Japanese Society for Rights of Authors, Composers, and Publishers (JASRAC)

The *mechanical-right society* and *performing-right society* in Japan.

Jargon

Terminology, slang references, and abbreviations commonly used and understood by people professionally engaged in a particular business, which may not be understood by those with little knowledge of the business. Also called *trade language*. See also *legalese*.

JASRAC

Acronym for *Japanese Society for Rights of Authors, Composers, and Publishers*.

J-Card

A cardboard sheet cut and folded to fit inside an audiocassette case. (The fold resembles the shape of the letter J.) For commercially released audiocassettes, J-cards generally have cover artwork printed on the side facing out; copyright details and track-listings (title, artist, songwriter, publisher, playing time, copyright notices, etc.) are printed on the reverse. For blank audiocassettes, the J-card is blank, so that a purchaser can detail whatever information is applicable to the tape's ultimate recorded contents.

Jeep

A *hip-hop* term used to describe beats. Derived from the vehicle Jeep, which became popular in inner-city hip-hop communities because of the space available for mounting big speakers.

Jewel Box

A transparent plastic case designed to hold a compact disc and accompanying printed materials (*inlay cards* or *tray cards*, and *booklets*). The case, disc, and printed materials are *shrink-wrapped* when packaged for sale. See also *longbox*, *Digipak* and *Eco-Pak*.

Jingle

A short, catchy tune or *ditty*. The term is commonly

applied to music written specifically for a broadcast commercial advertising spot.

Some large *ad agencies* employ staff writers and producers to create jingles for clients, while others *commission* jingles from independent songwriters and jingle production companies. When commissioning music from third parties, advertising agencies typically work with a select group of experienced writers or producers who can work fast and provide complete turnkey packages at one inclusive price. Jingle production companies often own their own studio facilities, and either employ or have access to producers, songwriters, lyricists, musicians, singers, and arrangers.

Ad agencies frequently present a storyline and suggest a musical genre to several writers and jingle producers, and invite them all to submit demo ideas. Commission fees to creators of the winning idea range from the low $100s for local radio spots to $10,000 or more for national television commercials containing as little as 30 seconds of music. Superstar writer/producers may command even higher fees, ranging upwards to $100,000 for a full-scale nationwide television ad campaign.

JLO

Abbreviation for *Jukebox License Office*.

Jobber

A middleman in the distribution and sale of merchandise; one who buys product directly from manufacturers and resells it wholesale to retailers. See also *rack jobber*.

Joint Administration

Pertaining to copyrights that are co-owned or copublished by two or more music publishers, joint administration is when each of the owners assumes responsibility for managing its own share of the copyright. A joint-administrator can issue *nonexclusive* licenses, insuring that the other administrator is properly accounted to, but neither joint administrator may issue an exclusive license without the other's consent. See *co-owned copyright*, *copublishing* and *administration rights*.

Joint Authorship

The shared responsibility or credit for the contents of a creative work by two or more people.

Joint Venture

A business partnership entered into for a specific purpose and for only the limited duration it takes to accomplish that purpose. A joint venture differs from a *general partnership* in that a joint venture is formed to achieve a specific goal, as opposed to being an ongoing business. When this specific goal is fulfilled, the joint venture comes to an end. All other similarities with general partnerships apply, however, with regards to responsibilities, shares of assets, profits, losses, liabilities, and disposal of assets when the venture is dissolved.

Joint ventures are useful when two companies pool resources to further a project that benefits them both. For example, a record company and publishing company might finance a film production company to produce a movie featuring music owned by the publisher and performed by the record company's artists. The joint venture benefits (1) the film production company, which gets financing to produce the film; (2) the publishing company, which earns a share of the film's profits while exploiting its copyrights; and (3) the record company, which gets rights to the soundtrack album, gains exposure for its artists, and shares in the film's profits.

Joint-Work

A creative work, such as a song, that is authored by two or more people. See also *collective work*.

Jukebox

A coin-operated device, which plays phonograph records or compact discs, and which provides a selection of recorded music from which patrons may choose.

Jukebox License

Before the *Copyright Act of 1976*, jukebox operators were exempt from paying royalties to publishers whose works were played on the boxes. Section 116 of the Copyright Act of 1976 provided for a *compulsory license* to publicly perform nondramatic musical works by means of coin-operated phonorecord players (jukeboxes). Under this provision, jukebox operators were required to obtain licenses and pay an annual fee to the *performing-right societies* for distribution to song copyright owners. The fee was initially $8 for each jukebox in operation. The *Copyright Royalty Tribunal* was authorized to review and escalate the fee periodically; licensing and fee-collections were handled by *ASCAP*, *BMI*, and *SESAC*. By 1990 the fee had increased to $63 per box, and ASCAP, BMI, and SESAC collected more than $14 million for their members on an estimated 225,000 jukeboxes in the US.

The *Berne Convention Implementation Act* (effective March 1, 1989) amended the US Copyright Act to allow negotiated licenses between jukebox operators and copyright owners. Negotiated licenses now take precedence over the compulsory license. Presently, jukeboxes are covered by *blanket licenses* issued by the *Jukebox License Office* (JLO).

Jukebox License Office (JLO)

Under the *Copyright Act of 1976*, jukebox operators were required, under a *compulsory licensing provision*, to obtain a *performing-right license* and pay an annual fee to the *performing-right societies* for distribution to members whose works were publicly performed on coin-operated phonographs (jukeboxes); the *Copyright Royalty Tribunal* was authorized to review and escalate the fee periodically. The 1976 Act was amended with the *Berne Convention Implementation Act* (effective March 1, 1989) to allow negotiated licenses between jukebox operators and copyright owners. Presently, jukeboxes are covered by *blanket licenses* issued by the Jukebox License Office (JLO) to cover repertoire from all three performing-right societies. The JLO is a panel of members comprising appointees from each of the performing-right societies and the *Amusement and Music Operators Association (AMOA)*.

Juke

(1) Slang for a bar, tavern, or roadhouse that features cheap food, alcoholic beverages, and music for dancing. (2) To patronize a roadside bar that features jukebox music for dancing.

Juke Joint

Slang for a bar, tavern, or roadhouse that provides jukebox music for dancing.

Jungle

Term originating from the Tivoli district of Kingston in Jamaica, is applied to an electronic dance music genre surfacing in the *Bristol* area of southwestern England during the mid-1990s. The style is a blending of *hip-hop* drum *samples*, *hardcore techno*, and *dancehall* chants, with thundering bass lines.

Juno Awards

Presented annually by CARAS in various categories, the Juno Awards are the Canadian equivalent to the Grammy Awards in the United States.

Jurisdiction

(1) The statutory authority to interpret and apply the laws of a district, region, or territory. (2) The extent or range of authority. (3) A legal district, such as a city, county, state, territory, or country in which the laws of the district apply to contracts made, actions taken, or disputes that arise within the district. See also choice of forum.

Karaoke

A form of entertainment featuring a device or machine that plays audio tapes and/or videos containing musical tracks with no lead vocal, designed for sing-along. The machines are placed in public, commercial establishments, such as nightclubs skating rinks, amusement arcades, etc., where customers take the stage and sing along with the music. Karaoke machines are also sold, along with instrumental tracks of hit songs, for home use.

Since the appeal of karaoke rests with using well-known songs that members of the public enjoy singing, virtually all tracks produced for these machines consist of existing songs licensed from music publishers, as opposed to new works commissioned especially for the format.

Licenses for karaoke sing-along tapes and discs are akin to *mechanical licenses*, with the *statutory mechanical rate* paid for each copy distributed. However, the appeal of karaoke is sing-along, which means the customer base needs access to the lyrics of each song. So, in addition to the statutory mechanical rate, the licensor pays an additional 2¢ to 6¢ per copy when lyrics are printed or displayed electronically in conjunction with the music. A video version may pay as much as 10¢ to 12¢ per copy. Videos produced for use in karaoke machines are called programs. Licenses for music used in karaoke recordings are called *karaoke synchronization licenses*.

Karaoke Synchronization License

See *karaoke video booth*, below.

Karaoke Video Booth

Karaoke video booths are attractions at carnivals, theme parks, arcades, malls, etc., where customers can have video clips made of their sing-along performances. Since customers' vocal performances are *synchronized* with their visual images, some form of *synchronization license* is needed from the copyright owners of the songs used. This is often covered by incorporating synchronization rights within the karaoke music license itself, and charging a *fixing* fee of around $200 to $300. Typically, music publishers are paid a 50¢ royalty per video clip sold to customers.

Key

The dominating or governing *scale* in which a musical work, or a passage within a musical work, is written or performed. The key is normally determined by the *tonic* or *keynote* (C, E, etc.) of the scale.

Key-Man Clause

Provision in a contract that protects a recording artist or songwriter who signs to a company primarily because of one person (the "key man"), without whose presence the writer or artist would not want to be bound to the company. A key-man clause provides that if the named individual should leave the company during the term of the artist's or songwriter's contract, the artist or songwriter may have the option to terminate the contract without legal or financial repercussions. To be fair to the company, such a clause may also require the artist or songwriter to repay any outstanding advances and/or to fulfill a product commitment in order to terminate the contract early.

Key-Man Insurance

A life insurance policy designed to compensate investors, lenders, partners, employers, employees, and any other named beneficiaries, who stand to lose financially when a venture is derailed through the death or incapacity of a "key man." Often, an entire venture may be jeopardized when an organization loses just one key member. This is especially true in a small entrepreneurial company driven by the ideas and talents of one or two people, or in a musical act dependent upon the star power of one or two members of the group.

Key Signature

A sign or symbol consisting of the "accidental(s)" (sharps or flats) of the notes in the governing scale of a musical work. The key signature is placed on the staff after the clef at the beginning of a work and indicates the *key* in which the work is to be performed.

Keynote

(1) The principle or *tonic* note of a scale in which a musical work (or a passage therein) is written or performed, and which determines the *key*. See also *scale*. (2) A speech designed to focus an audience's attention on the primary issues of a convention, meeting, or assembly and to inspire enthusiasm for the shared goals of the assembled audience.

Kickback

A payoff given by one who receives a sum of money for services rendered or goods sold to one who was in position to influence an employer to make the purchase or contract for the service. A kickback is normally a percentage of the money that was received, and is usually paid as a bribe, and often as a result of pressure from the person receiving the kickback. Because kickbacks are generally illegal, and can result in prosecution for commercial bribery and loss of employment, they are typically made *under the table*.

KODA

The *performing-right society* in Denmark.

KOMCA

Abbreviation for *Korea Music Copyright Association*.

Korea Music Copyright Association (KOMCA)

The *performing-right society* in South Korea.

Label

(1) A recording company ("record label"). (2) The area of a disc or cassette on which is printed the name and logo of the manufacturer, product identification (title, artist, master and catalog numbers, copyright notice, etc.), and credits. (3) A category or description.

Label Copy

Information supplied by a producer or record manufacturer detailing what should be printed on a disc *label* (i.e., master number, catalog number, copyright notice, titles, artists, writers, publishers, performing-rights affiliations, producers, etc.).

Label Credit

Acknowledgment printed on a product label for work done, such as production, authorship, arrangement, etc.

Label Deal

Agreement between a record company and an independent producer whereby the producer delivers finished masters to the company and the company manufactures and distributes the masters under the producer's own logo. See also *distribution deal*, *pressing & distribution (P&D) deal*, and *production company*.

Label Information

See also *label copy*. Product details printed on a *label*, including *credits*, *copyright notice*, catalog numbers, etc.

Lacquer

A durable natural varnish. Lacquer is used to coat aluminum discs used in *disc mastering*. See also *master lacquer*, *reference lacquer*, and *acetate*.

Lamination

A coating process used on album covers to protect against scratches and scuffing and to give the covers a shiny, glossy look.

LAN

Acronym for *local area network*.

Lapse

(1) The expiration of a right, privilege, or termination of an option when it is not exercised within an agreed time period. (2) The termination of a right or privilege due to one party's failure or neglect to fulfill its obligations during the time allowed.

Lapsed

An option, right, privilege, contract, license, or insurance policy that has expired or been terminated and is no longer in force.

Laserdisc

Also known as an *optical disc*, a laserdisc stores digitalized data, including text, audio, and visual images. The data is etched onto the disc's surface in microscopic pits, which are "read" with a laser scanning device. Types of optical laser discs include *CDs*, *CD-ROMS*, *CD-Is*, *CD-WORMs*, and *video discs*.

Laser Video

Also called *videodisc*. A type of *optical laserdisc* capable of reproducing audio and visual images. Videodiscs cannot record television programs off the air, but their sound and visual reproduction is digitalized and therefore of better quality than that of *analog* videotapes used in *VCRs*.

LASS

Abbreviation for *Los Angeles Songwriters Showcase*.

Last Refusal

A right given to one party to exercise an option, distribute a product, license a copyright, sign an artist, or purchase an asset, etc., by matching a price or other terms offered by any other party. Also called *first refusal*.

LATGA-A

The *performing-right society* in Lithuania.

Latin

Abbreviated reference for Latin America, and used generically for (1) the Latin American market (i.e., Mexico, Central America, and South America, and Hispanic Americans), and (2) for music produced by and popular among Latin Americans. Also called *Latino*.

Latino

See *Latin*.

Lawyer

An *attorney* or *solicitor* licensed to practice law. See *attorney*, *attorney at law*, and *attorney in fact*.

Lead

(1) To conduct, direct (a band, for instance). (2) To be the featured performer in a group of performers (i.e., lead singer, lead guitarist, lead role, etc.). (3) The primary focus. (4) A *tip* or a piece of information given by someone with inside knowledge of record companies, producers, and others needing new song material.

Lead Sheet

Musical notation containing a song's melody line, together with lyrics and chord symbols, but not fully orchestrated. Also called a *top line* or *professional copy*. See also *fake book*.

Lead Time

(1) Time needed to complete a task. (2) The cut-off time for submission of press releases and advertising copy prior to publication date of a periodical or newspaper. For instance, Sunday newspapers may require receipt of copy 7 to 14 days prior to publication; a monthly magazine might require copy to be submitted 6 to 8 weeks ahead of the issue date.

Leader

(1) The conductor or director of an orchestra, a band, or vocal group. (2) In engagements involving union musicians, one musician is designated as leader, and is responsible for all dealings with the employer. Union leaders must file copies of engagement contracts with the union *local*, and see that each member collects agreed wages and pays *work dues* to the local. (3) The *first chair* or principal performer in an orchestral section. (4) A *leader tape* (see below).

Leader Tape

A short length of unrecordable plastic film or tape spliced onto either end of a reel of film or tape, and/or at the beginning and end of a track or take contained on the reel (or cassette), in order to (1) facilitate threading or winding; (2) cue the actual start of a take or track; and/or (3) separate different tracks or takes contained on the reel. (Leaders are usually of a different color than the actual film or tape, in order to distinguish the beginning and end of a track or take.)

Leading

(1) In the first rank. (2) Top billing, starring, featured, headlined, in the spotlight. (3) Giving direction or guidance. See also *lead*.

Leading Edge

Same as *cutting edge* or *state of the art*; in the vanguard; ahead of the crowd; most up-to-date.

Leakage

In broadcasting or recording, when sound emanating from one source (i.e., an instrument or amplifier) is picked up by a microphone placed to pick up sound from another source. Also called "bleed," "bleeding," or "bleed through."

Lease

A contract agreement whereby one party (the *lessee*) obtains the right to use a property owned by another party (the *lessor*) during the stated term of the lease in exchange for specified payments, such as rent, or for royalties based on a percentage of the income derived from the use of the property. At the end of the lease period, the lessee retakes possession of the property. See also *master lease*.

Lease Deal

An agreement between a recording company and producer whereby the company obtains exclusive rights to reproduce, distribute, and sell a recording for a stated period of time, after which those rights *terminate* and *revert* back to the producer. The producer furnishes a completed master recording; in some cases, the producer also furnishes camera-ready artwork (*mechanicals*) for album covers. The record company assumes the responsibility and expenses of manufacturing, marketing, and distribution, paying the producer a percentage of each unit sale (based either on the wholesale or the recommended retail price). The producer is generally responsible for paying artist royalties from the gross income received from the record company. The record company typically assumes responsibility for paying *mechanical royalties* to music publishers that control the song copyrights on the recording.

LED

Abbreviation for *light emitting diode*.

Ledger

A book of ruled pages or a record of accounts containing financial transactions posted in the form of *debits* and *credits*.

Legal Affairs

Name used in some companies for a department or person managing contracts, licenses, leases, corporate matters, and other business transactions of a legal nature. The head of legal affairs is generally an attorney versed in copyright and entertainment law who supervises staff attorneys and paralegals and works with outside legal firms hired on retainer or brought in from time to time for nonrecurring issues.

Legal Consideration

A payment given, promise made, or service rendered in return for something else promised, given, or done, the exchange of which makes an agreement between two parties a legally enforceable contract. Also referred to as "good" or "sufficient" consideration. See also *inducement* and *consideration*.

Legal Department

See *legal affairs*.

Legalese

Terminology, specialized words or phrases, slang references, and abbreviations commonly used and understood by lawyers in their professional capacity, which may not be understood by those with little formal knowledge of the law. See also *jargon* and *trade language*.

Legit

Slang for *legitimate*. A term often used in reference to classical music or classical theater, as opposed to popular music or (in theater) to *burlesque*, *vaudeville*, and *musical comedy*.

Legitimate Theater

See *legit*.

Lessee

A party to a *lease* agreement who receives temporary possession or use of a property or right from the *lessor*.

Lessor

A party to a *lease* agreement who grants temporary possession or use of a property or right to the *lessee*.

Letter Agreement

Also called "letter of agreement." A contract or license in letter form wherein the sender proposes and describes the terms, conditions, considerations, and warranties of agreement, and the recipient, by signing and returning a copy of the letter to the sender, acknowledges, approves, and agrees to the terms, conditions, considerations, and warranties of agreement. Contracts and licenses in letter form are generally (but not always) shorter and more informal than standard or *long-form contracts* and licenses, often omitting much of the *boilerplate* and *legalese* common in standard contract formats. Characteristically, letter agreements refer to the parties as "we" and "you" as opposed to such impersonal terms as *licensee* and *licensor*, *assignor* and *assignee*, etc. Because letter-form agreements are usually simpler, they are more common in licensing (where a *nonexclusive* privilege or permission to use a copyright is given). Standard, long-form contracts are more common where *exclusive assignments* of services or property rights are involved.

Letter of Acceptance

A letter accepting an offer of contract or settlement. A letter of acceptance is considered binding once it is deposited in the mail. See also *letter of consent*, *letter of intent*, and *acceptance*.

Letter of Attorney

A letter granting the legal authority to act on behalf of, represent, sign for, or stand in for another. Also called *power of attorney*.

Letter of Consent

A letter agreeing to, or approving of, something planned or done by another. A written statement of permission for another party to pursue a course of action.

Letter of Intent

A statement that the sender will enter into a formal agreement with the recipient for some business arrangement or transaction, based upon a preliminary understanding (as summarized in the letter).

Letter of Transmittal

A cover letter sent with a document, contract, license, proposal, shipment, etc., summarizing the item or items being *transmitted* and/or the purpose of the *transaction*.

Liability

(1) An obligation, a debt, or a legal responsibility. (2) An exposure to the risks of failing to honor a debt, fulfill an obligation, or assume a responsibility. (3) A responsibility, obligation, burden, penalty, debt, or charge incurred as the result of a breach of

contract, an act of negligence, or the commitment of an act causing damage, injury, or loss to another. (4) A shortcoming, defect, or handicap.

Liable

(1) To be legally responsible for a debt, action, or inaction. (2) To be obligated to perform a service, honor a debt, or pay a judgment. (3) To be held accountable. (4) To risk the consequences of some action or inaction.

Libel

A *defamation*; to make malicious and unjustified statements about someone in fixed or permanent form (written, recorded, pictured). (An orally expressed defamation is called *slander*.)

Librarian

A person in charge of compiling, cataloging, and maintaining a *library* and its operating system.

Librarian of Congress

The official title of the director of the *Library of Congress*. Under a law enacted in 1802, the Librarian of Congress is appointed by the President of the United States and approved by the Senate, and is the person solely responsible for making the library's rules and regulations and overseeing its operating system.

Library

(1) A systematically arranged collection of literary, artistic, and reference materials, such as books, magazines, newspapers, catalogs, sheet music, records, CDs, cassettes, and tapes. (2) A collection of compositions or prerecorded musical segments available for licensing in productions not requiring original music. Typical libraries contain instrumental fragments capturing a range of moods, such as lush orchestrations of romantic themes or music that builds suspense, tension, and fear. Users pay licensing fees to "drop" musical segments into productions, which range from training films to local radio programming. Also called *recorded music library*, *transcription library*, *library service*, *production music library*, and *music supply house*.

Library Music

Prerecorded music tracks available from *recorded music libraries*. Also called *needledrop music*, *production music*, or *canned music*. Producers of low-budget films, documentaries, training films, television programs, commercials, etc. frequently license canned music tracks from library services, which provide master quality recordings and rights to use the track and the underlying music copyright, all at one relatively low fee.

Library of Congress

The de facto national library of the United States. Established in 1800 as a service agency of the United States Congress, the Library of Congress now occupies three buildings in Washington, DC, and is the world's largest library, with a collection of 97 million items in more than 400 languages, including books, film, maps, photographs, recordings, music, manuscripts, and graphics. From 1870, all US copyright activities were centralized at the Library, with the requirement that two copies of every book, pamphlet, map, print, and piece of music registered for copyright be deposited in the Library. (See also *Copyright Formalities*.)

Library Service

See *recorded music library*.

Librettist

Person who writes a *libretto*.

Libretto

The *book*, script, or literary text of a dramatic musical work, such as an opera, operetta or a musical comedy.

License

(1) To authorize the use of a copyrighted work; to grant permission to do or use something. (2) An official sanction, permission, or authorization to do, use, possess, or sell something.

License by Operation of Law

The creation of a license in fact by virtue of succession to a right or privilege by a will or through inheritance as a lawful heir to someone who dies intestate. A license may also come into existence through operation of law by application of the *compulsory licensing* provision of the *Copyright Act*. See also *statutory beneficiary*.

License Extension

An authorization to continue doing, using, or selling something for an additional term beyond the original term of authorization.

License Renewal

The creation of a new license following the termination of an existing one. Technically, a renewed license constitutes an entirely new right to use, sell, or do something, as opposed to an *extension* of the original license for an additional period of time beyond the initial term.

Licensed Territory

The country or geographical area in which a permission to use, do, or sell something applies.

Licensee

A person or company granted a right or an authorization to do, use, or sell something.

Licensing

The act or process of granting authorization, or of obtaining authorization to do, use, or sell something.

Licensor

A company, governing body, or person that grants permission, authority, and rights to do, use, or sell something.

Life Cycle

In marketing, the life of a product or of a business, beginning with inception (or conception), and continuing through incubation (development), introduction, nurturing, growth (expansion), maturity, saturation, decline, and abandonment (death):

(1) Inception (or conception): The idea for the product is generated and evaluated. A cost analysis and a sales forecast are required to justify committing funds for development.

(2) Incubation (or development): Once the idea is accepted as viable, funds are committed and development begins. Expenses might include advances, demos, preproduction, recording, mixing, mastering, artwork, and manufacturing. Simultaneously, marketing plans are finalized, a release date set, and prerelease promotion and publicity begin in accordance with a marketing calendar. At this stage, much money is invested with no opportunity yet for sales.

(3) Introduction: With the product's launch into the marketplace, costs continue to rise as initial marketing steps are executed. Testing begins in earnest, and orders may trickle in, but sales aren't sufficient to recoup investment.

(4) Nurturing: The product is still in its infancy. Positive feedback from testing is used to nurture the product by pyramiding initial successes throughout the marketplace. Further promotion and marketing costs are incurred, still out of proportion to return, but in line with the amount of positive results demonstrated thus far. (The marketer tries not to get too far ahead of the curve by committing heavy marketing expenses until the concept is proven valid.)

(5) Growth (or expansion): Now the product begins to fulfill its promise with positive sales results, so that full-scale marketing can be committed with confidence. The rising line of sales income closes in on the line of product expenditures.

(6) Maturity: The product is established and is profitable. It may still be possible to re-enter the growth phase if more marketing resources are committed, but only if careful analysis shows further growth potential is great enough to justify additional expense.

(7) Saturation: Sales reach a plateau as the marketplace is saturated. The product has gone as far as it can. Further marketing expenditures are not justified, because the product has peaked. New investment would only reduce return on investment, without spurring additional sales.

(8) Decline: The product has reached old age, sales are rapidly falling off, ultimately to a trickle. The product is maintained mainly as a catalog item.

(9) Abandonment (or death): The product has died. Inventory maintenance costs more than its worth, and the product is shelved, or (in the case of recorded product) deleted from the catalog, scrapped, or sold as cut-outs.

Life of Author

In statutory copyright law, the determining factor in the term of copyright protection for a creative work (the *life of copyright*), which currently extends from the time the work is created until 50 years from the date of the author's death (or the date of the death of the last surviving author in the case of *joint-authorship*). As of 1998, Congress was considering legislation to extend copyright protection to 70 years from the date of the author's death.

Life of Copyright

The term of copyright protection afforded a creative work under statutory copyright law. See *life of author* (above), *copyright duration*, *copyright term*, and *copyright renewal*.

Lift

An excerpt or edited version of a broadcast commercial, used for shorter spots (i.e., a 30-second spot edited down from a 60-second commercial).

Ligature

(1) A device on a reed instrument, such as a saxophone, which holds the reed in place on the mouthpiece. (2) A musical phrase played by a slurring of successive, connecting notes.

Light Emitting Diode (LED)

A semiconductor diode that converts voltage to illuminated digital displays of data, such as those used for calculators, cell phones, recording consoles, etc.

Light Music

Music, such as waltzes, airs, or marches, which is deemed not quite as high-brow as so-called *serious music*.

Light Opera

A musical theatrical production with spoken dialogue and songs, having many of the same characteristics as an *opera*, but which is geared more to parody, satire, frivolity, and/or sentimentality. Also called *operetta*.

Light Rotation

In radio programming, *rotation* is a term used to describe how often a recording is featured (aired) on a current *playlist* each week. Recordings that receive the most airplay are categorized as having *heavy rotation* (30+ plays), followed by those with *medium rotation* (15 to 29 plays), and then those with *light rotation* (less than 15 plays).

Limitation

(1) A restriction or prohibition, as specified by contract or law. (2) The statutory time allowed for a law to be applied (the *statute of limitations*) or for a lawsuit to be filed. (3) A shortcoming, lack, flaw, or defect.

Limitation of Liability

A law or provision in a contract or license that restricts, caps, or places a ceiling on the extent of legal *liability* for specific types of damages, losses, injuries, etc. See also *limited liability* and *statute of limitations*.

Limited Company (Ltd.)

A legal form of company registration, especially in Great Britain, which is equivalent to *incorporation* in the United States, and which provides *limited liability* to owners (shareholders) of the company.

Limited Distribution

The restriction, either through marketing choice, lack of access to distribution outlets, or through contractual or licensing provisions, of a product's distribution to a narrowly defined geographical region or to specific types of marketing. For instance, masters and songs might be licensed to a *premium* album marketer on condition that the album be used as a bonus giveaway to purchasers of a certain product and not be made available to consumers as retail merchandise. Or, a new recording might be test marketed in a regional area and not made available nationally.

Limited Edition

A book, print, record album, or other work whose publication is restricted to a specific number of copies, each of which usually bears a unique identifying serial number.

Limited Liability

The underlying principle of statutory protection afforded investors in and owners of corporations and partnerships. In a *limited partnership*, *corporation*, or *limited company*, the personal assets of owners (or limited partners) are shielded from any liabilities incurred by the business. In the event of business failure, liquidation, or bankruptcy, the most any owner (or limited partner) can lose is the amount of capital he or she has already invested in the business. Limited liability, in effect, separates the person of the owner from the company, whereas, in a *sole proprietorship* or *general partnership*, the owners and company are treated as one. See also *unlimited liability*.

Limited Partnership

A partnership in which some of the partners have limited liability for the business's obligations. At least one partner acts as *general partner*, assuming total responsibility for managing the venture. The remaining, "limited" partner(s) must not have any say or role in managing the venture. Whereas general partnerships are formed by like-minded individuals who collectively contribute assets, capital, expertise and/or time to the company, limited partnerships usually arise where one party seeks to raise money to pursue a specific venture. The function of the limited partners is to provide operating capital.

Limited partners are repaid a percentage of the venture's profits. Normally a limited partnership has a finite life. Limited partnerships may be formed to finance specific projects (i.e., an album production, a series of productions, the purchase of a copyright catalog, or the launch of a record company).

However, once limited partners receive a pre-agreed return on investment, or a certain period of time lapses (or both), the limited partnership is dissolved. Usually, the assets then become the property of the general partner, and the limited partners have no further association with the venture.

Should the venture fail, limited partners lose only their investment; they are not liable for losses or damages beyond what they put into the venture. However, if a limited partner makes management decisions, he ceases to be a "limited" partner, and exposes himself to the full liability of a general partner.

Limiter

In audio technology, a circuit or *signal-processing* device that flattens peaks in volume by preventing the *amplitude* of a *waveform* from rising above a set level.

Line

(1) In a musical arrangement, a melodic part or harmony part taken by, or assigned to, an instrument or group of instruments, or to a vocalist or group of vocalists (i.e., a sax line, horn line, or bass line). (2) In a song or poem, a phrase or segment of lyrics distinguished from other phrases or lyric segments by (a) a visual break on the page, and (b) rhyme scheme, length, or meter. (3) In a script, a part or section of dialogue or narration assigned to a character or an announcer. See also *product line*.

Line Art

A drawing representing the outline or shape of an object, without detailed features, shading, or color.

Line Cut

An engraving process used to make prints. The design or artwork is cut directly into the surface of a metal plate, from which prints are made. See also *line engraving*.

Line Dance

A style of dancing emerging from country music in the late 1980s with continuing popularity into the 1990s. It involves club patrons forming lines to join in choreographed dance steps, often at the direction of dee-jays. Though associated with country music clubs, the concept has spread to other types of dance music and clubs.

Line Drawing

See *line art*.

Line Engraving

The process of making prints by cutting (engraving) a design or drawing directly into the surface of a copper plate, from which prints are made.

Line Producer

A record, radio, play, film, video, or television producer who actually works "on the floor" of the production with the performers and crew. Line producers are usually employed "in-house" by record labels, music publishers, or production companies, or hired to take charge of one-off projects put together by *executive producers*.

Liner Notes

Biographical or other introductory information printed on the reverse or inset of an album cover pertaining to the music and artist(s) heard on the recording. See also *blurb*, *credits*, and *label credits*.

Lineup

(1) The composition of a band, orchestra, ensemble, vocal group, etc. (2) The order of appearance by a number of different performers on a program. (3) The arrangement of track selections or songs on a tape, disc, or album. (4) A list of cast members. (5) A sequence of events. (6) A schedule of television programs, coming attractions, tour dates and venues, etc.

Lip Synch

Also called *sync* and *lip sync*. To simulate a vocal performance, either live or on film, by mouthing the words to a song in *synchronization* with a pre-recorded vocal on a music track. See also *pantomime*.

Liquidate

To convert assets into cash; to settle or pay off business debts and obligations in order of priority with cash raised from collecting accounts receivable and selling all or part of the firm's assets.

Liquidation of Reserves

Record companies, sheet music publishers, and other firms that sell product for which royalties must be paid routinely withhold a portion of those royalties as a contingent fund to offset product returned for credit (as in the case of goods that are damaged in shipment, or goods shipped on *consignment* and returned unsold, etc.). The portion of royalties withheld is called a *reserve fund*, or *reserves*. When a reserve fund is open-ended, the date that the royalty earner ultimately receives full payment for every royalty-earning piece of product can be indefinitely postponed. Therefore, many royalty-earners try to negotiate contracts and licenses that require reserves to be *liquidated*. Ideally, the liquidation time frame will be specifically defined (i.e., within 12 to 24 months). At the end of a liquidation period, the royalty-earner must receive a full accounting for all funds held in reserve: either unsold and returned product, for which no royalties are due, is numerated and written off, or the balance of the reserve fund is paid over to the royalty-earner. Some liquidation provisions call for a series of *prorated* declining-balance payments by which a reserve fund is paid down to the royalty earner.

List Price

The suggested retail price of an item as published or advertised by the manufacturer to the consumer, but which may be discounted at the retailer's discretion. The difference between the list price and the price paid by the retailer to the distributor or wholesaler is the retailer's margin of operating profit. Also called "sticker price," "list," "suggested retail price," "published retail price (PRP)," and "recommended retail price (RRP)."

Literary Content

The *book*, *libretto*, *script*, *choreographic* directions, *dialogue*, and/or *lyrics* of a musical play, dramatic work, opera, operetta, ballet, song, etc.

Literary License

The creative range of artistic expression in speech, writing, performance, or artistic interpretation, which may bend the rules of common practice, tradition, expectation, or author's original intent, and which is employed to achieve a certain effect on an audience. Also called *artistic license* and *poetic license*.

Literary Work

A body of creative or scholastic writing, either in prose or verse.

Live

An unrecorded performance, or a performance being recorded (or broadcast) as it takes place in front of an audience.

Live-on-Tape

A recording or filming of a live performance, which can be (or is intended to be) edited before actual manufacture and sale of the recording or before being broadcast on radio or television.

Living Stage

Live theatrical productions of plays, musicals, operas, operettas, and ballets—but not dramatizations that are recorded, filmed, or broadcast.

LOA

Abbreviation for *letter of agreement* or *letter of acceptance*.

Loan-Out Corporation

Primarily a tax-saving device used by a recording artist to shelter income from a recording contract. Instead of signing directly with a record company, the artist signs to his or her own corporation. The corporation then "loans" the artist's services via an agreement with the record company, and the record company pays royalties to the corporation. The corporation, in turn, pays the artist a salary or some other type of compensation structured to minimize tax liabilities for the artist. The corporation may also provide other benefits to the artist. such as insurance, pension fund contributions, etc. See also *flow-through clause* and *inducement letter*.

Local

(1) A district chapter or branch office of a national trade organization, union, or guild, which has oversight and direction of members within that district. Both the *AFM* and *AFTRA* divide the country into geographical districts in which locals are granted charters to operate relatively independently of locals in other districts. Union members in each district belong to the local that governs their area. AFM locals are identified by numbers (i.e., Local 47 in Los Angeles), while AFTRA locals take the name of the district they serve. (2) A broadcast confined to the geographical area of a radio or television station's transmission range. (3) An audience or a market resident to one area, district, or city.

Local Area Network (LAN)

A group of personal computers and workstations linked by local cabling (as opposed to over communication lines). See also *wide area network (WAN)*.

Local Cover

A song licensed to a foreign music publisher (a *subpublisher*), which is recorded by an artist based in the subpublisher's territory.

Local Marketing Agreement

In broadcasting, an agreement where a radio or television station owner leases original programming to another station.

Local Promotion

One of three layers of record promotion. A local promotion person generally covers a specific region or territory on all types of product released by a record company. (A *national promotion* person usually concentrates on a specific genre or market segment, such as R&B, and an *indie promotion* person is hired to promote a specific release.)

Local Station

A radio or television station broadcasting to a geographical area centered on the station's location. There are approximately 13,000 local radio stations in the United States and about 1,500 local television stations.

Local television stations operate either on *UHF* or *VHF* bands. Most are affiliated with one of the national networks (ABC, CBS, Fox, NBC), and carry network programming interspersed with locally produced programs, *syndicated* programs, reruns, and movies. Independent stations (non-network) rely on syndicated programs, reruns, and movies for the bulk of their programming.

Local radio stations operate on either *FM* or *AM* bands. Though some are network-affiliated, the vast majority are independently owned and operated. Most local radio programming centers on playing prerecorded music and listener call-in talk shows, which are either locally produced or picked up through *syndicators*.

More than 90% of all local television stations and 75% of all local radio stations are commercial enterprises, relying on the sale of airtime to national and local advertisers for operating revenues and profits. The remaining, noncommercial, stations are funded by educational institutions, local governments, nonprofit civic organizations, corporate donations, listener contributions, and the *Corporation for Public Broadcasting*, which channels federal funding to *National Public Radio (NPR)* and *Public Broadcasting Service (PBS)*.

See also *network, superstation, cable television, syndication, public radio*, and *public television*.

Local Television Per Program Performance License

A modified *blanket license* offered by *performing-right societies* to local television stations as an alternative to the comprehensive blanket licenses required previous to the *Buffalo Broadcasting* case. Under this type of license, a station pays performance fees only for those shows that actually use songs in the societies' repertoire. Stations opting for this type of license must pay monthly fees based on *cue sheets* submitted to the societies, listing titles, songwriters, music publishers, performing-right affiliations, time of broadcast, playing times of each performance, and nature of performances.

Local Writer

A songwriter based in a foreign *subpublisher*'s territory who is hired to translate or adapt lyrics of an *original publisher*'s song in order to enhance its market appeal and commercial potential in the territory. In music publishing *subpublishing* agreements, an overseas subpublisher usually has the right to *translate* lyrics of subpublished works, in which case the subpublisher assigns a local writer to do the translation.

Locale

A place, venue, scene, site, location, or vicinity.

Location

A site where recording or filming takes place away from a studio. See *on location*.

Lock In

To guarantee, or to be given a guarantee. For instance, a film producer may lock in an *option* to use a song copyright at a fixed price by paying the copyright owner a non-returnable advance or an option fee; or, a prospective purchaser may lock in an option on a song catalog by paying *earnest money* to the seller.

Lock-In Date

The date at which an interest rate, royalty rate, exchange rate, etc. will be used to calculate a payment. Many recording contracts lock in the date at which a *statutory mechanical* rate is in effect as the basis for calculating *mechanical royalties* on *controlled compositions*. The statutory mechanical royalty rate is periodically increased by the *Copyright Arbitration Royalty Panel (CARP)*. In order to avoid paying a higher royalty rate if and when CARP increases the statutory rate, record companies may contractually lock in the rate as of the date of release, the date of the finished master's delivery by the artist, the date the recording is begun (or completed), or the date on which the contract is signed.

Lo-Fi

Associated with *indie rock* bands, lo-fi is essentially barebones production derived from the "do-it-yourself" recording techniques cash-poor bands used to cut records in home-based four- and eight-track recording studios.

Log

A schedule listing kept by radio stations of all recordings played or programmed during broadcasting hours, including titles, artists, and performing-right affiliations of the music publishers.

Logging Procedure

Method used by *performing-right societies* to determine broadcasting usage of music copyrights and to calculate *performance royalties* due music publishers and songwriters. Logging procedures differ according to methods established by each society, but encompass various forms of statistical *sampling* derived from airplay on randomly selected radio stations, census counts of titles logged on *cue sheets* supplied by television stations and networks, and census counts of titles gathered via *BDS*. See also *sampling*, *weighting formula*, *credit system*, *performance survey*, and *credit weighting formula*.

Logo

A name, design, symbol, or trademark created to establish and reinforce public recognition of a product, company, or organization.

Lone Ranger

Essentially a one-person outfit, especially in music publishing, such as writer-publishers, artist-publishers, producer-publishers, and entrepreneurs who single-handedly acquire material and hustle it into the marketplace. Many lone rangers do their own copyright administration, licensing, and collections, while others enter into joint-ventures or contract arrangements with larger publishers or service organizations to handle specific functions.

Long-Form Contract

A formally worded contract (i.e. containing *boilerplate* and *legalese*) setting forth in great detail all terms and conditions of an *assignment* or *transfer of copyright*, the provision of exclusive services, the legal relationship being established between the parties, etc. Contrasts with *letter agreement* and *short-form assignment*.

Long Playing Phonograph Record (LP)

A 33 1/3 rpm vinyl record, usually 12 inches in circumference. Before its introduction in the late 1940s, an album of songs required several 10-inch 78 rpm discs, but the slower rpm speed of "long playing" records provided more playing time so that an entire album of songs could be reproduced on one disc.

Long Term Assignment

An assignment of a copyright or other property, or of certain rights or interests, usually for a period of more than five years, after which all rights and interests revert to the assignor.

Longbox

A 6 x 12-inch cardboard package for marketing CDs. In use between 1980 and 1993, longboxes were dropped by the industry as a cost-cutting move and in response to environmentalists concerned by the millions of pounds of garbage created by consumers throwing them away. Longboxes were really redundant, since *jewel boxes* containing the CDs were packaged inside.

Loop

To splice or digitally link sections of a recording or program back to back so that they are repeated over and over again. Each repeated loop is called an *iteration*.

Loophole

A provision in a contract or license that is worded in such a way that one party may use it as a means of legally avoiding or evading an obligation or restriction.

Looping

The process of linking repeated sections (*iterations*) of a recording or computer program.

Los Angeles Songwriters Showcase (LASS)

Los Angeles Songwriters Showcase recently merged with *National Academy of Songwriters* (NAS), a trade organization for more than 3,000 professional songwriters, located at 6255 Hollywood Blvd., Hollywood, CA 90028. Tel: (213) 463-7178. NAS now offers all LASS services as well as promoting the LASS weekly showcase. LASS as a separate organization has ceased to exist.

Loudspeaker

An electromechanical device through which sounds are converted into acoustic (sound) waves from amplified audio voltages. Most loudspeakers are "dynamic," and contain voice coils of light wire mounted within electromagnetic fields; signal passes through the coil, varying the magnetic force between the coil and the magnetic field, and paper diaphragms attached to the voice coils vibrate to generate sound.

The loudness and sound quality of a loudspeaker depends upon the design properties of the enclosure or cabinet in which it is contained. Some speaker cabinets contain two or more loudspeakers of varying size. Larger speakers, called woofers, offer better replication of low notes and bass tones; smaller speakers (tweeters) are better for high notes and treble tones.

Lounge Act

A performer or band hired as featured entertainment in casinos, hotels, resorts, etc.

Love Song

Usually, a ballad containing romantic lyrics and presented with a warm, melodic arrangement.

Low Bias

Also called *standard bias* or *normal bias*. Bias is the calibration of a magnetic field applied during the recording process to a *magnetic tape*. High-frequency voltage combined with an audio signal reduces distortion in tape recording. *Audiocassettes* are graded according to dynamic range, *signal-to-noise ratio*, and *frequency response*. See also *ferric*, *chrome cassette*, *metal cassette*, *bias*, and *normal bias*.

LP

Abbreviation for *long playing phonograph record* (typically a 12-inch, 33 1/3 rpm vinyl record).

Lump Sum

A one-time payment or receipt of money, as opposed to incremental payments spread out over time.

LV

Abbreviation for *laser video*.

Lyric Magazine

A mass-circulation magazine featuring collections of lyrics from the latest hits. Some of these magazines are devoted to Pop music, while others concentrate on Country, Rock, or R&B songs. Charlton Publications of Connecticut is perhaps the most prominent publisher in this field, with a number of lyric-magazine titles under their imprint.

Licenses to reprint lyrics in periodicals usually are limited to one year. Average lyric reprint fees for such periodicals are in the $100 range, but if a work reaches the upper Top 20 of a recognized Top 100 chart (such as *Billboard*) additional payments of, say, $50, may be chargeable.

In some cases, a royalty-based license is used, which might pay an advance on either the expected number of magazine sales or the number of paid subscribers. For instance, if the magazine's cover price is $1.50, the total royalty may be 18¢. If there are 30 song lyrics contained in the issue, each song earns a *prorated* 6/10ths of one cent. If the magazine has a circulation of 50,000, the advance would be $300 (50,000 x .006).

There are also magazines that contain sheet music (the music is printed along with the lyrics).

Licenses for these types of magazines may be offered on a royalty basis of around 12.5% of the cover price prorated among the number of songs included in the issue.

Lyric Reprint

Publication of a song's lyrics, without the music. Music publishers are frequently asked to license song lyrics for publication in books, magazines, newspapers, greeting cards, print advertisements, etc. Permission to reprint lyrics are most often granted individually on a *per use, nonexclusive* basis. See also *lyric magazine*, above.

Lyric Sheet

A page containing the lyrics to a song or a number of songs. When music publishers submit demos of new songs to *A&R* personnel, producers, and recording artists, it is common practice to include a lyric sheet with the demo tape. Frequently, record companies reproduce the lyrics to songs contained on an album, either by reprinting them on the album cover itself, or by including a separate lyric sheet as an insert. Music publishers generally give record companies nonexclusive *gratis* licenses to reproduce lyrics in this fashion.

Lyricist

Person who writes the words of a song.

Lyrics

The words of a song.

M
Music format abbreviation for *metal*.

MACP
Abbreviation for *Music Authors Copyright Protection*.

Macromarketing
The integration of a concept (for a business, product, or service) into a grand strategy designed to create a desired identity or public perception (for the business, product, or service). See also *micromarketing*.

Made-For-Hire Work
Also called *work for hire* and *work made for hire*. A copyright can be a work for hire in one of two ways. In many exclusive songwriter agreements, for instance, the writer is "hired" (an *employee for hire*) to create songs within the scope of his or her employment. Officially, this means there must be a continuing business relationship during the creative process in which the employer guides, supervises, and oversees the writer and/or provides facilities, equipment, and materials.

The other approach is when the employer *commissions* the writer to create works for a specific use, such as a film or television production, a jingle, a translation, or an adaptation, etc. Once the commissioned work is completed, the relationship officially ends. The commissioned material is a *work made for hire*, though the creator is not an employee, since there is no ongoing relationship.

Normally, when a song is written, the creator is automatically vested with copyright ownership. The writer can assign copyright interest to a publisher, but still be eligible to recapture the copyright under certain conditions of statutory copyright law (i.e., after lapse of a prerequisite number of years, and/or other conditions of assignment between the writer and publisher). But, under a work for hire agreement, the writer has no vested interest in the copyright. The writer was hired or commissioned to write the song *prior* to actually writing it. The writer is never eligible to recapture the copyright, because he never had it in the first place. If the employer or commissioner fails to meet all obligations laid down in the contract, the writer's only recourse is to sue for damages (although such a suit might include a demand that the copyright be assigned to the writer).

Though the publisher is credited as *author* in the copyright claim to a work for hire, the songwriter receives full songwriting credit on all label copy, sheet music, film credits, registrations, licenses, etc. And, the songwriter's share of royalty and fee income is not normally affected when a song is a work for hire.

Maestro
(1) An orchestra conductor, a band leader, a director. (2) A *master* in an art, such as music.

Mag Stock
Vertical strip on a motion picture film onto which the soundtrack is imprinted.

Magnetic Recording
The most common method of *sound recording*, by which transformed sound waves are amplified and made to magnetize a recording tape. The magnetization fluctuates according to the *frequency* and *intensity* of the recorded sound. See also *electromagnetic recording*, *digital recording*, *magnetic recording tape*, *mechanical recording*, and *optical recording*.

Magnetic Recording Tape
A thin, plastic tape coated with a layer of magnetic material, such as iron oxide, which is used to record electric signals or impulses of sound, video, or data. As the tape passes across an electromagnetic *head*

in the recording process, it is magnetized with the *frequencies* and *amplitude* of the original electronic signal. In playback mode, the tape passing across the head relays the stored impulses to an amplifier, which converts them into a reproduction of the original source. Magnetic tapes are manufactured in cassette, cartridge, or reel-to-reel formats, and can be reused by erasing, or demagnetizing, the recorded impulses.

Magnum Opus
"Great work." A masterpiece.

Mail Order
Method of marketing product directly to customers, bypassing distributors and retailers, by (a) mailing solicitations to names on a mailing list, or (b) advertising product in various media with invitations to potential customers to purchase directly from the advertiser by phoning or mailing in an order. *Record clubs* use mail-order marketing exclusively to sell music product, and many independent, *niche market* labels augment sales by building up a mail-order customer base. Also, numerous *compilation* albums are packaged for mail-order sales via television advertising.

Mail Out
See *mailing* and *mailer*.

Mailer
(1) A sheet of cardboard or other light material used to protect disks, records, books, etc. when mailed or shipped. (2) A protective shipping container, such as a cardboard tube or bubblepack. (3) A new product announcement or advertising brochure, leaflet, or circular mailed with invoices, letters, and product.

Mailing
A press release, product announcement, promotional item, advertisement, or solicitation distributed by mail to a select group of names.

Mailing List
A list of names and addresses of companies, organizations, and individuals selected to receive *mailings* of a particular nature, and which are compiled and grouped by demographics, occupations, interests, or business relationships.

Mailing Service
A company that is contracted to package, address, and mail items to mail-order customers or names on a mailing list.

Mainstream
The prevailing fashion, current taste, most popular activity, culture, or influences.

Major
Something of first rank importance, significance, size, or dominance (i.e., a major hit, a major artist, etc.) A "major company" is one that ranks among the leaders in a particular industry (in market share, revenues, product range, distribution network, etc.). In the record business, for instance, the term is used in reference to one of the six* so-called major labels, or corporate groupings of labels, which include BMG (RCA, Arista, etc.), CEMA (Capitol, EMI, Virgin, Chrysalis, Liberty, etc.), MCA (MCA, Uni, Decca, etc.), PolyGram (Mercury, Phonogram, Polydor, Motown, A&M, Island, etc.), Sony (Columbia, Epic, etc.), and WEA (Warner Bros., Reprise, Elektra, Atlantic, Asylum, etc.).

Virtually every one of the six major record companies are divisions of still larger corporations. They maintain national distributing networks (see *branch operations*), regional offices, international divisions, and own related music industry companies (music publishing companies, studios, manufacturing plants, merchandising companies, record clubs, etc.), and distribute numerous smaller labels through *label deals*, *distribution deals*, *pressing* & *distribution deals*, and *joint-ventures*.

The six major labels dominate the recorded music market and account for the vast majority of recorded product sold in the United States. Each of the majors has staff numbering in the 100s covering every facet of the record business (administration, finance, legal, marketing, promotion, advertising, design, A&R, manufacturing, sales, operations, international, copyright, shipping, information systems, merchandising, etc.).

Note: In mid-1998, it was reported that MCA and PolyGram were merging.

Major Market
Reference to a metropolitan area with a consumer base of several million people (i.e., New York City, Chicago, Los Angeles, etc.) A "major market station" is a radio station located in a major market. See also *primary station* and *secondary station*.

Major Territory
In a licensing agreement, where overseas *territories* are involved, the countries of Germany, Japan, United Kingdom, France, The Netherlands, Italy, and Australia are usually considered to be "major territories." Groupings of certain smaller countries sometimes are also considered to constitute major territories, such as Benelux (The Netherlands together with Belgium and Luxembourg), Scandinavia (Sweden, Norway, Denmark, Iceland, and, sometimes, Finland), and G.A.S. (Germany together with Austria and Switzerland).

Make Ready

To assemble resources prior to use; to put together; to prepare. In color printing (for album covers, posters, etc.), "making ready" refers to running a quantity of paper through the printing press prior to starting the production run in order to test for ink registration and color application.

Manage

(1) To administer and supervise the affairs of a business or venture. (2) To direct, lead, guide, and handle the professional career and related business affairs of an artist, actor, etc. (3) To exercise executive authority. (4) To accomplish, succeed, achieve (as in "manage to get a deal" or "break a record," etc.).

Management

(1) Person or persons in charge of business administration and operations. (2) The executive supervision, direction, leadership, and control of a business, organization, project, or venture. (3) A person or company engaged in directing, leading, guiding, and handling the professional careers and related business affairs of artists, actors, etc. See also *personal manager, business manager, copyright management, administration.*

Management Game

A technique used for honing management skills and negotiating strategies with mock scenarios or hypothetical business models. A management game is both a training exercise and a method to shape a desired management style.

Participants can tackle a range of issues from problem solving to opportunity assessment, and learn from mistakes without the real world costs of making wrong decisions. Management games can also be played by dividing participants into adversarial teams representing two sides of a contract negotiation or conflict resolution. It often helps to have the game presided over by an outside consultant who brings special expertise to the subject and impartial judgment about the outcome.

Management Information Systems (MIS)

A system or process by which a company or an organization produces, organizes, stores, and distributes information, such as market research, sales, billings, expenses, revenues, inventory, personnel records, customer accounts, royalty receipts and payments, etc. An MIS includes all the tools and personnel necessary for developing and maintaining information vital to functional operations and strategic planning (i.e., hardware, software, networks, data processors, etc.) See also *data, data processing, database, information services, information system,* and *information system.*

Manager

(1) Person in charge of business operations or of one of several departments, divisions, or branches of a corporation. (2) Person authorized to conduct the business affairs of another, or who is given the responsibility to direct, control, and oversee something (such as copyright administration, studio operations, etc.) See also *management, business manager, personal manager, professional manager, road manager,* and *stage manager.*

Managing Director (MD)

Senior director of a *limited company*, equivalent of a company president or *CEO*.

Manchester

Industrial city in northern England associated with the rise of guitar-driven dance bands in the late 1980s, and with earlier post-*punk* and *acid house* bands.

Manufacture

To process or fabricate raw materials into a finished product, especially where the product is mass-produced for sale and distribution to the public.

Manufacturer

A company that *manufactures* product. The term is frequently used in the music business to reference record companies that mass-produce finished product such as CDs, audiotapes, etc., even though the company may contract out the actual manufacture of its product to independently-owned factories.

Manuscript (MS)

Author's original version (of a book, article, document, script, musical piece, or other composition), either handwritten, typewritten, or composed on a wordprocessor, which is submitted for publication.

MAP

Acronym for *minimum advertised price.*

Market

(1) To promote or advertise a product or service. (2) To offer for sale. (3) A geographical area where a product or service is offered (i.e., the local market). (4) A segment or portion of the population deemed to be potential customers for a product or service (i.e., the college market). (4) A segment or portion of the population considered to be a likely audience for a type of music or entertainment (i.e., *MTV* viewers).

Market Price

Price of a product or service that has been established by customer acceptance and/or prevailing prices for similar products or services as determined by supply and demand.

Market Research

The process of collecting and evaluating population statistics (*demographics*) in order to determine the size, characteristics, and likely market potential for a product or service. (2) The process of determining the potential interest in a specific product or service within a defined market segment. See also *test marketing*.

Market Segment

A portion of a population defined by *demographics* (i.e., age, race, gender, education, profession, marital status, tastes, habits, buying power, geographical location, etc.).

Market Share

A percentage of total sales generated by a particular industry (i.e., one company's sales as a percentage of all sales generated within the industry), or a percentage of all sales of a particular type of product sold by all companies within a range of products in a particular industry.

Market Universe

The entire scope or total size of the population potentially interested a particular product. See also *market segment*.

Market Value

The amount an asset is appraised to bring on the open market, as opposed to *book value*, which is the monetary value of the asset on a company's books. When there is no established *market price*, the market value is an estimation of the best and most reasonable price a seller can expect to get from a potential purchaser.

Marketing

The process of conceiving, developing, promoting, and selling a product or service. This process includes (a) making the product, (b) researching and defining the market, (c) devising a strategic *marketing concept* to promote the product or service, (d) devising and carrying out the tactical *marketing plan* (actual steps used to carry out the promotion), and (e) *fulfillment* (distributing the product from point of manufacture down the line to the customer). See also *marketing plan*, *macromarketing* and *micromarketing*.

Marketing Campaign

A series of planned and coordinated steps to market a product or service, starting with a marketing concept, and continuing with tactics set forth in a marketing plan to promote, sell, and deliver the product to customers. See also *marketing plan*, *macromarketing* and *micromarketing*.

Marketing Concept

A theme or strategic plan devised to market a product, service, company, artist, etc.

Marketing Department

Division of a company whose functions are to devise marketing concepts and plans, and to coordinate and carry out campaigns to market the company's products or services, including market research, promotion, publicity, advertising, distribution, and sales.

Marketing Plan

A marketing plan focuses on (a) how to position a company, product, or service in the marketplace; (b) optimum ways to expose a company, product, or service to the public; (c) the image or message the company, product, or service should project; (d) the mechanics of projecting that image or message; and (e) exactly what steps must be taken to sell and deliver the product or service.

There are essentially two types of marketing plans. (1) A *macromarketing* plan defines the *strategies* by which a product can be seen, heard, and bought. It may be reduced to a one- or two-page document, laying down principle guidelines without all the nuts-and-bolts details of the marketing process. (2) A *micromarketing plan*, on the other hand, can be quite comprehensive, and might run 10 to 20 pages, or more. It defines and elaborates on the tactics required to fulfill the strategic marketing concept (i.e., specific marketing tools and media used, frequency of use, costs, milestones, and objectives).

Marquee

(1) A porch-type structure at a hotel, club, auditorium, or theater entrance, on which signs are erected advertising or announcing the entertainment and/or coming attractions offered inside the establishment. (2) A large open-sided tent where entertainment is featured.

Marquee Value

A performer whose reputation is sufficiently well established to draw fans to a performance or to purchase a product bearing his/her name. Same as *name value*. See also *star power*.

MASA

Acronym for *Mauritius Society of Authors*.

Mass Market

(1) The population taken as a whole, without segmenting by age, income, gender, race, region, occupation, education, etc. (2) To market a product or service to the entire population, as opposed to concentrating marketing efforts on narrowly defined segments of the population.

Mass Media

Media that offers means of public communication to the population as a whole (i.e., newspapers, radio, television, general interest magazines, etc.), as opposed to media geared to narrowly targeted audiences, such as *trade magazines*, *fanzines*, specific interest newsletters, *closed-circuit* television, etc.

Mass Production

The manufacture of a product in large quantities, using standardized parts and assembly-lines or automated fabrication techniques.

Master

(1) An original of something (such as a sound recording) from which copies are made. (2) A device used to control various parts of a machine or mechanism, or to control a group of other devices (a master switch, a master *fader*). (3) A highly skilled or proficient artist or performer (a *maestro*).

Master Lacquer

An aluminum disc coated with lacquer onto which grooves are cut with a stylus in the *disc-mastering* process. Master tapes are "tuned" by a mastering engineer using a disc-mastering *console* to adjust equalization, sound and tone levels, etc. As the master tape is played, a *stylus* cuts the spiral grooves into the master lacquer disc. A separate *lacquer* is cut for each side of the record, and then sent to the pressing plant where the master lacquers are converted to *stampers* that duplicate the grooves onto vinyl discs as they are "pressed" or manufactured.

Master Lease

An agreement between a recording company and producer whereby the company obtains exclusive rights to reproduce, distribute, and sell a recording for a stated period of time, after which those rights *terminate* and *revert* back to the producer. The producer furnishes a completed master recording; in some cases, the producer also furnishes camera-ready artwork (*mechanicals*) for album covers. The record company assumes the responsibility and expenses of manufacturing, marketing, and distribution, paying the producer a percentage of each unit sale (based either on the wholesale or the recommended retail price). The producer is generally responsible for paying artist royalties from the gross income received from the record company. The record company typically assumes responsibility for paying *mechanical royalties* to music publishers who control the song copyrights on the recording.

Master Number

Number assigned to a finished *master tape* by the record company. The master number is used to identify the master internally (i.e., for filing in the tape vault, work orders to manufacturing plants and mastering labs, etc.), as opposed to a *record number*, which is assigned to the finished product made from the master tapes. See also *matrix number*.

Master of Ceremonies (MC or Emcee)

A person or performer who hosts an event or conducts a program by making opening and closing remarks, announces entertainments and activities as they are offered, and formally introduces guests and other performers to the audience.

Master Purchase

An agreement between a recording company and producer whereby the company buys exclusive rights in perpetuity to reproduce, distribute, and sell a recording, as opposed to a *master lease* agreement whereby the company obtains those rights only for a stated period of time, after which those rights terminate and revert back to the producer.

Master Tape

The original tape recorded version of a sound recording, which is used to make copies, including *parts*, such as *lacquer discs*, with which to manufacture copies for commercial release.

Master Use License

Permission given from the copyright owner of a *master* (i.e., a record company) to another party to use the master in any of a variety of ways. For instance, a motion picture producer may wish to use an original hit recording in a movie soundtrack; a television marketer of compilation albums will need such a license from the owners of each recording included on the compilation; an advertising agency may wish to use an original hit recording in a television and/or radio commercial.

Mastering

The process of transferring audio from a *master tape* to a *lacquer disc* and/or other parts used to manufacture copies of the recordings. See also *compact disc mastering*.

Mat

See *matrix*.

Matching Folio

A published collection of song arrangements issued in conjunction with a recorded album release, reproducing the album cover on the folio cover, and including all the songs contained on the album.

Matching Rights

A right given to one party to exercise an option, distribute a product, license a copyright, sign an artist, or purchase an asset, etc., by matching a price or other terms offered by any other party. See also *buyout rights* and *right of first refusal*.

Material
(1) The essence, basis, or substance(s) used to create a finished work (i.e., song material performed by a recording artist to make a *master*). (2) Something that is necessary, goes to the heart of a matter, affects an outcome, or is essential.

Matrix
(1) In phonorecord manufacturing, an *electroplated* impression of a phonograph record, which is used as a mold to *press* finished records. (2) In printing, a metal plate made from a mold taken from positive impressions of typefaces and/or illustrations, which is used to duplicate the impressions in the printing process. (Also called a *mat*.)

Matrix Number
Unique number assigned to a *matrix* in order to identify each side of a recording in the manufacturing process. The matrix number is printed on the label of a phonorecord to identify which label goes on which side of the disc. In many cases, the matrix number is the same as the *record number*, except that it is preceded or tagged with either "A" or "1" for the first side of the disc or "B" or "2" for the reverse side.

Matrixing
Also called *plating*. The process of making a *matrix* (i.e., casting a mold or metal plate from positive impressions) in order to duplicate a recording or a page of typeface. See *plating*, *master lacquer*, *mother*, and *metal stamper*.

Mauritius Society of Authors (MASA)
A *copyright collective* based in Mauritius.

Maxi-Single
A longer-than-standard length recording released in cassette format, equivalent to a 12" vinyl single.

MC
(1) Prefix used to denote an audiocassette in a product catalog numbering system. (2) Abbreviation for *master of ceremonies*. (Also called *emcee*.)

MCPS
Abbreviation for *Mechanical Copyright Protection Society*, a *mechanical-right society* in Great Britain.

MCSC
Abbreviation for *Music Copyright Society of China*, the *performing-right society* and *mechanical-right society* in China.

MCSK
Abbreviation for *Music Copyright Society of Kenya*, the *performing-right society* and *mechanical-right society* in Kenya.

MCSN
Abbreviation for *Music Copyright Society of Nigeria*, the *performing-right society* and *mechanical-rights society* in Nigeria.

MCT
Abbreviation for *Music Copyright Thailand*.

MD
(1) Abbreviation for *music director*. (2) Abbreviation for *managing director*.

Mechanical
(1) Type of royalty paid to song copyright owners by record manufacturers for the sale of sound recordings. (2) Final *camera-ready* artwork or graphic layout material prepared to make a plate or offset for printing. (3) An uninspired, unemotional performance, as if done by a machine.

Mechanical Copyright Protection Society (MCPS)
The *mechanical-right society* in Great Britain, which also covers the Bahamas, Bermuda, British Virgin Islands, India, Ireland (Eire), Jamaica, Kenya, Nigeria, Uganda, Northern Ireland, and Zimbabwe.

Mechanical License
Authorization or grant of permission for the mechanical reproduction, distribution, and sale of a song copyright in audio-only form (i.e., records, tapes, compact discs, piano rolls, microchips, etc.). See also *compulsory mechanical license*, *negotiated mechanical license*, and *statutory mechanical royalty*.

Mechanical Recording
In the now obsolete mechanical method of recording sound, sound waves directly actuated a cutting needle (*aka* stylus or cutter) to engrave a pattern of wavy-lines (corresponding to the sound-waves) on a disk or cylinder made of wax, metallic foil, or shellac. The stylus was attached to a very light diaphragm, which was set into a vibrating motion when the sound waves directly struck it. A disk or cylinder was rotated under the point of the stylus as it cut a spiral groove into the disk or cylinder. The groove was a mechanical replica of the sound waves that struck the diaphragm.

In the modern indirect mechanical method of making phonograph records, a microphone converts sound to electrical impulses, which are then amplified to actuate the stylus or cutting needle by electromagnetic means. The cutting needle engraves a shellac master disk, which is then used to make the metal molds needed to press vinyl records.

Mechanical Reproduction

The duplication or manufacture of sound recordings by mechanical means. Permission to record and reproduce recorded copies of song copyrights by mechanical means is called a *mechanical license*.

Mechanical Right

One of the *bundle of rights* vested in copyright ownership, giving a song copyright owner control over the *mechanical reproduction* of a song, subject to the *compulsory licensing* provision of the *Copyright Act*. See also *mechanical license*.

Mechanical Right Agency

Same as *mechanical-right society*.

Mechanical Right Society

An organization formed to license mechanical rights to record manufacturers and others on behalf of affiliated song copyright owners, music publishers, and songwriters. Mechanical-right societies collect mechanical royalties from licensees and periodically distribute the earnings to members; they also audit licensees to insure proper accounting, and act to protect the mechanical rights of members through identifying and prosecuting copyright infringers and lobbying lawmakers with regards to statutory changes in copyright law. Virtually every country has at least one society to license mechanical rights on behalf of local music publishers and songwriters, and virtually every mechanical-right society has reciprocal agreements with societies in other countries for international mechanical-right licensing and royalty collections. See also *Harry Fox Agency*.

The following is a partial list of mechanical-right societies around the world: *AEPI** (Greece); *ACODEM* (Colombia); *AMCOS* (Australia and New Zealand); *AUSTRO-MECHANA* (Austria); *CASH** (Hong Kong); *CMRRA* (Canada); *COMPASS** (Singapore); *GEMA** (Germany, Austria, Poland, Hungary, etc.); *COSGA** (Ghana); *HARRY FOX* (USA); *JASRAC** (Japan); *MCPS* (Great Britain and Ireland); *MCSC** (China); *MCSK** (Kenya); *MCSN** (Nigeria); *NCB* (Scandinavia); *NCB TEOSTO* (Finland); *RAIS* (Russia); *SABAM** (Belgium); *SADAIC** (Argentina); *SARRAL* (South Africa); *SBACEM** (Brazil); *SDRM* (France and French-speaking African countries); *SGAE** (Spain); *SODRAC* (Canada); *SIAE** (Italy); *SPA** (Portugal); *STEMRA* (Holland); *SUISA** (Switzerland); *VAAP* (former Soviet Union). ** Indicates a society that licenses both performance and mechanical rights.*

Mechanical Royalty

A *royalty* paid to song copyright owners by record manufacturers and others for the sale of mechanically reproduced copies of songs (i.e., vinyl records, compact discs, audiotapes, videocassettes, CD-ROMs, music boxes, etc.). The maximum mechanical royalty rate for *phonorecords* is established by *statute* and incorporated into copyright law. The *statutory mechanical rate* in the United States is periodically adjusted by the *Copyright Arbitration Royalty Panel* (CARP), which is appointed by the *Librarian of Congress*.

In the United States, the amount of the mechanical royalty is defined in each mechanical license in terms of dollars and cents (i.e., 7.1¢ or \$.071 per unit sold as of 1998, but see also *statutory mechanical royalty rate*). In most other countries, the mechanical royalty is usually based on a percentage of either the recommended retail price or the dealer price of each unit sold.

Mechanical income and *performance* income are the two main sources of revenue for most music publishers and songwriters. See also *statutory mechanical royalty rate*.

Media

A collective reference to various groups of individuals and companies engaged in the communications industry (i.e., journalists, newspapers, magazines, television, radio, etc.).

Media Buyer

Person employed by an ad agency, or by the marketing department of a company, whose job is to purchase print space and broadcast time for advertisements. A media buyer seeks to place ads where they can have the most impact on a targeted *market segment* within the advertising budget allotted for a *marketing campaign*.

Media Event

(1) An event or circumstance that receives widespread, prominent coverage by the news media. (2) An event or circumstance staged or arranged to achieve the widest possible media coverage.

Media Hype

Widespread, prominent coverage by the media of an event, product, personality, or circumstance, through excessive and exaggerated publicity, extravagant promotion, and/or inflated claims.

Media List

A list of key people and organizations in the *media* who are deemed important to the marketing and promotion of a product and are thus targeted to receive review copies, press releases, promo kits, invitations to promotional events, complimentary tickets to performances, etc.

Mediate

To *arbitrate*; to intercede between two or more parties in a negotiation or a dispute in order to help settle the issues dividing them.

Medium

(1) A mode of artistic expression determined by the materials or techniques used in the creative process (i.e., watercolors, charcoal, oils, etc.). (2) A method or means by which something is accomplished or communicated (i.e., songwriting as a medium of expression). (3) One segment of the *media* (i.e., the print medium, referring to newspapers or magazines).

Medium Rotation

In radio programming, *rotation* is a term used to describe how many times a recording is featured (aired) on a current *playlist* each week. Recordings that receive the most airplay are categorized as having *heavy rotation* (30+ plays), followed by those with *medium rotation* (15 to 29 plays), and then those with *light rotation* (less than 15 plays).

Medley

A composite musical arrangement of melodies or fragments of melodies taken from two or more songs.

MEIEA

Abbreviation for *Music & Entertainment Industry Educators Association*.

Melody

The lead musical line, or recognizable theme, of a song or an instrumental work.

Member

A person who belongs to an organization (i.e., a labor union, trade guild, band, etc.). A company affiliated with a trade group, such as *NARAS*. Music publishers and songwriters affiliated with *ASCAP* are called "members." (Publishers and songwriters affiliated with *BMI* are called *affiliates*.)

Membership

Those belonging to an organization, a union, guild, class, type, or a group as a whole.

MENC

Abbreviation for *Music Educators National Conference*.

Merchandise

(1) Product that is bought wholesale and resold retail (commercial goods). (2) To buy product for resale; to trade commercially; to sell by promoting, advertising, and displaying a product.

Merchandiser

A firm (or person) engaged in commercial trade (i.e., buying goods wholesale to sell retail).

Merchandising

(1) The process of buying product wholesale and selling it retail; the process of selling by promotion, advertising, and displaying goods. (2) The sale of goods tied in to an artist's *album tour cycle*, such as souvenir programs, T-shirts, badges, sweat shirts, jackets, calendars, posters, bags, mugs, cups, dolls, toys, etc. bearing the artist's name, logo, and/or likeness. Besides selling artist-related goods at live performances, merchandise can also be sold in retail outlets or by mail order, etc.

Merchandising Agreement

An agreement between an artist and a merchandising company whereby the company manufactures and sells goods bearing the artist's name, likeness, logo, and/or biographical information. Such agreements are usually tied in with an artist's *album tour cycle*, and, in fact, the proceeds quite often provide initial funding for the tour itself, particularly for newer artists and in cases where the record company does not supply sufficient *tour support*. In some cases, record companies insist on acquiring merchandising rights as part of an artist's recording agreement. If the record company does not have its own merchandising division, it *sublicenses* these rights to a merchandising company. Typical merchandising agreements provide for an advance to the artist, recoupable from royalties earned on the sale of each piece of merchandise, which may encompass a range of items, such as souvenir programs, T-shirts, badges, sweat shirts, jackets, calendars, posters, bags, mugs, cups, dolls, toys, etc. bearing the artist's name, logo, and/or likeness. Besides selling artist-related goods at live performances, merchandising companies might also sell merchandise to consumers indirectly through retail outlets and directly by mail order. Some merchandising agreements are specific as to where and how merchandise is sold. So-called *tour merchandise agreements*, as the name implies, are restricted to sales at concerts in a tour cycle (though there may be sell-off provisions for surplus merchandise at the end of the cycle). *Retail merchandise agreements*, on the other hand, allow merchandising through normal retail channels, as well as mail order.

Mersh

Abbreviated reference for *commercial* spot or a recording with commercial appeal.

MESAM

The *performing-right society* in Turkey.

Metal

A highly energetic, loudly amplified electronic *rock music*. See also *heavy metal*, *hard rock*.

Message Song

A song with lyrics promoting a cause, idea, philosophy, or espousing a lifestyle; usually of a positive or uplifting nature, though sometimes to decry social injustice or human frailties.

Metal Cassette

One of three basic types of cassette tape (the others being *ferric* and *chrome*). Ferric tape is the most common, but metal and chrome offer higher playback quality. However, chrome and metal each require cassette players that are *calibrated* to play them, because of their higher *bias* and *EQ* requirements. In addition to being more expensive than ferric, chrome and metal cassettes are abrasive, which causes wear on the recording and playback *heads*.

Metal Mold

See *metal part* and *metal stamper*, below.

Metal Part

Any one of various types of metal components used in manufacturing recordings, collectively called *parts*. In manufacturing records, a *metal mold* made either from a *master lacquer* or a *mother*. A negative impression of the grooves cut into a master lacquer is cast in a metal mold, which is electroplated in a nickel solution. This "master" mold then makes a second, electroplated mold (a *mother*) containing positive impressions of the grooves. A *metal stamper* (with negative groove impressions) is then cast from the mother.

Metal Stamper

A *metal mold* containing negative impressions of the grooves cut into a *master lacquer*. Stampers are cast from *mothers*, and are mounted on pressing machines used to stamp out, or press, vinyl phonograph records during the manufacturing process.

Meter

(1) The rhythm pattern of a musical composition, or section of a composition, as determined by the number of beats to a measure and the time value assigned to each note. (2) In poetry or spoken lyrics, the rhythm of delivery as determined by the number of syllables in a line and the accent or stress assigned to each syllable.

Method Book

A book of musical arrangements for a particular instrument with playing instructions, hints, and tips, published primarily for students or learners. Also called a *music instruction book*.

Mic

(1) An abbreviation for microphone. (2) To strategically place a microphone close to the origin of a sound (i.e., a voice, or instrument) in order to most faithfully capture, reproduce, transmit, or record the sound.

Micromarketing

The tactical functions of moving individual products, ideas, and services through channels of distribution into the marketplace. These tactical exercises include pricing, placing, and promoting product in order to create a demand that results in sales. It is not so much force-feeding the customer as it is tailoring the presentation of the product to match consumers' desires or needs, so that they want to purchase it. See also *macromarketing* and *marketing*.

Middle Eight

Musical term referring to the passage between a chorus or *hook* and a verse, or between a hook and a repeat of the hook. A transitional passage between two sections of a song. Also called a *bridge*.

Middle of the Road (MOR)

(1) A musical genre akin to *easy listening*, which is characterized by soft arrangements of melodic material. (2) A radio station format focusing on MOR or Easy Listening music. (3) A market segment for this type of music.

MIDEM

Acronym for an annual trade show held in Cannes, France, whose English translation is *International Record and Music Publishing Market*. Established in 1966, the event is held each January, and is the oldest, continuous international music business market, attended by most major and leading independent record companies and music publishers from some 90 countries around the world. The US office of MIDEM is located at 475 Park Ave. South, New York, NY 10016. Tel: (212) 689-4220.

MIDI

Acronym for *Musical Instrument Digital Interface*.

MIDI Rights License

Permission to use a composition in a *MIDI sequence*. The license permits the user to make and distribute copies in what is called the *MIDI sequence market*. Specifically, this refers to the sale, lease, license, use or other distribution of MIDI sequences directly or indirectly to individuals for playback through a hardware *sequencer* or personal computer connected to a MIDI-capable *synthesizer* using MIDI software or any similar devices.

Since MIDI software reproduces copyrights for sale in tangible form, a per unit royalty based on sales is paid, much like a *mechanical license*. However, the *compulsory licensing provision* of the *Copyright Act* does not apply to MIDI as in the case of *phonorecords*. So, each licensing situation is negotiated between the copyright owner and user.

A typical MIDI rights license grants the user permission to arrange, orchestrate, record, and re-record the musical composition for use in a MIDI sequence, and make and distribute copies of the MIDI sequence program throughout the licensed territory.

MIDI Sequence

A computer data file of one particular *MIDI* data recording capable of playback through a computer. See *Musical Instrument Digital Interface*.

MIDI Sequence Market

See *MIDI rights license*.

Midline Album

Album priced to sell at around 20% to 40% less than a full-priced or *top line* album. Record company contracts with artists often provide that artist royalties for midline album releases will be based on around 75% of the royalty paid on top line albums. See also *budget line*.

Military Sales

Also called *PX* sales. PX is an abbreviation for *post exchange*. PX sales of recorded product are made on military bases and ship's stores to military personnel and their immediate relatives. Wholesale prices to military bases are generally discounted, because post exchanges and ship's stores resell product at prices lower than those charged by civilian retailers.

Mime

(1) A play, skit, or other performance in which performers act out a story using only gestures and facial expressions in order to communicate without speaking. (2) To tell a story silently, using bodily movements, gestures, and facial expressions. (3) To mimic; to ridicule by exaggerated imitation; a farcical portrayal. See also *panto*, *pantomime*, and *lip sync*.

MiniDisc

A digital audio disc developed by Sony for release 1993. Smaller than a conventional *compact disc*, the MiniDisc is capable of recording as well as playing prerecorded material, and contains up to an hour's playing time.

Minimum Advertised Price (MAP)

A stated retail price from a record company, which may be lower than its *recommended retail price (rrp)*, but which retailers are ostensibly not allowed to undercut. For example, the company may recom-

mend that a new *boxed set* of CDs retail at $49.99, but instructs dealers that the MAP must not be less that $39.99.

Minimum Delivery Commitment

An obligation imposed by contract on an artist, a songwriter, or producer to deliver to a record company or music publisher a minimum number of finished masters or songs during the contract term. Depending upon the specific contractual remedies available to the company, failure to meet a minimum delivery commitment can result in withholding advance payments, suspension of the contract until delivery commitments are fulfilled, a demand for repayment of advances already made, and/or termination of the contract.

Generally, the delivered songs or masters must meet commercially acceptable standards, as deemed by the company. Requiring product to meet the company's standards of commercial quality prevents disgruntled artists, writers, or producers from fulfilling delivery commitments with junk. And, in a songwriter's contract, particularly, the number of songs accepted as fulfilling the requirement are *prorated* to reflect the percentage of authorship. For example, the writer's percentage of a cowritten song should count toward the commitment in relation to the percentage belonging to other cowriters (i.e., 1/2 or 1/4 of one song).

Minimum/Maximum Advance Formula

A sliding-scale method of computing the amounts of advances payable during each contract option period. Instead of stating the exact dollar size of the advance to be paid for picking up a renewal or extension option, the artist (or songwriter or producer, etc.) is guaranteed to receive at least $X (the minimum), but the amount of the advance may escalate up to as much as $Y (a pre-agreed maximum), depending upon the previous period's royalty earnings. The amount payable above the minimum, if any, is calculated on a percentage of income generated during the previous period.

For instance, a songwriter's contract might provide for a first term advance of, say, $25,000, with the music publisher having the option to renew the agreement after one year upon payment of either a minimum amount of $30,000, or 75% of earnings up to a maximum of $50,000, whichever is higher.

Thus, if the writer's first year's royalty earnings are $25,000, the publisher could pay $30,000 to pick up the option for a renewal period. If, however, the first period's royalty earnings were $50,000, the publisher would have to pay $37,500 ($50,000 x 75%) in order to pick up the option. But, if the writer's royalty earnings were $75,000, 75% of that would be $56,250, so the publisher could renew the agreement upon payment of the maximum amount of $50,000.

Minimum/Maximum Royalty Formula

A sliding-scale method of computing royalties payable. The artist (or songwriter or producer, etc.) is guaranteed to receive at least $X (or X%, if the royalty is percentage-based), but the amount of the royalty may escalate up to as much as $Y or Y% (a pre-agreed maximum), depending upon the number of units sold or the amount of royalties earned during the previous period.

For instance, a record company's master-lease agreement with an independent producer might start at a minimum royalty based on 12% of the record's retail price on 90% of all sales. Then, percentage points—or half-points—may be added incrementally for sales above a certain level (i.e., a minimum 12% for the first 500,000 units and .5% more for each 500,000 units thereafter up to an agreed maximum). Alternatively, 12% might be paid for the first album with incremental rises for each album option exercised by the record company. See also *escalator clause*.

Minimum Recording Obligation

(1) A contractual obligation imposed on a record company to record or finance the recording of a minimum number of sides during the term of a recording artist's contract with the company. Normally, such a provision gives the company discretion as to when to call a session, where the recording shall take place, and under what circumstances (i.e., producer, budget, studio, etc.) A minimum recording obligation is not the same as a *minimum release obligation* (see below). (2) In an *artist development* contract between a songwriter-artist, a music publisher (or other party, such as an independent producer, management company, etc.) commits to record, or to finance the recording of, a minimum number of sides during the term of agreement. See also *pay or play*.

Minimum Release Obligation

A commitment by a songwriter, artist-songwriter, or producer-songwriter that a certain number of recordings written during the term of a music publishing agreement will be commercially released. Quite often, music publishers sign songwriters who are also artists or producers on the expectation that their collateral work will generate commercially released material assigned to the publisher. In such situations, advances may be payable as and when songs are actually released.

Minimum Royalty

Also called *floor*. A royalty base rate (as opposed to *ceiling*, which is a maximum amount), which is set forth in an *escalation clause* or *royalty fee structure*. See also *cap*.

Minor

A person under legal age; not yet an adult. A contract with a minor is invalid unless a parent or legal guardian cosigns the agreement and/or signs a separate *letter of consent*.

MIS

Abbreviation for *management information system*.

Mix

(1) To combine and blend two or more separately recorded tracks into one or two equalized tracks. (2) To combine two or more separate channels of sound into one or two equalized channels. (3) One or two equalized tracks or channels "mixed down" (combined, blended, merged) from two or more separately recorded tracks or channels.

Mix Down

See *mix*.

Mixed Folio

A *folio* or *songbook* publication containing arrangements of songs by different writers, and/or songs popularized by different recording artists.

Mixed Media

(1) An artistic work created by using two or more techniques or *media*, such as oil and watercolor, etc. (2) See also *multimedia*.

Mixer

(1) A recording engineer specializing in *mix downs*. (2) An electronic device used to combine (mix) several audio signals onto one or more tracks on a magnetic tape, or to one or more channels amplified through a loudspeaker system.

Mixing Console

A *board*, *desk*, or panel housing the mixing device and mixing controls (sliders, faders, manuals, knobs, buttons, toggle switches, etc.) used to mix several audio signals onto one or more tracks on a magnetic tape, or to one or more channels amplified through a loudspeaker system.

Mobile

A recording, broadcasting, or filming unit capable of being moved to sites away from a studio base for *remote* broadcasts or *on location* recording or filming.

Model Release

A document signed by a model or other person appearing in a photograph allowing or authorizing the use of their likeness in a publication, advertisement, album cover, poster, etc.

Modem
Device linking telephone lines to computers so that data can be transmitted to, and received from, one computer to another, or transmitted to, and received from, a network of computers.

Modification
An alteration made to the language of a provision in a contract or license that clarifies, limits, or expands the agreement.

Modifications Clause
A contractual provision stating that the agreement cannot be altered, amended, or canceled except by a written instrument signed by all parties to the agreement. See also *integration clause*.

Modify
To change, alter, or qualify the language of an agreement.

Modulate
(1) In music, to change keys; to pass from one key to another by means of melodic or chord progression. (2) In electronics, to change the character of a sound wave by varying its *frequency, amplitude,* or *phase.*

Modulation
(1) In music, a change from one key to another by means of melodic or chord progression. See also *transition.* (2) In electronics, particularly in radio transmission, an intermittent *frequency* or *amplitude* change of a radio carrier wave, as determined by the audio characteristics of the signal being transmitted, such as music or a voice.

Modulator
An electronic device used to change the *frequency* or *amplitude* of a *waveform.*

Mold
(1) In record manufacturing, a hollow form or *matrix* into which vinyl or hot liquid styrene is poured, shaped, then baked and cooled (cured). (2) In printing, a hollow form or matrix into which molten metal is poured and shaped before casting typeface. (3) Something which gives shape, form, or pattern to, or which distinctively influences the development of something else. *Example:* "His vocal style is in the mold of Ray Charles."

Mom & Pop
Reference to a small retail outlet independently owned and operated by one person, group, or family.

Monaural
(1) The recording, reception, or playing of sound recordings through one channel or speaker. (2) The

mixdown of two or more sound tracks or channels into one channel or track. Also called *mono* and *monophonic.*

Monitor
(1) A video display device, a computer display screen, or an audio speaker. (2) A device used to observe and/or listen. (3) To check the quality or content of a performance, transmission, or data entry. (4) To supervise, control, and regulate a process, function, or performance.

Mono
Abbreviated reference for *monaural.*

Monophonic
See *monaural.*

Monopolize
(1) To acquire or maintain exclusive control over a commercial activity. (2) To dominate a situation or activity to the exclusion of others.

Monopoly
(1) A product, commodity, or service controlled by one company, group, or person. (2) A company, group, or person that has exclusive control over the manufacture, distribution, and sale of a product. (3) The right of exclusive commercial control over a product or service.

MOR
Music format abbreviation for *middle-of-the-road.*

Moral Rights
Sometimes referred to by its French translation *droit moral,* moral rights is a concept incorporated into the copyright laws of several European countries. Droit moral essentially gives the author of a work creative veto over any changes or alterations to the work by others. For instance, a songwriter would be able to prevent his or her music publisher from authorizing a translation, adaptation, synchronization, or other usage of a song (in a commercial, for instance) if the songwriter felt the changes or usage harmed the work's integrity.

Morality Clause
Also called "morals clause." A usually broadly worded and infrequently enforced contractual provision borrowed from the film industry that requires an artist, songwriter, producer, or other service provider to conduct himself or herself in a manner conforming to public laws, morals, and conventions, and to not commit any act that might bring discredit or opprobrium on the company because of its association.

Mortgage Recordation

The procedural formality of lodging a mortgage or lien against a copyright when it is used as a security or collateral for a loan. The procedure is essentially the same as lodging a written assignment detailing a change of copyright ownership with the *Copyright Office*. (See also *transfer of copyright*.) The lender should record a mortgage with the Copyright Office within a month from the date of the loan. Though liens and mortgages should also be recorded locally in jurisdictions where the transactions take place, the lender can obtain a national record of its security interest by a single filing with the Copyright Office and the payment of a single recordation fee. The lender sends a copy of the mortgage document, a *letter of transmittal* requesting recordation, and the required fee of $10 for documents of 6 pages or less (50¢ per each additional page and 50¢ for each additional song title over one).

Most Favored Nation Clause

A contract or licensing provision stipulating that a *licensor* or *assignor* will automatically be extended the benefits of any better terms, conditions, advantages, or compensation granted to a *third party* in a similar agreement. *Example*: Where a music publisher licenses the use of a song in a commercial video release, this clause insures that if, during the term of the license, the distributor agrees to pay any other publisher a higher *fixing fee* and/or royalty rate to use another song in similar fashion in the same video, then that higher fee and/or royalty rate shall also apply to the composition in question, and that higher fee and/or royalty rate shall be retroactive to the date of the license. In such event, the distributor shall immediately pay the publisher the difference between the original fee and/or royalty with regards to past sales, and the distributor must continue to pay the publisher at the higher royalty rate for all copies distributed thereafter.

Mother

In manufacturing vinyl records, a *master lacquer* is prepared for conversion into a *stamper* used to duplicate the grooves on the master disc when copies are pressed. The conversion process involves (1) "making a master" (electroplating the master lacquer in a nickel solution, then stripping away the plating, leaving a negative impression of the grooves as a *metal mold*); (2) "making a mother" (electroplating the master to make a positive mold of the grooves exactly like the original); then (3) making negative metal stampers from the "mothers" to press the records. See also *father*.

Motion Picture

A filming technique that captures moving objects in a series of individual frames; when projected on a screen in rapid succession, the individual frames produce an optical effect that seems to duplicate the original, continuous movement of the filmed objects. The making of motion pictures (or movies) is both an art and an industry, encompassing a wide range of skills, including technical, creative, management, financing, legal, marketing, and distribution. The term "motion picture" normally is used in reference to a *feature film*.

The first motion pictures were made in France by E.J. Marey in the 1880s. *Thomas Edison* invented the Kinetoscope, which used rolls of celluloid film, for peep-show viewing in 1889, . The first movie theater, called a *nickelodeon*, opened in Pittsburgh in 1905. Motion pictures with sound evolved in the 1920s, and color was introduced in the 1930s. Exhibition of motion pictures outside of theaters expanded to television in the 1950s and by the late 1970s, the introduction of *VCRs* enabled consumers to buy or rent movies on videotape for home viewing. Advances in computerized digital technology in the early 1990s made interactive motion pictures possible whereby audiences could control certain scenes and change some aspects of the storyline.

MOU

Abbreviation for *memorandum of understanding*. See also *Addendum to a Regional Memorandum of Understanding*, *Fox Agency International*, *deal memo*, and *heads of agreement*.

Movie Producer

Person or organization that creates or causes the creation of a motion picture; that assembles, finances, guides, and shapes the elements of the film product from concept to actuality; a provider, an originator, a maker, or a creator of motion pictures.

MPA

Abbreviation for *Music Publishers Association*.

MPPA

Abbreviation for *Music Publishers Protective Association*.

MS

Abbreviation for *manuscript*.

MSO

Abbreviation for *multiple system operator*.

MTV

A cable television channel (*Music Television*) established in 1981, which programs video clips produced by record companies. Located at 1515 Broadway, 24th Floor, New York, NY 10036. Tel: (212) 258-8000; Fax: (212) 258-8100.

Multi-Format

A song or recording that initially sees success in one particular market segment and then "crosses over" to achieve success in one or more other market segments. *Example*: A record that hits the R&B charts then crosses over to hit the Pop charts as well. Also called *crossover*.

Multilateral Agreement

An agreement between three or more parties (as opposed to a *bilateral agreement* involving two parties).

Multilateral Treaty

An agreement, such as a trade agreement, between three or more countries, as opposed to a bilateral treaty between just two nations. See also *copyright convention*.

Multimedia

(1) The combination of several *media* (i.e., movies, animation, music, graphics, text) used for entertainment or education. (2) In marketing, the combined use of different *mass media*, such as television, radio, and print, for advertising or publicity. (3) In computing hardware, a combination of devices for input and output, such as a video accelerator, external speakers, headphones, a sound card, CD-ROM drive, microphone, keyboard, etc.

Multimedia Company

A company engaged in producing, marketing, and/or distributing entertainment and information products in several *media*, such as records, music publishing, newspapers, magazines, television, radio, films, video, etc.

Multimedia License

Any type of license granting permission to reproduce a copyrighted musical work in a *multimedia* format (i.e., interactive CD-ROMs, karaoke machines, video games, computer games, etc.).

Multi-Platinum Record

In the United States, a recording certified by the *RIAA* has having sold two or more million units. See also *hit, silver record, gold record, platinum record,* and *diamond record*.

Multiple

The value, price, or asking price of a company or an income-producing asset (such as a copyright), divided by average annual earnings. For instance, if a copyright catalog generating an average annual income of $200,000 is sold for $1 million, the multiple used to arrive at the selling price was five ($1 million ÷ $200,000 = 5). A "multiple" is also called the *price/earnings ratio* (*P/E*), particularly when valuing the price of corporate stock (i.e., the price of the company's stock divided by its earnings per share).

A copyright catalog's appraisal value hinges on the multiple of its average annual net earnings. The multiple used to appraise a music publishing catalog, for example, is commonly between 4 and 10 times the average annual net receipts. Different appraisers might use different multiples to value the same catalog, just as one appraiser might value two catalogs with identical average annual earnings differently.

There can be no argument about the average annual net income, since this is derived from simple, indisputable math. But there may be a natural tug-of-war between negotiating parties over which multiple produces a fair market value. Buyers and lenders tend toward caution. Since they don't want to risk loss of profit, they use a conservative multiple to value the copyrights. Sellers and borrowers, on the other hand, want to raise the maximum amount of money possible, so they argue for a higher multiple.

Ultimately, an appraiser of a copyright catalog arrives at a multiple by considering the following factors: (a) duration of ownership rights to key copyrights; (b) contractual commitments to pay advances to writers; (c) advances owed to the copyright catalog owner by writers; (d) advances owed to licensees by the owner; (e) contractual commitments by licensees to pay additional advances to the owner; (f) income trend over previous 3 to 5 years (rising or falling?); and (g) the appraiser's expert opinion of the catalog's future commercial potential.

Multiple Use

A licensing situation where a copyright is to be used more than once in the same project. For instance, a film producer might request to use a song several times in a movie. Each use requires a fee, but that doesn't necessarily mean that if the copyright owner charges $X for one use, the producer should be charged three times X for using the song three times. Generally, a fee scale is formulated between the parties, which reduces the fee for each additional use. For example, a film producer requesting to use a song three times might be charged, say, (a) $X for the first use; (b) $X + (X x 75%) for the second use; and (c) $X + (X x 75%) + (X x 50%) for the third use. Translated, this might work out to, say: (a) $10,000 for one use; (b) $17,500 for two uses; and (c) $22,500 for three uses. Of course, this assumes all three uses are relatively equal in terms of duration and type of use.

Multiplex

(1) A building housing several compartmentalized units serving the same basic functions. *Examples*: A multiplex cinema containing separate theaters; A

multiplex studio containing separate rooms for simultaneous mixing and recording projects. (2) A communications system capable of transmitting two or more signals or messages simultaneously over the same wire, line, or radio frequency channel.

Multitrack

(1) A studio, recording device, or tape capable of recording and playing back several, parallel tracks either simultaneously or individually. Each track on a multitrack tape can be edited or enhanced without affecting data recorded onto other tracks, and, ultimately, all tracks are *mixed down* to one or two tracks for *monaural* or *stereo* reproduction. (2) A situation or circumstance involving several separate issues, potentials, or functions, such as a multitrack career, or multitrack contract negotiations.

Music & Entertainment Industry Educators Association (MEIEA)

Association formed to bring together educators and the leaders of the music and entertainment industry to prepare students for careers in these fields. The goal of the organization is to provide a forum for ideas, strategies, and original concepts in education to meet the professional challenges of the 21st century. MEIEA promotes interaction among individuals and institutions involved with music industry education, establishes standards of excellence among individuals and institutions involved with music industry education, encourages interaction between the educational community and the music industry, and assists institutions in the development of programs in music industry education.

Music & Media

A music industry trade magazine focusing on the European market. Published by Billboard Publications, with US offices located at 1515 Broadway, New York, NY 10036. (212) 764-7300.

Music Authors Copyright Protection (MACP)

The *performing-right society* in Malaysia.

Music Box

Also called *musical box*. A spring-driven mechanism that plays music by means of pins plucking tuned steel teeth arrayed on a revolving cylinder. Most music boxes are activated by lifting the lid, though some are operated with manual cranks. Similar music-making mechanisms are housed in toys, dolls, figurines, cigarette lighters, etc. Music boxes are usually programmed to play melodies of well-known songs. These songs are often in *public domain*. But, if the song is in copyright, the music box manufacturer is required to obtain a *mechanical license* from the copyright owner. Music boxes are

enduring examples of the earliest technology for mechanically reproducing music.

Music Centre

British term for a home *hi-fi* system or stereo unit, when all components (turntable, CD player, cassette deck, radio tuner, amplifier, and speakers) are grouped together or assembled as one piece of domestic furniture.

Music City

Nickname for Nashville, Tennessee.

Music City News

A consumer oriented magazine geared towards fans of *country music*; located at 50 Music Square West, Nashville, TN 37203.

Music Clearance

The process of tracking down music-rights owners, and negotiating licenses and fees to use music for recordings and other types of productions, such as film, television, advertising, *karaoke*, *electrical transcriptions*, etc. See *clearing house*.

Music Connection

A music industry trade periodical, with particular focus on issues of interest to those breaking into the business. Located at 6640 Sunset Blvd., Hollywood, CA 90028.

Music Contractor

Person engaged by a producer or record company to hire session musicians, and who serves as the go-between for payments, compliance with union regulations, and arrangement of working conditions. Contractors' fees are double the minimum *union scale* for a musician. Often, a session musician will also act as contractor, in which case he or she is paid double the minimum scale.

Music Coordinator

A consultant or staff employee of a film or television production company whose duties include selecting or suggesting music for a production, clearing music rights, overseeing *synchronization*, preparing *cue sheets*, etc.

Music Copyright Society of China (MCSC)

The *performing-right society* and *mechanical-right society* in China.

Music Copyright Society of Kenya (MCSK)

The *performing-right society* and *mechanical-right society* in Kenya.

Music Copyright Society of Nigeria (MCSN)

The *performing-right society* and *mechanical-right society* in Nigeria.

Music Copyright Thailand (MCT)

Music rights agency in Thailand.

Music Cue

(1) Brief musical segment used to introduce or *underscore* the action or dialogue of a scene. (2) A musical signal or prompt to alert a performer to enter or exit the stage or to begin singing, playing, speaking, or dancing. (3) Music used to introduce a person or event on a radio or television broadcast.

Music Cutter

In television or film production, a person who cuts, assembles, and *splices* music tracks to *synchronize* with film or videotape. Also called *music editor*.

Music Director

(1) At a radio station, person that screens and selects recordings for airplay. See also *program director*. (2) Person hired by an artist to rehearse and lead backing bands on the road. (3) Person who scores and arranges music for films, television programs, commercials, or *library services*, and who usually also conducts the orchestra recording the music for such usages. (4) Person employed by hotels, resorts, theaters, churches, arts centers, community centers, etc. to organize musical events, book musicians and orchestras, lead in-house orchestras, etc. (5) A *conductor*.

Music Editor

(1) In film, video, and television production, person who chooses, cuts, assembles, and splices music soundtracks to synchronize with film or videotape. See also *music cutter*. (2) In music print publishing, a person who makes editorial decisions on material to be published, including choice of material and preparation for publication (i.e., adaptations, corrections, revisions, proofreading, and supervisory coordination of design, printing, collation, binding, and marketing.)

Music Format

The type of programming focused on by a radio station (i.e., *CHR*, *quiet storm*, *urban contemporary*, etc.). See below.

Music Format Abbreviations

The following are commonly used abbreviations to denote the style of music programmed by a radio station or reviewed in a periodical:

AAA - Adult Album Alternative
AC - Adult Contemporary
B - Blues
BG - Bluegrass
C - Country
CH - Christian
CHR - Contemporary Hit Radio (Top 40)
CL - Classical
D - Dance
E - Ethnic
F - Folk
G - Gospel
I - Industrial
J - Jazz
M - Metal
NA - New Age
NAC - New Adult Contemporary
QS - Quiet Storm
R - Rock
RA - Rap
R&B - Rhythm & Blues
R&R - Rock & Roll
RG - Reggae
SW - Spoken Word
UC - Urban Contemporary
WB - World Beat

Music Hall

In Great Britain, a widely popular forum for musical and variety entertainment, especially between the mid-1800s and the outbreak of World War I in 1914. Like *vaudeville* in America, music hall offered comedy skits, song-and-dance acts, magicians, jugglers, acrobats, mimes, etc. Though the music hall tradition is still found in some areas of northern England, the term now refers to a musical style or type of act reminiscent of music hall's heyday.

Music House

See *music supply house*.

Music Instruction Book

A book of musical arrangements for a particular instrument with playing instructions, hints, and tips, published primarily for students or learners. Also called a *method book*.

Music Jobber

Also called a *selling agent*. Company or independent contractor appointed to sell printed music to retailers on behalf of a music publisher. While a music jobber may only be a distributor, a selling agent is also usually a print publisher with expertise in designing, printing, distributing, and selling sheet music. Instead of licensing the original music publisher's works in return for a royalty on sales, however, the production costs are paid by the publisher and the agent pays all sales revenue to the publisher less a commission, usually in the range of 25%.

Music Performance Trust Fund

Under the *Phonographic Trust Agreement* between the *AFM* and *signatory* record labels, record companies are required to pay a small percentage of the price of each recording sold into the Music Performance Trust Fund. The purpose of the fund is to employ union musicians to perform in public places, such as parks, veterans' homes, schools, etc. These performances provide free entertainment for public benefit, promote live music, and provide income for union members.

Music Preparation

The process of reproducing a *score* and its various parts for an orchestra, including the copying out of individual parts for each instrument, proofreading, collating, binding, and delivery.

Music Publishers Association (MPA)

(1) Founded in 1895, the Music Publishers' Association is the oldest music trade organization in the United States, fostering communication among publishers, dealers, music educators, and all ultimate users of music. MPA focuses on issues pertaining to every area of music publishing for the advancement of standard, contemporary, and educational music. The MPA serves the industry through its presence at and cooperation with various important organizations such as CMPA, MSENC, MTNA, MLA, ACDA, RSMDA, ASCAP, BMI, SESAC, International Federation of Serious Music Publishers, and through its relations with the *National Music Publishers Association* (NMPA). (2) MPA is also the name of the British trade association of music publishers.

Music Publishers Protective Association (MPPA)

Original name of what is now called the *National Music Publishers Association* (NMPA).

Music Rights Organization

An agency or society formed to license mechanical, synchronization, performance, and/or other rights on behalf of music copyright owners and to collect fees and royalties from licensees. *Examples*: BMI and *ASCAP* (*performing rights*) and *The Harry Fox Agency* (*mechanical* and *synchronization rights*).

Music Row

Area of Nashville, Tennessee where the principal record companies, music publishers, studios, agents, and management companies are located.

Music Supervisor

Person in charge of music for a film, television, or theatrical production. Duties include selecting the music or composers, clearing rights from music copyright owners, and/or booking musicians, perform-ers, rehearsal halls, studios, etc. See also *music coordinator*.

Music Supplier

See *music supply house*, below.

Music Supply House

Also called *music house* or *music supplier*. A music production company that creates custom music for film producers, broadcasters, advertisers, et al, using staff or contractors (composers, arrangers, and performers) who work to *specs* submitted by clients. Many supply houses also maintain libraries of ready-made recorded music for clients to choose "off the shelf." See also *recorded music library*.

Music Television

See *MTV*.

Music Theater

A modern musical work, somewhat similar to opera, combining visual and dramatic elements and requiring a staged presentation.

Music Theory

A systematic, analytical study of music, including its classifications, characteristics of various genres and instruments, and its accepted principles and rules.

Music Therapy

The theory, research, and study of clinical and practical applications of the power of music to heal and music's impact on physical, cognitive, emotional, and spiritual well-being.

Music Trades

A trade periodical catering to professionals in the music business, located at 80 West Street, Englewood, NJ 07631.

Music User

Any company, organization, or individual who licenses music from copyright owners for commercial usage. *Examples*: record companies, recording artists, record producers, broadcasters, film producers, advertising agencies, software developers.

Music Video

A videotaped performance of a recorded song, typically featuring choreographed dancers, actors or models, imaginative sets or location shots, and characterized by stylized cinematography, quick cuts, and computer imaging. "Short-form" music videos (also called *clips*, a performance of one song only) are most often produced by record companies to promote new releases, and are therefore geared to younger audiences who are more likely to purchase the most current and fashionable records. "Long-form" video albums may also be produced for commercial release.

Music videos are frequently more expensive to produce than the recordings they are used to promote. They have developed into an innovative art form, and their production techniques have had much influence on advertising, television, and film production. Originally popularized by screenings on *MTV* and *VH-1* cable networks catering to pop and rock viewers, they are now common to all popular music genres (i.e., R&B, rap, country, etc.). See also *video rights* and *promotional music video*.

Music Week

A trade magazine catering to the music business in Great Britain, located at Greater London House, Hampstead Road, London NW1 7QZ, England.

Musical

A play or movie incorporating music, chorus dancing, and topical numbers woven into the storyline. The plot is developed by dialogue as well as the lyrics of the songs, and the music is thus an integral part of the overall production, rather than being merely incidental. Musicals are essentially an evolution of *operetta* as a form of entertainment, relying on memorable songs, duets, and choruses to achieve popular success. Also called *musical comedy*. See also *musical play* and *grand rights*.

Musical Comedy

See *musical*, above, and *musical play*.

Musical Instrument Digital Interface (MIDI)

An international standard communications protocol for exchanging information between computers and electronic music instruments. MIDI transmits commands that control sounds by affecting parameters such as pitch, tone, reverb, and timing. MIDI has evolved into a widely available, relatively inexpensive technology used by many professional musicians, producers, and artists to enhance recording projects. Modern electronic music is commonly produced using MIDI-controlled *synthesizers* and instruments to simulate pianos, organs, guitars, brass, strings, bass, and drums, etc., as well as electronic instruments connected to one another and to computer-driven *sequencers*, synthesizers, *samplers*, *drum machines*, and *signal-processing* devices.

Musical Notation

A system of universally accepted symbols arranged on a *staff* of five lines to comprise a written record of musical sounds so musicians can perform the music as the composer or arranger intended. In addition to symbols for each tonal *pitch*, other symbols indicate time value, meter, rhythm, key, ex-

pression, and dynamics. Notations often are accompanied by phrases, usually in Italian, indicating tempo and interpretation. In *electronic music*, standardized notations may be combined with specially adapted rhythm and pitch notations and/or written instructions. Also called *nomenclature*. See also *Nashville Number System*.

Musical Play

A play that incorporates music as an integral part of the plot or storyline (as opposed to a *play with music*, which is a dramatic play that uses music to set the atmosphere, but not to develop the action of the story). In a musical play, the music is essential to the development of the storyline and therefore to the production; in a play with music, the music is *incidental* to the story (i.e., it enhances the performance, but is not essential). See also *musical*, *musical comedy*, and *grand rights*.

Musical Product

Music created for and converted into commercially available, tangible formats, such as sheet music, records, CDs, audiotapes, music boxes, musical toys and games, etc. See also *musical product license*, below.

Musical Product License

Permission authorizing the *mechanical reproduction* of a copyrighted musical work as an integral part of a consumer product, such as a doll, toy, music box, novelty items (doorbells, cigarette lighters, greeting cards, etc.) that play music upon activation. Musical product licenses may take the form of a *mechanical license* in audio-only formats, or, where sound is *synchronized* with vision, the license may be similar to a *videogram license*.

Musical Revue

A stage or cabaret show incorporating skits, songs, and dances, linked by dialogue, narration, or a monologue, though there is no plot or storyline. Revues typically incorporate previously written songs, often by different songwriters.

Musical Switch

A medley consisting of just a few bars each of several popular tunes, with each melodic fragment neatly dovetailed into the next, thereby "switching" from one tune to another.

Musical Works Fund

Under the *Audio Home Recording Act of 1992*, one-third of all taxes collected on the sale of digital recorders and blank digital recording tape are placed in this fund for distribution to songwriters and copyright owners of the songs recorded and distributed on digital recordings. Of the revenues placed in the

Musical Works Fund, songwriters receive 50% and song copyright owners the other 50%.

The remaining two-thirds of revenues collected under the act goes into the *Sound Recording Fund* for distribution to copyright owners of sound recordings distributed in digital formats, and to the featured artists, and nonfeatured backing vocalists and musicians whose performances are included on digital recordings. Nonfeatured vocalists are allocated 1.375% of revenues placed in the Sound Recording Fund; nonfeatured musicians receive 2.725%; featured artists receive 38.36%; and copyright owners of the sound recording (usually the record company) receive 57.54%. See also *Digital Audio Recorders and Tape (DART)*.

Musicale

A "musical evening" of social entertainment with music as the focal point.

Musicality

(1) Having an ear or talent for music. (2) A musical quality.

MUSICAUTOR

The *performing-right society* in Bulgaria.

Musician

A magazine catering to professional musicians, focusing on performance techniques, new technologies, reviews, and interviews, located at 49 Music Square West, Nashville, TN 37203. Tel: (615) 321-9160; Fax: (615) 321-9170.

Musician's Incentive Agreement

An agreement between a record producer or record company and studio musicians that gives the musicians a *royalty override* in sales of recordings they play on.

Musicology

The study of music as a field of knowledge, as opposed to practical application. See also *music theory*.

Mutual Consent

Where all parties are in accord, in agreement, in consensus.

Muzak

Trademarked name of a *background music service* company that supplies recorded music in over 60 formats to business subscribers via wire or FM radio links. Located at 400 N. 34th Street, Suite 200, Seattle, WA 98103. Tel: (206) 633-3000; Fax: (206) 633-6210.

MVPA

Abbreviation for *Music Video Producers Association*.

N Form

Under the *Copyright Act of 1909* (as amended in 1972), copyright claims for sound recordings were registered with the *Copyright Office* using Form N. Under the *Copyright Act of 1976*, effective January 1, 1978, however, copyright claim registrations for sound recordings are made with *Form SR*. The N Form is now obsolete.

NA

Music format abbreviation for *new age*.

NAB

Abbreviation for *National Association of Broadcasters*.

NAC

Abbreviation for *New Adult Contemporary* (*New Age*).

NAFTA

Acronym for *North American Free Trade Agreement*.

NAIRD

Acronym for *National Association of Independent Record Distributors*. See also *Association For Independent Music (AFIM)*.

Name Artist

A recording artist who has established a large market base of fans; one who has *marquee value* or *name value*.

Name Rights

The right to use the name of a personality in order to promote, publicize, and advertise a product. The right to use a name in merchandising and endorsements can be a valuable asset. While names can't be copyrighted, they can be protected in various ways, principally through established professional and trade usage, which can shield rights to a name under *trademark*, and *unfair competition* laws. Where the name of a group or band is involved, individual members should have a written agreement defining how ownership of the name is to be shared, what happens to the share of a member who leaves the group, who owns the name in the event the group disbands, etc.

Name Value

(1) A performer whose reputation is sufficiently well established to draw fans to a performance or to purchase a product bearing his/her name. Same as *marquee value*. (2) The appraised worth of a company over and above its tangible assets, which is attributable to *goodwill* (the reputation established over the years, resulting in a market base of loyal customers for the company's product).

Namibian Society of Authors & Composers of Music (NASCAM)

The *performing-right society* in Namibia.

NAMM

Acronym for *National Association of Music Merchandisers*.

NAPM

Abbreviation for *the National Academy Of Popular Music*.

NARAS

Acronym for *National Academy of Recording Arts & Sciences*.

NARM

Acronym for *National Association of Record Merchandisers*.

Narration

(1) A running commentary for a movie, documentary, or performance. (2) A *spoken word* recording.

Narrowcasting

The *transmission* (especially by *cable* or *closed-circuit* delivery) to a select audience of viewers, listeners, or subscribers, of programs tailored to the specific interests and tastes of the audience—as opposed to *broadcasting*, which transmits programs indiscriminately to the population as a whole. The term has also come to mean programming to the tastes of a narrowly focused audience even though the mode of transmission is a broadcast available to all.

NAS

Abbreviation for *National Academy of Songwriters*.

NASCAM

Acronym for *Namibian Society of Authors & Composers of Music*.

Nashville Number System

A method of *musical notation* associated with Nashville *session musicians*, which essentially assigns numbers, rather than letters, to chords, and which allows musicians to quickly follow a song's chord changes and to improvise parts and *head arrangements* in any key.

Nashville Songwriters Association International (NSAI)

A nonprofit trade organization established in 1967 for professional songwriters. Currently representing over 4,500 songwriters worldwide, NSAI educates its members on copyright and contract issues, puts on workshops, and lobbies for stronger legislative copyright protection. NSAI's offices are located at 15 Music Square West, Nashville, TN 37203. Tel: (615) 256-3354.

NASM

Abbreviation for *National Association of Schools of Music*.

National Account

(1) An advertising agency client whose ads are featured in national media, as opposed to local or regional outlets. (2) A large wholesale customer, such as a national chain of record shops, who buys product centrally for resale at branch or franchised locations throughout the country.

National Academy of Recording Arts & Sciences (NARAS)

Trade organization of companies and individuals professionally active in the recording industry, including ancillary professions, such as management, music publishing, songwriting, music videos, album artwork, etc. Founded in 1957, NARAS currently has over 8,000 members. It maintains the NARAS Foundation, which promotes the archiving and preservation of original sound recordings, stages Grammy in the Schools to educate students about the recording industry, manages MusicCares, provides scholarships, research grants, educational materials, and workshops. The organization produces the annual *Grammy Awards*, has several regional chapters, and is headquartered at 3402 Pico Blvd., Santa Monica, CA 90045. Tel: (310) 392-3777. See also *Grammy* and *Grammy in the Schools*.

National Academy of Songwriters (NAS)

Trade organization for more than 3,000 professional songwriters, located at 6255 Hollywood Blvd., Hollywood, CA 90028. Tel: (213) 463-7178. Formerly *Songwriters Resources and Services*, the Academy has operated a *song registration service* since 1974 to provide a method of documenting copyright claims to musical works, which is less expensive than registration fees required for filing copyright claims with the *Copyright Office* of the *Library of Congress*. Upon receipt of a tape, disc, or lead sheet, NAS issues a registration number for the work, seals it, and files it in a vault. The service is bonded to insure against unauthorized tampering with registered songs. The service is used primarily by authors of unpublished works. When an NAS registered work is published, the author usually then proceeds with formal copyright registration with the Library of Congress.

NAS recently merged with *Los Angeles Songwriters Showcase* (*LASS*), and now also offers all LASS services as well as promoting the LASS weekly showcase. LASS as a separate organization has ceased to exist.

National Association of Broadcasters (NAB)

Trade organization for the radio and television industries, NAB's mission is to maintain a favorable governmental, legal, and technological climate for the constantly evolving and dynamic business of free over-the-air broadcasting. The Association represents members' interests before Congress, the FCC and other federal agencies, the courts, and on the international front. NAB is located at 1771 "N" Street NW, Washington, DC. Tel: (202) 293-3500.

National Association of Independent Record Distributors (NAIRD)

Now called *Association For Independent Music* (*AFIM*). A trade organization consisting of non-major, independent record distributors and record labels. Founded in 1972, the association's mission is to strengthen the clout of *indie* operations, offering information and co-op support on marketing, promotions, advertising, and manufacturing activities. AFIM stages a convention every spring where distributors and labels can solidify relationships, exchange views, attend educational seminars, buy and sell product, etc. AFIM is located at P.O. Box 568, Maple Shade, NJ 08052-0568. Tel: (609) 547-3331.

National Association of Music Merchandisers (NAMM)

Trade association comprising retailers, distributors, and suppliers of musical instruments, equipment, accessories, and music-related publications and software. The organization stages trade shows twice a year where manufacturers, suppliers, and publishers can introduce new product to distributors and retailers. Also provides market research, business training, and industry publications. Located at 500 N Michigan Avenue, Chicago, IL 60611. Tel: (312) 527-3200.

National Academy Of Popular Music (NAPM)

Founded in 1969, the Academy is the custodian for the *Songwriters Hall of Fame*. The membership consists of songwriters and artistic and business figures within the music industry. NAPM stages an annual induction and awards ceremony for songwriters. Each year, a nominating committee selects candidates for induction into the Songwriters Hall of Fame. Only writers who have actually been engaged in the profession for a minimum of 20 years, and who have written an extensive catalogue of hit songs are eligible. The 20-year limit is waived in the consideration of posthumous awards if the writer in question made a major impact on the course of popular music before achieving two full decades of productivity. NAPM also maintains extensive archives of songwriter memorabilia, publishes a newsletter, awards scholarships, and sponsors songwriter showcases and workshops.

National Association of Record Merchandisers (NARM)

Trade organization consisting of over 1,000 companies involved in the sale and distribution of recorded product and related services and accessories. Members include record companies, distributors, wholesalers, one-stops, rack jobbers, retailers, and merchandising suppliers. NARM stages an annual trade convention where distributors and labels can solidify relationships, exchange views, buy and sell product, etc. It also stages seminars, lobbies legislatures on industry concerns, publishes a newsletter, and supplies merchandising materials and tips to members. NARM is located at 10008 F. Astonia Blvd., Cherry Hill, NJ 08034. Tel: (609) 427-1404.

National Chart

A recognized, definitive listing of the currently most popular recordings in the country, such as those published by *Billboard* and *Cash Box*.

National Code of Fair Practices for Phonograph Recordings

An agreement regulated by *AFTRA*, which binds record labels who sign the agreement to pay *union scale* to vocalists on recording sessions. Union wage-scales vary according to the number of songs recorded, type of session (i.e., masters, demos, film scores, etc.), number of instruments played, time of day session takes place (i.e., after regular business hours, weekends, holidays, etc.), number of hours the session lasts, etc. Union members are prohibited from working for record companies that don't sign the agreement, and are also prohibited from working with non-union vocalists on recording sessions. See also *Phonograph Record Labor Agreement*.

National Conference of Personal Managers (NCOPM)

A trade association of personal managers in the United States, comprising regional and national offices. The organization sets standards for conduct and provides model contract forms.

National Educational Television (NET)

Now called *Public Broadcasting Service* (PBS), a network association of public, noncommercial television stations. PBS became government-financed under the aegis of the *Corporation for Public Broadcasting* in 1968, and today receives a large portion of its funding through viewer subscriptions and corporate underwriting, thus circumventing the commercial pressures of achieving the audience ratings necessary to attract paid advertisers. As such, public television concentrates its programming on documentaries, panel discussions, children's educational shows, and the arts. See also *National Public Radio* (NPR) and *Corporation for Public Broadcasting* (CPB).

National Endowment for the Arts (NEA)

A funding agency established by Congress in 1965 to promote wider access to the arts through subsidies granted to museums, symphony orchestras, ballet and opera companies, artists, musicians, composers, etc. The agency is located at 1100 Pennsylvania Avenue NW, Washington, DC 20506. Tel: (202) 682-5400; Fax: (202) 682-5617.

National Music Council (NMC)

An umbrella association of approximately 50 commercial and noncommercial music trade groups, including *ASCAP*, *BMI*, *SESAC*, *NMPA*, *RIAA*, *CMA*, *ACA*, *AFM*, etc.

National Music Publishers Association (NMPA)

Trade organization for music publishers, founded in 1917 as the *Music Publishers Protective Association*. The association founded the *Harry Fox Agency* in 1927, which it continues to operate as a wholly-owned subsidiary. The NMPA actively addresses copyright issues arising from infringement and technological changes, lobbies for stronger statutory copyright protections, and takes advisory roles with *CARP*, the *Copyright Office*, *CISAC*, and other industry and governmental organizations. Located at 205 E. 42nd Street, New York, NY 10017. Tel: (212) 370-5330.

National Promotion

One of three layers of record promotion. A *national promotion* person usually concentrates on a specific genre or market segment, such as R&B. (A *local promotion* person generally covers a specific region or territory on all types of product released by a record company, and an *indie promotion* person is hired to promote a specific release.)

National Public Radio (NPR)

A network association of local nonprofit public radio stations, which produces and transmits news and other programming on a noncommercial basis, and which is funded through the *Corporation for Public Broadcasting,* individual contributions, and underwriting from corporate and foundation donors. Located at 635 Massachusetts Avenue NW, Washington, DC 20001. Tel: (202) 414-2000; Fax: (202) 414-3329.

National Sound Archive

A British organization founded in 1948 as an archival depository for sound recordings. The organization's mission is to obtain, catalog, and preserve copies of every recording produced in every genre, and to make them available for research. Formerly known as the *British Institute of Recorded Sound.*

National Television Standards Committee (NTSC)

Organization that sets and oversees technical standards for video and television transmissions. The NTSC standard is used in North America and Japan, contrasting with *PAL (Phase Alternation by Line)* adopted in Europe.

Nature of Use

A definition or exact description as to how a copyright is used by a *licensee.* In licensing copyrights, copyright owners narrowly define the scope of the permission being granted, and licenses must be very specific about how, where, when, and under what conditions copyrights can be used. One of the determining factors as to how much the *licensor* should pay the copyright owner for use of a work is the "nature of use" (i.e., exactly how the licensee intends to use the work).

Typical usages of music copyrights include *performance* (broadcast, jukeboxes, background music, live entertainment), *mechanical reproduction* (records, tapes), *synchronization* (audiovisual productions, such as movies, documentaries, videotapes), *print* (sheet music, lyric reprints), *transcriptions* (recorded library services, in-flight entertainment, background music services) etc. The nature of use may be further defined within the scope of a license. For instance, a synchronization license for a song used in a movie may restrict the permission to a maximum amount of playing time (i.e., 30 seconds), and exposure (i.e., incidental background usage as opposed to a performance featured onscreen), etc.

NCB

Abbreviation for *NORDISK Copyright Bureau,* the *mechanical-right society* in Scandinavia.

NCB TEOSTO

The *mechanical-right society* in Finland.

NCOPM

Abbreviation for *National Conference of Personal Managers.*

NEA

Abbreviation for *National Endowment for the Arts.*

Needle

On the *tone arm* of a phonograph record player, a small *stylus* that picks up vibrations from the grooves of a turning phonograph record. The vibrations are transmitted through circuitry in the tone arm and converted into audio signals that are amplified through loudspeakers.

Needle Drop

Term used to describe the insertion of a short prerecorded sound effect or musical passage from a *recorded music library* into a broadcast program, commercial, or film.

Needle Drop Music

Prerecorded music tracks available from *recorded music libraries.* Also called *canned music, library music,* or *production music.* Producers of low-budget films, documentaries, training films, television programs, commercials, etc. frequently license canned tracks from library services, which provide master quality recordings and rights to use the track and the underlying music copyright, all at one relatively low fee.

Needle Time

British broadcasting term used to describe the amount of airtime allotted for playing phonorecords.

Negative

A film or photographic plate containing a reverse image whose light areas appear dark and dark areas appear light, from which "positive images" are produced. In film developing, the negative is photographed and processed to reverse the shading, thereby producing the final print (the positive image).

Negative Cash Flow

The condition of having spent more cash for expenses and other transactions during an accounting period than a company or individual takes in through earnings and other receipts. See also *cash flow* and *positive cash flow*.

Negative Cost

Production and delivery costs of a film or television program before promotion expenses are factored.

Negative Master

A metal *stamper* created from an *electroplated* positive master (a *mother*), which is used to *press* phonorecords. Also called a *father*.

Negative Tour Support

An arrangement between a recording company and a recording artist whereby the company advances the artist a sum of money equal to the difference between income generated by a tour and the artist's expenses.

Negotiated License

A permission to use a copyright under terms negotiated and agreed between the copyright owner and the *user*. The term itself normally refers to a *mechanical license* issued by a music publisher to a record company when both parties agree to waive the *compulsory licensing* provision of the *Copyright Act of 1976*. This provision states, in effect, that once a song is recorded and commercially released, the copyright owner cannot prevent others from also recording and releasing it, as long as new users (a) serve a *notice of intention* on the copyright owner (before any recordings are distributed and within 30 days after recording the work); (b) pay *mechanical royalties* at the *statutory rate* by the 20th of each month for all recordings distributed in the preceding month; (c) make each monthly accounting sworn under oath; (d) make cumulative, annual statements, certified by a *CPA*.

The terms of the compulsory licensing provision are rather cumbersome for record companies to comply with, and, in practice, most publishers issue mechanical licenses to legitimate record companies under terms of a "negotiated" mechanical license. In contrast with a statutory compulsory license, negotiated licenses do not require record companies to serve notices of intention, accountings don't have to be under oath, cumulative annual accountings certified by a CPA are not required; also, royalties may be paid quarterly, rather than monthly, and the mechanical royalty rate may be less than statutory, if the copyright owner agrees.

Neighboring Rights

Also called *related rights*. In the use of copyrighted song material, the *user* typically generates either tangible or intangible properties which have rights in and of themselves, and which belong to the user, not the *author* of the copyrighted material. *Examples*: rights stemming from a performance belong to the performer; copyright in a sound recording belongs to the producer of the recording; copyright to a television program belongs to the program's producer.

Neighboring Rights Collective of Canada (NRCC)

A music rights agency that collects and distributes royalties arising from *neighboring rights* (see above) in the *public performance* and *telecommunication* of sound recordings in Canada.

Neo-

A prefix used to describe a style reminiscent of, or representing a return to, an earlier genre. *Example*: neo-classical.

Net

(1) Abbreviated reference to a *network*, as in a radio, television, or telephone network. (2) The bottom line, as in the "net result" or final outcome. (3) The amount of income left after all expenses are deducted (i.e., the net profit, or the net loss). (4) To make a profit.

Net Sales

Amount of gross income collected from sales less returns, allowances, cash discounts, and shipping.

NET

Acronym for *National Educational Television*.

Network

(1) A group of radio or television stations linked by wire or microwave relay to broadcast programs originating from one source. (2) A radio or television company that produces and transmits programs for affiliated stations to broadcast locally. (3) A group of people or organizations informally linked through mutual interests, who interact for mutual assistance or support. (4) To informally interact with others for mutual assistance or support. (5) Two or more computers linked by cables, modems or other devices in order to share or exchange data, hardware, and/or software resources. In computing, a *local area network* (*LAN*) links two or more personal computers (PCs) over dedicated, private lines; a *wide area network* (*WAN*) links large numbers (or networks) of computers via communications equipment.

Networking

The use of an informal group of *contacts* within a group of people who share common interests, concerns, and professional activities in order to gather information, develop business or job prospects, or seek assistance.

New Adult Contemporary (NAC)
Alternative name for *New Age* music. See below.

New Age
(1) A 1980s movement promoting spiritualism and holistic solutions to health and ecology concerns. (2) A musical genre associated with the New Age movement, chiefly characterized by ethereal instrumental improvisations on synthesizers and/or acoustic pianos, guitars, etc., and sometimes blended with ethnic rhythm and/or wind instruments. Also called *New Adult Contemporary*.

New Country
A musical genre that blends traditional country music with modern pop and rock.

New Entry
A song or recording making its first appearance on a sales or airplay *chart*.

New Media
Term broadly applied to newer technologies, such as MIDI, CD-ROM, Internet applications, video games, karaoke, interactive television, etc.

New Music
A late 20th century musical genre characterized by *atonal*, nontraditional harmonies, free-form rhythms patterns and meter, etc., and frequently composed and performed using sound synthesis computer software, *synthesizers*, *sequencers*, etc. See also *electronic music*.

New Music Seminar (NMS)
Now defunct, NMS was a popular showcase and music industry forum for upcoming artists, indie labels, etc. It was held in New York City every summer from 1980 to 1994.

New On The Charts
Monthly trade magazine listing details of *new entries* to national Pop, R&B, and Country record and video charts, including contact addresses and phone numbers of companies, producers, publishers, agents, etc. Located at 70 Laurel Place, New Rochelle, NY 10801. Tel: (914) 632-3349.

New Punk
Variant of *house music*, sometimes called *acid house*, a music genre and lifestyle gaining favor between 1987 and 1991. It represented a reaction to status-conscious dress codes and superstar recording artists of the earlier 1980s.

New Use
The use of copyrighted material in new formats or media other than that for which it was originally licensed. For example, a *mechanical license* granted to a record company by the song copyright owner does not apply to the new use of the sound recording. For instance, the use of a hit single in a television commercial constitutes a new use requiring new licenses from the copyright owner of the song, as well as the copyright owner of the sound recording. And, when a music service, such as *Muzak*, uses original recordings for *foreground music* transmission, rather than re-recording songs with custom arrangements, as for *background music*, a new use license must be acquired from the copyright owners of the song and of the sound recording. Producers of films and television movies wishing to *synchronize* a hit single in a production must also negotiate new use licenses as well as new use payments to artist's and musician's unions, such as *AFTRA* and *AFM*.

New Wave
A genre of rock music characterized by synthesized instruments, repetitive or sequenced beats, and (often) aggressive vocal renditions of lyrics dealing with social issues and alienation with popular culture, etc. New Wave emerged in the mid-to-late 1970s as the American counterpart to, and concurrent with, the *Punk Rock* movement in Great Britain.

New Wave of New Wave
A mid-1990s British reaction to *dream pop*, which became a forerunner of the *BritPop* music movement.

Next of Kin
The person(s) most closely related by blood to another person. Next of kin are normally entitled to share the personal assets of someone who dies *intestate* (i.e., without a legal will). Thus, a deceased copyright owner's royalties must be paid by a licensee to the next of kin, absent a will directing otherwise. See also *statutory beneficiary*.

Niche
(1) A narrowly defined area of specialization or interest. (2) A particular activity or interest that best matches a person's natural talents or abilities.

Niche Market
A narrowly defined audience, or area of consumer demand, for a musical style, product, or some type of service. The term is frequently used to describe a situation where a company or individual parlays a special expertise or talent into a dominant share of a relatively small *market universe*, and the market is too small to attract serious competition.

Nickelodeon
(1) Term originally applied to movie theaters early in the 20th century when typical admission cost a nickel, and to five-cent coin-operated player pianos

located in bars and cafes. The term was adapted to apply to *jukeboxes*, which replaced player pianos. (2) A cable television channel, located at 1515 Broadway, 20th Floor, New York, NY 10036. Tel: (212) 258-8000; Fax: (212) 258-7666.

Nielsen, A.C.

The A.C. Nielsen Company, Inc. conducts research into local and national markets to determine the size of an audience tuned into a selected broadcast program, station, or network. The company is located at 299 Park Avenue, New York, NY 10071. Tel: (212) 708-7500; Fax: (212) 708-7795.

Nielsen Rating

The result, expressed in percentages of audience share, of research conducted by the *A. C. Nielsen Company, Inc.*, which rates the popularity of a particular broadcast program, station, or network as of the period of time in which the research was carried out. See also *sweeps*.

Nineteen-Year Extension

Under the *Copyright Act of 1976*, copyrights then in existence, which were eligible for 28-year renewal terms under the *Copyright Act of 1909*, were given an additional 19 years of copyright protection so that, with renewal, they would have a total term of protection for 75 years (28 years original term, plus 28 years renewal, plus 19 years extended renewal).

Nintendo

An electronic game maker, located at 4820 150th Avenue NE, Redmond, WA 98052. Tel: (206) 882-2040; Fax: (206) 882-3585.

NMC

Abbreviation for *National Music Council*.

NMPA

Abbreviation for *National Music Publishers Association*.

NMS

Abbreviation for *New Music Seminar*.

Noise Reduction System

An electronic device used to filter out, cancel, or reduce high-frequency background noises and *hiss* on *analog* tape recordings. See *Dolby system* and *dbx*.

Nom de Plume

A *pen name* or *pseudonym*.

Nomenclature

A system of universally accepted symbols arranged on a *staff* of five ledger lines to comprise a written record of musical sounds so musicians can perform the music as the composer or arranger intended. See *musical notation*.

Nonbinding

(1) A decision, resolution, or understanding which has no force in law. (2) A situation or circumstance which imposes no legal obligation. (3) A contract or license *voided* by mutual agreement of the parties involved or by a judicial ruling.

Noncommercial

(1) A product that proves to have no market demand, or is judged to be without commercial appeal. (2) A service rendered, performance given, or product made for free and/or delivered or distributed without a profit motive.

Noncommercial Station

A not-for-profit local television or radio station that is funded by individual and corporate contributions, subscriptions, endowments, and/or government subsidies, and which does not rely on advertisers for operating costs. Also called a *public station*. See also *Public Broadcasting Service*, *National Public Radio*, and *Corporation for Public Broadcasting*.

Noncommercial Transmission

The not-for-profit broadcast of a television or radio program or announcement (i.e., not paid for by viewers, listeners, or advertisers). Examples include *public service announcements (PSA)*, emergency broadcasts, and programming via *National Public Radio*, *Public Broadcasting Service*, college radio and/or local public stations.

Nondisclosure Agreement

(1) An agreement or contract provision (aka *confidentiality clause*) in which one party acknowledges it is, or will be, entrusted with another's *proprietary* information (such as financial position, product development and marketing plans, contractual terms with artists or songwriters, etc.), and agrees not to disclose such information to any other party without permission. Such an agreement or a provision often is part of a business plan, sale prospectus, financing proposal, private stock placement, employment agreement, or partnership agreement. (2) A contractual provision in an agreement between an artist, songwriter, producer, or other party and a record company, music publisher, etc., which prohibits either party from disclosing the terms of the agreement to anyone other than their respective legal and financial advisers and government agencies. The reason for such a clause, from the company's viewpoint, is that the size of an advance and/or royalty given to one artist (or songwriter, producer, etc.) may upset other signees who received less, or may be used as benchmark negotiating positions by others the company wants to sign in the future.

Nondramatic Performance

The performance of a song *as* a song, as opposed to a song being performed as an integral part of a dramatic production. For instance, even though the song "Memories" is an integral part of the musical play *Cats*, it can be extracted from the play and used in numerous nondramatic contexts (i.e., a recording played on radio, a live piano bar rendition, a background music transcription, etc.). By contrast, a *dramatic performance* is where a song is performed in the context of a musical play or otherwise rendered by acting out the storyline. See *small rights* and *grand rights*.

Nonexclusive

A license, service, or circumstance that does not exclude similar licenses being issued for the same work, or similar services being performed for others, or similar circumstances from arising. For instance, a *mechanical license* is nonexclusive, meaning that a copyright owner can license the same song to several record companies simultaneously, resulting in several recordings of the song being released by different artists on different labels. Another example is that of an independent producer who produces recordings by different artists for different record companies without conflict of interest.

Non-Musical Play

A theatrical production where music (for themes, cues, segues, etc.) is commissioned after the play is written. *Plays with music* are dramatic plays that use music to set the atmosphere, but not to develop the action of the story. In both types of productions, the music is incidental: It enhances the presentation, but is not essential to the story.

Nonprofit

Something produced, formed, or presented without motive for financial gain.

Nonprofit Performance

Under the *Copyright Act of 1976*, copyright owners maintain licensing rights to songs *publicly performed* at not-for-profit events, such as charity balls, school dances, fraternal lodge parties, religious broadcasts, etc. There are, however, four exceptions where *nonprofit* public performances are exempt from licensing requirements: (1) religious services that are not broadcast; (2) performances at events where there is no admission fee, either directly (ticket sales), or indirectly (contributions, club membership, etc.), and no direct or indirect fee is paid to performers; (3) classroom teaching by nonprofit educational institutions; and (4) certain nonprofit educational and governmental public service broadcasts of instructional materials. See also *performance license, performance royalty, performance fee*, and *performing-right society*.

Non-Returnable Advance

An advance against potential royalty earnings, which is only *recoupable* against royalty income that actually materializes. The recipient isn't obligated to repay the balance of any unrecouped portion of the advance. Where advances are paid in music business deals and licensing agreements, they are almost always done so on a non-returnable basis.

Non-Returnable Deposit

A fee paid to secure an option to acquire an object or the right to use something, and which does not have to be refunded in the event the depositor decides not to take full possession of the object or to acquire the right.

Example: A movie producer might want to base a movie script on the title and lyrics of a song. Since the song is essential to the film project, the film producer takes an *option* on the song, so the publisher won't license it to others while production details are finalized.

The option may require the producer to pay the publisher a deposit equal to a percentage of the ultimate *synchronization fee* as a *non-returnable advance*. Alternatively, the publisher may insist on a deposit as an option *fee*, rather than an advance. The fee pays for the privilege of holding the song without regard to the amount paid for the full synchronization fee. Option payments made as fees may not be deducted from the ultimate synchronization fee. In either case, if the project doesn't materialize, the publisher does not have to return the deposit.

Non-Theatrical Synchronization

A musical work *synchronized* with a noncommercial film or videotaped production. Many large corporations and government agencies make audiovisual programs for training, informational, and business-to-business promotional purposes. No commercial use is intended, in so far as exhibition to the paying public or sale of *videograms*.

Distribution of the work is usually restricted to in-house screenings or *closed circuit* videoconferencing—as opposed to commercial, or *theatrical* showings. If the *user* desires to make videocassettes for distribution to employees, trainees, or prospective clients, an additional fee is charged, usually based on the number of copies to be made.

Nonunion

(1) A person who does not belong to a trade, craft, or labor union, and is not subject to a union labor agreement governing minimum wages, hours, and other conditions of employment. (2) A company that does not recognize the right of a trade union to dictate its conditions of employment, and does not, therefore, employ union members. See also *closed shop* and *open shop*.

NORDISK Copyright Bureau (NCB)

A *mechanical-right society* based in Denmark, also covering Sweden, Norway, Finland, and Iceland. Located at: Frederiksgade 17, Copenhagen DK 1265. Tel: (01) 12.87.00.

Normal Bias

Also called *standard bias*. Bias is the adjustment of the strength of a magnetic field applied during the recording process to a *magnetic tape*. High-frequency voltage combined with an audio signal reduces distortion in tape recording. Audiocassettes are graded according to dynamic range, *signal-to-noise* ratio, and *frequency response*. Types 0 and 1, called normal bias, use *ferric* tape and are subject to more *hiss*. *High bias* tapes (types 2 and 3 *chrome* and type 4 *metal*) provide the best frequency responses, wider dynamic ranges, and lower hiss. See also *ferric*, *chrome cassette*, *metal cassette*, *bias*, and *high bias*.

Normal Retail Channels

Permanent locations where recorded product is offered at full price to consumers (i.e., record stores and record departments of variety stores). The term "normal retail channels" is used in recording contracts to define the artist's *royalty base* in contrast with marketing situations where the royalty might be reduced (i.e., sales through record clubs, military sales, overseas licensing, etc.).

North American Free Trade Agreement (NAFTA)

A *multi-lateral treaty*, effective January 1, 1994, which established a North American free-trade zone for the countries of Canada, Mexico, and the United States. The agreement's purposes are to eliminate tariffs on goods produced by the signatory nations by the year 2005 and to reduce red tape for cross-border investments and transfers of goods and services. The agreement includes provisions to add other countries to the free trade zone.

Norwegian Black Metal

A violently anti-Christian, Satanist movement among certain youth in Scandinavia, which includes a musical movement and genre of the same name.

Nostalgia

An interest in, or yearning for, things of the past. It is the basis for the *oldies* market (i.e., popular hits of yesterday) in radio programming, compilation albums, etc.

Notarial Acknowledgment

Statement by a *notary public* declaring that he/she has taken an affidavit, witnessed the signing of a document, or has had sight of the original document for which a copy is being submitted, etc. The acknowledgment includes the notary's name and signature, the date of the acknowledgment, and the date the notary's commission expires.

Notarize

To have a *notary public* certify the authenticity of a document, signature, or affidavit, etc.

Notary Public

A person legally empowered to witness signatures to agreements, validate authenticity of documents, and take affidavits.

Notation

(1) A system of symbols used to represent musical tones, key signatures, time values, etc. See *musical notation* and *Nashville Number System*. (2) An annotation or brief note in the margin of a contract or license, which summarizes, clarifies, or further explains the adjacent contents.

Notice

A written advisement from one party of a contract or license to the other party, such as the intention to exercise an option, a demand to *cure* a failure to perform in a timely manner as agreed, etc. All contracts and licenses provide (or should provide) clarity as to whom, how, when, and where notices must be given.

Notice of Copyright

Under the copyright law in effect before 1978 (The *Copyright Act of 1909*), all published copies of a work were required to bear a *copyright notice* affixed in such manner and location as to give reasonable notice of the owner's copyright claim. The *Copyright Act of 1976* continued this requirement, but it is no longer mandatory for works published on or after March 1, 1989 as a result of the United States joining the *Berne Convention*. Notice of copyright is still required on all copies of works published before March 1, 1989, however.

Copyright notice (except for sound recordings) consists of the symbol © (the letter C in a circle), the word "copyright," or the abbreviation "copr.," the year of first publication, and the name of the copyright owner. *Example*: © 1998 Smith Music.

For sound recordings, copyright notice consists of the symbol (P) (the letter P in circle), the year of first publication, and the name of the copyright owner, visible on the surface of the phonorecord, its label, or container. *Example*: (P) 1998 Smith Record Corp.

If the copyright notice is omitted or given with erroneous information, copyright will not immediately be forfeited, but it must be corrected within certain time limits. However, persons or companies misled by copyright notice omissions or errors may be immune from liability for infringement.

Prior to the effective date of the 1976 Act (January 1, 1978), if a work was published without the required notice, copyright was lost immediately (though some works were granted "ad interim" protection). Once copyright is lost, it can only be restored in the United States by special legislation.

Though the required notice of copyright has been abolished for works published on or after March 1, 1989 under the accords of the Berne agreement, voluntary use of notice is strongly recommended. When a copyright notice is displayed, an infringer cannot claim to have "innocently infringed" a work, and may then be liable for damages the infringement caused the copyright owner.

The *Berne Convention Implementation Act of 1988* is not retroactive, meaning that all works published before March 1, 1989 must comply with the notice requirements of the 1976 Act. If a work was first published without notice between January 1, 1978 and February 28, 1989, it must be registered within five years after publication and the notice added to all copies distributed in the United States after discovery of the omission.

Notice of Intention

Before a record manufacturer can distribute a copyrighted work under terms of the *compulsory licensing* provision of the *Copyright Act*, a notice of intention (to record and distribute the work) must be served on the copyright owner. Notice must be sent at least 30 days before the work is actually recorded. Failure to notify the copyright owner voids eligibility to use the work under the compulsory licensing provision, and, if the manufacturer issues the record anyway, it becomes an actionable *infringement*. If the manufacturer cannot locate the copyright owner, and the Copyright Office has no record of ownership, the manufacturer can file a notice of intention with the Copyright Office and thereby comply with the compulsory licensing provision.

Notice of Use

(1) Another name for *notice of intention* (to use). (2) Under the *Copyright Act of 1909*, song copyright owners filed a "notice of use" (*Form U*) with the Copyright Office once a song had been commercially recorded and released, so that anyone else wishing to record the work would be subject to the *compulsory mechanical licensing* provisions of the Copyright Act. Under the *Copyright Act of 1976*, there is no requirement for copyright owners to file a U Form.

Notice Omission

Prior to the effective date of the *Copyright Act of 1976* (January 1, 1978), if a work was published without the required *copyright notice*, copyright was lost immediately. The omission of a copyright notice was fatal, because once copyright is lost, it can only be restored in the United States by special leg-

islation. Under the 1976 Act, if the copyright notice is omitted or given erroneously, copyright will not immediately be forfeited, but it must be corrected within certain time limits. Copyright notice is not mandatory for works published on or after March 1, 1989 as a result of the United States joining the *Berne Convention*. Notice of copyright is still required on all copies of works published before March 1, 1989, however.

Novelty Advertising

Also called *specialty advertising*. An advertising medium by which items are given away to promote or draw attention to a specific product (i.e., a record release or a recording artist), or to a company in general. Advertising novelties are akin to *institutional ads* in that they are image builders and keep the name of a company, performer, or product before the public. However, like *institutional ads* in trade directories, they have the benefit of repeat advertising, since they are produced at a one-time cost, and recipients usually keep or use them for some period of time.

Novelty giveaways include items like calendars, desk-sets, pens, pencils, T-shirts, sweat-shirts, jackets, caps, jewelry, rulers, paperweights, wall clocks, watches, cigarette lighters, scratch-pads, mugs, cups, playing cards, toys, ashtrays, bags, buttons, stickers, belt buckles, matchbooks, boxes of candy or other foodstuffs, key chains, and so on. Needless to say, the advertiser's name, address, phone/fax numbers, and logo are imprinted on each item.

Novelty Record

A record produced to spoof or parody current events, personalities, or issues, or relate a comedic storyline.

Novelty Song

A song written to spoof or parody current events, personalities, or issues, or relate a comedic storyline.

NPR

Abbreviation for *National Public Radio*.

NRCC

Abbreviation for *Neighboring Rights Collective of Canada*.

NSAI

Abbreviation for *Nashville Songwriters Association International*.

NTSC

Abbreviation for *National Television Standards Committee*.

Null

Something of no consequence, amounting to nothing. A contract that is null has no legal force.

Null and Void

A contract or license that has no legal force, that has been invalidated, annulled, declared by a competent legal body to be void, untenable, etc.

Nullify

To *void* or cancel an agreement or a provision thereof. To make *null and void*; to invalidate.

O&O
Abbreviation for *owned and operated station*.

O-Card
Cardboard envelope or sleeve used to package *cassingles*, as opposed to inserting the cassette in a plastic case with a *J-Card*. O-Cards are open-ended on either side.

Octave
On a musical *scale*, an interval of 8 whole tone notes, counting the bottom and top notes. To arrange, sing, or play music in octaves means that each note is doubled one or more octaves above and/or below.

Off-Broadway
Term used for professional theatrical productions staged in small New York City venues outside the mainstream *Broadway* theater district. Off-Broadway productions are generally low budget, compared to full-scale Broadway shows, and are often somewhat more experimental in content.

Offset
Something used to counterbalance or compensate for a deficiency or risk. *Examples*: The financial gains from one big hit may offset the losses from several flops; a higher royalty rate may offset a lower advance; the use of a company car and other *perks* might offset a lower salary.

Offset Printing
A process that indirectly prints images to paper by first transferring ink to a metal or paper plate, which is then used to ink a rubber cylinder that transfers (offsets) the images to paper.

Off the Shelf
A product already available when needed, rather than having to be made from scratch or tailored to match special needs. For instance, *recorded music library* services provide off-the-shelf (prerecorded) music for certain low-budget productions, such as training films, etc.

Oldie
An old song or record that was once popular. See also *nostalgia*.

OMDA
The *performing-right society* in Madagascar.

ONDA
The *performing-right society* in Algeria.

On Hold
(1) A song is placed "on hold" when a music publisher agrees not to exploit or license it to others because a record company, producer, or recording artist plans to record it. (2) A project or planned activity is placed "on hold" when it is suspended, postponed, or delayed for any reason, but not (yet) canceled or scrubbed. (3) To be kept waiting for a decision about the acceptance of a deal or for the *greenlight* on a project.

On-Hold Music
Recorded music that is played over a telephone line when a caller is placed "on hold."

On Location
To make a recording or shoot a film scene on a site away from a studio.

On Spec
To do something on a *speculative* basis; to produce (a record or film) without assurance of distribution or of recouping expenses or making a profit. *Example*: an independent producer may finance a recording ses-

sion "on spec," hoping to be reimbursed if and when a record distributor leases the finished masters. See also *spec deal*.

On the Shelf

(1) A project that has been *shelved*. (2) A product no longer in demand, which has been taken out of circulation, but kept in inventory. (3) Product that is ready to be shipped.

One-Color Printing

A printing process using one color with white (i.e., red on white, white on blue, white on black, etc.), or using the darkest and lightest extremes of the same color (i.e., black and gray, red and pink, brown and tan, etc.).

One-For-Ten Policy

A sales incentive to bulk buyers, whereby one free item is supplied with the purchase of ten like items. Such a policy amounts to giving the purchaser a 10% discount.

One-Hit Wonder

(1) An artist who scores one hit record, but no more. (2) One who achieves a degree of sudden success, then fails to perpetuate that success or build upon it as expected or hoped; a *flash in the pan*.

One-Nighter

Typically, an engagement by a performer in a privately booked club or other venue for a one-night event, such as a party, dance, concert, convention, prom, etc.

One-Off

An event, such as a sale, performance, or *limited edition* publication, which is offered or done only once, and will not be repeated or reproduced.

One-Off Song Contract

A contract between a songwriter and music publisher covering one song, as opposed to a catalog agreement or exclusive songwriter's agreement. Also called a *single-song contract*.

One Sheet

Slang term for a one-sheet *blurb* and list of tracks contained on an album, which is sent out in promo mailings of a new album release.

One-Stop

A record wholesaler that stocks product from many different labels or distributors for resale to retailers, *rack jobbers*, and jukebox operators. (Buyers can acquire merchandise stocks from a one-stop source, rather than having to go several different manufacturers or distributors.)

One-Time Payment

(1) A fee paid to acquire a license or the rights to a performance or copyright, without further compensation due, as opposed to royalties or periodic advances, etc. (2) A nonrecurring expense.

Online

(1) A personal computer or workstation that is connected to a computer network (see *LAN* and *WAN*). (2) A database or information service that is accessible via *modem* directly to personal computers or to personal computers via a computer network. (3) A project that is underway, in the *pipeline*, or scheduled to take place as planned.

Open Shop

A business whose employees are not required to be union members. See also *closed shop*.

Opening Act

On a concert bill, a warm-up act for the headliner. See also *close* and *closing act*.

Opening Credits

Acknowledgments for work done, services rendered, and rights licensed, displayed at the beginning of a motion picture, television show, or publication, or announced at the beginning of a broadcast. See also *credits* and *closing credits*.

Opera

(1) A dramatic theatrical work set to music. Though many operatic works contain spoken dialogue, the music is more often continuous, using solos, duets, choruses, etc. to further the storyline and dramatize the action. (2) Plural form of the word *opus*.

Opéra Bouffe

French name for comic opera.

Opera Buffa

Italian name for comic opera.

Operating Costs

Same as *overhead*: the expenses of continuing in business, including outlays for rent or lease payments, utilities, taxes, insurance, maintenance, etc.

Operations

A company division responsible for planning, overseeing, and maintaining ongoing functional areas of the business.

Operetta

A musical theatrical production with spoken dialogue and songs, having many of the same characteristics as an *opera*, but which is geared more to parody, satire, frivolity, and/or sentimentality. Also called *light opera*.

Optical Disc

Also called *laserdisc*, an optical disc is coated with a transparent plastic film, and stores digitalized data, including text, audio, and visual images. The data is etched onto the disc's surface in microscopic pits, which are "read" with a laser scanning device. Types of optical laserdiscs include *CDs, CD-ROMS, CD-Is, CD-WORMS*, and *videodiscs*. See also *optical recording*, below.

Optical Recording

In the optical method of sound recording, a microphone converts sound waves into equivalent electrical impulses, which are amplified to operate a device that changes the intensity and/or size of a light beam. As the beam of light varies, it is directly focused onto a moving film, which is then developed to provide a photographic track with varying intensity and density but constant width. In order to reproduce the sound track, a light source is focused on the film, while a photoelectric cell is placed behind it. As the light passes through the film, a fluctuating electric current is generated in the photoelectric cell, which is amplified and converted into sound through loudspeakers.

Opticals

Term used for the visual effects created for film and videotape productions.

Option

(1) A right to license, acquire, buy, or sell something within a specified time for a stated price and/or other stated conditions, such as adopting a stated pricing or royalty formula. (2) To grant to another, or acquire from another, the right to extend or renew a current agreement, or to enter into an agreement, upon fulfillment of certain conditions.

Option Deal

Also called an *step deal*. This is a variation of a *spec deal*, where a songwriter (for instance) receives a partial payment towards a *creative fee* for writing a song for a film production, commercial, or other project. Upon completion of the song, the writer submits a demo to the company. If the company approves the song, a further payment is made and the song is recorded for *synchronization*. Final payment is made if and when the song is actually synchronized or otherwise used in the completed project. If the song is not used, the songwriter keeps the initial payment(s), and usually retains full rights to the work, though there may be conditions.

Opus

A creative work, such as a musical composition.

Oral Agreement

See *oral contract*, below.

Oral Contract

An unwritten, verbal agreement; expressed in spoken words rather than in writing. In most circumstances and in most jurisdictions, oral contracts are legally enforceable, except where real estate is involved.

Oral License

See *oral contract*, above.

Orchestra

(1) A relatively large group of formally organized musicians, usually including string players and led by a *conductor*. (2) The forward section of seats occupying a theater's main floor.

Orchestra Pit

In a theater, a sunken area occupied by an orchestra, between the stage and audience.

Orchestrate

(1) To compose or arrange music. (2) To organize, direct, and control.

Orchestration

An arrangement of music for performance, wherein written parts are assigned to specific instruments.

Orchestrator

An arranger; one who writes or *scores* the various instrumental and/or vocal parts to music, often composed by someone else.

Original

(1) Something that is created firsthand and not copied from another source. (2) The source from which something is derived, copied, or begun. See also *originality*.

Original Cast Album

A recording of songs from a musical play, featuring the original cast from a live stage, television, or feature film production.

Original Publisher

A music publisher who grants or assigns *administrative*, *copublishing*, or *subpublishing* rights in a song, or catalog of songs, to another publisher. The first publisher (the original publisher) maintains full copyright control, subject to the rights assigned to the *administrator, copublisher,* or *subpublisher*, and the rights granted by the original publisher are usually limited in scope, duration, and/or territory. See also *chain of title*.

Original Term

(1) The term of a license, contract, or an agreement, exclusive of any option periods, extensions, or renewals. (2) The statutory 28-year term of copyright protection extended to pre-1978 copyrights, exclusive of any renewal period.

Originality

The state of being *original*, which is a necessary ingredient for copyright eligibility in a creative work. The degree of originality does not have to extend to an entire work in order to make the work copyrightable. For instance, an *adaptation* of a work in *public domain* can be copyrighted if there is sufficiently new and original material added to it (such as lyrics, melodic variations, etc.).

OSA

The *performing-right society* in the Czech Republic.

Oscar

Nickname for an *Academy Award*, derived from the name given to the golden statuettes awarded annually by the *Academy of Motion Picture Arts and Sciences* for excellence in the field of motion pictures. Awards are given in numerous categories, including Best Picture, Director, Actress, and Actor; Supporting Actress; Supporting Actor; Art Direction; Cinematography; Costume Design; Documentary (Feature); Documentary (Short Subject); Editing; Foreign-Language Film; Makeup; Music (Original Score); Music (Song); Original Screenplay; Adapted Screenplay; Short Subject (Live Action); Short Subject (Animated); Sound; Sound Effects; Visual Effects; et al.

Out Take

(1) A complete recorded version of song that is shelved in favor of another version (the *final take*). (2) A filmed scene dropped from the final theatrical version of a movie. (3) A videotaped scene dropped from the final broadcast version of a television production. (4) A complete short-form videotaped performance that is shelved in favor of another version (the *final take*).

Outboard Equipment

External recording, signal processing, or *mixing* devices patched through a studio *control board* or *console* in order to provide additional audio control options for the producer, engineer, or mixer.

Outdoor Concert

A performance presented in a stadium or other open-air setting, as opposed to indoor venues, such as auditoriums or theaters.

Output

(1) Work production (i.e., a catalog of songs created by a songwriter over a period of time, or the number of recordings produced, manufactured, and released by a record company). (2) The level of volume generated by an amplifier. (3) The power-generating capacity of an electrical device. (4) Data produced, or processed from *input*.

Output Impedance

The impedance measured across the output terminals of a device.

Outside In

The conventional mode of disc playback using a turntable and tonearm, with the *stylus* moving from the outer edge or rim of the disc towards the center of the disc as it revolves on the turntable. See also *inside out*.

Outside Material

Songs recorded by an artist that were written by persons not directly connected to the artist or his/her record company, publisher, or producer—as opposed to songs recorded by the artist that were self-penned, or written by his/her producer, or by someone on his/her label's or publisher's staff. Also called *third-party material*.

Outtake

See *out take*.

Over the Top

Extreme, exaggerated; an outlandish performance. A *hyped* promotion.

Over the Transom

Term describing the receipt of *unsolicited material*, as if someone tossed the submission package through the open (transom) window over an office door. Audition tapes sent or received without prior arrangement between the sender and recipient.

Overcall Album

A request by a record company for an artist to record an album in addition to the number of albums called for by contract.

Overdub

To record new parts in synchronization with previously recorded material (i.e., to overdub a lead vocal onto a rhythm track).

Overdubbing

The process of recording or adding vocals, instruments, or sound effects to previously recorded tracks.

Overhead

Same as *operating costs*: the expenses of continuing in business, including outlays for rent or lease payments, utilities, taxes, insurance, maintenance, etc.

Override

A commission or royalty paid to someone over and above a commission or royalty earned by the person who directly created or generated the work. For instance, a sales manager might be given an override for sales generated by his/her sales force, which is in addition to the commissions earned by the salesmen in the field. Or, as part of an agreement whereby a record company sells an artist's contract to another label, the first company might receive a royalty override on sales of the artist's releases by the second company for a stated period of time.

Overscale Employee

A musician, vocalist, arranger, etc., who receives more than minimum *union scale* for work on a project.

Overseas

Same as *foreign*, referring to licensing, collections, marketing, sales, distribution, etc. outside one's own country.

Overt Lyrics

Lyrics that deal directly with the subject, as opposed to *allegorical lyrics*. In popular Christian music, for instance, overt or vertical lyrics would speak directly to and of God or Jesus and/or about prayer and the Christian faith. Also called *vertical lyrics*.

Overtracking

Similar to *overdubbing* and *doubletracking*: The process of recording an instrument or vocal part two or more times on separate tracks in *unison*, *octaves*, or in harmonic accompaniment with another, previously recorded instrument or vocal part, in order to produce the effect of a larger *ensemble*.

Owned & Operated Station (O&O)

Term used for radio and television stations that are wholly owned and managed by a broadcasting network.

Owned Composition

Also called *controlled composition*. A term used in recording-artist contracts in reference to a song written in whole or in part by the artist, and/or published by a publishing company owned or controlled in whole or in part by the artist, and/or otherwise owned or controlled directly or indirectly in whole or in part by the artist. See also *controlled composition clause*.

Ownership

The legal right to possess and control a property. Ownership is represented by a deed or bill of sale, in the case of *tangible* properties, or by a copyright or patent, in the case of *intangible* properties.

P&D

Abbreviation for *pressing and distribution*.

P&L

Abbreviation for *profit and loss*.

P&L Statement

A financial statement summarizing business revenues, expenses, and net profit (or loss) for an accounting period. Also called *earnings statement*, *earnings report*, *income statement*, or *operating statement*.

P/E

Abbreviation for *price/earnings ratio*. See also *multiple*.

P.A.

Abbreviation for (1) *personal assistant*; (2) *public address system*; (3) *press agent*; (4) *production assistant*; (5) *power of attorney*; and (6) *per annum*.

PA Form

A form for registering copyright claim information with the Copyright Office. Under the *Copyright Act of 1976*, Form PA is used for registering both published and unpublished songs.

Pacific Rim

A reference to countries that border the Pacific Ocean, as well as island nations situated in the Pacific Ocean. As a group, Pacific Rim countries have experienced significant economic growth since the 1980s, and most of them belong to APEC (Asia-Pacific Economic Cooperation), established in 1989 to facilitate cooperation on trade and copyright matters. See also *Fox Agency International*.

Package

(1) To put together a group of related items or services. (2) A deal or an offer comprising several related items or services at one umbrella price. For example, a promoter may pay a booking agent one inclusive fee for a group of different acts "packaged" to appear on the same concert bill. Or, a jingle production company might offer a *package deal* whereby one fee covers compensation for composing the jingle; paying singers, arrangers, and musicians; and studio costs of recording and copying.

Normally, a package offer must be accepted as a whole in order to realize any cost benefit; individual items or services are not offered on a *prorated* basis. For instance, a compilation album packager might be offered a package deal of ten masters in return for an advance of $10,000, as opposed to licensing each master individually for $1,500.

Package Deal

See *package*, above.

Packager

A person or agency who puts together all elements of a *package deal*; or, one who assembles the components of a package, such as selecting and licensing various masters for a compilation album.

Packaging

(1) The process of putting together a *package deal*, or of compiling all the elements of a package. (2) Materials used to protect goods during shipping. (3) Containers used for storing or shipping product.

Packaging Deduction

Also called *container charge*. A charge against an artist's royalties by a record company for the costs of packaging a record album, including the costs of covers, *J-cards*, envelopes, slipcases, sleeves, *jewel boxes*, jackets, inserts, shrink wrapping, etc. Record companies typically deduct around 25% from the price of a CD before calculating royalties payable (see *royalty base*). Packaging deductions for cassette tapes are in the 20% range. Record companies defend this deduction by contending the artist should only be paid on sales of the recording, not of the packaging.

Paid Attendee
Member of an audience at a performance who pays full price for an admission ticket.

PAL
Abbreviation for *phase alternation by line*.

Palm Off
(1) To sell, trade, or dispose of by deception (i.e., to deal in counterfeit recordings; to claim someone else's work as one's own). (2) To impose an unwanted task or responsibility on another.

Pan
(1) To place a sound signal from left to right, right to left, or to the center of a stereo image. (2) To follow a moving object with a movie, television, or video camera. (3) To sweep a scene from one side to another with a camera in order to create a panoramic visual effect. (4) To give a bad review, or to negatively review a performance, book, movie, play, or recording.

Pan Pot
Abbreviation for panoramic potentiometer, a variable device on a recording or mixing *console*, used to *pan* sound signals between left and right channels.

Panto
Abbreviation used in Great Britain for *pantomime*, where the term is used in reference to entertainment featuring comic mimicry, frequently consisting of farcical songs, bawdy dialogue, and ludicrously exaggerated gestures.

Pantomime
(1) A play, skit, or other performance in which performers act out a story using only gestures and facial expressions in order to communicate without speaking. (2) To tell a story silently, using bodily movements, gestures, and facial expressions. See also *lip sync*.

Pantone Matching System (PMS)
Standardized numbering system used by printers to match ink colors with the exact colors chosen by designers for album artwork, logos, posters, brochures, advertisements, etc.

Paper Business
Segment of the music publishing business that deals in printed editions (*piano copies, sheet music, method books, folios,* orchestral arrangements, etc.).

Paper the House
To give away numerous free tickets to a live performance or concert in order to ensure a capacity audience or full house.

Parallel Import
A recording manufactured in one country and imported for sale into another country where the recording is also being manufactured and sold. (The *Copyright Act* prohibits importation of records containing copyrighted musical works owned by Americans without specific permission of US copyright owners. See *import license*.)

Parallel Rights
Arrangers are typically paid a flat fee and derive no further rights or compensation for their creative contributions to a *derivative work*, such as an arrangement of a recorded song. In some European countries, however, arrangers have what is called "parallel rights" in the contributions they make to derivative works, which entitles them to a royalty share of *mechanical* and *performance* earnings from the recorded versions of their arrangements.

Parametric Equalizer
In recording, a parametric equalizer enables a sound engineer to isolate a specific frequency (or bandwidth) in order to alter its accent or *attenuation*. This contrasts with a *graphic equalizer*, which controls fixed bands of frequencies simultaneously.

Paraphrase
A summary, restatement, truncation, abridgment, condensation, or rewording of something already written or said.

Parody
A take-off or comic slant given to an existing work for the purpose of spoofing or making fun either of the work itself or of some currently newsworthy event or person. A parody necessarily involves changing lyrics or in some other way altering the work, which requires special permission from the copyright owner. In other words, if the parody is to be a recorded performance, *compulsory mechanical licensing* does not apply.

Parodies are usually made only of songs that are instantly recognizable. This means the song has previously achieved hit status, and is thus an important copyright. If a publisher allows such usage, full ownership of the copyright in new lyrics is usually (but not always) vested in the publisher. Sometimes, however, the adapter may successfully negotiate partial ownership of the new work.

Part

(1) That part of a musical arrangement written specifically for one particular instrument or voice. (2) A section (such as a chorus or introduction) taken, excerpted, or extracted from a complete arrangement. (3) A share, portion, cut, or piece (as in an equal part of copyright ownership to a song). (4) A portion of a broadcast or broadcast day (see *day part*). (5) In manufacturing records, a *metal mold* made either from a *master lacquer* or a *mother*. Also called *metal parts*.

Part Song

(1) A choral work arranged for harmonic voices. (2) A *polyphonic* song.

Partial Ownership

A share, right, claim, stake, or an interest amounting to less than 100% of an asset, such as a copyright, or of a business venture.

Partial Performance

(1) The partial fulfillment or incomplete execution of an obligation, a responsibility, a duty, or an act required by contract. (2) A *partial use*.

Partial Use

The use of less than 100% of a song, recording, videotaped performance, etc. *Example*: Thirty seconds of a song used as background music in a movie scene is a partial use.

Participate

(1) To share (as in having *partial ownership* of a copyright, or having a *cut-in* [percentage] of the *mechanical royalties* received from the sale of a recording, etc.) (2) To contribute to, or take part in, the creation of a work (i.e., to cowrite a song, coproduce a record, etc.). (3) To contribute to, or take part in, the management or direction of an enterprise (i.e., to share authority and/or legal responsibility).

Participation

Taking part in, contributing to, or having a share of something. See *participate*.

Participation Agreement

See *participation deal*, below.

Participation Deal

An agreement, such as a *cut-in*, whereby one party receives a share of profits or royalties arising from a venture, production, or work, usually given in return for some contribution towards the situation that generates those profits or royalties.

Parties

See *party*. Persons or groups who enter into an agreement, join to pursue some venture, or are involved in a legal proceeding.

Partner

A person or group joined with another or others in a common activity or venture. See also *partnership*, *general partner*, *limited partner*, and *silent partner*.

Partnership

A venture or activity involving two or more persons or groups who share, to some degree, responsibilities, liabilities, and rewards of the venture's success or failure. See also *partnership*, *general partnership*, and *limited partnership*.

Party

Term frequently used in legal parlance as a substitute for a person or company or other entity. *Examples*: *Parties* to a contract; a *plaintiff* in a lawsuit is said to be an injured party seeking redress from the alleged guilty party (the *defendant*).

Pass

(1) To turn down or reject a submission or offer. (2) A complimentary ticket or an authorization for free admission to an event.

Patent

(1) A government grant made to an inventor, originator, and/or a proprietor of a new product idea, process, or technology, which bestows the sole right to use, manufacture, and sell that invention, or to authorize others to do so. Any "original and useful device or process" is eligible for a US patent, which is valid for 17 years. (2) The official document granting a patent holder monopolistic control over the use of a patented device or process. (3) To apply for and obtain a patent.

Patent & Trademark Office

Bureau of the United States government that reviews patent claims and trademark registrations, grants patents and trademark clearances to successful applicants, and maintains records of patents and trademarks. Located at Crystal Park, Arlington, VA 22202. Tel: (703) 308-4357; Fax: (703) 305-6369.

Patter

Slang term for a *dee-jay*'s *spiel* or chatter; rapidly *ad libbed* comments by an *emcee*.

Patter Song

A song, usually comic in nature, characterized by rapidly delivered lyrics, with the musical accompaniment being secondary to the performance.

Pattern

(1) An arrangement or structure (as in a rhythm pattern, or the order of verses and hooks in a song, etc.). (2) A specimen, type, or kind. (3) To copy, emulate, or imitate using something else as a model. (i.e., "he patterned his vocal style on that of Rod Stewart.")

Pay or Play

Provision in a recording artist contract giving the company an option to pay off the artist without recording any tracks. Most recording contracts don't require the company to actually record the artist. Instead, under a so-called pay-or-pay provision, the company can pay the artist *union scale* for a recording session, or (depending upon the contract's terms), pay the artist any outstanding balance remaining in the *recording fund*. If the company doesn't want to release any recordings by the artist, it is obviously cheaper to pay off, rather than incurring additional expenses (studio, session musicians, producers, mastering, manufacturing, etc.). See also *minimum recording obligation*.

Pay-Out

See *buyout*, *cash pay-out*, and *contingent pay-out*.

Pay-Per-View (PPV)

Special, optional programming available via cable television to viewers who choose to pay one-off fees in addition to regular cable subscription charges.

Pay Television

A delivery system for television programming, available only to paid subscribers (i.e., cable television), as opposed to *free television*, which viewers can receive without charge via "over the air" broadcasts from local network affiliates and independent local stations. See also *pay-per-view*.

Pay To Play

A requirement by some clubs, particularly in the Los Angeles area, that up-and-coming bands pay to play in the venue. The system was put in place by club owners who felt they were losing money booking bands that had yet to establish a following, and was grudgingly accepted by young bands eager to *showcase* their talent. Essentially, the band buys a specified number of admission tickets, which they then give away to key A&R personnel, producers, and others who may be helpful in furthering their career. The band may also resell tickets at a markup in order to make up their *take* for the night. The tickets sold to the band by the club are called *pre-sells*.

Payment Schedule

A supplemental statement appended to a document, such as a contract, which details the dates on which royalty accountings or advance payments are due. A schedule listing due dates for advances or fees normally includes the amount of each payment.

Payoff

(1) A payment fulfilling a monetary obligation or liability. (2) A monetary settlement satisfying a liability or dispute. (3) A bribe.

Payola

An illegal gift of money, goods, services, or other benefits, used to bribe a disc jockey to play a record.

PBS

Abbreviation for *Public Broadcasting Service*.

PCM

Abbreviation for *pulse code modulation*.

PD

(1) Abbreviation for *program director*. (2) Abbreviation for *public domain*.

Peak

To reach a maximum level. For example, "the record peaked at number 20 on the charts;" or "sales peaked at 100,000 units."

Pen Name

A writer's *pseudonym*. Also called *nom de plume*.

Pension & Welfare Fund

Under the *Phonograph Record Labor Agreement*, employers of union musicians for recording sessions are required to pay up to 10% of the gross scale wages paid for each session into the *AFM Employers Pension & Welfare Fund*, which provides pension benefits to participating members.

Per Annum

(1) Payment made once a year. (2) Total sum(s) earned in one year.

Per Broadcast

Method of computing royalty or licensing fees, based on the number of times a copyrighted work is aired on television or radio. See *per program* and *per program performance license*.

Per Copy

Method of computing royalty or licensing fees, based on the number of copies (*units*) of a copyrighted work manufactured, printed, distributed, and/or sold.

Per Diem

(1) A daily rate of pay. (2) An expense allowance,

set aside as a reimbursement for expenses (over and above regular compensation) incurred for each day on a job or project.

Per Program

(1) Method of computing software royalty or licensing fees, based on the number of copies (*units*) of a copyrighted work manufactured, distributed, and/or sold. (2) Method of computing royalty or licensing fees, based on the number of times a broadcast program containing a copyrighted work is aired (see *per program performance license*, below).

Per Program Performance License

A modified *blanket license* offered by *performing-right societies* to local television stations as an alternative to the comprehensive blanket licenses required previous to the *Buffalo Broadcasting* case. Under this type of license, a station pays performance fees only for those shows that actually use songs in the societies' repertoire. Stations opting for this type of license must pay monthly fees based on *cue sheets* submitted to the societies, listing titles, songwriters, music publishers, performing-right affiliations, time of broadcast, playing times of each performance, and nature of performances.

Per Unit

Method of computing royalty or licensing fees, based on the number of copies (*units*) of a copyrighted work manufactured, printed, distributed, and/or sold.

Percentage

(1) A proportion, part, or share of something, based on 100 percentage points equaling a whole. For instance, 15% of \$1,000 = \$150 (\$1,000 ÷ 100 percentage points = 10 x 15 percentage points = 150). (2) A *royalty, commission, participation*, or an *override* based on a proportion of total revenues, profits, or sales.

Perform

(1) To render, act, recite, sing, play, or dance, whether directly (as before a live audience) or indirectly through a "device or process" (as with a sound recording, film, videotape, broadcast, etc.). (2) To fulfill an obligation, responsibility, duty, or act as required by, and according to the terms of a contract.

Perform Privately

The nonpublic use of a copyrighted work (i.e., a sound recording or song). Playing or performing a musical work in a private setting, such as a home, and not for the benefit of the public, particularly where paying customers are present. The performance of a work in a setting not available for public use, control, or participation. Private use of a copyrighted work, as among close friends or family, does not require permission from, or payment to, the copyright owner.

Perform Publicly

To play, perform, or broadcast a copyrighted work for the entertainment of paying customers or others outside of a social circle of close friends and family members who might constitute either a direct or indirect audience in a public place. The public use of a copyrighted work requires permission from the copyright owner.

Performance

(1) The public presentation of a musical work, film, play, program, dance, etc., whether directly (as before a live audience) or indirectly through a "device or process" (as with a sound recording, film, videotape, broadcast, etc.). (2) The fulfillment of an obligation, responsibility, duty, or act as required by, and according to the terms of a contract.

Performance Clause

A contractual provision requiring one party to perform or cause to perform some service or act or to achieve some goal. *Examples*: A record company may be required to release at least one album by an artist within a set period; a recording artist might be required to deliver to a record company a stated number of commercially acceptable finished masters within a set period; a music publisher may be required to get a minimum number of a writer's songs recorded and released within a specified time period.

Performance Fee

A fee paid to a copyright owner for the use of a work in a *public performance*. Performance fees from broadcasters, jukebox operators, arcade owners, nightclubs, concert halls, background music services, airlines, etc., are paid to *performing-right societies*, such as *ASCAP* or *BMI*, under *blanket licensing* systems. The societies then allocate performance royalties due individual copyright owners and songwriters whose works were publicly performed.

Most major countries—but not the US—also have copyright legislation providing payment of performance fees or royalties to owners of *neighboring rights* in a copyright. For instance, a recording artist will receive performance fees or royalties when his or her recordings are publicly performed, even though the underlying copyright in the song belongs to someone else.

The United States also is an exception to rule with regards to performance fees for music integrated with movies when publicly performed in movie theaters. ASCAP and BMI operate under *con-*

sent decrees preventing them from requiring movie theaters to obtain blanket performance licenses for *theatrical exhibitions*. Thus, authorization to exhibit a film with music included must be obtained by the film's producer or distributor directly from the copyright owner, which usually requires the payment of a flat performance fee. The theatrical exhibition performance fee is normally equal to the *synchronization fee*, though some publishers request up to 200% of the size of the synchronization fee. Though they are separate issues, the grant of performance rights for US theatrical exhibition is often included in the synchronization license issued to the film production company. See also *performance right, performance right exclusions,* and *performance royalty.*

Performance License

A grant of permission authorizing the *public performance* of a copyrighted musical work.

Performance Minimum

In a *merchandising agreement,* an artist guarantees the *merchandiser* that he or she will perform before a minimum number of *paid attendees* during the course of a tour.

Performance Obligation

A requirement imposed by contract on a party to achieve a stated goal or to perform or cause to be performed some act or service. See *performance clause.*

Performance Right

Also called *performing right.* One of the *bundle of rights* vested in copyright ownership, giving a song copyright owner authorizing control over the *public performance* of a song.

Each *public performance* requires the *user* to pay a fee or royalty to the copyright owner and songwriter. Most of the royalties amount to just a few cents in each case, but it all adds up. There are many types of performance usages, and any song achieving commercial success inevitably earns income from several categories of performing-right users. On any given day, one hit song may be broadcast on hundreds of radio and television stations across the country; performed live in nightclubs, concert halls, and arenas; played on countless jukeboxes in bars and cafes; played on tape decks in aerobic and dance studios, hair salons, and boutiques; used as background music in restaurants, elevators, malls, supermarkets, offices, and factories, etc.

Under the *Copyright Right Act of 1976,* copyright owners maintain licensing rights to songs even when publicly performed at not-for-profit events, such as charity balls, school dances, fraternal lodge parties, religious broadcasts, etc. There are, however, four exceptions where nonprofit public performances are exempt from licensing requirements: (1) religious services that are not broadcast; (2) performances at events where there is no admission fee, either directly (ticket sales), or indirectly (contributions, club membership, etc.), and no direct or indirect fee is paid to performers; (3) classroom teaching by nonprofit educational institutions; and (4) certain nonprofit educational and governmental public service broadcasts of instructional materials.

See also *performance license, performance royalty, performance fee,* and *performing-right society.*

Performance Right Exclusions

The *Copyright Act of 1976* specifically exempts owners of sound recordings from being vested with performance rights in the recordings. Thus, while songwriters and copyright owners of songs are paid performance royalties when recordings of their songs are broadcast or otherwise publicly performed, the copyright owners of the sound recordings themselves are not entitled to similar compensation. The American copyright law in this regard does not follow the example of almost every other developed country, where performers and copyright owners of sound recordings receive performance royalties from broadcasters.

The U.S. copyright law is also out of step with laws of other countries with respect to performance royalties paid for music used in motion pictures shown in movie theaters. In most countries, theater owners pay performance royalties to music publishers and songwriters based on box office receipts. In the United States, however, music copyright owners must negotiate a one-time *performance fee* with a film producer or distributor at the time a *synchronization license* is negotiated.

Performance rights are licensed separately from synchronization rights in the United States, because *ASCAP* and *BMI* operate under *consent decrees* preventing them from requiring movie theaters to obtain *blanket* performance licenses for *theatrical exhibitions*. A flat performance fee for US theatrical exhibition is often included in the synchronization license, to be paid by the film production company. The performance fee is normally equal to the synchronization fee, though some publishers request up to 200% of the size of the synchronization fee.

Performance Royalty

Each commercial performance of a copyrighted musical work requires the user to pay a performance royalty to the copyright owner and songwriter. There are many types of performance usages, including radio and television broadcasts; live performances in nightclubs, concert halls, and arenas; juke box plays; background music in restaurants, elevators, malls, supermarkets, offices, and factories, etc. Performance royalties are collected on behalf of copyright owners and songwriters by *performing-right societies*. Mechanical royalties and performance royalties are the two main sources of revenue for most music publishers and songwriters.

Many publishers find that their largest and most consistent source of income is performance royalties. In the United States, $750 million is collected annually in performance royalties on behalf of publishers and songwriters. Worldwide, performance licenses generate more than $2 billion each year, accounting for more than 40% of all publisher/writer income.

A song that reaches number one on the *Billboard* Top 100 chart can earn performance royalties of between $100,000 and $400,000 in the first year alone, just from radio *airplay*. (Radio performance royalties usually account for between 80% and 90% of all domestic performance royalties from a song that hits the Top 100.)

Hit songs in niche markets (i.e., Country, R&B, Easy Listening) earn lesser amounts, but generate significant performance royalties nevertheless. But, if a song crosses over to hit number one on the Pop, R&B, Country, and Adult Contemporary charts, gross US performance royalties from the first year could reach $600,000.

Foreign performance royalties can equal the American earnings, assuming widespread international success. Although performance royalties fall off substantially after the first couple of quarters of peak activity, a hit song might still be generating as much as 10% of its first year earnings in the 20th year of release. See also *performance fee*, *performance right*, and *performance right exclusions*.

Performance Survey

Method by which *performing-right societies* calculate *performance royalty* earnings attributable to specific music copyrights. For instance, individual radio station *playlists* and television programmers' *cue sheets* are surveyed to identify copyright titles aired during each royalty accounting period, including the *nature*, broadcast time, and *duration* of each performance, the size of the station and its market, or the number of network stations carrying the broadcast in which a performance is aired. Not all stations are surveyed at the same time, so various sampling techniques are used to arrive at statistical estimates of the number and types of performances nationally. Nor do performing-right societies survey actual performances at the thousands of venues where live music is performed. It is more cost-effective to issue *blanket licenses* to such venues. Performance royalties collected from blanket licenses are distributed to copyright owners and songwriters in proportion to their respective broadcast royalty

earnings. See also *sampling*, *weighting formula*, *credit system*, *logging procedure*, and *credit weighting formula*.

Performing Art

An art form that is staged for presentation before an audience (i.e., music, dance, drama).

Performing Right

See *performance right*.

Performing-Right Society

An organization that licenses *nondramatic* performance rights and collects performance royalties on behalf of music publishers, composers, and songwriters. There are three performing-right societies in the United States: *ASCAP* (*Association of Composers, Authors & Publishers*), *BMI* (*Broadcast Music, Inc.*), and *SESAC* (*Society of European Stage Authors & Composers.*)

Every active music publisher and professional songwriter belongs to a performing-right society. The collective strength of thousands of members enables performing-right societies to negotiate *blanket licenses* to broadcasters and venues where music is used or performed, and to effectively *administer* licenses and collect royalties on behalf of publishers and writers. Virtually every country has at least one society to license performance rights on behalf of local of music publishers and songwriters, and virtually every performing-right society has reciprocal agreements with societies in other countries for international performing-right licensing and royalty collections.

The following is a partial list of performing-right societies around the world: *ACAM* (Costa Rica); *ACDAM* (Cuba); *ACUM* (Israel); *AEPI** (Greece); *AGADU* (Uruguay); *AGAYC* (Guatemala); *AKM* (Austria); *APA* (Paraguay); *APDAYC* (Peru); *APRA* (Australia); *ARTIJUS* (Hungary); *ASCAP* (USA); *BMDA* (Morocco); *BMI* (USA); *BSDA* (Senegal); *BUMA* (Holland); *BURIDA* (Ivory Coast); *CASH** (Hong Kong); *CHA* (Taiwan); *COMPASS** (Singapore); *COSGA** (Ghana); *COTT* (*Trinidad & Tobago*); *EAU* (Estonia); *FILSCAP* (Philippines); *GEMA** (Germany); *HDS* (Croatia); *IMRO* (Ireland); *IPRS* (India); *JASRAC** (Japan); *KODA* (Denmark); *KOMCA* (S. Korea); *LATGA-A* (Lithuania); *MACP* (Malaysia); *MCSC** (China); *MCSK** (Kenya); *MCSN** (Nigeria); *MESAM* (Turkey); *MUSICAUTOR* (Bulgaria); *OMDA* (Madagascar); *ONDA* (Algeria); *OSA* (Czech Republic); *PRS* (Great Britain); *RAO* (Russia); *SABAM** (Belgium); *SACEM* (France); *SACERAU* (Egypt); *SACM* (Mexico); *SACVEN*; (Venezuela); *SADAIC** (Argentina); *SAMRO* (South Africa); *SAYCO* (Colombia); *SAYCE* (Ecuador); *SBACEM** (Brazil); *SCD* (Chile); *SESAC* (USA);

SGAE* (Spain); *SIAE** (Italy); *SOBODAYCOM* (Bolivia); *SOCAN* (Canada); *SOCINADA* (Cameroon); *SODACT* (Tunisia); *SONECA* (Congo [Zaire]); *SOZA* (Slovakia); *SPA** (Portugal); *STEF* (Iceland); *STIM* (Sweden); *SUISA** (Switzerland); *TEOSTO* Finland); *TONO* (Norway); *UCMR* (Romania); *ZAIKS* (Poland); *ZIMRA* (Zimbabwe).
* Indicates a society that licenses both *performance* and *mechanical rights*

Performing-Right Society, The (PRS)

British *performing-rights society*, formed in 1914, and located at 29/33 Berners Street, London W1P 4AA, England. Tel: (0171) 580-5544.

Periodical

A publication, such as a magazine, that is issued at regular intervals of more than one day apart (i.e., weekly, monthly, quarterly, etc.), as opposed to a daily publication, such as a newspaper.

Perk

See *perquisite*.

Permission

A *license* or authorization to use a copyrighted work, or to use a name or likeness. See also *special use permit*.

Permit

(1) To license, authorize, allow, consent, or grant permission. (2) A written form of consent, such as a license or certificate, which authorizes someone to do something.

Perpetuity

An indefinite period of time; no cut-off date; forever.

Perquisite

Term frequently referred to in abbreviated form as *perk*, which is the same as *fringe benefit*. A benefit or method of compensation that is in addition to, but not part of, an employee's salary or commission. *Examples*: use of a company car, insurance coverage, stock options, etc.

Personal Manager

A person or company engaged in directing, leading, guiding, and handling the professional careers and related business affairs of artists, actors, etc. Personal managers generally are given *power of attorney* by clients, and are authorized to act on the client's behalf in all professional matters in a *fiduciary* capacity. Managers are in effect *CEOs* of the client's business (the client being the chairperson). They generally have supervisory control over others working for the client (i.e., lawyers, accountants, *business managers*, *talent agents*, *publicists*, etc.), and they represent the client in dealings with their record company, music publisher, and other employers. Personal managers are typically compensated with *commissions* of between 15% and 20% of all income received from the professional activities of the client, though there may be certain exclusions. Some managers may receive higher percentage-based commissions from less established clients, particularly those to whom the manager advances money to help further their careers.

Personal Property

All movable property, including *tangible* and *intangible* assets (but not real estate) owned by an individual, as opposed to that owned by a corporation.

Personal Service Contract

An agreement whereby one party agrees to personally perform an ongoing service for another. For instance, in an exclusive songwriter agreement, a songwriter agrees to provide services (songwriting) to a music publisher during the term agreed.

Personal service contracts can't be open-ended; there must be a cut-off date where the service provider is free to re-negotiate or take his or her services elsewhere. Most such contracts bind service providers to an initial one-year term, with options to extend the agreement. The number of options is usually limited to between two and four additional one-year terms. Some states invalidate personal service contracts that extend beyond a set number of years. California, for instance, caps personal service contracts at seven years. New York's limit is ten years. Members of the *AFM* cannot enter into a personal service contract (such as a recording agreement) for terms longer than five years without prior approval by the union.

Aside from limiting the duration, some states also require that service providers be guaranteed a minimum level of income during each year of an agreement. This means, for example, that an exclusive songwriter (or a recording artist, etc.) must be provided an annual advance equal to at least the minimum income required by the state in the event royalty revenue does not meet the statutory threshold.

California courts have ruled personal service contracts unenforceable when the provider's annual income from the services provided falls short of $9,000. So, for an exclusive songwriter agreement to be enforceable in California, the publisher must cap the duration of agreement at seven years and guarantee the writer will receive at least $9,000 in each year. The monetary guarantee can, of course, be in the form of a non-returnable advance, recoupable from royalty earnings.

The legal motivation of these statutes is to protect the service provider's ability to earn a livelihood. Continuing the example of an exclusive songwriter's contract, since the writer has in effect become the publisher's exclusive property, he or she is ostensibly prohibited from earning a living through the exercise of his or her craft for anyone other than the publisher during the term of agreement. In addition, since most exclusive writer agreements require the writer to assign all works in his or her back catalog that have not been previously published, the writer is further restricted from pursuing outside opportunities to earn money from his or her work.

Personality Folio
A softbound, folio publication of songs or musical compositions written by a particular songwriter or made popular by and associated with a particular recording artist, featuring photos and biographical material of the songwriter or artist.

Personnel
(1) People employed by a company or active in a venture. (2) A department or division within an organization whose function is to deal with employees and employment matters.

Phase
(1) A period of time or a stage of development. (2) "To phase in" (begin the first stage of a project or policy) or "to phase out" (end a project or policy). (3) To *synchronize*, regulate, coordinate. (4) The polarity of a sound wave.

Phase Alternation by Line (PAL)
European standard for color-television broadcasting, contrasting with *NTSC* (*National Television System Committee*) adopted in North America and Japan. PAL is also a videocassette format used in Europe.

Phase Modulation
The electronic variation of a radio carrier wave so that information contained in the signal can be transmitted. See also *pulse code modulation*.

Phase Shifter
A *signal-processing* device used in recording and mixing to delay an audio signal slightly then recombine it out of phase to give the effect of a swooshing sound.

Phoner
An interview conducted over the telephone rather than in person.

Phonogram
An early term used for a sound recording. It is a combination of terms derived from the Greek words for "sound" or "voice" (phone) and "something written" (gramma), and was coined to describe the technology whereby sounds are "written" (recorded) onto devices from which they can be "read" (played) back. The word phonogram, probably adapted from the word telegram, was first used in 1879 in reference to a sound recording made by a *phonograph*, and was later inverted to form the word *gramophone*, the name given to a device patented in 1884 by *Emile Berliner*.

Phonograph
Also called *record player*, a device that reproduces sounds recorded onto discs etched with spiral grooves. The discs (records) are rotated on the record player's *turntable*, and a *tone arm*, containing a *stylus* at one end, picks up vibrations from the grooves as the record rotates. The vibrations are converted by a *transducer* into corresponding electrical signals, which are expanded by an *amplifier* then converted to sound by a loudspeaker. The first phonograph, which used cylinders rather than discs, was devised by *Thomas Edison* in 1877. *Emile Berliner*'s *Gramophone* (1884) was the first sound reproduction device to use discs, and is the forerunner of the modern record player.

Phonograph Record Labor Agreement
An agreement regulated by the *AFM*, which binds record labels who sign the agreement to pay *union scale* to musicians on recording sessions. Union wage-scales vary according to the number of songs recorded, type of session (i.e., masters, demos, film scores, etc.), number of instruments played, time of day session takes place (i.e., after regular business hours, weekends, holidays, etc.), number of hours the session lasts, etc. Union members are prohibited from working for record companies who don't sign the agreement, and are also prohibited from working with non-union musicians on recording sessions. The agreement also obligates employers to pay stated amounts to the *Phonograph Record Manufacturers Special Payments Fund*, the *AFM Health & Welfare Fund* and the *AFM Employers Pension Fund*. See also *National Code of Fair Practices for Phonograph Recordings*.

Phonograph Record Manufacturers Special Payments Fund Agreement
An agreement between the *AFM* and *signatory* record labels requiring the record companies to pay a percentage of the price of each recording sold into a special fund set up to distribute extra payments to union members each year based on the number of union sanctioned recording sessions each recipient has played on in the previous year. The fund distributes an average of between $250 and $300 to each of the approximately 40,000 eligible union members annually.

Phonographic Trust Agreement (AFM)

An agreement between the *AFM* and *signatory* record labels requiring the record companies to pay a small percentage of the price of each recording sold into the *Music Performance Trust Fund*. The purpose of the fund is to employ union musicians to perform in public places, such as parks, veterans' homes, schools, etc. These performances provide free entertainment for public benefit, promote live music, and generate income for union members.

Phonolog Reporter

A cross-referenced publication, available by subscription, listing all nationally distributed phonorecords currently released in the United States. Weekly update supplements detail all nationally distributed new releases. Listings include artist; title; record label (and the company's address); category (pop, country, R&B, etc.); format (CD, cassette, LP, etc.); catalog number; song titles; durations of each song; songwriters; *performing-right* affiliation, etc. Along with the *Schwann Record and Tape Guide*, Phonolog Reporter provides a definitive reference for locating and ordering commercially released recordings. Phonolog is located at 10996 Torreyana Road, San Diego, CA 92121.

Phonorecord

An all-encompassing term for material objects produced through *sound recording* (i.e., phonograph records, compact discs, audiotape cassettes, etc.).

Photo Essay

See *photo story*.

Photo Opportunity

An event staged especially to allow photographers to take pictures. Also called "photo op."

Photo Story

A newspaper or magazine feature article that uses a group of photographs with *captions* to develop a theme or tell a story, and in which written copy is subordinate to pictorial material. Also called *photo essay*.

Photog

Abbreviated term for *photographer*.

Phrase

(1) A musical segment extracted from a larger work. (2) A method of expressing, pacing, or interpreting a musical passage. (3) A division of a musical work. (4) A division or unit of dance movements within a choreographed work. (5) A method of expressing a thought orally or in writing, (6) To express, pace, or perform.

Piano Bar

An intimate lounge area of a hotel, nightclub, or bar where entertainment is provided by a pianist.

Piano Copy

A musical composition arranged for solo piano and published in *sheet music* format on unbound sheets of paper.

Piano Roll

A spool of perforated paper encoded with a musical composition. As the spool is rotated by the mechanical system of a *player piano*, the perforations actuate a mechanism that causes the piano keys to automatically play back music encoded on the paper. Also called *player roll*.

Piano-Vocal

A *piano copy* or *sheet music* publication of a song arranged for vocalist with piano accompaniment.

Pick

(1) Term used by reviewers to distinguish a newly released recording as having potential for commercial success, especially compared with other recordings released at the same time (i.e., a "pick hit"). (2) To pluck a stringed musical instrument such as a guitar, violin, or banjo. (3) A small, wedge-shaped, flat plastic implement used to pluck a stringed instrument, usually a guitar.

Pickup

(1) A musical note or series of notes used to introduce a *phrase*, passage, or section of a composition. (2) A device in a record player's *tone arm* that converts the oscillations from the *stylus* into electrical impulses, which are then converted to sound. (3) A device in an electric musical instrument, such as a guitar, which converts movements into electrical impulses in the reproduction of sound. (4) The reception of a sound signal or visual image for broadcast transmission on radio or television. (5) The site of a broadcast. (6) The equipment used to transmit a *remote* broadcast back to the broadcasting station.

Pickup Band

A group of musicians temporarily assembled to perform or back up a performer for a limited engagement.

Picture Disc

A *vinyl* record manufactured with a picture or some form of artwork baked into the vinyl playing surface (as opposed to the traditional solid black vinyl). Picture discs were particularly popular during the 1980s, before the advent of compact discs made vinyl records largely obsolete.

Picture Sleeve

Paper envelope for 45 rpm records that is printed (usually) with a photograph of the artist or some other type of artwork relating to the artist or subject matter of the song.

Ping Pong

In recording, to *mix* two or more tracks together in order to free up tracks for additional recording or *overdubbing*. See also *submix*.

Piped Music

Music transmitted by wire or cable from a central location to another location. See *background music*.

Pipeline

(1) The process, channels, or steps through which something passes before completion or receipt. For instance, when a record company collects income for the sale of recordings, but has not yet made royalty payments to artists, producers, and music publishers for those sales, the royalties are *in the pipeline*. (2) A private or direct source of information.

Piracy

(1) Unauthorized sale, receipt, use, or reproduction of copyrighted material; the theft of copyrighted material. See also *bootleg*, *counterfeit*, and *copyright infringement*. (2) Broadcasting radio or television programs from an unlicensed transmitter.

Pirate

(1) A person or organization that appropriates, sells, receives, uses, or reproduces copyrighted material without authorization and without compensating the copyright owner. (2) An unlicensed radio or television broadcasting operation, often located outside a government's *jurisdiction* but transmitting programs back into the jurisdiction.

Pit

In a theater, a sunken area occupied by an orchestra, between the stage and audience.

Pit Orchestra

The backing musicians for featured performers in theatrical productions, usually occupying the *orchestra pit* between the stage and audience.

Pitch

(1) The true position of a musical tone on a scale as defined by the tone's frequency of vibration (i.e., the true pitch of *A* above middle *C* vibrates at 440 cycles per second). Pitch may also be relative to another tone used to "tune" an instrument. A musician or vocalist who sounds a note slightly under or above an intended tone is "off pitch." (2) To plug, promote, or attempt to sell (a song, master, script,

concept, or deal, for example). (3) A *spiel* (i.e., a sales pitch).

Place a Song

To successfully *pitch* a song (get a *cover* version recorded) with an artist, producer, or record company.

Plagiarism

The act of appropriating, copying, stealing, or adapting another person's ideas, words, music, or other creative work and passing it off as one's own. When the appropriated work is copyrighted material, plagiarism constitutes an act of *copyright infringement*. See also *piracy* and *fair use*.

Plagiarize

To appropriate, copy, steal, or adapt another person's ideas, words, music, or other creative work and then claim authorship.

Plaintiff

A party who files suit against another in a court of law; a *complainant* or accuser.

Plating

Also called *matrixing* and *electroplating*. A process used in manufacturing vinyl phonograph records whereby the *master lacquer* is coated with a silver film and bathed in a nickel solution through which a current is passed. The nickel plating is then stripped away to leave a negative impression of the grooves on the master disc. This is used as a mold or matrix to make a second, electroplated mold (a *mother*) containing a positive impression of the grooves. A *metal stamper* (with negative groove impressions) is cast from the mother, then mounted on a pressing machine to stamp out, or press, copies of the recording onto vinyl discs.

Platinum Album

A phonorecord album that is certified by the *RIAA* to have sold one million units. Music industry associations in various countries set the number of units that must be sold in order to achieve *gold* or platinum status. For instance, in the United Kingdom 300,000 sales warrants a platinum record award; 50,000 sales are needed for such an award in Norway. For a listing of sales requirements needed to obtain gold and platinum status in various countries, see *hit*. See also *silver record*, *gold record*, *multi-platinum*, and *diamond record*.

Platinum Single

A *single* recording that is certified by the *RIAA* to have sold one million units. Historically, one million sales of a commercially released single recording earned a *gold record* award in the United States. In recent years, however, sales of singles have declined in favor of album purchases, so a single now needs only 500,000 sales to be certified gold. For a listing of sales requirements needed to obtain gold and platinum status in various countries, see *hit*. See also *silver record, gold record, multi-platinum record*, and *diamond record*.

Platter

Slang term for phonograph record.

Play

(1) The broadcast of a recording over the air. (2) To broadcast a recording. (3) To perform (either musically or dramatically). (4) To operate a coin-operated amusement device, such as a jukebox or an arcade game. (5) A dramatic literary work written for the stage. (6) To perform with a musical instrument (i.e., play the piano). (7) An audience reaction (the song "played" well with the concert audience). (8) To act or assume a role.

Play with Music

A dramatic play that uses music to set the atmosphere, but not to develop the action of the story. *Non-musical plays* are productions where the music is *commissioned* after the play is written. In both types of productions, music is incidental to the story. It enhances the presentation, but is not essential to the play itself.

Playback

(1) The process of playing recorded audio. (2) The system by which a sound recording is monitored.

Player Piano

A mechanically operated piano that automatically plays music encoded on a perforated paper roll. See *piano roll*.

Player Roll

See *piano roll*.

Playing Time

(1) The duration (in minutes and seconds) of a sound recording. (2) The amount of time allotted for the broadcast of a performance or sound recording.

Playlist

(1) A schedule of recordings slated for broadcast on a radio program. Playlists are usually changed each week, adding some recordings, dropping others. They also indicate the *rotation* each recording has during the period (i.e., heavy, medium, or light). (2) To add a recording to a radio station playlist.

Plot

The storyline, or main story points, of a literary or dramatic work.

Plot Line

Dramatic dialogue or lyrics essential to the *plot* development of a story or a song.

Plug

(1) To promote, tout, or advocate the commercial use or broadcast of a song or recording. (2) A favorable public announcement regarding a product, business, upcoming performance, or appearance, etc.

Plugger

Person who *plugs* a product. *Examples*: A *songplugger*; a record promotion person.

Plugola

(1) A bribe or under-the-table payment given to a journalist, editor, or reviewer in order to get favorable publicity or reviews. (2) An advertisement or commercial message broadcast on radio or television that is not paid for like regular advertising.

PMS

Abbreviation for *Pantone Matching System*.

Poetic License

The creative range of artistic expression in speech, writing, performance, or interpretation, which may bend the rules of common practice, tradition, expectation, or author's original intent, and which is employed to achieve a certain effect on an audience. Also called *artistic license* and *literary license*.

Point

A percentage. One point equals one percent, or 1/100th of a total amount.

Point Arrangement

An agreement whereby a party receives a percentage of income generated by the sale or use of a product or asset, or a percentage of money raised from a financing arrangement, such as a loan, investment, or advance, etc. Each point received equals one percent. See also *point*.

Point Person

Person designated to act as a liaison, go-between, or spokesperson for an organization in its dealings with others.

Point of Purchase (POP)

A marketing technique used to stimulate impulse sales. POP materials are visually positioned to attract customers' attention when they've already come into a store. POP materials include special boxes with pop-up displays, racks, bins, posters, banners, streamers, stickers, balloons, pennants, window displays, etc. In-store play of recorded product is another, effective type of POP marketing.

Autograph signings and personal appearances by artists at retail outlets are also good focal points for POP marketing.

Point of View (POV)

(1) The state of mind, feeling, disposition, or attitude of a song's singer or a story's narrator, as expressed through lyrics, text, or dialogue. (2) Perspective, conveyed by a camara shot.

POLI

Acronym for *Publishers Online Information*, an online service offered by the *Harry Fox Agency* to music publishers represented by the agency to access the information database maintained by *HFA*. See also *POLI-Plus*, below.

POLI-Plus

Acronym for *Publishers Online Information-Plus*, an interactive online service offered by the *Harry Fox Agency* as an upgrade to *POLI*, enabling music publishers represented by the agency to not only access information on *HFA*'s database, but to also make online authorizations for issuing licenses.

Polyphonic

A musical work arranged for several different melodies to be played or sung simultaneously by different instruments or voices. From the Greek word *polyphony*, meaning "many sounds."

Polystyrene

A thermoplastic resin, used in the *injection method* of manufacturing phonograph records.

Polyvinyl Chloride (PVC)

A thermoplastic resin, used in the *compression method* of manufacturing phonograph records.

Poor Man's Copyright

The "poor man's copyright" is so-called because it is an attempt to save the $20 fee required to register a claim for copyright under the *formalities* of the *Copyright Act*. Instead of filing the claim with the *Library of Congress*, a copy of the work is placed in a sealed envelope, which the claimant sends to himself or herself by *certified mail*. The idea is to be able to prove that a copyright claim was made on a certain date, and that the work in question, therefore, could not have been cobbled together later in order to make a spurious claim against someone else's work. It is hoped the postmark certification will validate the copyright claim when the seal is broken and the envelope is opened in a court of law.

This method of copyright-claim documentation is sometimes acceptable by courts attempting to settle rival claims, but it is an iffy way to establish copyright ownership. It is always preferable to register a copyright claim with the Library of Congress, following the formal procedures laid down by the 1976 Copyright Act. Otherwise, a copyright owner may not have legal status to claim damages and royalties earned from unauthorized usages of the work.

Pop

Abbreviated reference for *popular* music, the genre most in fashion at any given time to *mainstream* audiences.

POP

Acronym for *point of purchase* and *proof of purchase*.

Popkomm

International music market and trade show held annually in Germany. Contact address is POPKOMM, Rottscheider Strasse 6, D-5600 Woppertal 11, Germany. Tel: (020) 227-8310.

Popular

A fashion, style, or genre that is widely liked or appreciated, or which is geared to the current tastes of a large, *mainstream* segment of the population.

Positive Cash Flow

When more money is received during an accounting period than is paid out during the same period. See also *cash flow* and *negative cash flow*.

Post Exchange

See *PX*.

Post Production

The third of the three stages of record production (preceded by *pre-production* and *production* or "in the studio"). The postproduction phase involves *mastering*; securing *mechanical licenses*; delivering master tapes to record company; delivering *label credits*, liner notes, copyright information, etc. to record company; paying outstanding bills for studio, mastering, tapes and supplies, equipment rental, personnel, etc.; working with graphic artists, photographers, and others for album *artwork*, etc.

Poster

Traditionally, a placard, sign, billboard, or banner used in advertising an event, such as a concert or sale, or in advertising a product, such as an album release. In recent years, posters have also become commercial and sought-after promotional items in their own right, either replicating early advertisements for classic movies (i.e., *Casablanca*, *Gone With the Wind*, etc.), early appearances by pop icons (i.e., Beatles concerts, etc.), or featuring blow-up likenesses of past and current pop and film stars (i.e., Elvis, James Dean, etc.).

Posthumous Work

A creative work published or released after the author's death.

Pot

A variable control, often on a recording console, used to *pan* sound signals; a *pan pot*.

POV

Abbreviation for *point of view*.

Power Broker

A person who is able to make or affect high-level changes, deals, decisions, appointments, etc., by virtue of having attained a position of influence or control over a company's management, or over a network of influential contacts.

Power of Attorney

The legal authority to act on behalf of, represent, sign for, or stand in for another. Also called *letter of attorney*.

Power Play

A manipulation of others achieved through the use, or threatened use, of authority, influence, or control.

Power Trip

An action taken solely for the gratification of being able to exercise authority over others.

PPD

Abbreviation for *published price to dealers*.

PPV

Abbreviation for *pay-per-view*.

PQ Subcode

Digital sub-code on a compact disc, which, when read, offers index information about the disc being played (i.e., number of tracks on the disc, their start and stop times, frequency-boost data, etc.) See also *premastering* and *SMPTE*.

PR

Abbreviation for *public relations*.

Preamp

Abbreviated reference for *preamplifier*.

Preamplifier

A control device used with an *amplifier* to amplify signals too weak for the amplifier to handle.

Pre-Clear

To get *permission* to use copyrighted material in a project before starting production. See also *clearance* and *clearing house*.

Premastering

The first phase in the process of manufacturing compact discs from a recorded master.

Premiere

(1) A *debut* or introductory performance; the first public appearance; the first in a series of performances (i.e., "opening night").

Premium

(1) A bonus give-away item or a product sold at discount as an incentive for customers to purchase other items. (2) An amount paid for something over and above its *market price*. (3) High quality; extra value.

Premium Channel

A *cable television* channel offered to subscribers by a cable provider at a supplementary fee above the *basic cable* subscription price. *Examples*: HBO, the Disney Channel, Cinemax, Showtime, et al.

Premix

A recording technique for maximizing the number of tracks available for multitrack recording. Instead of each instrument being assigned a separate track, several instruments are simultaneously recorded and mixed together onto one track. This technique thus frees up other tracks for other instruments and/or for overdubbing later. See also *submix* and *ping-pong*.

Pre-production

The first of the three stages of record production (followed by *production* and *post production*). Preproduction involves devising a concept or direction in which the artist is matched with suitable song material, musicians, arrangers, etc.; preparing a recording budget; securing the funding for the session; booking a studio and engineer; hiring backing musicians and vocalists, etc.; insuring that all accessories (recording equipment and instruments) are available; and rehearsing the artist and accompanists.

Prequel

A literary, cinematic, or dramatic work created as a backstory or prelude to an existing work. Opposite of *sequel*.

Prerecord

(1) To tape a radio or television program for later broadcast. (2) To record music, effects, or other material for later use.

Prerecorded Tape

Commercially released recordings in a tape format, such as audiocassettes, reel-to-reels, etc., as opposed to blank tape purchased for the purpose of recording.

Prerecorded Videocassette

Commercially released videotapes in cassette format, as opposed to blank videotapes purchased for the purpose of recording television broadcasts or use in *camcorders*, etc.

Pre-Screen

(1) To informally audition with a talent scout, A&R scout, or producer's assistant before being recommended for a full-scale audition before the scout's or assistant's employer. (2) To go through submissions (of *demos*, for instance) and cull those worthy of further consideration.

Pre-Sells

Admission tickets a club sells to a band in advance of the band's performance at the club. See *pay to play*.

Present

(1) To *emcee*, introduce, announce (a program, performance, revue, production, etc.). (2) To produce, put on, stage (a concert, program, performance, revue, production, etc.). (3) To make an award in a formal setting.

Presenter

Someone who produces, puts on, stages, *emcees*, announces, or introduces a program, show, performance, production, etc.

Press

(1) To manufacture phonograph records or videodiscs using a mold or *matrix*. See *pressing*. (2) A generic reference to the news *media* (i.e., people and organizations active in gathering, publishing, and broadcasting the news).

Press Agent

A media specialist employed to write press releases and advertising copy, and generate publicity.

Press Conference

An on-the-record question-and-answer session between members of the *media* and a person or group. Also called a *news conference*.

Press Kit

A package of promotional materials (i.e., photographs, review copies, bios, clippings, background information, etc.) distributed to the *media* in order to generate publicity or *plug* an upcoming performance or a new release.

Press List

A list of individuals and organizations in the *media* who are targeted to receive publicity materials, review copies, and/or invitations to performances, release parties, premiers, press conferences, and/or other events.

Press Release

An announcement distributed to the *media* for the purpose of generating publicity (i.e., for a new signing, etc.) or to plug a new release, a performance, or other event.

Pressing

(1) The process of manufacturing phonograph records. There are two principal methods and materials used to press records: the *compression method* (using *polyvinyl chloride*), and the *injection method* (using *polystyrene*). See also *master lacquer*, *stamper*, *mother*, and *plating*. (2) A phonograph record or videodisc manufactured from a master mold or *matrix*. (3) A quantity of phonograph records or videodiscs manufactured at one time (i.e., a "first pressing," as in a "first edition").

Pressing & Distribution Deal (P&D)

A type of *distribution deal* in which an *indie* label delivers finished *masters* and *artwork* to the distributor, and the distributor then assumes responsibility for manufacturing, packaging, and distributing the finished product. Generally, P&D deals also provide that the distributor is to handle all marketing of the product, and the indie label is paid a royalty (typically 16% to 20% of the product's retail price). If the indie does its own marketing, the distributor generally retains a royalty ranging from 20% to 30% of the wholesale price of each unit sold, and either charges direct marketing costs back to the indie or deducts these costs from the indie's share of sales revenues. See also *label deal*, *distribution deal*, and *production company*.

Pressing Plant

A factory where phonograph records are manufactured from a master mold or *matrix*.

Price Discrimination

A discount offered to, or a surcharge imposed on, one customer but not others. Conditions where discounts are granted or surcharges are imposed must apply to all customers to avoid price discrimination, which is a violation of the *Uniform Commercial Code* (*UCC*).

Price/Earnings Ratio (P/E)

Also called *multiple*. The value or price of a company or an income-producing asset (such as a copyright), divided by average annual earnings. For instance, if a copyright catalog generating an average annual income of $200,000 is sold for $1 million, the multiple derived from the P/E used to arrive at the selling price was five ($1 million ÷ $200,000 = 5). Also, the price of corporate stock (i.e., the price of the company's stock divided by its earnings per share).

Price Fixing

An unlawful conspiracy between competing manufacturers or dealers whereby an agreement is reached to charge identical prices for their respective products.

Pricing

A key element of marketing whereby the price of a product is set in order to generate the most sales at optimum profits. Consumers will resist overpricing, yet very low pricing risks generating a perception of inferior goods.

Primary Station

Radio station with a broadcast market reach to a population of 500,000 or more. (A *secondary station* serves a market of less than 500,000.)

Prime Time

The time of day when the audience of television viewers is at its *peak* (usually between 8 PM and 11 PM) Monday through Friday and between 7 PM and 12:59 AM on weekends. (The peak time for radio audiences is called *drive time*, when people commute to and from work listening to their car radios.)

Print

(1) Generic reference to the publication of music in various printed formats. (2) A reference to printed publications, such as newspapers or magazines. (3) A copy of a photograph, film, or movie. (4) To produce text copies using a printing press or other replication process. (5) To produce copies of photographs, films, or movies.

Print License

Permission to make and sell printed copies of a musical work or catalog of works. As noted in *print rights* below, there are numerous formats in which music can be published in print.

Print Media

Referring to journalists, editors, and publishers of newspapers, magazines, newsletters, etc.

Print Rights

Among the rights vested in copyright ownership is the right to publish or authorize others to publish a work in any printed format. With regards to music copyrights, hit songs often appear in several printed formats simultaneously, and there are some 30 to 50 different formats in which a single song can be published in print, including: *piano copies, concept folios, educational* or *method books, mixed folios, fake books, personality folios, matching folios,* as well as arrangements for marching bands, combos, dance bands, solo instruments, choirs, vocal ensembles, stage bands, brass bands, string orchestras, etc. In addition, print rights also include the authority to publish or license the publication of lyrics only in magazines, books, greeting cards, print advertisements, etc.

Prior Use

A condition necessary before the *compulsory licensing* provisions of the *Copyright Act* apply. Once a song has been recorded and released, the copyright owner cannot prevent anyone else from recording and releasing the song, as long as the new *user* obtains a *mechanical license* to do so. Without such prior use, however, the copyright owner can forbid anyone from recording the work. See also *first use, compulsory licensing,* and *compulsory mechanical license.*

Private Performance

See *perform privately.*

Privilege

A legitimate claim, right, title, license, or prerogative.

PRMSP Fund

Abbreviation for *Phonograph Record Manufacturers Special Payments Fund.*

Pro

Abbreviated reference for *professional.*

Pro Forma Financial Statement

A statement of financial projections, or predictions of financial performance, based on an analysis of expected revenues, costs, and market potential.

Pro Rata

A proportional division or distribution, as of income, rights, shares, benefits, etc. For instance, mechanical royalties are typically divided between copublishers of a song in proportion to their respective shares of copyright ownership.

Pro Rate

See *prorate.*

PROCAN

Canadian *performing-right society,* an affiliate of *BMI,* which was merged with *ASCAP's* Canadian affiliate, *CAPAC,* into a single Canadian performing-right society called *SOCAN.*

Produce

(1) To create or cause to be created. (2) To oversee, supervise, and finance creative efforts from concept to actualization. (3) To create, present, stage, or make something, such as a recording, movie, television show, concert, play, etc., by putting the necessary elements together and directing, guiding, shaping, or molding them to a desired outcome. (4) To provide, originate, manufacture, make, or fashion a product.

Producer

Person or organization that stages an event, or that creates or causes to be created a product or service; that assembles, finances, guides, and shapes the elements of a product from concept to actuality; a provider, an originator, a maker, or a creator.

Product

Something that is *produced*. In the music business, product can be a reference to an *intangible* creative work, such as a song, but most often it is a reference to tangible, manufactured goods resulting from a creative work, such as a compact discs, printed folios, or videocassettes.

Product Code

Also called *bar code* or *universal product code*. A computer coding system used to identify products, and to track inventory and facilitate delivery of product. Product codes consist of printed patterns of lines or bars representing a string of unique identifying numbers or letters that are assigned to each product, account, or mailing piece. The codes are read by computer-linked optical scanners, which provide and record information, such as price or quantity sold, etc. Most retailers require manufacturers to supply product with bar codes so that inventory control, pricing, and sales can be tabulated by in-house databases.

Product Life Cycle

In marketing, the life of a product beginning with inception (or conception), and continuing through incubation (development), introduction, nurturing, growth (expansion), maturity, saturation, decline, and abandonment (death).

(1) Inception (or conception): The idea for the product is generated and evaluated. A cost analysis and a sales forecast are required to justify committing funds for development.

(2) Incubation (or development): Once the idea is accepted as viable, funds are committed and development begins. Expenses might include advances, demos, preproduction, recording, mixing, mastering, artwork, and manufacturing. Simultaneously, marketing plans are finalized, a release date set, and prerelease promotion and publicity begin in accordance with a marketing calendar. At this stage, much money is invested with no opportunity yet for sales.

(3) Introduction: With the product's launch into the marketplace, costs continue to rise as initial marketing steps are executed. Testing begins in earnest, and orders may trickle in, but sales aren't sufficient to recoup investment.

(4) Nurturing: The product is still in its infancy. Positive feedback from testing is used to nurture the product by pyramiding initial successes throughout the marketplace. Further promotion and marketing costs are incurred, still out of proportion to return, but in line with the amount of positive results demonstrated thus far. (The marketer tries not to get too far ahead of the curve by committing heavy marketing expenses until the concept is proven valid.)

(5) Growth (or expansion): Now the product begins to fulfill its promise with positive sales results, so that full-scale marketing can be committed with confidence. The rising line of sales income closes in on the line of product expenditures.

(6) Maturity: The product has become established and is profitable. It may still be possible to re-enter the growth phase if more marketing resources are committed, but only if careful analysis shows further growth potential is great enough to justify additional expense.

(7) Saturation: Sales reach a plateau as the marketplace is saturated. The product has gone as far as it can. Further marketing expenditures are not justified, because the product has peaked. New investment would only reduce return on investment while not spurring additional sales.

(8) Decline: The product has reached old age; sales are rapidly falling off, ultimately to a trickle. The product is maintained mainly as a catalog item.

(9) Abandonment (or death): The product has died. Inventory maintenance costs more than its worth, and the product is shelved, or (in the case of recorded product) deleted from the catalog, scrapped, or sold as cut-outs.

Product Line

The range of various products and services produced, sold, or offered by a company.

Product Manager

Person in charge of coordinating, overseeing, and/or directing the manufacture and release of product. A record company product manager's duties include the assembly of master tapes, label copy, copyright information, credits, liner notes, graphics, artwork, etc., which are forwarded to the pressing plant, mastering lab, and printers. Product managers work closely with other departments to schedule release dates and coordinate marketing activities.

Product Mix

The specific types or varieties of products or services comprising a company's *product line*. For instance, a record label may have a product mix of artists appealing to several different market profiles (i.e., Pop, Blues, Country, Rock, Rap). *Niche market* companies tend to have a very limited product mix (i.e., one or two types of products or services geared to narrow segments of the population). A limited product mix carries the risks of rising competition in, or a drop in demand from, a narrow audience, whereas a "full-line" product mix offers alternative marketing opportunities.

Production

The second of the three stages of record production (preceded by *preproduction* and followed by *post production*). The production (or "in the studio") phase involves recording basic tracks; overdubbing lead vocals and instrumental solos; overdubbing sweeteners (background voices, strings, horns, etc.); selecting final takes; mixing; making reference copies; filing required paperwork (W-4 forms, union contracts, etc.).

Production Company

An organization that produces recordings, films, or television programs for licensing to a distributor or manufacturer. A typical record production company signs artists directly, then enters into a production agreement with a record label to furnish finished masters by the artist. See also *pressing & distribution deal (P&D)*, *distribution deal*, *label deal*, *flow-through clause*, and *inducement letter*.

Production Coordinator

Person who administers paperwork and logistical details for a producer, production company, or record label, such as booking studios, scheduling sessions, hiring session musicians, making travel arrangements, forwarding invoices, checks, and contracts, etc.

Production Deal

(1) An agreement between an independent producer or production company and a record company whereby the producer furnishes finished masters by one or more artists signed directly to the producer or production company. See also *pressing & distribution deal (P&D)*, *distribution deal*, *label deal*, *flow-through clause*, and *inducement letter*. (2) An agreement where an artist signs directly to a production company (as opposed to signing directly to a record company). The production company finances and produces the recording and arranges manufacturing, marketing, and distribution, either through a network of independent distributors or through an arrangement with a record company, such as a *pressing and distribution deal*. The production company is paid a royalty on sales from the distributor, from which a portion is paid to the artist. For example, the record company might pay the production company 18% of the suggested retail price of each unit sold, and the production company in turn pays the artist 50% of that (or 9% of the suggested retail price per unit sold).

Production Manager

Person in charge of coordinating business affairs for a film, television, stage, or music production. See also *product manager*.

Production Music

Prerecorded music tracks available from *recorded music libraries*. Also called *needledrop music*, *library music*, or *canned music*. Producers of low-budget films, documentaries, training films, television programs, commercials, etc. frequently license canned tracks from library services, which provide master quality recordings and rights to use the track and the underlying music copyright, all at one relatively low fee.

Production Music Library

Also called *recorded music library*. A collection of prerecorded musical segments available for licensing in productions not requiring original music. Typical libraries contain instrumental fragments capturing a range of moods, such as lush orchestrations of romantic themes or music that builds suspense, tension, and fear. Users pay licensing fees to "drop" musical segments into productions, which range from training films to local radio programming. Also called *transcription library*, *recorded music library*, *library service*, and *music supply house*.

Professional Copy

A *lead sheet* or *top line* of a song, made available to artists, producers, arrangers, and other professional music users for demonstration purposes, but not for sale to the public. See also *DJ copy*.

Professional Manager

Person who manages and markets songs for a music publisher (also called *songplugger*, *catalog manager*, or *creative manager*). In addition to promoting (or plugging) songs, the position might also include other duties, such as scouting, signing, and developing talent, producing demos, and liaison with licensees.

Professional Musician

Person who performs as a livelihood, as opposed to one who plays without pay or as a hobby.

Professional Songwriter

Person whose songwriting activity and royalty earnings provide a livelihood, as opposed to one who writes songs as a hobby.

Profit & Loss Statement

A financial statement summarizing business revenues, expenses, and net profit or loss for an accounting period. Also called *earnings statement* or *operating statement*.

Program

(1) A public presentation. (2) A radio or television show. (3) A schedule of events, performers, performances, and other relevant information to be presented in a program. (4) A set of coded instructions for a computer; the software instructing a computer to process data or perform a sequence of operations. (5) To devise a schedule of activities, or plan an order of performances. (6) To select and schedule the order of events or performances on a public presentation, show, or broadcast. (7) To design software or write a set of coded instructions for computer data processing.

Program Consultant

An independent expert hired by radio stations to increase audience share. Program consultants may devise or revise a station's format, playlists, image, marketing strategy, etc.

Program Director (PD)

In broadcasting, the person in charge of planning and scheduling programs, and who has ultimate responsibility for the material and personnel selected for programs. See also *music director*.

Program Music

Music chosen or written specifically because it foreshadows, enhances, punctuates, sets off, or suggests a scene's mood, actions taking place, or the mental state of the characters being portrayed.

Programmer

(1) Person who writes coded instructions for computer software. (2) A *program director*.

Programming

(1) The broadcasting output of a radio or television station or network. (2) The process of planning, selecting, and scheduling a program or series of programs. (3) The coded instructions or language used in computer operations. (4) The process of designing and writing computer software or instructions for computer-driven operations.

Progressive Rock

A 1970s rock music genre characterized by grandiose arrangements and anthem-like hooks, typified by bands such as Pink Floyd, Styx, Genesis, and Emerson, Lake & Palmer, etc.

Prohibition

(1) A contractual provision that forbids a party from doing something. (2) A law or judicial order forbidding a party from doing something. See also *restriction* and *re-recording restriction*.

Promo

(1) Abbreviated reference for *promotion*. (2) A television or radio spot promotional announcement. (3) A personal appearance intended to promote something, such as a recording, film, or book. (4) A promotional presentation intended to generate sales, build an audience, or increase a market for something. See also *promo record*, *DJ copy*, and *professional copy*.

Promo Copy

A copy of commercially released product (such as a recording, book, or music publication) given away for promotional purposes only (i.e., to reviewers or broadcasters, etc.). Promo copies are usually stamped or marked "not for sale" or "for promotional use only." No royalties are paid on promo copies. See also *promo record*, *DJ copy*, and *professional copy*.

Promo Kit

A package of promotional materials, such as press releases, review copies, photos, bios, clippings, etc.

Promo Pack

See *promo kit*.

Promo Record

Also called *DJ copy*. A copy of a commercially released recording given away for promotional purposes only (i.e., to reviewers or broadcasters, etc.). Promo records are usually stamped or marked "not for sale" or "for promotional use only," etc., and/or have a hole punched through the label, in order to prevent unauthorized sale. No royalties are paid on promo records. See also *promo* and *professional copy*.

Promo Reel

An audiotape or videotape used to showcase the work of a performer, songwriter, choreographer, producer, director, etc., or to show highlights of a performance, show, film, etc., or to demonstrate a product or service.

Promo Spot

A commercial announcement, as on television or radio, which touts a coming attraction, a program, a product, a service, a company, etc.

Promo Video

A videotaped performance by an artist used to promote a new recording; a video *promo reel*. See also *music video*, *promotional music video*, and *video clip*.

Promote

(1) To publicize, advertise, advocate, or plug a product, service, event, or person in order to make sales and/or increase popularity. (2) To stage a concert or show. (3) To raise financing for a venture.

Promoter

(1) Person who publicizes, advertises, advocates, or plugs a product, service, event, or performer in order to make sales and/or increase popularity. (2) Person or organization who stages or produces a concert or show. (3) Person who raises financing for a venture.

Promotion

(1) The process of publicizing, advertising, marketing, or plugging a product, service, event, or person in order to make sales and/or increase popularity. (2) Advertising, publicity, and other efforts or materials used to attract popularity and generate sales. (4) A concert or show that is staged or presented for a paid audience. (3) The process of raising capital for a venture.

Promotion Department

Division of a company charged with promoting the company's products or services.

Promotion Expenses

The costs of promotion, including materials, artwork, photography, design, graphics, preparation, travel, advertising, consultants' fees, etc. When promotion is carried out by a record company or music publisher using staff and in-house facilities (i.e., to promote records to radio stations or plug songs to producers, etc.), the costs are usually shouldered by the company as an operating business expense. However, most recording and publishing contracts provide for *recoupment* of all or a portion of all third-party or extraordinary promotion expenses. Thus, some or all of the costs of hiring independent promotion firms, producing music videos, retaining outside publicists, placing television advertisements, etc., may be treated as a *recoupable* advance against the artist's royalty account.

Promotion Person

Person who specializes in promoting a product, and who may either be a staff employee or independent contractor hired to work a specific product for a specific period of time and/or in a specific medium. Promotion personnel usually work an assigned territory, which may either be local or regional, under the direction of a regional or national promotion manager. Their activities are concentrated most heavily on getting radio and video airplay in order to generate exposure for the product and thereby create a sales demand. See also *independent promotion*, *regional promotion*, and *national promotion*.

Promotion Restriction

A contractual prohibition against a music publisher exploiting a songwriter's works in certain media or for certain types of usages with out the writer's permission. Typical promotion restrictions include licensing works for commercials (or for certain types of products, such as alcohol, tobacco, or political advertising), for use in X-rated films or material, etc.

Promotional Music Video

Also called a *clip*. A short audiovisual work, usually encompassing the performance of one song, as produced by a record company to promote an artist's recording on television and cable networks, such as MTV, BET, CMT, VH-1, etc. *Synchronization licenses* issued by the copyright owners of songs used in such videos are usually issued for 2 to 5 year terms with renewal provisions and are limited to a performance duration that is the same as the commercially released recording. The synchronization fees are generally nominal, since the copyright owner shares the same goal as the record company, which is to use the video as a promotional vehicle to drive sales of the recording. See also *music video*.

Proof

(1) A trial printing of material run off for "proofreading" (corrections) before final printing. (Also called a "proof sheet" or *galley proof*.) (2) A trial print of a photograph.

Proof of Purchase

A receipt showing date, place, price, and item purchased.

Prop

Shorthand reference for *property*. See below.

Property

(1) Something to which an individual or a business has a legal title of ownership and the exclusive right to possess, enjoy, and dispose of. (2) A performer or writer under contract. (3) A copyright, a book, a script, a film, a play. (4) A physical object (except costumes or scenic backdrops) used in a play, film, or television show, such as furniture, a bottle, a gun, etc., commonly called a *prop* for short.

Proprietary

(1) Information or data developed by, or belonging exclusively to, a private individual, company, or corporation. (2) Something that is owned exclusively. (3) Information protected by a patent, copyright, or trademark.

Proprietary Interest
Ownership or a share thereof.

Proprietary Rights
All rights associated with ownership.

Proprietor
An owner, usually of a business; one who possesses legal title.

Proprietorship
An unincorporated business owned by one person. A *sole proprietorship*.

Prorate
To assess, divide, distribute, pay, or charge in proportion to *pro rata* shares of ownership or liability. For example, if a publication containing arrangements of 20 songs pays an inclusive royalty of $1.00 for each unit sold, each song's copyright owner is paid a prorated royalty of 5¢ per unit.

Prospectus
A formal document or business proposal summarizing key details of a venture or project, intended for the use of potential investors, lenders, partners, customers, or buyers.

Protection
The preservation, guardianship, and safekeeping of a right, title, or interest, such as is given to creative works by copyright law, which prohibits use, reproduction, or sale without the owner's authorization. See also *copy protection*, *copyright*, *patent*, and *trademark*.

Provision
In a contract or license, a clause that guarantees, promises, stipulates, specifies, or qualifies a condition of agreement, or a law that prohibits, restricts, or limits some action.

Proviso
A *provision* in a contract, deed, or legal statute that imposes a condition, restriction, or limitation.

PRS
The *performing-right society* in Great Britain.

Prudent-Man-Rule
To handle assets and money prudently, seeking to preserve capital and avoiding speculation. See *fiduciary responsibility*.

PSA
Abbreviation for *public service announcement*.

Pseudonym
A *pen name*, *nom de plume*, *stage name*, *assumed name*.

Pseudonymous Work
A work copyrighted or otherwise publicly credited to an author using a *pen name*, *nom de plume*, *stage name*, *assumed name*, or *pseudonym*. Under the *Copyright Act of 1976*, a work by an author whose identity is concealed by a pseudonym is granted copyright protection for a term of either 75 years from date of publication or 100 years from the date of creation, whichever comes first. If the author's identity is later revealed in the records of the Copyright Office, copyright protection is altered to extend for the duration of the identified author's life plus 50 years. (As of 1998, Congress was considering legislation to extend copyright protection for nonpseudonymous works to life of author plus 70 years.)

PTY
Abbreviation for *proprietorship* or *proprietary*.

Public
The people at large; the entire population of a community, district, county, city, state, country, etc. Any unrestricted portion of the community at large. Something is made public when it becomes open to the knowledge and scrutiny of the community as a whole. A public performance, for instance, is one that is open to all (though audience members may have to pay for admission), as opposed to a private performance that is limited to those with invitations. A publicly owned company is one whose stock is available to all who are willing to buy it.

Public Access Television
Cable television channels allocated to nonprofit organizations and private citizens, as required by the 1984 Cable Act, in order to promote programming of local community interests and prevent cable monopolization by commercial interests. In addition to making channels available to nonprofits and individuals, local cable franchise holders must also provide studio space, equipment, and technical assistance.

Public Address System (P.A.)
An electronic device consisting of microphone(s), amplifier, and speaker(s), used for closed-circuit broadcasting in public areas.

Public Broadcaster
A noncommercial television or radio broadcasting station or network. See *Public Broadcasting Service*, *public television*, *public radio*, and *National Public Radio*.

Public Broadcasting Service (PBS)

A network association of public, noncommercial television stations. Originally called *National Educational Television (NET)*, PBS became government-financed under the aegis of the *Corporation for Public Broadcasting* in 1968, and today receives a large portion of its funding through viewer subscriptions and corporate underwriting, thus circumventing the commercial pressures of achieving the audience ratings necessary to attract paid advertisers. As such, public television concentrates its programming on documentaries, panel discussions, children's educational shows, and the arts. See also *National Public Radio (NPR)* and *Corporation for Public Broadcasting (CPB)*.

Public Domain (PD)

Any publication, creative work, intellectual property, product, or process that is not protected by patent or copyright. Once copyright or patent protection expires, a work or process is said to be in the "public domain." Any member of the public may make use of a PD work or process without permission or payment. No one may claim ownership, right, or title to a PD work or process.

Public Performance

See *perform publicly*.

Public Radio

Local, nonprofit radio stations, which produce and transmit news and other programming to the public on a noncommercial basis. Most public radio stations are affiliated with *National Public Radio (NPR)*, which is funded through the *Corporation for Public Broadcasting*, individual contributions, and underwriting from corporate and foundation donors.

Public Relations (PR)

The process of establishing a favorable public image, and the activities undertaken to do so. Public relations as a process occurs virtually any time there are dealings with the public (those outside of a company or an organization), including attending conventions, making charitable donations, taking someone to lunch (networking), and publicity.

Public Service Announcement (PSA)

An announcement or noncommercial spot broadcast on television or radio for the benefit of the public, which the broadcaster does without charge. PSAs are used to fill unsold commercial time, while promoting nonprofit organizations or governmental agencies or information deemed to be beneficial for the public interest.

Public Station

A local television or radio station supported by public funds and private donations as opposed to selling airtime for paid advertisements. See *noncommercial station*, *public television*, *public radio*, *Public Broadcasting System*, and *National Public Radio*.

Public Television

Local, nonprofit television stations, which produce and transmit news and other programming to the public on a noncommercial basis. Most public television stations are associated with *Public Broadcasting Service (PBS)*, which is funded through the *Corporation for Public Broadcasting*, individual contributions, and underwriting from corporate and foundation donors.

Publication

(1) A volume or an edition of printed material issued for sale or distribution to the public. (2) Something made known to the public. (3) The act of publishing. (4) A recording, film, or other tangible representation of a creative work made available to the public by display, sale or other form of distribution. (5) A public declaration, announcement, broadcast, or other type of communication by which information is disseminated to the public.

Publicist

Person employed to generate *publicity* for a company, organization, or individual.

Publicity

Information that becomes public knowledge, whether deliberately disseminated or not. When generated by design, publicity is a form of advertising or promotion, used to gain acceptance, increase popularity, or stimulate sales. In contrast to paid advertising, publicity can result in free space or broadcast time through press releases, interviews, articles, feature stories, and reviews. Although publicists, press agents, and PR reps can fashion publicity campaigns to achieve the widest possible media exposure, publicity can't be controlled. Since media outlets aren't paid to publicize a message, there is no way to dictate when or if it will be used, how it is presented, or whether it will be accurate; nor is there any way to censure bad publicity or reviews.

Publicity Release

See *press release*.

Publicity, Right of

A contractual provision giving a record company or music publisher the right to use the name and likeness and background information of an artist, songwriter, or producer for the purposes of promoting and marketing works covered by the agreement.

Publish

(1) To prepare and issue material for display, distribution, or sale to the public. (2) To make known. (3) To bring to the attention of the public. (4) To spread information via public advertisement or announcement. (5) To publicize or broadcast. (6) To issue a publication.

Published Price to Dealers (PPD)

A record company's stated price to be charged by wholesalers or distributors to retail merchants for the product they resell to consumers. Some companies use the PPD as a base upon which to calculate royalty payments; other companies base royalties on the product's *suggested retail list price (SRLP)*.

Publisher

A company or individual engaged in preparing and issuing material for distribution or sale to the public.

Publishers Online Information (POLI)

See *POLI*.

Publishers Online Information-Plus (POLI-Plus)

See *POLI-Plus*.

Publisher's Share

Net income from copyrights after deduction of royalty payments to writers.

Publishing

(1) Preparing and issuing material for distribution or sale to the public. (2) Making known. (3) Bringing to the attention of the public. (4) Spreading information via public advertisement or announcement. (5) Publicizing; broadcasting. (6) Issuing a publication.

Puff Piece

Writing containing high praise of its subject matter, such as found on book jackets, album covers, press releases, etc., which is created to generate favorable publicity or to promote a product, project, or individual. See also *blurb*.

Pulse Code Modulation (PCM)

A form of *digital* modulation in which an input signal is translated into pulses of varying length according to *binary* code.

Punch In

To depress (punch) a recording key on a *console* and activate a microphone or synchronization device in order to insert or overdub new or additional material.

Punch Out

To depress (punch) a control key on a *console* and deactivate a microphone or synchronization device in order to stop overdubbing.

Punch Up

(1) To add excitement or otherwise enhance a musical arrangement or script. (2) To punch holes in labels or packaging of product (i.e., record labels, album jackets) to mark the product as promotional copies, not intended for sale.

Punk Rock

British rock music genre that gained notoriety in the 1970s, characterized by spare production, hard-driving aggressiveness, and angry lyrics expressing alienation with societal conventions and popular culture. See also *New Wave*.

Purchase License

Permission to use prerecorded music, granted by a producer or *recorded music library* in return for a one-off, upfront fee.

Pure Jazz

Jazz music performed in the traditional manner, usually instrumental, *improvised*, and using *acoustic* instruments. Also called *classic jazz*.

Push

To aggressively market, publicize, advertise, promote, and plug a product, service, or person in order to stimulate sales and/or increase popularity.

Put on Notice

To send a written *notice* advising a party to a contract or license of the sender's demands or intentions, as required by the terms of the contract or license. For example, the sender may be required to put the other party on notice when it intends to exercise an option, terminate an agreement, or demand the *cure* of a failure to perform in a timely manner as agreed, etc. All contracts and licenses provide (or should provide) clarity as to whom, how, when, and where notices must be given.

PVC

(1) Abbreviation for *polyvinyl chloride*. (2) Abbreviation for *prerecorded videocassette*.

PX

Abbreviation for *post exchange*. PX sales of recorded product are made on military bases and ship's stores to military personnel and their immediate relatives. Wholesale prices to military bases are generally discounted, because post exchanges and ship's stores resell product at prices lower than those charged by civilian retailers.

QS
Music format abbreviation for *quiet storm.*

Quad
Abbreviation for *quadraphonic.*

Quadraphonic Recording
A system for recording and playing back four independent channels of sound through speakers placed in each of four corners of a listening area. Quadraphonic's developers envisioned consumers rushing to replace their *stereo* systems with *quad,* but the format failed to achieve commercial success.

Qualified
(1) Person eligible to do something, such as practice a profession or join an organization, by virtue of training, examination, licensing, or meeting other requirements. (2) A conditional acceptance of an offer (i.e., acceptance contingent upon the other party agreeing to certain modifications of the terms). (3) An approval, endorsement, certification, or opinion that is limited, conditioned, or restricted to certain conditions having been met or to verification of information provided. (4) A right, privilege, permission, or license that is limited, conditioned, or restricted in scope.

Qualified Works
In the *credit weighting system* used by *ASCAP* to calculate *performance royalty* payments, songs that generate a specified number of featured performances during a five-year survey period are called "qualifying works," which means they are assigned higher credit values.

Quarter-Track Stereo
A tracking format for recording stereo channels in one direction on a quarter-inch *magnetic tape,* so that two stereo channels can be recorded in the other direction when the tape is flipped over.

Quarterly
(1) An accounting period, occurring four times a year at three-month intervals. (2) A publication issued four times yearly at regular three-month intervals.

Query
An inquiry, usually relating to ownership or availability of rights, authorship credits, or division of royalty shares.

Questionnaire
In marketing, a list of questions to be answered by participants of a market survey in order to gauge commercial strength of a product or service. Responses are used to compile quantitative and/or qualitative statistical information for market research. See also *reply card, response card,* and *bounce-back card.*

Quid Pro Quo
"Something for something." A situation where one party provides a service or something of value to another party in return for some other service or thing of value.

Quiet Storm

A genre of contemporary R&B music, or radio station program format, characterized by soft ballads, smooth arrangements, and romantic lyrics.

Quitclaim

A legal transfer of a title, right, or claim from one party to another, in which the first party irrevocably renounces (quits) all claim to a possession or right.

Quote

(1) A booking price, royalty rate, licensing fee, studio rate, producer's fee, etc. given in response to a *query* from a potential client or music user. (2) To cite an excerpt from a review, article, book, song lyrics, etc.

R
Music format abbreviation for *rock*.

R Form
Form used to file *copyright renewals* with the *Copyright Office*. Under the *Copyright Act of 1909*, statutory copyright protection was given for an initial term of 28 years with the right to renew copyright protection for an additional 28 years. Form R is obsolete for works created on or after January 1, 1978, since the *Copyright Act of 1976* grants statutory copyright protection for one term only (currently life of author plus 50 years, but Congress was considering legislation in 1998 to extend this to life of author plus 70 years), with no renewal options.

RA
Music format abbreviation for *rap*.

R&B
Music format abbreviation for *Rhythm & Blues*.

RAB
Abbreviation for *Radio Advertising Bureau*.

Rack
(1) A free-standing metal frame or case used to house or mount audio and computer equipment. (2) A portable shelving unit or case used to display merchandise, such as CDs or cassettes. (3) To stock merchandise in portable display units. See *rackjobber*, below.

Rackjobber
A salesperson or sales organization that buys product from *one-stops* or distributors to sell directly to consumers off of free-standing display racks in retail establishments. Retailers typically receive sales commissions or rental fees in return for providing rack space.

Rack Up
(1) To score big sales or chart success. (2) To fill sales *racks* with stock. (3) To make prerecorded spots ready for broadcast.

R&D
Abbreviation for *research & development*.

Radio
Term applied to the transmission and reception of radio waves. In radio transmission, sound waves are transformed into electromagnetic waves, which are picked up by a receiving antenna, then converted back into sound waves.

Every radio broadcasting station is allocated one of two types of modulated frequency to carry information: *amplitude modulation (AM)* or *frequency modulation (FM)*. In FM, the frequency of the carrier is made to fluctuate: in AM, the strength of the carrier is made to fluctuate in time with the audio signal.

FM transmissions are not sensitive to atmospheric interference and electrical disturbances that cause static in AM radio broadcasting. In addition, FM broadcasting stations can be operated in very-high-frequency bands that are in a range much wider than the standard broadcast AM bands, allowing for a greater number of broadcasting stations in a given area without mutual interference. The superior reception of FM, and the ability to broadcast in stereo, together with comparatively inexpensive broadcasting equipment, have resulted in the rapid growth of FM stations and radio audiences at the expense of AM broadcasting. Approximately 5,250 radio stations broadcast on AM in the United States, compared with around 7,750 FM stations.

Traditionally, radio has been the primary mode of introducing new musical recordings to consumers. In recent years, however, other marketing methods (such as video clips broadcast on television) have become increasingly important.

Radio Advertising Bureau

Trade association of radio broadcasters and advertisers. Publishes an annual report called *Radio Facts*, which updates statistical information on current radio station formats. Located at 304 Park Avenue South, 7th Floor, New York, NY 10010. Tel: (212) 387-2100; Fax: (212) 254-8908.

Radio & Records

Weekly *trade magazine*, offering reviews of new releases, charts, and playlist surveys from radio stations focusing on *CHR, AOR, AC, jazz, country, rock, R&B, New Age*, etc. located at 1930 Century Park West, Los Angeles, CA 90067. Tel: (310) 553-4330; Fax: (310) 203-9763.

Radio Facts

See *Radio Advertising Bureau*, above.

Rag

(1) A *ragtime* composition. (2) Slang term (usually derogatory) for a newspaper or magazine.

Ragga

Also called *dancehall*, ragga is a very uptempo, hard-driving dance genre characterized by aggressive rap deliveries and synthesized rhythms married to roots reggae.

Ragtime

Early form of jazz music popular from 1890s to the 1920s.

Rainbow

A full-color artwork proof used to check ink colors, layout, and typesetting before a print run is started. Though a rainbow may serve the same purpose as a *color match*, it is not printed directly from a negative, thus the colors may not exactly match the inks. See also *Pantone Matching System* and *color match*.

RAIS

The *mechanical-right society* in Russia.

RAO

Abbreviation for Russian Authors Society. The *performing-right society* in Russia.

Rap

A sub-genre of contemporary R&B music characterized by spoken delivery of improvised rhyming lyrics integrated with funky, hip-hop music tracks. Rap originated in the late 1970s among East Coast African-American and Hispanic performers, and gained widespread popular appeal during 1980s and 1990s.

R&R

Music format abbreviation for *rock & roll*.

Rate

(1) A price or fee, usually computed on a *per use* or *per unit* basis. A royalty rate may be expressed in dollars-and-cents (i.e., a rate of 50¢ per unit), or as a percentage of a unit's recommended retail or dealer price (i.e., 10% of retail). A *mechanical royalty rate*, thus, is the amount paid to a song copyright owner for each unit (phonorecord) sold. Note, however, that the term "rate" is frequently used in the music publishing business to signify a mechanical royalty rate that is lower than *statutory*. If a record company executive requests a "rate" from a publisher, he or she is asking for a discount of from 25% to 50% off the statutory royalty amount. (2) To value, assess, appraise. See also *rate of interest*, *rate of exchange*, and *flat rate*. (3) The price or fee charged for use of a studio, equipment rental, and/or for the performance of certain services; rates are often computed hourly, daily or weekly.

Rate Card

A summary of charges for advertising space or time, issued by newspapers, magazines, and broadcasters to potential advertisers.

Rate of Exchange

The value of one unit of currency from one country measured against one unit of currency from another country. Also called *exchange rate*.

Rate of Interest

(1) A percentage of a loan amount charged to the debtor by the lender. (2) A percentage of an amount of money on deposit, such as in a savings account, which is earned by leaving the money on deposit. Also called *interest rate*.

Rating

A ranking, an assessment, or an appraisal of worth measured against items in the same category. (2) An assessment of one's creditworthiness. (3) The percentage of surveyed listeners or viewers tuned into a particular radio or television program, station, or network at any given time. See also *Arbitron*, *Nielsen*, *sweeps*, and *audience share*.

RDP

Abbreviation for *recommended dealer price*.

Real Property

Real estate; land and all attached property, such as buildings, houses, garages, wells, walls, fences, and all improvements, as well as natural features, such as trees, shrubs, lakes, etc.

Real Time

(1) The monitoring of something, such as a recording session, while it is in progress. (2) To duplicate a recording using a copying process at the same *ips* or *rpm* as the original (as opposed to *highspeed duplication*). In other words, if the original or master is 30 minutes long, it takes 30 minutes to make the copy. Though time-consuming, real-time duplication produces the highest possible sound quality, because the master's frequency response and dynamic range are almost exactly replicated on the copy. (3) The actual time required for a controlled process, from inception to completion.

Rear Window Decision

Name given to Supreme Court decision in a case called *Stewart v. Abend*, which concerned copyright renewal rights to a song used in the classic Alfred Hitchcock film *Rear Window*, starring Jimmy Stewart and Grace Kelly. The upshot of the decision affected songs written before 1978 (when the *Copyright Act of 1976* took effect). Prior to January 1, 1978, songs were given copyright protection for a 28-year term with the right to renew copyright protection for a further 28 years. The Supreme Court ruled that if a pre-1978 song was used in a motion picture during its initial 28-year copyright term, and the writer(s) died during the initial term, the *heirs* of the writer(s) are entitled to terminate the *synchronization license* during the renewal period. As a result, many film studios found themselves having to delete certain pre-1978 songs from film soundtracks if they couldn't get heirs to agree to new licensing terms. In addition, studios are reluctant to license pre-1978 songs for new films unless they can get heirs to co-sign synchronization licenses. See also *renewal expectancy*.

Re-assignment

A contract provision whereby an *assignor* can have copyrights or masters transferred back from the *assignee* under certain conditions, such as *default*, bankruptcy, sale of company, or *termination* of the contract. See also *reversion*.

Rebroadcast

(1) A program that is repeated, rerun, or relayed to another station. (2) To repeat, rerun, or relay a broadcast.

Recapture of Rights

See *reversion* and *reassignment*.

Receipts

The total amount of money received by a business or venture, as from sales of product, services, tickets, royalties, etc. See also *take* and *gate*.

Receipts-Basis Royalties

Royalties calculated and paid on the basis of monies actually received, as opposed to being calculated on credit sales, *receivables*, shipments, or *at source* royalty earnings.

Receivables

Money owed, due, and awaiting payment for product sold or shipped on credit, or for services rendered on credit.

Reciprocal

An obligation, service, action, or recognition that is mutual or interchangeable, to be performed, exchanged, or experienced by both parties to an agreement.

Recital

(1) In a contract or license, a *whereas clause*, which cites the underlying reason for the transaction. *Example*: "Whereas, the Publisher is engaged in the business of publishing, selling, and exploiting songs, and Whereas the Writer is a composer of musical compositions, Therefore, in consideration of the mutual covenants herein contained and other good and valuable consideration, it is hereby agreed..." (2) In a lawsuit or legal pleading, a statement by the *plaintiff* introducing a complaint or an allegation. (3) A musical performance by a soloist or a duet.

Recommended Retail Price (RRP)

Same as *list price* and *suggested retail list price (SRLP)*. The suggested retail price of an item as published or advertised by the manufacturer to the consumer, but which may be discounted at the retailer's discretion. The difference between the RRP and the price paid by the retailer to the distributor or wholesaler is the retailer's margin of operating profit. Also called "sticker price," "list," "suggested retail price," and "published retail price (PRP)."

Record

(1) To produce, create, or copy a performance on to media, such as audio tape or CD. (2) A *recording*, in any format, of information, data, sound, or video. *Note*: Although the *vinyl record* format is no longer the primary mode of merchandising music recordings, the term "record" is now used in generic reference to all recorded music product, including compact discs, audiocassettes, vinyl discs, video, etc. See also *phonorecord* and *recording*. (3) A collection of related items of information treated as one unit. See also *database*.

Record Bin

A divided or partitioned container for display storage of recorded product in retail stores.

Record Club

Mail order record companies that offer selected phonorecords to members from monthly catalog mailings, usually containing special offers, discounts, bonus opportunities, etc. Major record clubs, like Columbia Record Club and BMG Music Service, license recordings from other labels to offer along with product distributed by their parent companies (Sony and BMG/RCA, respectively). The clubs manufacture the recordings using original artwork and logos of the licensors, paying licensors a royalty on each unit sold. The clubs are also responsible for paying *mechanical royalties* to music publishers whose works are contained on the recordings.

Club membership enrollment plans enable new members to purchase several recordings of their choice for a nominal sum, such as $1 plus shipping, usually tied to an obligation to buy a certain number of other recordings at club prices within a specified period of time. To encourage additional purchases, members are frequently offered special discounts, bonus records (buy two, get one free), etc.

Record Mailer

(1) A sheet of cardboard or other light material used to protect *phonorecords* when mailed or shipped. (2) A protective shipping container, such as a cardboard envelope, carton, box, or bubblepack.

Record Number

A serial or catalog number assigned by a record company to a particular release in order to identify the release for purposes of manufacturing, licensing, inventory, sales, shipping, royalty accounting, etc. A record number identifies the product as a collective whole, as opposed to a *master number*, which identifies *master tapes* of individual tracks, or a *matrix number* used to identify individual manufacturing parts. Record numbers usually are given slight variations to identify the type of format in which a product is released. For instance, an album might be given the record number 1000, with MC-1000 assigned to audio cassettes, CD-1000 to compact discs, and LP-1000 to vinyl LPs.

Record Player

Also called *phonograph*, a device that reproduces sounds recorded onto discs etched with spiral grooves. The discs (records) are rotated on the record player's *turntable*, and a *tone arm*, containing a *stylus* at one end, picks up vibrations from the grooves as the record rotates. The vibrations are converted by a *transducer* into corresponding electrical signals, which are expanded by an *amplifier*, then converted to sound by a loudspeaker. The first sound-reproducing device (called a *Phonograph*), used cylinders rather than discs, and was devised by *Thomas Edison* in 1877. *Emile Berliner's Gramophone* (1884) was the first sound-reproducing device to use discs, and was the forerunner of the modern record player.

Record Producer

Person or organization who produces sound recordings. See *producer* and *independent producer*.

Record Sales

Generic reference to sales of recorded music in all formats (i.e., CDs, cassettes, vinyl, etc.).

Record Week

Canadian music industry *trade magazine*, located at 216 Carlton, Toronto, Ontario, Canada.

Record/CD Rental

See *rental*.

Recordation

See *recordation of transfer*, below.

Recordation of Transfer

The procedural formality of lodging a written assignment detailing a change of copyright ownership with the *Copyright Office*. (See also *transfer of copyright*.) Recordation was previously a prerequisite to bringing an *infringement* suit. Though this is no longer the case, the benefits of recordation are unchanged, since recordation places the transfer document on public record, and helps establish *chain of title* and priorities between conflicting transfers and licenses. See also *mortgage recordation*.

Recorded Music Library

A collection of prerecorded musical segments available for licensing in productions not requiring original music. Typical libraries contain instrumental fragments capturing a range of moods, such as lush orchestrations of romantic themes or music that builds suspense, tension, and fear. Users pay licensing fees to "drop" musical segments into productions, which range from training films to local radio programming. Also called *transcription library*, *library service*, *production music library*, and *music supply house*.

Recording

(1) The process of producing, creating, or copying sound and/or visual images in any permanent format whereby the recorded material can be reproduced by mechanical or electrical means. (2) A medium, such as compact disc or magnetic tape, on which sound and/or visual images have been recorded. (3) An account, statement, testament, or memorial. See also *magnetic recording tape*, *phonorecord*, and *record*.

Recording Artist

A singer or musician whose creative abilities, talents, and skills are applied to creating and recording works of commercial and/or aesthetic value.

Recording Arts

The activities, skills, crafts, disciplines, studies, principles, and methods applied to conceptualizing and recording creative works of commercial and/or aesthetic value. This field of endeavor includes technical (engineering, mixing, etc.) as well as creative aspects (performing, producing, arranging, etc.). See also *recording sciences*.

Recording Budget

An itemized allocation of money to cover costs of a recording session, including studio and equipment rental, technical personnel, creative personnel, etc. While recording budgets are generally worked out between a record company and producer (and/or the artist), artists' and producers' advances are not included. Many record companies, however, now provide all-inclusive *recording funds* instead of budgets; the funds include the advances.

Recording Costs

Expenditures related directly to recording: studio rental, tapes, cartage, engineers and other technical personnel, talent (musicians, singers, arrangers, etc.), support personnel (copyists, caterers, etc.), logistics (transportation, parking, storage, lodging, etc.).

Recording Fund

An all-inclusive financial commitment by a record company to an artist, which combines a recording budget and artist's advance. By combining the two, the record company forces the artist to control recording costs, since any money spent on recording in excess of the budget reduces the amount left over for the artist's personal use. See also *all-in advance*.

Recording Industries Music Performance Trust Funds (RIMPTF)

An independent trust created in 1948 as part of an agreement between the *AFM* and the recording industry. It supports and promotes music appreciation and education through the presentation of live musical performances and school workshops. Funding comes from contributions of recording companies of a small percentage of their revenues. RIMPTF is the largest single sponsor of live music in the world. Concerts provided through RIMPTF are free to the public, and take place throughout the US and Canada in concert halls, clubs, parks, schools, etc.

Recording Industry Association of America (RIAA)

Trade association established in 1952 in order to promote and protect the interests of record companies, particularly with regards to counterfeiting, bootlegging, and piracy. The organization also certifies sales of recordings in order to officially award *gold* and *platinum* discs, and provides extensive research on the markets for recorded music product. All major record companies belong to the RIAA, as do most of the successful indie labels. In fact, 90% of all recorded product sold in America is produced by RIAA members. Located at 1020 19th Street NW, Washington, DC 20036. Tel: (202) 775-0101.

Recording Scale

Minimum fees for musicians, vocalists, et al engaged in recording, as agreed between record manufacturers and unions, such as the *AFM* and *AFTRA*. AFM members (musicians, leaders, contractors, copyists, arrangers, orchestrators) receive scales based on the *AFM Phonograph Record Labor Agreement*. Vocalists are covered by AFTRA agreements. Scales are set for regular sessions of 3 hours (basic scale), special sessions (1.5 hours max), sessions of more than 3 hours (overtime scale), and sessions occurring outside of "regular" business hours (premium scale), which include holidays, after midnight, after 1 PM on weekends, etc. Double scale is paid to session leaders and contractors, and additional payments are made to those who play more than one instrument on a session (*doubling*), and those who have to bring in heavy equipment or large instruments (*cartage*). Different types of scales are set for demo sessions, symphonic recordings, movie soundtracks, television taping, and commercials.

Recording Sciences

The systematic field of study and/or practical application of recording technologies. Includes studio and equipment design, engineering, acoustics, electronics, mixing, etc. See also *acoustics* and *recording arts*.

Recording Session

A time scheduled to make a recording; the process of recording a performance.

Recoup

(1) To receive back a sum equal to an investment, an advance, a loan, or a loss. (2) To deduct or withhold an amount equivalent to a loan, a loss, an advance, or an investment. (3) To be reimbursed.

Recoupment

A reimbursement for a loan, a loss, an investment, or an advance.

Reel

A plastic or metal *spool* onto which a roll of tape or film is wound for storage.

Re-Entry

A song or recording that enters a chart listing of best sellers after having once appeared on that chart and then losing its position.

Reference Copy

A copy of a recording made solely for reference or demonstration, as opposed to being used as a master from which other recordings will be made.

Reference Lacquer

A metal disc coated with lacquer made from cellulose resin, used in the *disc mastering* process as a reference to check the transfer quality of sound from a master tape to disc before approving the manufacture of vinyl records. Reference lacquers are fragile; their sound quality deteriorates noticeably with repeated playings. Also called an *acetate* or *test pressing*.

Refrain

(1) A melody. (2) A recurring theme. (3) A verse or chorus repeated at intervals throughout a song. (4) To hold back, to keep from doing something, to abstain.

Reggae

A genre of popular music originating in Jamaica in the 1960s, characterized by looping, offbeat rhythm patterns and lyrics frequently dealing with sociopolitical matters and/or tenets of the Rastafarian movement.

Regional

(1) Pertaining to a geographical area or district. (2) Characteristics peculiar to or identifiable with a particular geographical area or district, such as accents, dialects, grammar, vocabulary, tastes in foods or music, etc.

Regional Distribution

A song, recording, book, movie, etc. that is marketed and distributed in one or more specific geographical areas or districts, but not nationally.

Regional Distributor

A wholesaler or supplier of product to retailers in a specific geographical area or district.

Regional Hit

A song, recording, book, movie, etc. that achieves commercial success and popular appeal in one or more specific geographical areas or districts, but not nationally.

Regional Testing

A song, recording, book, movie, etc. that is marketed on a limited basis in one or more specific geographical areas or districts, in order to gauge commercial acceptance and hone marketing tactics before committing to an expensive, national marketing campaign.

When test marketing doesn't succeed within the test region, the marketer has either failed to get the marketing concept properly focused or there is a product failure. Either case is a red flag, indicating barriers to success on a national level, and a clear sign that rolling out big bucks for a full-scale marketing campaign will be a wasted expenditure, since there is no proven commercial acceptance of the product or service. See also *market research* and *test marketing*.

Register

(1) A roll or book containing an official listing of related events, names, titles, items, or actions. (2) To record in writing a series of related events, names, titles, items, or actions. (3) In music, a range of notes that an instrument can play or a voice can sing. (4) An organ stop (i.e., a pull-key that regulates a tuned set of pipes or emulates the sound of a tuned set of pipes.). (5) To record a claim of copyright. See also *registration*, *recordation of transfer*, *copyright formalities*, and *copyright registration*.

Register of Copyrights, The

Head of the *Copyright Office* section of the *Library of Congress*, who is charged with overseeing the formalities of copyright registration.

Registered Mail

Mail officially recorded and tracked by the post office to insure safe delivery.

Registration

One of the *formalities* of establishing a claim of copyright ownership under the *Copyright Act of 1976* is the registration of claims in the *Copyright Office* of the *Library of Congress*. A registration is not the same as making a *deposit*, which is a separate formality. Registration may be made at any time during the term of copyright. Under the accords of the *Berne Convention*, which the United States joined effective March 1, 1989, registration is not required to establish a copyright claim, nor is it any longer a prerequisite for bringing a court action against alleged infringers. However, copyright claimants may not be fully eligible for awards of statutory damages and attorney's fees for acts of infringement that occur before a registration is made. For this reason, it is recommended that copyright claims be registered with the Copyright Office at the first opportunity. See also *register*, *recordation of transfer*, *copyright formalities*, and *copyright registration*.

Regrind

To melt down defective phonograph records in order to reuse the vinyl in the *compression method* of *pressing* phonograph records.

Reissue

(1) To re-release a recording. See also *repackaging*. (2) To re-press or manufacture new copies of a recording in order to make it available again. (3) To publish something anew. (4) A second or subsequent printing.

Reject

(1) To turn down, pass on, decline to accept. (2) To throw out, set aside, or discard because of a flaw, defect, or substandard quality. (3) Something that has been turned down or discarded.

Rejection Letter

A notice received from or sent by one who turns down or declines to accept a submission, offer, or proposal.

Related Rights

In the use of copyrighted song material, the *user* typically generates either tangible or intangible properties which have rights in and of themselves, and which belong to the user, not the author of the copyrighted material. *Examples*: rights stemming from a performance belong to the performer; copyright in a sound recording belongs to the producer of the recording; copyright to a television program belongs to the program's producer. Also called *neighboring rights*.

Release

(1) To publish, issue, distribute, or make available for sale, use, or performance. (2) Something that is published, distributed, or made available (i.e., a recording, book, movie, press release, etc.). (3) To let go, to set free from an obligation or debt (i.e., to release from a contract). (4) A document certifying the discharge or forgiveness of an obligation or a debt, or the relinquishment of a right or a claim. See also *model release* and *quitclaim*.

Release Commitment

Provision in a recording contract requiring the company to release product by the artist within a specified time frame. If the company fails to release product within that period, the artist can put the company on notice to *cure* the inaction. The artist can then *terminate* the contract if the company fails to act within the cure period. See also *performance obligation*, *release guarantee*, and *minimum release obligation*.

Release Guarantee

(1) A contractual provision in which a publisher, producer, or distributor guarantees the commercial publication or issuance of a song, recording, film, etc. Such a provision may also include a time frame for release and/or a minimum number of songs, recordings, films, etc. to be so released as well as the territories in which the release(s) shall take place. See also *release commitment*, above, and *performance clause*. (2) A *minimum release obligation*: a commitment by a songwriter, artist-songwriter, or producer-songwriter that a certain number of recordings written during the term of a music publishing agreement will be commercially released. Quite often, music publishers sign songwriters who are also artists or producers on the expectation that their collateral work will generate commercially released material assigned to the publisher. In such situations, advances may be payable as and when songs are actually released.

Release Phrase

Musical term referring to the passage between a chorus or *hook* and a verse or a repeat of the hook. A transitional passage between two sections of a song. Also called a *bridge*. See also *middle eight*.

Release Requirement

See *release guarantee*, *release commitment*, *minimum release obligation*, and *performance clause*.

Religious Music

Music written and published for religious ceremonies or services. See also *religious performance*, *gospel*, and *spiritual*.

Religious Performance

A performance of a copyrighted musical work during a non-broadcast religious service. Under the *Copyright Right Act of 1976*, copyright owners maintain licensing rights to songs publicly performed at not-for-profit events, such as charity balls, school dances, fraternal lodge parties, religious broadcasts, etc. There are, however, four exceptions where nonprofit public performances are exempt from licensing requirements: (1) religious services that are not broadcast; (2) performances at events where there is no admission fee, either directly (ticket sales), or indirectly (contributions, club membership, etc.), and no direct or indirect fee is paid to performers; (3) classroom teaching by nonprofit educational institutions; and (4) certain nonprofit educational and governmental public service broadcasts of instructional materials.

See also *performance license*, *performance royalty*, *performance fee*, and *performing-right society*.

Remake
A new version of an old song. A new movie based on and adapted from an earlier movie.

Remaster
Usually, to master a previously released recording for release in a new format (i.e., an old vinyl release being re-released on compact disc).

Remedy
(1) To set right a wrong committed; to rectify, counteract, correct an error, or *cure* a *default* under a contract. (2) A contractual provision stating precise terms of compensation, relief, or avenues for redress open to one party in the event the other party fails to act or perform as agreed.

Remix
Usually, to mix a master recording to create a different version of a commercial release for release in another format (i.e., a 12-inch single "disco mix;" a "radio mix," etc.)

Remote
A site away from a studio where filming, taping, recording, or broadcasting takes place "on location." The term is also used in reference to portable equipment (cameras, recorders, microphones, etc.) and/or trucks, trailers, or vans from which the equipment is operated on location.

Remote Broadcast
A live radio or television broadcast originating from a location outside of a studio.

Render
(1) To perform, deliver, present, express, interpret, or translate. (2) To provide, give, or offer. (3) To make a submission or make available. (4) To repay, fulfill an obligation, satisfy a debt.

Rendering
A performance, offering, delivery, presentation, interpretation, representation, payment, or submission.

Rendition
A version, translation, interpretation, or performance of a musical work.

Renegotiate
To seek to revise the terms of an existing contract or license.

Renewal
(1) The creation of a new legal relationship following the termination of an existing one. Technically, a renewed contract or a renewal agreement constitutes an entirely new agreement, as opposed to an *extension* of the original contract for an additional period of time beyond the initial term. (2) Under the *Copyright Act of 1909*, creative works were given *statutory* copyright protection for an initial period of 28 years, which could be renewed for an additional 28 years. See *copyright renewal*.

Renewal Assignment
Under the *Copyright Act of 1909*, creative works were given *statutory* copyright protection for an initial period of 28 years, which could be renewed for an additional 28 years. A copyright owner could assign (give, sell, transfer) the copyright to another party during the original term, just as any other type of property right could be transferred. However, a copyright owner had no rights per se in the work beyond the original term unless and until those rights were renewed for a renewal term. Therefore, the copyright owner had only an "expectancy" of continuing rights beyond the original copyright term, contingent upon renewal. In order, then, to assign those future rights before they existed, the copyright owner could only make an assignment of *renewal expectancy*.

Assuming the copyright owner made such an assignment, and was still living at the expiration of the original copyright term, the original owner was bound by the terms of the assignment. The rights vested in the copyright upon the renewal date would then become the property of the *assignee*. If, however, the copyright owner died before expiration of the original term, the rights vested upon renewal belong to the *statutory beneficiaries* of the deceased's estate.

If, for example, a music publisher wished to obtain renewal rights from a songwriter, the publisher would have to also obtain the renewal expectancies of the writer's statutory beneficiaries (normally, the spouse and children) at the same time. Even this was not foolproof, because, if the writer *and* the spouse and children had died by the time of renewal, the expectancies would pass to *their* statutory beneficiaries. The issue could be further complicated by the writer having additional children or re-marrying after the publisher had received assignments of renewal expectancy from the original statutory beneficiaries.

The *rule of expectancy* applies only to songs in their original terms of copyright as of the effective date of the Copyright Act of 1976 (January 1, 1978). Works created after that date are provided with one term of copyright protection, and there are no renewals.

Renewal Claim
Under the *Copyright Act of 1909*, statutory copyright protection was given for an initial term of 28 years with the right to renew copyright protection for an additional 28 years. A claim for copyright

renewal was made using *Form R*, which is obsolete for works created after January 1, 1978, since the *Copyright Act of 1976*, now in effect, grants statutory copyright protection for one term only (currently life of author plus 50 years, though in 1998 Congress was considering extending this to life plus 70 years), with no renewal options.

Renewal Expectancy
See *renewal assignment*.

Renewal Option
A right to extend a current agreement upon fulfillment of certain conditions, which, technically, creates a new legal relationship. See also *renewal* and *extension*.

Renewal Period
The period of time (or term) for which an existing legal relationship continues after termination through the creation of a new contract or license. See also *copyright renewal*.

Renewal Term
Same as *renewal period*.

Rental
An arrangement whereby one party obtains temporary use of a property from its owner in return for an agreed payment or schedule of payments. Copyright owners are paid on the *first sale* of products embodying their copyrights (i.e., CDs, audiocassettes). Purchasers then own the physical product, though not the copyright. The concept of first sale is the legal basis video stores use to buy recorded product and videos that they in turn rent out and ultimately resell as used. In 1984, however, legislation was enacted to prohibit the rental of sound recordings, which put an end to a then-burgeoning record rental business akin to video rentals.

Repackaging
Reissuing noncurrent catalog product in new *configurations* with new artwork. Many record labels repackage older masters in *best of* series, or *compilation albums* for retail at *midline* or *budget* line pricing. Numerous television-marketing companies lease older masters from record companies and repackage them as concept or "greatest hits" compilations to sell via television mail-order advertising.

Repertoire
Also called *repertory*. (1) A selection or stock of songs an artist performs or records. (2) A catalog of material.

Repertory
See *repertoire*, above.

Replay Fee
A *reuse fee* paid *AFTRA* members for rebroadcasts of recorded performances.

Reply Card
In marketing, a *questionnaire* card given to participants of a market survey in order to gauge commercial strength of a product or release. See also *response card* and *bounce-back card*.

Report
(1) An account or record. *Examples*: an expense report, a sales report, an airplay report, etc. (2) To give an account of something.

Reporting Period
(1) A time during which a radio station must supply detailed logs of music broadcast on air to a *performing-right society*. (2) A time covered in an account (i.e., expenses incurred, sales generated, royalties earned, radio stations *adds* achieved, etc.)

Reporting Station
(1) A radio station that reports *adds*, *rotations*, and *playlists* to national chart compilers and to various *tip sheets* and other *trade publications*. Reporting stations are heavily targeted by record promotion people. When a sufficient number of influential reporting stations begin to play a new release, the recording starts to show up on airplay charts, and other stations can be more easily persuaded to play the record. As national airplay gathers steam, sales pick up and the record may emerge as a hit. (2) A radio station that submits detailed logs of music broadcast during a *reporting period* to a *performing-right society*.

Representation
(1) In a contract, license, or prospectus: a statement, warranty, or claim made by one party as fact. (2) A power of attorney, agency, or authority to act for another as agent, representative, spokesperson, subpublisher, etc.

Repro
A copy; a *reproduction*.

Reproduce
To copy or make copies.

Reproduction
A copy.

Reproduction License
A grant of permission to make copies of a copyrighted work.

Re-recording Restriction

A contractual provision prohibiting an artist from re-recording any work recorded under the agreement for any other record company within a specified number of years of the agreement's termination. Typical re-recording restrictions prohibit re-recordings for at least five years from the date of the original recording or for at least two years after termination of the agreement, whichever comes first. See also *prohibition* and *restriction*.

Re-release

To reissue a recording, film, movie, etc. in the same format.

Rerun

A rebroadcast of a television program.

Resale

(1) To sell at *retail* something that was bought at *wholesale*. The commercial resale of goods requires a seller's permit or *resale license* from the state, county, and/or city in which a business (seller) is located. (2) To sell the same merchandise or property again, after repossessing it from a first purchaser who *defaults* on payments. See also *first sale*.

Resale License

Also called a seller's permit. See *resale*, above.

Reservation

(1) The withholding or limitation of some right or interest from among other rights or interests that are granted. (2) A right or interest that is withheld, restricted, or limited. See also *reserved rights*. (3) A *conditional* grant of a right or interest, or an agreement based on certain conditions being met by the other party, or of certain circumstances having first occurred.

Reserve Fund

(1) A percentage of royalties withheld in order to meet possible *returns* of royalty-earning product. Since most record sales are made on *consignment*, artist contracts with record companies allow the company to withhold royalties on a reasonable amount of product shipped so that the company doesn't end up paying royalties on unsold goods. Contracts don't always specify the percentage withheld, and different companies have different policies, usually based on their own experience. A new artist, whose market acceptance is not yet established, may be subject to a higher *holdback* than the company applies to an established artist's royalty account. Reserve funds might range from a low of 20% for proven artists to as high as 50% for *baby acts*. See also *liquidation of reserves*. (2) A percentage of investment or working capital set aside to meet contingencies.

Reserved Rights

In a contract or license, a *reservation* provision specifying any rights or interests withheld, restricted, or limited from among other rights or interests that are granted. Though the reservations may be narrowly defined, a broadly worded *catch-all* phrase is usually included in the provision to the effect that: "all rights and interests not herein specifically granted are reserved by the *licensor*."

Reserves

The anticipated percentage of product shipped on *consignment* that will be returned unsold. Artist contracts with record companies generally provide royalty payments only on product actually sold and paid for. The common practice of allowing retailers and distributors to return unsold product results in significant quantities of product coming back to the record company, for which no royalties are payable. See *reserve fund* and *liquidation of reserves*.

Reserves Against Returns

See *reserves* (above) and *returns*.

Residual

An additional payment due a performer, producer, writer, or director each time their work (on a television show or commercial, etc.) is rebroadcast. See also *reuse fee* and *replay fee*.

Response Card

In marketing, a *questionnaire* form given to participants of a market survey in order to gauge commercial strength of a new product or release. Also, a card enclosed with promotional copies of new product sent to disc jockeys and reviewers to gauge reaction. See also *reply card*, *bounce-back card*, and *questionnaire*.

Rest of World (ROW)

Language used in contracts and licenses as a *catch-all* to cover those countries not specifically excluded or included by name in the *licensee's* operative *territory*.

Restoration of Copyright

Under the *Copyright Act of 1909*, the term of *copyright protection* in the United States was limited to 56 years maximum (a 28-year term plus a 28-year renewal). Many foreign copyrights thus fell into *public domain* in the United States, either because renewal *formalities* weren't taken properly or because 56 years lapsed, even though the works were still under copyright protection in their countries of origin. Since the United States joined the *Berne Convention* in 1989, copyright owners of songs originating in countries that are *signatories* to the Berne Convention (or which are members of the *World*

Trade Organization) can have copyright protection restored to works that fell into the public domain, as long as those works are still in copyright in their countries of origin. Copyright restoration is accomplished by filing a *GATT form* with the *US Copyright Office*.

Restriction

A specific limitation or exclusion stated in a contract or license that prohibits one party from engaging in or participating in something. See also *prohibition* and *re-recording restriction*.

Résumé

Same as *CV* and *curriculum vitae*. A brief summary of professional qualifications, experience, and accomplishments, as opposed to a *biography*, which is usually fleshed out with more personal anecdotal information to present a profile for publicity purposes.

Retail

The sale of product directly to consumers. See also *dealer*, *resale*, and *wholesale*.

Retail Merchandise Agreement

A *merchandising agreement* that allows merchandising through normal retail channels, as well as mail order. *Tour merchandise agreements*, on the other hand, are restricted to sales at concerts in a tour cycle (though there may be sell-off provisions for surplus merchandise at the end of the cycle). See *merchandising agreement*.

Retail Price

The price charged to consumers for products and services, which may nor may not be the same as *list price* (the price suggested by a product's manufacturer, which a dealer may raise or lower at discretion). The retail price is set by the dealer so as to provide a profit margin after factoring in the wholesale price of the product and operating costs.

Retailer

(1) An establishment, such as a store, shop, boutique, etc., where goods are sold directly to consumers. (2) A person who buys goods wholesale for resale to consumers. (3) The final link in the distribution chain between a product's creator and its *end-user*.

Retain

(1) To deduct, keep, withhold, or maintain possession. See *retention*. (2) To hire or engage a professional adviser, such as an attorney, by paying a fee in advance of services rendered.

Retainer

An advance fee paid to engage the services of a consultant, such as an attorney, or of an independent service provider, such as a promotion person.

Retention

Something kept, withheld, or retained. See *retention rights* and *retention period*, below.

Retention Period

The term or period of time in which *retention rights* apply. See below.

Retention Rights

A contractual or licensing provision allowing one party to retain certain rights granted by the other party beyond the term of the agreement. For instance, in many exclusive songwriter agreements, the music publisher retains publishing rights to all songs created under the agreement for a stated period beyond the contract's termination date. Some contracts allow retention rights if advances have not been recouped at the end of the term.

Retention rights are most often *conditional* (i.e., they apply only if certain conditions have occurred or have been met). In a foreign *subpublishing* agreement, for example, the subpublisher may have retention rights for a stated period of time to *local covers* (songs the subpublisher gets recorded and commercially released in the territory, or that the subpublisher gets included in a film, local television production or television commercial). The right of retention may be further conditioned to apply only to those songs released within 12 to 18 months of the agreement's termination date, and/or to those songs that achieve specified milestones or are successful by some definitive yardstick, such as chart positions, sales levels, or income generation, etc.

Continuing the example of a subpublishing agreement, a normal retention period ranges from one to two years—especially in the case of local covers. The reason for retentions is that subpublishers should be able to benefit from efforts expended to secure and promote local releases. Otherwise, as an agreement nears its end, a subpublisher won't consider such promotional efforts to be commercially viable.

Sometimes retention is limited to *pipeline income*. Money in the "pipeline" is income earned during the agreement that has not yet been received from licensed *users* at time of termination. The right to collect pipeline income is usually limited to 6 to 18 months from the date of termination.

A pipeline situation could arise in which an *original publisher* guarantees that a certain number of songs would be released in the subpublisher's territory. The subpublisher might be induced to enter into the agreement because the original publisher's writers have producer or artist deals with release commitments in the territory. However, if a number of these guaranteed releases don't occur until the final 6 months of the term, the original publisher technically meets the release guarantee, but, in reality, the subpublisher does not have time remaining in the agreement to profit. The solution, then, is for the subpublisher to have retention rights to any guaranteed release issued within the final year of the agreement. The retention period might reasonably be 6 to 12 months from the date of release, or from the date of termination, whichever is later.

Return

(1) A product that is returned by a retailer for credit to a manufacturer, distributor, or wholesaler, or merchandise returned by a consumer to a retailer. The common record industry practice of *consignment* sales (allowing retailers and distributors to return unsold product, resulting in significant quantities of product coming back to the record company, for which no royalties are payable) requires record companies to set up a *reserve fund* for each artist's royalty account. See also *liquidation of reserves*. (2) The amount of profit made on an investment or on the sale of product.

Return of Copyrights

See *reversion* and *re-assignment*.

Return of Masters

See *reversion* and *re-assignment*.

Return Privileges

A condition of sale on *consignment* that allows a retailer or distributor to return unsold merchandise to the manufacturer for credit or refund. Some sales may be made on the basis of limited return privileges (i.e., only a certain percentage of product ordered may be returned for credit). See *return, reserves, reserve fund*, and *liquidation of reserves*.

Returnable

(1) A condition of sale that allows the buyer to return merchandise for credit or refund. See *return, return privileges, reserves, reserve fund*, and *liquidation of reserves*. (2) A condition of a loan, advance, lease, rental, etc. that requires the recipient to restore the sum or item within a specified time. See also *non-returnable advance* and *non-returnable deposit*.

Returns

See *return, return privileges, reserves, reserve fund*, and *liquidation of reserves*.

Reuse

(1) To use a recorded performance in media other than the original medium in which the performance

was recorded. (2) To rebroadcast a recorded performance.

Reuse Fee

(1) A payment charged by the owner of a recorded performance for the right to *reuse* the recorded performance. (2) Fees paid union members for rebroadcasts or reruns of recorded performances. For instance, under the *AFM Television, Video Tape Agreement*, musicians receive 75% of the basic scale amount paid for the original work when a program is rebroadcast the second and third time; 50% of scale for the fourth, fifth, and sixth reruns; 10% for the 7th rerun; and 5% for each additional rerun thereafter. Such payments are also called *residuals*. *AFTRA* members receive *replay fees* for rebroadcasts of recorded performances, formulated on a *sliding scale* similar to AFM reuse fees.

Revamp

To revise, rework, or reinterpret an original work.

Revenue

The total amount of income generated by a product, line of products, activity, or investment.

Reverb

(1) To *reverberate*. (2) Abbreviated reference to a reverberator, an electronic device used in recording and sound systems to simulate natural reverb effects.

Reverberate

To resound or re-echo; the repeated reflection of sound waves in quick succession.

Reverberation

The *reverberating* effect caused by electronic or natural means.

Reversed Area

In printing, the application of colored or black type or images to paper in such a way that they appear light against a colored background or white against a black background.

Reversion

Also called *recapture of copyright*. The return of a copyright or master to an *assignor* after a contract, license, or assignment expires or is voided. Some recording and publishing contracts provide for reversion of masters or song copyrights after a stated period of time and/or fulfillment of certain conditions by the assignor and/or failure of the *assignee* to perform or achieve certain milestones within a stated period of time. See also *reassignment*.

Revert

To return or reassign a copyright or master to its original owner or *assignor*.

Review

To examine, listen, watch, or read (i.e., a work of art, recording, performance, manuscript) for the purpose of evaluation, criticism, analysis, reporting, recommendation, or correction.

Review Copy

A copy of a commercial edition of a creative work (i.e., a recording, book, etc.), which is supplied free of charge for the purposes of critical review or promotion, and which is normally marked in some way so as to prevent its being offered for retail sale.

Reviewer

Person who offers critical commentary on, and analysis of, newly issued creative works (often employed to do so by various media outlets, such as newspapers, magazines, broadcasters, etc.).

Revolutions Per Minute (RPM)

Measurement of speed at which a phonograph turntable revolves (i.e., 45 rpm, 33-1/3 rpm, etc.).

Revue

A stage or cabaret show incorporating skits, songs, and dances, linked by dialogue, narration, or a monologue, though there is no plot or storyline. Revues typically incorporate previously written songs, often by different songwriters.

RG

Music format abbreviation for *reggae*.

Rhythm

(1) A pattern in music or speech, characterized by recurring alternations of contrasting accents or stresses on certain beats, sounds, words, or syllables. See also *cadence* and *meter*. (2) The patterned evolution or development of a musical, literary, or dramatic work produced through repetition of certain themes, motifs, incidents, words, phrases, symbols, and images.

Rhythm & Blues (R&B)

A music genre primarily developed by African-Americans, characterized by strong backbeat with blended elements (to lesser or greater degrees) of blues, jazz, gospel, pop, and other genres.

Rhythm Section

The backbone of a band or orchestra, around which other instruments (i.e., horns, woodwinds, strings) and vocals are added. Rhythm instruments include piano, bass, drums, guitar, mandolin, and banjo.

Rhythm Track

A *basic track*, or group of *tracks*, containing rhythm instruments recorded as the foundation of a recorded performance, and which are later overdubbed with vocals, *sweetening*, and/or other effects.

RIAA

Abbreviation for *Recording Industry Association of America*.

RIAA Certification

Official authentication and recognition by the *Recording Industry Association of America* that a recording has sold sufficient units to be awarded a *Gold* or *Platinum* Disc. When a record company wishes a release to be awarded a gold or platinum disc, the RIAA conducts an independent audit to verify that sales warrant certification of the award. A single selling at least 500,000 units merits a gold record; one million sales merits platinum status. An album merits a gold certification upon sales of 500,000 units plus revenues of at least $1,000,000 based on 33-1/3% of suggested list price; one million sales merits a platinum award. A multi-platinum award is certified for albums and singles selling two million units or more.

Rider

A clause, amendment, or addition to a contract or license.

Riff

A rhythmic, repetitive musical pattern, sometimes improvised.

Right

A legally recognized claim, title, or ownership interest in a property, which allows the holder of the right to prohibit others from using or possessing the property. A right may be conferred on the owner by *statutory law*, *common law*, *operation of law*, tradition, or nature, and the owner may subsequently sell, transfer, lend, or assign the right to another party. Permission to use the property is called a *privilege* and is granted by the owner in the form of a *license*.

Right of First Refusal

A right given to one party to exercise an option, distribute a product, license a copyright, sign an artist, or purchase an asset, etc., by matching a price or other terms offered by any other party. See also *buyout rights* and *matching rights*.

Right of Last Refusal

Same as *right of first refusal*.

Right of Publicity

Privilege granted by one party to another to use a name, likeness, and background information in order to promote and market a product or product line. Essentially, a person may not prevent the use of his or her likeness or name in dissemination of news, editorial comment, reviews, or information deemed to be in the *public interest*. However, a person does have the right to control commercial exploitation of his or her own name or likeness. Courts have ruled that where a person exploits his or her own celebrity by licensing the use of name and likeness in, say, merchandising or commercial endorsements, then the right of publicity survives that person's death and may continue to be protected and exploited by his or her heirs or estate.

Right of Renewal

A privilege granted to one party by another to *renew* (recreate) a legal relationship upon termination of an existing agreement or license. A right of renewal may be *conditional* and/or may be incorporated in a *right of first refusal*.

Right of Retention

See *retention rights*.

Right-to-Work Law

A law prohibiting the institution of a *closed shop*, thus guaranteeing the right of someone to work without being forced to join a union. See also *open shop*.

Rights

See *right* and *bundle of rights*.

RIMPTF

Abbreviation for *Recording Industries Music Performance Trust Funds*.

Road Crew

Personnel employed by touring bands to transport, load, unload, set up, operate, and maintain equipment, etc.

Road Manager

Person in charge of a *road crew*, and who coordinates the logistical requirements of touring (transportation, lodging, catering, etc.).

Road Show

(1) A touring theatrical production; a troupe of traveling performers. (2) A presentation, demonstration, or promotional event carried out in a series of different localities.

Roadie

Member of a *road crew*.

Rock & Roll Hall of Fame

Located in Cleveland, Ohio where dee-jay Alan Freed coined the word rock-and-roll in the 1950s. Founded in 1985, the institution began annually inducting rock and roll luminaries in 1986, and opened its physical museum and premises in 1995.

Rock Music

Popular music genre that germinated in the 1950s with a merging of various American regional and ethnic musical genres, notably blues, country, jazz, and gospel. The genre has continued to evolve and develop into various subgenres (rockabilly, hard rock, heavy metal, soft rock, grunge, alternative, country rock, blues rock, folk rock, pop rock, et al).

Rockabilly

A blending of rock and country ("hillbilly") music, especially popular in the mid-to-late 1950s.

Rolling Fee

A variation of a *rollover advance*, except money paid is considered a *fee* for so many units sold as opposed to a *per-unit royalty*.

Rolling Stone

Monthly magazine founded in 1967 for the counterculture rock movement, that has survived to become recognized as perhaps the premier journal of rock culture.

Rollover

To reinvest profits received from one project, product, or activity into another, similar project, product, or activity.

Rollover Advance

An advance against royalties given by one party to another as and when a previous advance is recouped. Normally, the advance equals an agreed royalty rate times a certain level of sales, with another like sum advanced each time that sales plateau is reached. For instance, a rollover advance to a music publisher on 15,000 unit sales at 6¢ per song would be $900 (6¢ x 15,000 units). When 15,000 units are sold, an additional $900 is paid; then, a further $900 is paid when the next 15,000 units are sold, and so on.

Rolodex

Trademarked name for a rotary desktop device containing removable file cards of contact names, addresses, fax and telephone numbers.

Rome Convention

A *copyright convention* in 1961 ultimately joined by 35 countries (but not the United States). The full name of the treaty is the Rome Convention for the Protection of Performers, Producers of Phonograms, and Broadcasting Organizations. The thrust of the agreement was to establish the legal concept that producers (i.e., recording companies) and performers are as much rights *owners* as they are rights *users*. That is, while they produce and perform licensed music and are thereby copyright users, the recorded performances themselves are copyrightable with inherent rights of control, protection, and compensation. The convention established copyright protection to recorded performances for a minimum 20-year period after *fixation*, which has since been extended to 50 years in most member countries.

Roster

(1) A list, register, or roll of artists, songwriters, producers, etc. under contract to a company. (2) A catalogue, directory, or inventory of product, copyrights, releases, etc.

Rota

British term for *roster*.

Rotation

In radio programming, term used to describe how many times a recording is featured (aired) on a current *playlist* each week. Recordings that receive the most airplay are categorized as having *heavy rotation* (30+ plays), followed by those with *medium rotation* (15 to 29 plays), and then those with *light rotation* (less than 15 plays).

Route People

Salespeople assigned to service retail clients in specific sales territories. *Branch operations* of record distributors employ route people to sell and deliver product to retailers, help them set up *P.O.P.* merchandising displays, etc. Route people are usually paid with a base salary augmented by commissions or overrides on sales.

R.O.W.

Abbreviation for *rest of world*.

Royalty

Consideration or payment for the right to use copyrighted material, or compensation for services (such as those by a recording artist or record producer). In a contract or license, the royalty is usually specified either in dollars-and-cents for each unit used, manufactured, distributed, or sold, or as a percentage of receipts. Thus, a songwriter might receive, in exchange for the copyright on his or her compositions, a royalty of 50% of the net revenues collected by a music publisher. A recording artist might receive, in exchange for his or performance as an artist, a royalty of 10% of the net revenues realized from sales of his or her recordings, less stated deductions such as *container charges*, etc.

Royalty Advance

A sum of money paid for the use, manufacture, or sale of copyrighted material before the actual use, manufacture, or sale of the material takes place, or a sum of money paid for services before they are rendered. The party paying the advance expects to recoup the sum of money from royalties accruing to the other party from the use, manufacture, or sale of copyrighted material or from the product produced as a result of the services rendered.

Record companies and music publishers frequently offer royalty advances as *inducements* for songwriters and recording artists to assign their works to the company. Royalty advances are *interest-free* loans with no fixed repayment schedule. They are *recoupable* against royalty income that may or may not materialize. Advances are recouped piecemeal as and when royalties are earned by artists, writers, and producers over rather indefinite periods of time. Furthermore, royalty advances are usually *nonreturnable*—there is no recourse if not enough royalties are earned, because recipients aren't obligated to repay unrecouped royalty advances. In effect, when a company pays a royalty advance, it guarantees that the songwriter, artist, or producer will earn at minimum an amount equal to the advance, since the sum is nonreturnable.

Example: When a publisher advances a songwriter $1,000 as an inducement to assign a copyright, the publisher is entitled to withhold (recoup) the first $1,000 from the songwriter's royalties. The songwriter receives royalties only after the advance is repaid, but doesn't have to pay the publisher back at all if the song never earns a dime.

A royalty advance differs from a conventional loan, because conventional loans obligate borrowers to repay certain sums by certain dates, and are normally made on terms that include interest and some type of collateral that is forfeited if the loan is not repaid as agreed. See also *cross-collateralize*.

Royalty Artist

A person who is compensated for his or her services as a recording artist by royalties paid on each unit (*phonorecord*) manufactured, distributed, and/or sold. Under *AFM* agreements with record companies, a royalty artist is one that receives a royalty of at least 3% of the recommended retail price of recordings sold. AFM members who are classed as royalty artists receive basic *union scale* for recording sessions, but are not entitled to mandatory supplemental payments for *doubling, overdubbing, sweetening*, etc., which non-royalty union members are entitled to receive.

Royalty Base

The basis upon which royalties are calculated, which is not the same as a *royalty rate*. A royalty base frequently translates into a discount on the royalty rate. For instance, an artist's royalty rate might be agreed at 10% of the retail price of a compact disc album. However, the "base" on which the royalty is calculated might be 90% of sales, and there might be a further *packaging deduction* of 25%. Thus, on a CD retailing at $16, the royalty base is $16 - 25% x 90% = $10.80. So, instead of receiving 10% of $16 ($1.60) per unit, the artist receives 10% of $10.80, or $1.08. See also *uplift*.

Royalty Override

A royalty paid or collected by someone over and above a royalty earned by the person who directly created or generated the work. For instance, a sales manager might be given an override for sales generated by his/her sales force, which is in addition to the commissions earned by the salespeople in the field. Or, as part of an agreement whereby a record company sells an artist's contract to another label, the first company might receive a royalty override on sales of the artist's releases by the second company for a stated period of time. See also *musician's incentive agreement*.

Royalty Participation

An agreement, such as a *cut-in*, whereby one party receives a share of royalties earned by another party's venture, production, or work. A royalty participation is usually given in return for some contribution towards the situation that generates those profits or royalties. See also *cut-in, override, split*.

Royalty Rate

A price or fee, usually computed on a *per use* or *per unit* basis. A royalty rate may be expressed in dollars-and-cents (i.e., a rate of 50¢ per unit), or as a percentage of a unit's recommended retail or dealer price (i.e., 10% of retail). A *mechanical royalty rate*, thus, is the amount paid to a song copyright owner for each unit (phonorecord) sold. See also *royalty base*.

Royalty Statement

An accounting of royalty earnings, including amounts and sources of income, nature and amount of deductions or withholdings, net share due, etc.

RPM

Abbreviation for *revolutions per minute*.

RPM

A weekly Canadian music industry trade magazine, located at 6 Brentcliffe Road, Toronto, Ontario M4G 3Y2, Canada.

RRP

Abbreviation for *recommended retail price*.

Rule of Expectancy

See *renewal assignment*.

Russian Authors Society (RAO)

The *performing-right society* in Russia.

Ryman Auditorium

For more than 30 years, the home of WSM's *Grand Ole Opry*. Located in Nashville, Tennessee, the Ryman is often called the "Mother Church of Country Music."

SABAM

The *performing-right* and *mechanical-right society* in Belgium.

SAC

Abbreviation for *Songwriters Association of Canada.*

SACEM

The *performing-right society* in France.

SACERAU

The *performing-right society* in Egypt.

SACM

The *performing-right society* in Mexico.

SACVEN

The *performing-right society* in Venezuela.

SADAIC

The *performing-right society* in Argentina.

SAE

Abbreviation for *self-addressed envelope.*

Safety

A copy of a master made for security in case the original is damaged or lost.

SAG

Abbreviation for *Screen Actors Guild.*

Salary

Method of compensating someone for services rendered, paid in fixed amounts on a regular basis. Contrasts with compensation in the forms of fees, commissions, royalties, etc.

Sale or Return

Product accepted by or shipped to a retailer or distributor on *consignment* (i.e., payment is made only on completed sales; all unsold items are returned).

Sales

(1) Income received from the exchange of product or services during an *accounting period*. See also *gross sales*, *net sales*, *cash basis*, and *accrual basis*. (2) Activities involved in the process of selling product or services, including sales presentations, sales calls, fulfillment, invoicing, and collections.

Sales Department

Division of a company whose functions are to devise sales concepts and plans, and to coordinate and carry out campaigns to sell the company's products or services, and to manage the activities of sales personnel. See *sales plan*, below.

Sales Plan

An adjunct to a *marketing plan*, the sales plan is a tactical outline of steps needed to actually sell a product or service. The sales process might involve selectively targeted direct-mail shots to likely music users, telephone solicitations for leads, and networking with personal contacts. It can also include direct-response offers to consumers via mail or over the airwaves, or simply putting a "for sale" sign next to a stack of CDs on a table set up at a gig.

The sales plan describes the nature of sales presentations and sales calls, and the quotas or goals expected from sales efforts. Specific steps in the sales process can include a combination of two or more of the following exercises: *cold calls* (contacting potential clients or song users without knowing whether they're interested in the product or service); *getting leads* (gathering names of potential clients or music users that have reason to be interested in the product or service, which can come from referrals or responses to surveys, direct mailings, or coupons); *following up leads* with sales presentations, or pitching material by mail, telephone, or in person; *fulfillment* (the turnaround time from receipt of an order to the customer's receipt of the product); *after sales follow-up* (checking to see if the customer is satisfied, which can lead to still more sales, because proven customers are obvious targets for future sales).

A comprehensive sales plan might also address the following issues: *productivity* (making the most efficient use of the time and money to close each sale, a major factor of profitability); *goals* or *quotas* (set by the size of the target market and the productivity factor established); *training* (sales skills are an art practiced on different levels depending upon the sophistication of the product and/or the customer-sales personnel must be trained to accomplish sales goals); methods and amounts of *compensation* for sales personnel (salary, commission, or a combination thereof), and incentives offered to spur their productivity (bonuses, awards, stock, gifts, etc.).

Sales Volume

Total number of units sold or dollars received from sales; the amount of gross income from sales of a service, a product, or a product line during an accounting period.

Salsa

Music genre popularized in the 1970s on the US East Coast by Hispanic performers, characterized by Latin American musical influences and dance rhythms blended with rock and jazz.

SAMPAC

A trade guild formed to promote and protect the interests of producers and composers of commercial jingles.

Sample

(1) To digitally capture a sound or sounds, often from previously recorded material for the purpose of incorporating the sampled sound or passage with another recording. (2) A sound or sound fragment that has been digitally isolated. (A sampled sound can be electronically altered before being incorporated into another recording.) (3) A fragment, segment, portion, or piece of something that is representative of a whole. (4) To analyze characteristics of a representative sample in order to arrive at statistical estimates. See also *sampling*.

Sampler

An album containing several representative tracks by an artist or by several different artists. Samplers are generally used as promotional items to expose new artists, and are usually given away, sold at cost, or sold at prices well below prevailing retail prices for *top-line* albums. As promotional items, samplers don't require royalty payments to the artist(s), and music publishers may be persuaded to grant reduced mechanical royalty rates for the songs included. Indeed, music publishers also issue samplers to promote their songs to producers, A&R personnel, film and television producers, and other music users. Quite often, these samplers contain recordings that require licensing from record companies who may be persuaded to grant licenses at nominal fees for promotional use only.

Sampling

(1) A survey of attributes or characteristics taken from samples of something in order to determine statistically reliable estimates of that thing as a whole. For instance, a sampling of television viewers can be extrapolated to estimate the number of viewers tuned in to a specific program. An in-depth survey of viewers included in such a sampling might also yield reliable estimates of what percentage of viewers happened to be married females working full-time, etc. *Performing-right societies* routinely use sampling to estimate the number of broadcast and live performances a song receives during any given survey period in order to allocate performance royalties to music copyright owners. (2) The process of digitally isolating and recording a sound or sounds from previously recorded material for the purpose of incorporating the sampled sound or passage with another recording. (3) Audio gear designed specifically for the recording and playback of audio samples.

SAMRO

Abbreviation for South African Music Rights Organization, a *performing-right society*.

SARRAL

Abbreviation for South African Recording Rights Association Ltd., the *mechanical-right society* in South Africa.

SASE

Abbreviation for *self-addressed stamped envelope*.

Satellite

A device launched into space that links radio, television, and telephonic transmissions worldwide from an orbital position, thus avoiding the limitations on communications between ground-based facilities that are constrained by the earth's curvature.

Satellite Station

A radio or television station that receives a broadcast transmission on one wavelength and rebroadcasts it simultaneously over a different wavelength.

Satellite-Syndicated Transmission

Method of delivering *syndicated* radio programming, using a satellite to transmit prerecorded programs to several *satellite stations* simultaneously. Many small-to-medium market stations use these syndicated services to provide relatively low-cost high-quality programming. The syndicators insert individual *station IDs* and *call letters* for each satellite station in order to "localize" the programs, which otherwise are identical wherever broadcast. The programs feature seasoned announcers, celebrity interviews, national commercials, and empty time slots for local commercials sold by the receiving stations.

Satire

A literary device relying on irony, sarcasm, derision, or ridicule to expose human vice, pretension, pomposity, stupidity, or folly.

Save

(1) To make a *safety* copy. (2) To store modifications to a computer file.

SAYCO

The *performing-right society* in Colombia.

SAYCE

The *performing-right society* in Ecuador.

SAZAS

Abbreviation for *Society of Composers, Authors, & Publishers of Slovenia.*

SBACEM

The *performing-right society* and *mechanical-right society* in Brazil.

SCALA

Abbreviation for *Songwriters, Composers & Lyricists Association.*

Scale

(1) Minimum wage rate(s) or forms of compensation for union employees and contractors as specified in union agreements for specific types of employees or specific types of work. See *union scale* and *recording scale*. (2) In music, a series of musical notes progressing by tones and semitones, up or down from a central *keynote* or *tonic* note. Although musical scales vary according to forms and traditions, and there is no known definitive number of the different scales in use worldwide, most contemporary western music is based on three scales based on an octave (an interval of 8 whole tone notes, counting the bottom and top notes): the major scale, the minor scale, and the chromatic scale.

Scaling the House

Setting the ticket prices of seats in a concert hall, arena, or theater, ranging from least expensive upwards.

Scalp

To buy up tickets to a performance in order to resell them for a profit to those who cannot buy them otherwise.

Scalper

Person who *scalps* tickets to a performance.

SCAU

Performing- and *mechanical-right agency* in the Ukraine.

SCD

The *performing-right society* in Chile.

Schedule

(1) A list of supplemental details attached to a contract or license (i.e., song titles, writers, copyright dates, artists, producers, royalty breakdowns, advance payment dates, etc.). (2) To set an agenda or timetable, to make an appointment, set a release date, etc.

Schlock

Recorded product that is deleted from a record company's catalog and sold as *cut-outs* to bulk buyers who in turn resell the product to consumers at pennies on the dollar. No royalties are paid on cut-outs.

Schwann Record & Tape Guide

Twice-yearly publication listing all nationally distributed phonorecords released over the past two years that are still available for sale in the United States. Monthly supplements are issued listing all nationally distributed new releases. Listings include artist; title; record label (and the company's address); category (pop, country, R&B, etc.); format (CD, cassette, LP, etc.), catalog number, etc. Along with *Phonolog Reporter*, the Schwann Guide provides a definitive reference for locating and ordering commercially released recordings. Schwann Record & Tape Guide is located at 535 Boylston St., Boston, MA 02116.

SCL

Abbreviation for *Society of Composers & Lyricists.*

SCMS

Abbreviation for *Serial Copy Management System.*

Scope

(1) The extent of activities, services, or products provided or offered. (2) The extent of rights, permissions, obligations, commitments, or considerations covered by an agreement.

Score

(1) To arrange, orchestrate, and write out instrumental or vocal parts of a composition. (2) To compose, orchestrate, and record music for a film, television show, musical, or other production. (3) The music that is *synchronized* with an audiovisual work, such as a motion picture, or which has been composed for a *dramatico-musical work*. (4) An arranged composition or an orchestration. (5) To have a hit, to succeed.

Scout

To search, seek out, find, evaluate, and recruit talent and material.

Scrap

To cancel, discard, delete.

Scratch

To cancel, discard, delete, erase.

Scratching

The sound produced by a vinyl record being quickly turned backwards and forwards on a turntable while the stylus is in the grooves.

Screen

(1) To review, audition, appraise, and evaluate talent or material, in order to weed out that which is not worthy of further consideration. (2) To show a film. (3) A display device, such as a computer monitor or television screen.

Screen Actors Guild (SAG)

Trade union for film actors. Vocalists who perform in theatrical films are governed by terms of SAG's Theatrical Motion Picture Agreement. Located at 7065 Hollywood Boulevard, Hollywood, CA 90028. Tel: (213) 465-4600; Fax: 213 856-6603.

Screen Credit

Acknowledgments of work done, services rendered, and rights licensed, displayed at the beginning and/or end of a motion picture or television show. See also *shared card*, *separate card*, *credits*, *closing credits*, and *opening credits*.

Screen Extras Guild (SEG)

Trade union for film actors who work as *extras*.

Screening

A showing or presentation of a film production, especially for a select audience before general release.

SDRM

A *mechanical-right society* serving music publishers, composers, and songwriters in France, Andorra, Luxembourg, Monaco, and French-speaking African countries.

Search Organization

A company specializing in scouting and recruiting executive talent, or in locating owners of music rights. See also *clearing house*, *copyright search*, *title search*, and *due diligence*.

SECAM

A *videocassette* format.

Second Billing

A performer whose name appears below or after that of the star attraction; an opening act; a support act.

Second Edition

A book published again to meet sales demand, usually with revisions or additions to the first edition. See also *second printing*.

Second Engineer

Assistant to chief or head engineer in a recording studio.

Second Fiddle

An assistant or person whose function is secondary to someone else's.

Second Pressing

To manufacture an additional quantity of sound recordings to meet sales demand.

Second Printing

To print an additional quantity of books or other type of printed work to meet sales demand. See also *second edition*.

Secondary Station

Radio station with a broadcast market reach to a population of less than 500,000. (A *primary secondary station* serves a market of 500,000 or more.)

Secondary Transmission

The rebroadcast of a program over a different transmitting system. *Example*: A program produced for a major television network, which is also delivered by a cable television system.

Secular Music

Non-spiritual, not religious in content.

Security

(1) A stock certificate, bond, or other document representing ownership, an obligation, a pledge, or a guarantee. (2) *Collateral* used to guarantee repayment of a loan.

SEDRIM

Italian *performing-right society* taken over by and merged into *SIAE*, Italy's *mechanical-right society*.

SEG

Abbreviation for *Screen Extras Guild*.

Segment

(1) A musical phrase or section taken from a work. (2) A division or category within a *market universe*. For instance, markets for music product might be characterized by musical genres that appeal to certain audiences, such as R&B, country, pop, etc., and each of these "segments" may be further divided into more narrowly defined groups (i.e., contemporary country, traditional country, country rock, country & western, honky tonk, bluegrass, etc.). Markets may also be segmented by consumer profiles, such as young adult, preteen, baby boomer, *generation X*, et al.

Segue

(1) To make a smooth, direct transition from one musical section, selection, or theme to another. (2) To move directly and gracefully from one subject, condition, or situation to another. (3) The time lapse between the ending of one song and the start of another.

Sel Sync

A tape recorder function that records new tracks in *synchronization* with previously recorded tracks.

Selection

(1) A work chosen for performance or broadcast. (2) A group of works chosen from among many to make up one volume or album. (3) One track on an album.

Self-Addressed Envelope (SAE)

An envelope enclosed with a *submission* upon which the address of the sender is written, to facilitate the return of submitted materials.

Self-Addressed Stamped Envelope (SASE)

An envelope enclosed with a *submission* upon which the address of the sender is written, and which has return postage attached, to facilitate the return of submitted materials. See also *international reply coupon* (IRC).

Self-Contained Act

(1) An artist or a band that writes and records its own material. (2) A band or musical group that performs or records without the need of hiring backup musicians or singers.

Self-Produce

When an artist or a band produces its own recordings.

Self-Publish

When a songwriter, a band, or an artist owns a music publishing company to publish material he, she, or they record.

Sell Off

(1) To *liquidate*. (2) A sale of product at discounted prices in order to reduce excess inventory.

Sell-or-Return

See *sale-or-return* and *consignment*.

Selling Agent

Also called a *music jobber*. Company or independent contractor appointed to sell printed music to retailers on behalf of a music publisher. The selling agent is usually a print publisher with expertise in designing, printing, distributing, and selling sheet music. Instead of licensing the original music publisher's works in return for a royalty on sales, however, the production costs are paid by the publisher and the agent pays all sales revenue to the publisher less a commission, usually in the range of 25%.

Semiclassical

(1) A popular musical work written in *classical* style. (2) A pop arrangement of a classical music work.

Semidocumentary

A feature film or television movie that dramatizes or fictionalizes actual events, lives of real people, or real situations.

Seminal

A creative work, performance, or performer whose work is highly original and contributes to the development of a new standard, style, or genre.

Semipro

A *semiprofessional*.

Semiprofessional

One who is paid for his/her talents or services, but who does not earn a full-time living at that endeavor (i.e., a part-timer, not a full-time professional).

Semitone

The smallest interval between whole tones or musical notes in traditional European musical *scales*.

Separate Card

Also called *single card*. Reference to a *screen credit*. A separate card is when only one person's credit appears on screen. A *shared card* is when two or more people are simultaneously given credit on screen.

Sequel

A follow-up, a continuation. A work that picks up and continues the narrative or storyline of an earlier work. See also *prequel*.

Sequence

(1) A repeated melodic or rhythmic pattern, especially when programmed by a computer. (2) The order in which one thing follows after another. (3) An arrangement of related things, such as a series of photographs, which together form an artistic or dramatic whole.

Sequencer

A computer program or electronic device used to arrange and generate melodic or rhythmic phrases in repeated or linked *sequences*, with or without modifications to each sound or sequence of sounds. Coupled with a *synthesizer*, composers can program a long, complex compilation of sounds for live playback without recording or further editing.

Serial Copy Management System

A blocking program required to be encoded on every home digital recorder under the *Audio Home Recording Act of 1992* so that digital copies can't be made of digital recordings. Under the Act, it is illegal to circumvent the Serial Copy Management System in order to make unauthorized digital copies of digital recordings.

Serial Copying

As defined by the Audio *Home Recording Act of 1992*: the duplication in digital format of a copyrighted musical work from a digital reproduction of a digital recording.

Serial Music

A modern classical music genre characterized by arrangements of tone patterns and repeated series of pitches, rhythms, or dynamics. Also called *twelve-tone music*.

Serialism

The art of arranging and composing *serial music* or *twelve-tone music*.

Serious Music

Music associated with sophisticated, educated tastes, that appeals to connoisseurs of the arts. Examples: *grand opera, classical music, ballet*.

Service

(1) To provide goods, equipment, supplies, repairs, maintenance, information, facilities, expertise, or help. (2) To send promotional copies out, as in to "service" major radio stations with *d.j. copies* of a new recording. (3) The official delivery of a writ, summons, or other legal notice. (4) To make interest payments on a debt.

Service Mark (SM)

A registered logo used to distinguish one company from others in marketing its services.

Service of Accounts

To call on retailers in order to solicit sales orders, set up *POP displays*, restock display bins or racks, deliver product, etc.

SESAC

One of three US *performing-right societies*. SESAC is much smaller than its two competitors, *ASCAP* and *BMI*, and is the only for-profit corporation of the three. Founded in 1930 as the *Society of European Stage Authors and Composers*, SESAC is now owned by a private investment group. Until 1992, it licensed *mechanical* and *synchronization rights* on behalf of members, as well as performance rights, but now concentrates only on *nondramatic* performance rights, like BMI and ASCAP.

Since it is privately owned, SESAC is not required to disclose operating expenses or profits. But, its estimated revenues are between $7 million and $11 million per year, of which about 50% is distributed to affiliated publishers and writers. SESAC claims its royalty payments are competitive with ASCAP and BMI. SESAC's repertoire is only about 1% of the total licensed for performing rights in the United States. The organization's headquarters are located at 55 Music Square East, Nashville, TN 37203. Tel: (800) 826-9996; (615) 329-9627.

Session

(1) A period of time scheduled for a specific purpose, such as a recording session or photo session. (2) A gathering to discuss or explore an issue (or issues) without a formal agenda, such as a brainstorming session, question-and-answer session, etc. See also *jam session*.

Session Fee

(1) Fee charged by a musician or backup singer for a recording session, usually set by union contract. See *session scale*, above. (2) A performance payment made to a union performer or actor for a single advertising commercial broadcast.

Session Leader

The leader of musicians on the studio floor in a recording session.

Session Musician

A musician hired to provide instrumental backing on a recording *session*.

Session Scale

Minimum fees for musicians, vocalists, et al engaged in recording, as agreed between record manufacturers and unions, such as the *AFM* and *AFTRA*. AFM members (musicians, leaders, contractors, copyists, arrangers, orchestrators) receive scales based on the AFM *Phonograph Record Labor*

Agreement. Vocalists are covered by AFTRA agreements. Scales are set for regular sessions of 3 hours (basic scale), special sessions (1.5 hours max), sessions of more than 3 hours (overtime scale), and sessions occurring outside of "regular" business hours (premium scale), which includes holidays, after midnight, after 1 PM on weekends, etc. Double scale is paid to session leaders and contractors, and additional payments are made to those who play more than one instrument on a session (*doubling*), and those who have to bring in heavy equipment or large instruments (cartage). Different types of scales are set for demo sessions, symphonic recordings, movie soundtracks, television taping, and commercials.

Session Singer

A singer hired to provide vocal backing on a recording session.

Set

(1) A program of songs performed by a band during a portion of an overall performance (i.e., between intervals or intermissions). (2) A collection of songs grouped or sequenced in order to develop an overall artistic theme and/or tell a story. (3) A studio area containing props and backdrop, where a movie is filmed, a television show is broadcast or videotaped, or a commercial is made.

Seven-inch

Reference to the diameter of vinyl records usually configured to play at 45 rpm.

Seventy-eight (78)

Reference to a phonograph record format configured to play at 78 rpm, usually manufactured on ten-inch *shellac* discs.

Severability

A condition in which sections of a contract can be separated into legally distinct obligations or rights.

Severability Clause

A *boilerplate* provision in a contract stating that, in the event of a judicial determination that parts of the contract are invalid or unenforceable, the valid portions of the contract will remain in force.

Sforzando

See *stinger*.

SFX

Abbreviation for sound effects.

SGA

Abbreviation for *Songwriters Guild of America*.

SGAE

The *performing-right society* in Spain.

Share

(1) An *equitable* percentage, part, or portion of a property, right, benefit, sum, or royalty, either owned by, owed by, contributed by, or distributed to a person, company, or group. (2) To divide or apportion. (3) To participate. (4) A unit of joint-ownership.

Shared Card

Reference to a *screen credit*. A shared card is when two or more people are simultaneously given credit on screen; a *separate card* is when only one person's credit appears on screen.

Shark

Someone who takes advantage of another's inexperience or naiveté in order to obtain rights by deceitful means or on unfavorable terms. See also *song shark*.

Sheet Music

Musical compositions published in printed format of one song each on unbound sheets of paper. Often called *piano copy*, though sheet music is also arranged and published for other instruments and vocals.

Sheet Music Distributor

A *music jobber*. A company that distributes sheet music and music published in other printed formats to retailers. This can be an *independent distributor*, or *selling agent*, handling printed music publications for indie publishers, or a *major* music publisher that distributes its own publications as well as those licensed from other, smaller music publishers.

Sheet Music Magazine

A periodical whose main focus is to print collections of songs in each issue, perhaps including articles, interviews, and photos related to the songs featured.

Sheet Music Magazine

A *sheet music magazine* (see above), located at 223 Katonah Avenue, Katonah, NY 10536. Tel: (914) 232-8108; Fax: (914) 232-1205.

Shelf Talker

A cardboard strip printed with an artist's name, folded to highlight the section of a retailer's cassette rack where the artist's cassettes are stocked. Used as a *point-of-purchase* eye-catcher to draw attention to a particular artist's cassette releases, much like *bin cards* are used in compact disc bins.

Shellac

(1) A thin, protective varnish made from purified Lac, formerly used to coat phonograph records during the manufacturing process. (2) Slang term for a

78 rpm 10-inch phonograph record, which was coated with the substance during the manufacturing process.

Shelve

To cancel a project, postpone a decision, delete a product, put something aside.

Ship

To transport, send, or dispatch product in fulfillment of an order.

Shipment

A quantity of product that is transported, sent, delivered, or received.

Shipping

The process of sending, delivering, or transporting product from one place to another.

Shmooze

A form of *networking* or gentle persuasion to try and get people to do something for you (make a deal, play a record on the air, divulge information, etc.).

SHOF

Abbreviation for *Songwriters Hall of Fame.*

Shop

To plug songs to potential users; to submit masters or deal proposals to record distributors; to submit audition tapes, demos, masters, etc. in order to get a publishing or recording deal.

Shop Steward

See *steward.*

Shore-Pak Cover

Type of album cover with the *graphics* printed directly onto the cardboard, as opposed to gluing separately printed *slicks* onto heavier cardboard.

Short-Form Copyright Assignment

A summarized assignment of rights to a copyright that omits financial details of a contractual relationship between the parties. Short-form assignments are frequently used for recording copyright assignments with the *Library of Congress* and in other situations where it is necessary to establish a *chain of title.* They are usually executed in addition to a *long-form contract,* so that a copyright assignment can be made a matter of public record without disclosing what was paid, given, promised, or received in consideration of the assignment.

Short-Form Video

A video format of less than feature length, frequently used to showcase an artist's performance of a commercially released sound recording. See also *music video.*

Short Subject

A brief film (less than 30 minutes in duration) screened in cinemas before the main feature. Often called a "short."

Short-Term Assignment

An assignment of a copyright or other property, or of certain rights or interests, usually for a period of five years or less, after which all rights and interests revert to the assignor.

Show Bill

A poster, placard, billboard, or sign advertising feature performances or featured performers.

Showcase

(1) A presentation of, or performance by, new talent before a selected audience, such as reviewers, record company or music publishing execs, agents, dee-jays, and others who may be able to advance the talent's career. (2) A presentation designed for the exposure and promotion of new talent. (3) An opportunity for a performer to display his/her talents in the best light. (4) An occasion for a company to present a new product or line of products.

Shrink-Wrap

A thin, clear-plastic protective covering wrapped around a product, such as a CD or cassette, which is then constricted with the application of heat, moisture, or cold to seal the product's casing.

Shrinkage

(1) Product or merchandise lost through breakage, theft, damage, etc. (2) The value of product lost through depreciation, breakage, theft, damage, etc.

SIAE

The *performing-right* and *mechanical-right society* in Italy.

Side

(1) One side of a record, disc, or cassette tape (i.e., the *A side* or *B side*). (2) A term loosely used in reference to a recorded selection in much the same way that the word track is used (i.e., "the artist cut 12 sides," or "the album contains 12 tracks.")

Side Letter

Also called an *inducement letter.* When a recording artist is under contract to a *production company* or a *loan-out corporation* that enters into a contract with a record company to provide the artist's services, the artist simultaneously signs a side letter or inducement letter agreeing to be bound by the terms of the agreement in the event a flow-through clause is exercised. (A *flow-through clause* in a deal between a record company and a record production company or a loan-out company guarantees the artist will fulfill all recording obligations directly for the record company in the event the production or loan-out company is unable or unwilling to render its obligations under the agreement.) A flow-through clause protects the record company's investment if the producer or loan-out defaults, has a falling out with the artist, or goes out of business. If a flow-through clause is exercised, the artist's obligations are transferred to the record company. Among the events that trigger a typical flow-through clause are: bankruptcy or insolvency of the production or loan-out company; breach of the production agreement by the production or loan-out company; and any breach by the production or loan-out company of its agreement with the artist that adversely affects the record company's rights. If the production or loan-out company defaults on the contract with the artist, the record company must cure the default when it exercises its flow-through rights.

Sideline Musician

A musician hired to appear on camera (in a movie, video, television production, etc.) who simulates playing an instrument, but does not actually play. Union members appearing as sideline musicians are paid extra scale supplements for time spent fitting costumes, putting on makeup, rehearsals, etc., in addition to time spent on camera.

Sideman

(1) A backing musician on a recording session. (2) A nonfeatured member of a band.

Sideman Provision

In a recording contract, a clause permitting the artist to make nonfeatured guest appearances on recordings by other artists for other record companies. Generally, sideman provisions are coupled with certain restrictions and conditions, which may include: Written credit must appear on the album saying that the artist appears "courtesy of [name of his or her record company];" in a sideman capacity, the artist will not be featured as a lead singer, soloist, or in any other fashion in which his or her unique talents are distinctively prominent; the artist will not perform or contribute to any performance of a song that the artist has recorded for release by his or her own record company.

Signal

Audio and/or video information transmitted or received.

Signal Processing Equipment

A range of auxiliary devices used in recording and mixing to control, adjust, or alter sounds. Signal-processing equipment includes *compressors, equalizers, phase shifters, digital delay, reverb, echo, limiters, filters,* and *expanders,* etc.

Signal-to-Noise Ratio

The ratio of an audio signal level to unwanted noise, interference, or distortion. The higher the signal-to-noise ratio, the better the quality of sound reproduction or transmission.

Sign

(1) To approve a contract or license by affixing a signature. (2) To acquire rights or hire talent by obtaining the signature on a contract of a rights owner, an artist, a songwriter, a producer, etc. (3) To assign, transfer, relinquish, or sell a right, title, claim, or property, by affixing a signature to a document.

Signatory

One of two or more signers of an agreement.

Signature Tune

A theme song identified with a particular program, band, or performer, which is used to open and/or close a show or signal a performer's entrance and/or exit.

Signed

(1) To have validated an agreement or indicated approval thereof by affixing a signature to a document. (2) To be under contract.

Signing

The formal signing, sealing, and delivering of a contract or license, which makes the agreement valid.

Signing Bonus

A *lump sum* or *up-front* payment delivered as an *inducement* when a party signs an agreement.

Sign-Off

(1) The end of a broadcast, or the closing down of transmission from a broadcasting station. (2) To approve something.

Sign-On

(1) The start of a broadcast, or the opening transmission of a broadcasting station. (2) To agree to something, to enroll, enlist, register.

Silver Record

In the United Kingdom, a silver record award is earned by sales of 60,000 albums or sales of 200,000 singles. See also *hit, gold record, platinum record, multi-platinum record* and *diamond record.*

Sing-Along

(1) A recording of a song without lead vocals, produced for sale, or playback on a *karaoke*-type device, so consumers or audience members or club patrons can assume the role of lead vocalist. (2) A song with a catchy *refrain* or *hook*, which compels listeners to join in.

Singer-Songwriter

A performer who writes most the material he or she performs or records.

Single

A recording having one song on each "side." (In the case of a CD, two songs are listed chronologically.)

Single Card

Also called *separate card*. A film *credit* (such as the name of the director, producer, composer of the score, etc.) that appears on the screen by itself. See also *shared card*.

Single-Song Contract

A contract between a songwriter and music publisher covering one song, as opposed to a catalog agreement or exclusive songwriter's agreement. Also called a *one-off song contract*.

Singles Deal

A contract between a record company and an artist or a producer providing for one *single* release only, but usually containing options for additional singles and/or albums in the event the first single achieves commercial success. Singles deals for new, untried artists were fairly common when singles sales were meaningful. Today, however, singles are primarily released only to drive the sales of albums. As a result, record companies are more likely to enter into *development deals* (or *demo deals*) with newer artists who have yet to convince a company to commit to a full-scale album session.

SIR

Acronym for *Song Information Request*, an online service offered by the *Harry Fox Agency* to music users who are seeking information required for licensing requests (i.e., names of specific song titles represented by the agency). See also *SIR-Plus*, below.

SIR-Plus

Acronym for *Song Information Request-Plus*, an interactive online service offered by the *Harry Fox Agency* as an upgrade to *SIR*, enabling music users to locate information required for licensing requests (i.e., specific song titles represented by the agency), and make online licensing requests.

Site

A *location*; the place where something originates. See also on *location*.

1630 Tape

Also called *U-Matic Video Tape*. A digital audio video tape with a standard sampling frequency of 44.1 KHz, onto which an original master recording is sometimes transferred in the *premastering* phase of manufacturing compact discs.

Ska

Music genre originating in Jamaica in the early 1960s as a blend of calypso with American *R&B* and *pop*. Characterized by choppy off-beat rhythm patterns and melodic hooks.

Slander

An orally expressed *defamation*. To make malicious and unjustified verbal statements about someone. A defamation expressed and fixed in permanent form (written, recorded, or pictured) is called *libel*.

Slate

(1) To identify a cut, take, or track on an audiotape, videotape, or film. (2) A list, roster, or roll of artists or songs. (3) A schedule or designated order of events. (4) A test tone.

Sleeper

An artist, a recording, a song, a play, a film, or some other marketed product that achieves unexpected acclaim or delayed commercial success.

Sleeve

A protective case or envelope made to contain a phonograph record.

Slick

(1) Smooth, glossy photos, suitable for reproduction. (2) A glossy paper onto which the *graphics* of an album cover are printed, and which is then glued onto a cardboard backing. See also *Shore-Pak cover*. (3) A magazine printed on glossy paper. (4) A performance or production (often heavily produced) of superficial quality, lacking depth or *soul*.

Slider

A sound control device used to change a parameter value. Also called *fader*.

Sliding Scale

A range of compensation or prices that varies according to performance, productivity, or sales volume.

Slot

(1) A regularly scheduled time for a television or radio program. (2) A position, job, or role in an

organization, group, or venture. (3) The order in which something happens or appears in a sequence. (4) A *niche*. (5) To place, to schedule, to put into a position, to find a spot for.

SM

Abbreviation for *service mark*.

Small Performance

The performance of a musical work that is not construed as part of a *grand right* or *dramatico-performance. Examples:* A recording played on radio, a song performed in concert or on a nightclub stage, a song performed on a television variety program or in a movie. See also *grand right, dramatico-musical performance.*

Small Rights

Rights to *nondramatic* musical works or for works extracted from *dramatico-musicals* for nondramatic usages, including the rights to copy, perform, display, distribute, sell, broadcast, print, etc. See *bundle of rights* and *grand right.*

Smash

A big hit; a resounding critical and commercial success.

Smoothed-Out R&B

A contemporary *R&B* music genre characterized by vocal harmonizing and *quiet storm*-style arrangements of romantically-oriented songs.

SMPTE

Abbreviation for *Society of Motion Picture and Television Engineers.*

SMPTE Timecode

Used for scoring and synchronizing music with film and videotape, the SMPTE time code is "striped" onto reference film or videotape footage in order to provide the composer with exact start and stop timings. *Spotting notes* provided by the music editor tell the composer exactly where each music cue should start and stop using the SMPTE timecode. The code is displayed in hours, minutes, seconds, and frames. For instance, "00:12:15:12" translates to a cue that should start precisely at 0 hours, 12 minutes, 15 seconds, and 12 frames.

Soap

A "soap opera:" a serial drama produced on daytime television or radio, characterized by melodramatic performances of sentimental and predictable plot situations. The term originated with the fact that many of the earliest such programs were sponsored by leading soap and detergent manufacturers.

SOBODAYCOM

The *performing-right society* in Bolivia.

SOCAN

The *performing-right society* in Canada.

Sociedad General de Autores de España (SGAE)

The *performing-right* and *mechanical-right* society in Spain.

Societie des Auteurs, Compositeurs, & Editeurs (SACEM)

The *performing-right society* in France.

Society

An organization or association of companies and individuals brought together by mutual interests, activities, and profession, for the purposes of protecting and promoting those interests.

Society of Composers & Lyricists (SCL)

Organization formed in 1983 to promote and protect the works of composers and lyricists who create works for film and television productions. Services include workshops, and advice on creative, legal, and financial matters. Located at 400 South Beverly Drive, Suite 214, Beverly Hills, CA 90212. Tel: (310) 281-2812.

Society of Composers, Authors, & Music Publishers of Canada (SOCAN)

The *performing-right society* in Canada. See also Procan and CAPAC.

Society of Composers, Authors, & Publishers of Slovenia (SAZAS)

The *performing-right society* in Slovenia.

Society of European Stage Authors & Composers (SESAC)

See *SESAC.*

Society of Motion Picture and Television Engineers (SMPTE)

Trade association of recording technicians active in the film and television industries. SMPTE provides training opportunities, information and education exchanges, and standardization of recording and synchronization techniques.

Society of Professional Audio Recording Services (SPARS)

A trade association of studio owners, managers, and technicians promoting educational and training standards in audio recording.

SOCINADA

The *performing-right society* in Cameroon.

SODACT

The *performing-right society* in Tunisia.

SODRAC

A *mechanical-right society* in Canada.

Soft Copy

Data displayed on a monitor screen, as opposed to *hard copy*, which is printed out on paper.

Software

Computer programs that, when executed, perform functions. *Examples*: music *sequencer* software and games.

Soho

District in central London, which was traditionally the hub of the British music industry. See also *Tin Pan Alley, West End*, and *Denmark Street*.

Sole

Pertaining to one person or one company only; a right, interest, claim, or title that is exclusive, not shared.

Sole Proprietorship

An unincorporated business owned and operated by one person.

Sole-Selling Agent

A company or independent contractor having exclusive rights in a territory to sell product on behalf of another. See *selling agent*.

Solicit

To ask, seek, or request, as in to ask for submissions of new songs or talent.

Solicited

Demos, masters, and auditions that are requested by a company or someone seeking new talent or material.

Solo

(1) Music performed or written to be performed by a single instrument or voice with or without accompaniment. (2) A section of a musical work that features a performance by one vocalist or instrumentalist.

Solo Switch

On a recording studio console, a control device that allows an engineer to listen to any mixing channel in isolation without affecting the audio on other channels.

Soloist

A musician or vocalist who performs a solo, with or without accompaniment.

SONECA

The *performing-right society* in the Congo (Zaire).

Song Casting

(1) The process of trying to find and match suitable song material with recording artists or other music users, such as film or television producers, ad agencies, etc. (2) The act of *pitching* or *plugging* songs for a recording artist or recording session.

Song Folio

A large, softbound book containing arrangements of several songs. See also *matching folio* and *personality folio*.

Song Information Request (SIR)

See *SIR*.

Song Information Request-Plus (SIR-Plus)

See *SIR-Plus*.

Song Registration Service

A service operated since 1974 by *National Academy of Songwriters* (formerly *Songwriters Resources and Services*) to provide a method of documenting copyright claims to musical works, which is less expensive than registration fees required for filing copyright claims with the *Copyright Office* of the *Library of Congress*. Upon receipt of a tape, disc, or lead sheet, the work is issued a registration number, sealed, and filed in a vault. The service is bonded to insure against unauthorized tampering with registered songs. The service is used primarily by authors of unpublished works. When a registered work is published, the author usually then proceeds with formal copyright registration with the Library of Congress. Contact: *National Academy of Songwriters*, 6381 Hollywood Boulevard, Los Angeles, CA 90028. Tel: (213) 463-7178

Song Score

Usually, a film soundtrack featuring licensed master recordings of songs and records that were hits at an earlier time (as opposed to a score written specifically for the film). Song scores composed of hit records have proven popular modes of evoking a past era around which a film's storyline centers. Examples of movies using such soundtrack concepts include "American Graffiti" and "The Big Chill."

Song Shark

An unscrupulous music publisher who takes advantage of an inexperienced songwriter's naiveté in order to obtain copyrights by deceitful means or on terms unfavorable to the writer, or who charges a songwriter money to publish a song. Though not all song shark practices are illegal, they are considered unethical by legitimate music publishers.

Song Title

The name given to a musical composition. Even though titles are very important and sometimes unique, they cannot be copyrighted. (Titles of motion pictures, however, can be protected by registration.) Dozens of copyrighted songs share the same title. However, certain songs have become so famous that the *Library of Congress* may refuse to register a new song with a title that would be easily confused with an established song. For example, the Doctrine of *Unfair Competition* might apply if someone attempts to register a new song called "Rudolph the Red-Nosed Reindeer."

Songbook

Also called *folio*. A large, softbound book format for printed music, usually consisting of large sheets of paper each folded once in the middle to make two to four pages.

Songplugger

Person who markets songs for a music publisher (sometimes also called *professional manager, catalog manager,* or *creative manager*). In addition to promoting or plugging songs, the position might also include other duties, such as scouting, signing, and developing talent, producing demos, and serving as liaison with licensees.

Songsalive!

Organization based in Australia but representing active professional songwriters worldwide with the mission to provide mutual support, information exchange, and development resources.

Songwriter

Person who composes music and/or writes lyrics for songs in any genre.

Songwriters Association of Canada (SAC)

Organization founded by active professional songwriters in Canada for mutual support and information exchange, and to help develop, promote, and recognize Canadian songwriting talent.

Songwriters, Composers & Lyricists Association (SCALA)

Non-profit organization founded in 1987 to promote the creation of original music by providing support to songwriters, composers, lyricists, and *libretto* writers with information, workshops, and seminars.

Songwriters' Guild of America (SGA)

An organization established in 1931 to promote and protect interests of songwriters, their heirs, and estates. Originally called the *Songwriter's Protective Association*, the organization later changed its name to the *American Guild of Authors and Composers* (AGAC), then changed again in the 1980s to the *Songwriters' Guild of America* (SGA). Services to members include publisher audits, royalty collections, catalog administration under *CAP (Catalog Administration Plan)*, estate administration, songwriter workshops, collaborator-matching, catalog valuations, contract reviews, legal advocacy, legislative lobbying on copyright matters, group insurance, form contracts and licenses, etc. Located at 6430 Sunset Boulevard, Hollywood, CA 90028. Tel: (213) 462-1108; Fax: (213) 462-5430.

Songwriters Hall of Fame (SHOF)

Maintained by the *National Academy of Popular Music*, which stages an annual induction and awards ceremony for songwriters. Each year, a nominating committee selects candidates for induction into the Songwriters Hall of Fame. Only writers who have actually been engaged in the profession for a minimum of 20 years, and who have written an extensive catalogue of hit songs are eligible. The 20-year limit is waived in the consideration of posthumous awards if the writer in question made a major impact on the course of popular music before achieving two full decades of productivity.

Songwriters' Protective Association

Founded in 1931, the organization later changed its name to *American Guild of Authors and Composers (AGAC)*, then changed again in the 1980s to the *Songwriters Guild of America (SGA)*.

Songwriters' Resources and Services (SRS)

See *song registration service* and *National Academy of Songwriters*.

Soul Music

A subgenre of popular *R&B* music, usually attributed to African-American musicians and singers, blending elements of Southern gospel music and blues.

Soulful

A heartfelt, emotional performance, or a performer whose work expresses this characteristic.

Sound

(1) Reference to a style characteristically used by or identified with a particular era, region, artist, band, producer, studio, or record label (i.e., the "Motown sound" or "Nashville sound"). (2) A physical phenomenon caused by sound waves stimulating the sense of hearing. Human hearing perception occurs with frequencies vibrating at between 20 and 20,000 hertz.

Sound Box

Hollow chamber in the body of a violin, viola, cello, mandolin, or an acoustic guitar that intensifies tonal resonance.

Sound Camera

A movie camera capable of recording sound in *synchronization* with visual images.

Sound Effects

Artificially produced or modified sounds that simulate other sounds, such as car crashes, gunshots, thunder, etc.

Sound Engineer

See *engineer*.

Sound Level Indicator

A gauge, meter, dial, or other device for measuring the intensity or volume of sound.

Sound Mixing

Process of combining two or more separately recorded tracks into one or two *equalized* tracks, or combining two or more separate channels of sound into one or two equalized channels.

Sound Quality

The quality (*timbre*) of a voice, tone, or instrument is formed by the harmonic constitution of the sound generated, and is distinguished by a unique resonance that enables the human ear to recognize and identify individual voices, tones, or instruments. See also *CD-quality sound*.

Sound Recording

The conversion of sound vibrations into a *fixed* or permanent form from which they can be retrieved and reproduced in their original form. See also *electromagnetic recording, magnetic recording, mechanical recording, digital recording,* and *optical recording*.

Sound Recording Fund

Under the *Audio Home Recording Act of 1992,* two-thirds of all taxes collected on the sale of digital recorders and blank digital recording tape are placed in this fund for distribution to copyright owners of sound recordings distributed in digital formats, and to the featured artists and nonfeatured backing vocalists and musicians whose performances are included on digital recordings. Nonfeatured vocalists are allocated 1.375% of revenues placed in this fund; nonfeatured musicians receive 2.725%; featured artists receive 38.36%; and copyright owners of the sound recording (usually the record company) receive 57.54%.

The remaining one-third of revenues collected under the act goes into the *Musical Works Fund* for distribution to songwriters and copyright owners of the songs recorded and distributed on digital recordings. See also *Digital Audio Recorders* and Tape (*DART*).

Sound Stage

A soundproofed building or studio area used for filming or videotaping. See also *set*.

Sound Truck

A van, truck, or car equipped with a *P.A. system* for broadcasting commercial or political announcements.

Sound Wave

A linear vibration through a *medium*, with a frequency of 20 to 20,000 hertz, capable of being percieved as sound.

Sound-Alike Recording

A recording produced to sound as much as possible like another recording. Although record producers can copyright sound recordings and prohibit unauthorized reproduction (making copies) of the recordings themselves, there is no protection against someone recording another performance in imitation of the original, as long as no attempt is made to pass off the imitation as the original. For instance, an album called "Michael Jackson's Greatest Hits" featuring Jackson's photo on the cover but containing sound-alike recordings by someone else may constitute an actionable case of deceptive trade practice. Problems may also arise when a sound-alike of a hit record, imitating an artist's distinctive style, is used for purposes such as a television commercial. Some artists have sued on the grounds that this type of use, in effect, constitutes an unauthorized use of their "name, likeness, and voice."

SoundScan

A computer network service operated by *Billboard* that monitors and tabulates sales of recorded product by retailers and rack jobbers. When a compact disc or cassette is purchased, its bar code is scanned and the sale is reported to Soundscan's databank. Subscribers can track sales, searching the database by title, label, catalog number, or artist. Subscribers can tailor individual sales reports by artist, title, label, store, region, sales rankings, and comparisons with previous totals, etc. Like *BDS,* Soundscan's information provides feedback for evaluating sales, marketing, advertising, and promotional efforts. Located at 1515 Broadway, New York, NY 10036. Tel: (212) 536-5319; Fax: (212) 536-5351.

Soundtrack

(1) Music synchronized with visual images in a film. (2) A commercially released recording of music originally used in a feature film or television program. (3) A thin, vertical strip running the length of a motion picture film in which the sound recording is contained.

Soundtrack Album

See *soundtrack*.

Source-and-Receipts Basis

A method of calculating and paying royalties. For instance, if a songwriter's contract calls for 50% of all *net receipts,* and the publisher's German *subpublisher* retains 25% of earnings in that country, then the writer would receive 50% of 75% of income earned in Germany. But, if the writer is paid based on earnings *at source*, and the German subpublisher retains 25%, the writer's publisher must factor the subpublisher's share back into net receipts and pay the writer 50% of all income earned in Germany. The effect is that of all earnings in Germany, the writer receives 50%, the subpublisher retains 25%, and the publisher is left with 25%-instead of 37.5% (50% of 75%).

Source License

A nonexclusive *performance license* to use music in a movie or television program, which is granted by a music rights owner directly to the producer or owner of the work in which the music is used. This contrasts with *direct licenses* issued by rights owners to broadcasters (i.e., television stations or networks), and with *blanket licenses* issued to broadcasters by rights owners' *performing-right societies*. Music publishers are free to negotiate source licenses and direct licenses directly with broadcasters and owners of television programs as a result of *consent decrees* entered into between the Justice Department, *BMI*, and *ASCAP*. See also *Buffalo Broadcasting Case*.

Source Music

Term used to describe music used in a film or television program that appears to be emanating from a prop on the set, such as a jukebox, radio, television set, or record player, etc.

Source of Income

A specific copyright usage, performance, license, or contract from which money is derived. For instance, sources of income for music publishers include *mechanical licensing* (sales of recorded songs), *performance rights* (royalties from radio airplay), *print licenses* (sheet music), *synchronization* (use of songs in films), *transcriptions* (background music), *subpublishing* (foreign licensing), etc. Income sources for recording artists include record royalties, live performance fees (concerts, touring), *merchandising, endorsements*, etc.

Source Royalties

Royalties calculated directly at the *source of income*. For instance, a music publisher or record company may be contractually obligated to pay writer or artist royalties based on all gross income earned and collected by a *licensee* (the source of the income) as opposed to calculating and paying royalties on *net receipts* (income received after the licensee has deducted its percentage). See *at source* and *source-and-receipts* basis.

South African Music Rights Organization (SAMRO)

The *performing-right society* in South Africa.

South African Recording Rights Association Ltd. (SARRAL)

The *mechanical-right society* in South Africa.

South by Southwest (SXSW)

Annual music industry showcase and marketplace, located in Austin, Texas. P.O. Box 4999, Austin, TX 78765. Tel: (512) 467-7979.

Souvenir Merchandising

The sale of product bearing names and likenesses of celebrities, often in conjunction with their public appearances. *Examples:* Tee shirts, jackets, caps, lunch boxes, concert programs, badges, balloons, toys, etc. See merchandising agreement.

SOZA

The *performing-right society* in Slovakia.

SPA

The *performing-right* and *mechanical-right society* in Portugal.

SPARS

Abbreviation for *Society of Professional Audio Recording Services*.

Speaker System

A group of loudspeakers assembled to reproduce sound, such as those used hi-fi sets, radios, public-address systems, theater sound systems, etc. A loudspeaker is an electromechanical device through which sounds are produced from amplified audio voltages. Most loudspeakers are "dynamic," and contain voice coils of light wire mounted within electromagnetic fields. Attached to voice coils are paper diaphragms that generate sound waves as the coils vibrate.

The sound quality of a loudspeaker depends upon the design properties of the enclosure or cabinet in which it is contained. Some speaker cabinets contain two or more speakers of varying size. Larger speakers, called woofers, offer better replication of low notes and bass tones; smaller speakers (tweeters) are better for high notes and treble tones.

Spec

(1) Abbreviated reference for *speculate*. (2) To write, design, or provide *specifications*.

Spec Deal

When a songwriter is invited to write a song for a film production, commercial, or other project without a guarantee the song will actually be used. The company supplies criteria for the type of material needed and the parameters of a deal to be offered if they like the work. The writer receives no compensation if the company does not accept the finished work. See also *step deal*.

Special Distribution

An unscheduled payment of royalties or commissions, made in addition to payments due at the end of agreed accounting periods. Special distributions usually result from receipts of damage awards, audit recoupments, or other collections outside the normal course of business.

Special Insert

A brochure, advertisement, coupon, photo, poster, lyric sheet, or other printed item enclosed in a phonorecord album, catalog, magazine, etc.

Special Material

Music, lyrics, or dialogue specifically tailored and created for a performance or artist.

Special Payments Fund

A provision of the *AFM* agreement with record manufacturers requires manufacturers to pay a percentage of income received from sales of records by union members into a trust fund. After trust fund expenses are deducted, the funds are ultimately distributed to union members who participated in the recordings.

Special Products

A product, such as a CD or record album, created and manufactured at a client's direction, for one-off purposes, such as charity fund-raisers or *premium* giveaways (i.e., a bonus item used as a sales incentive to get customers to purchase other items). Special products are not for general, commercial release. Some major record companies have special product divisions that package premium albums for other companies.

For example, the Gizmo Corporation may want to give away specially packaged *compilation albums* to customers who buy Gizmo products. But, since Gizmo has no expertise in packaging or manufacturing recorded product, it would approach the special products division of a major phonorecord manufacturer like BMG or Sony, who would then license the tracks, design and print the covers, and manufacture the discs or tapes for Gizmo.

Special product divisions of record companies (and other types of companies) also package *theme-oriented* albums to release on their own labels. This process entails licensing masters from other labels and songs from a variety of publishers. Notable packagers who release theme-oriented albums under their own labels are Time-Life, Reader's Digest, and K-Tel.

In some cases, special product packagers can pick and choose which masters and songs to include on a theme-oriented album. For instance, albums with titles like *Soul Sounds of the Sixties, Ladies Sing the Blues, Going Country*, etc., give scope for the titles included on them. The packagers can pick and choose from virtually any R&B song, blues song, or country song, which gives them latitude to exclude tracks or songs whose copyright owners refuse to grant reduced royalty rates.

On the other hand, if the package is geared to a specific selection, such as *All the Top 10 Hits of 1977*, the packager is limited to songs that reached the Top 10 that year. This constraint gives the owners of the original masters and songs leverage to demand higher royalty rates.

Special Program

An incentive sales campaign, usually lasting 4 to 6 weeks, during which a record company increases its normal range of discounts or free goods offers in order to induce distributors, wholesalers, and/or retailers to purchase more copies of a specific release, or to stimulate overall catalog sales. See also *distributor-free goods*.

Special Use Permit

Also called *permission*, a license to use a music copyright (or a portion thereof) in a merchandising tie-in. Examples include lyrics printed on T-shirts, greeting cards, posters, etc., or lyrics and/or music incorporated in toys, computer games, etc.

Specialty

An item created and manufactured for *specialty advertising* purposes.

Specialty Act

Usually, a performer or group of performers who provide special types of entertainment, instead of, or in addition to, musical entertainment. *Examples*: magicians, clowns, acrobats, jugglers, ventriloquists, mimes, imitators, etc.

Specialty Advertising

Also called *novelty advertising*. An advertising medium by which novelty-type items are given away to promote or draw attention to a specific product (i.e., a record release or a recording artist), or to a company in general. Advertising specialties are akin to *institutional ads* in that they are image builders and keep the name of a company, performer, or product before the public. However, like *institutional ads* in trade directories, they have the benefit of repeat advertising, since they're produced at a one-time cost, and recipients usually keep or use them for some period of time.

Specialty giveaways include items like calendars, desk-sets, pens, pencils, tee-shirts, sweat-shirts, jackets, caps, jewelry, rulers, paperweights, wall clocks, watches, cigarette lighters, scratch-pads, mugs, cups, playing cards, toys, ashtrays, bags, buttons, stickers, belt buckles, matchbooks, boxes of candy or other foodstuffs, key chains, and so on. Needless to say, the advertiser's name, address, phone/fax numbers, and logo are imprinted on each item.

Specialty Publisher
A music publisher that focuses on a *niche market* or on material other than that geared to mass appeal. *Examples*: children's music, educational or *method books*, religious songs, etc.

Specialty Record Label
A recording company that focuses on a *niche market* or on material other than that geared to mass appeal. *Examples*: children's music, *spoken word* recordings, religious music, etc.

Specifications
(1) A detailed written description of materials and physical dimensions of a product, which is used for the product's manufacture, maintenance, repair, or installation. (2) A detailed statement of materials, dimensions, and operating methodology of an invention or product improvement, such as that filed with a patent application. (3) In recording equipment, specifications refer to physical attributes, and degree of accuracy the equipment can produce and transmit electrical and magnetic signals: *signal-to-noise ratio*, *distortion*, and *frequency response*.

Specs
Abbreviated reference for *specifications*.

Speculate
To invest time, money, and/or effort in a project or activity on a risk basis, with no guarantee of compensation or profit.

Speculation
An investment or effort made in a project or activity, taken on a risk basis, with no guarantee of compensation or profit.

Speculative
An investment, activity, or undertaking that has no guarantee of profit or success.

Spiel
A sales *pitch*; a disc jockey's *patter*; ad-libbed comments by an *emcee*.

Spin
To play a *phonograph record*.

Spindle
A pin or rod at the axis of a phonograph turntable that is inserted through the center hole of a phonograph record in order to lock the disc in place as it turns.

Spin-Off
(1) A byproduct, an offshoot, a derivative. (2) To create something new out of something else already existing. For example, a record company might "spin off" an in-house music publishing operation as a separate corporation.

Spiritual Music
Originally, folk hymns used in American religious revivals of the 18th and 19th centuries, the term now applies to African-American adaptations of those folk hymns and to more contemporary African-American religious music composed and performed in the same manner. See also *gospel music*.

Splice
To join or edit together, particularly in reference to film, audio, and video editing.

Split
(1) A jointly-owned copyright; a co-published work. (2) To divide ownership, income, or liabilities. (3) To share credit, billing.

Split Copyright
A copyright jointly owned by two or more individuals or companies.

Split Publishing
To copublish, to divide publishing rights.

Spoken Word
A recorded *narration*.

Sponsor
(1) A person, organization, or business that financially supports radio or television programming by paying for advertising time. (2) A person, organization, or business that financially supports an event, activity, project, or cause, either through donations or by purchasing advertising sold by organizers of the event, activity, project, or cause.

Spoof
(1) To satirize or parody something through humorous imitation. (2) A nonsensical, humorous take on something.

Spool
British term for *reel*. Also a British term for "wind," as in "spool (wind) the tape back to the beginning."

Spot
(1) A commercial broadcast announcement. (2) A short presentation on commercial television or radio between feature programming, such as a weather spot, news update, or announcements of community events. (3) A spotlight. (4) To indicate film segments for *underscoring*. (See *spotting notes*.) (5) To find talent.

Spot Advertising
Targeting specific audiences by placing paid advertisements in selective media and/or specific regions or localities.

Spot Check
To inspect on a random or limited to basis.

Spot Radio Rates and Data
Monthly publication detailing music formats, advertising rates, broadcast power and hours, audience demographics, and addresses of more than 8,000 commercial radio stations.

Spot Sale
A market or situation in which product is offered, a purchase decision is made, payment is given, and delivery is taken immediately ("on the spot").

Spotting Notes
A music editor's or film director's cue instructions to a composer, specifying where and when music should be scored or synchronized.

SR Form
A form for registering copyright claim information with the *Copyright Office*. Under the *Copyright Act of 1976*, Form SR is used for registering both *published* and *unpublished* sound recordings. (Claimants who wish to register a recorded performance and the songs rendered on the recording, may register both claims with this one form-rather than separately filing an SR for the recording and a *PA Form* for the song).

SRLP
Abbreviation for *suggested retail list price*.

SRO
Abbreviation for *Standing Room Only*.

SRS
Abbreviation for *Songwriters' Resources and Services*.

Staff
(1) Personnel employed to assist management in the running of a business, to undertake certain functions of an enterprise, to carry out an activity, or to complete a project. (2) Five horizontal lines used in *musical notation*, which, along with the spaces between the lines, serve to represent tonal pitches. Also called a *stave*.

Staff Arranger
Person employed full-time (by a production company, record company, music publisher, et al) to orchestrate music.

Staff Producer
Person employed full-time (by a production company, record company, music publisher, et al) to oversee recording sessions.

Staff Writer
(1) Person employed full-time (by a production company, record company, music publisher, et al) to compose original music, jingles, film scores, lyrics, and/or songs. (2) Person employed full-time (by a newspaper, periodical, ad agency, television or film production company, et al) to compose original articles, stories, ad copy, scripts, etc.

Stage
(1) To produce a live concert, show, play, etc. (2) Abbreviated reference for the theatrical or acting profession. (3) A raised floor or platform from which performances are presented.

Stage Director
Person who directs a theatrical performance.

Stage Fright
Extreme nervousness before or during a performance in front of an audience, a microphone, or a camera.

Stage Manager
(1) Person who coordinates technical and creative aspects of a theatrical production, supervises rehearsals, cues tech crews during performances, and "runs the show." (2) Someone who works behind the scenes to orchestrate a desired effect.

Stage Name
A *pseudonym* adopted for professional use in show business.

Stage Whisper
A remark made by an actor or performer that is intended to be overheard by the audience but not by the other actors or performers.

Stamper
A metal mold containing negative impressions of the grooves cut into a *master lacquer*. Stampers are cast from *mothers*, and are mounted on pressing machines used to stamp out, or press, vinyl phonograph records during the manufacturing process. A separate stamper is made for each side of the record. Stampers deteriorate with use and must be replaced after pressing between 1,500 and 2,000 records. See also master lacquer, matrixing, metal parts, mother, plating, and pressing.

Standard
(1) A song that has achieved widespread popularity

over the years, has been recorded by numerous artists, and is instantly recognizable by the public. Also called an *evergreen*. (2) A recognized measure by which something may be compared for quantity, quality, or value; a *benchmark*.

Standard Bias

Also called *normal bias*. Bias is the adjustment of the strength of a magnetic field applied during the recording process to a magnetic tape. High-frequency voltage combined with an audio signal reduces distortion in tape recording. Audiocassettes are graded according to dynamic range, *signal-to-noise ratio*, and *frequency response*. Types 0 and 1, called normal or standard bias, use *ferric* tape and are subject to more *hiss*. *High bias* tapes (types 2 and 3 *chrome* and type 4 *metal*) provide the best frequency responses, wider dynamic ranges, and lower hiss. See also *ferric, chrome cassette, metal cassette, bias,* and *high bias*.

Standing Room Only (SRO)

A sell-out event, for which seats are no longer available.

Stanza

A section or division (verse) within a poem, or set of lyrics consisting of lines sharing similar rhyme schemes and *meter*.

Star

(1) A performer who is widely known, recognized, and acclaimed. (2) The leading, featured performer in a theatrical, film, broadcast, or musical production. (3) To take the lead role, to be the center of attention.

Star Billing

A headline performer, one whose name is given top position and largest type size on programs, screen credits, album covers, theater marquees, posters, or advertisements.

Star Power

The ability or capacity to attract a large audience, to sell large quantities of product to loyal fans, to influence others through endorsements, to command special considerations or concessions from others in contract negotiations. See also *draw, marquee value,* and *name value*.

State of the Art

The latest, most up-to-date technology.

Statement

A written report detailing or summarizing a commercial or financial account of monies owed, being paid, accrued, earned, etc. See also *royalty statement*.

Station I.D.

A radio or television station's identification (its *call letters* and *frequency*). The *FCC* requires all radio and television stations to identify themselves at regular intervals by announcing their call letters and frequency assignments ("making a station I.D."). See also *station logo*.

Station Log

A listing kept by radio stations of all recordings played or programmed during broadcasting hours, including titles, artists, and performing-right affiliations of the music publishers.

Station Logo

A musical jingle, or *signature tune*, by which a radio station's call letters, frequency, and slogan are identified on air.

Statute

An act, doctrine, or rule given the force of law by legislative enactment and executive signature.

Statute of Anne

The first *statutory* copyright law enacted by an English-speaking country, which was passed by the British Parliament during the reign of Queen Anne in 1710. The law specifically addressed the printing, reprinting, or importing of books, giving copyright owners exclusive rights to their works for a limited number of years.

Statute of Limitations

A time frame set by law during which an action can be brought, and after which no legal action can be taken. For instance, most states require lawsuits claiming violations of written contracts to be filed within six years of the alleged violation, after which time the statue of limitations runs out and a *complainant* no longer has a right to sue.

Statutory

An activity, a process, or a type of transaction that is authorized, regulated, constrained, or governed by law through legislative enactment.

Statutory Beneficiary

One that receives by law, or has the legal right to receive, monies, property, or other benefits from a will, insurance policy, or assignment of interests, etc. See also *renewal assignment*.

Statutory Copyright

A song or other intellectual property protected by copyright legislation.

Statutory Mechanical Royalty Rate
See *statutory rate*, below.

Statutory Rate
The maximum royalty that music copyright owners can demand for *mechanical* reproductions, (though *mechanical licenses* may be granted at lower rates at a copyright owner's discretion). The rate is called *statutory*, because, unlike other types of royalties and fees, which are set by the marketplace and negotiations between copyright owners and *users*, the mechanical royalty rate is established by *statute* and incorporated into copyright law. The statutory mechanical rate is periodically adjusted by the *Copyright Arbitration Royalty Panel (CARP)*, which is appointed by the *Librarian of Congress*.

The statutory mechanical royalty rate currently in effect is 7.10¢ per song for each record, disc, or audio tape distributed, or 1.35¢ per minute of playing time, whichever is greater. Thus, for a recorded song of average length (3 minutes) released in America, the record company is obliged to pay the publisher 7.10¢ for each unit distributed. A recorded version of, say, seven minutes-as commonly issued on 12-inch-singles for the dance/clubs/disco market- would yield the publisher 9.45¢ per song for each unit distributed. A recorded song with playing time of between 7:01 and eight minutes would require a royalty of 10.8¢ per unit (8 x 1.35¢).

Under a 1997 agreement between the music publishing and recording industries, the statutory mechanical rate will increase by 3% a year, beginning 1999, through the year 2006, when the statutory rate will become 9.10¢ for each song.

Statutory Termination
The date at which copyright protection ends, as proscribed by law in the *Copyright Act of 1976* as amended. Under the old *Copyright Act of 1909*, copyright protection was given for an initial term of 28 years with the right to renew for a further 28 years. This offered a maximum copyright life of 56 years.

The 1976 Copyright Act (effective January 1, 1978) as amended by Public Law 102-307 (effective June 26, 1992), provides for automatic renewal of works published or registered between January 1, 1964 and December 31, 1977. Filing a renewal claim in the Copyright Office is now optional. Copyrights in their renewal term as of January 1, 1978 are automatically extended up to a maximum of 75 years. *Unpublished* works in existence on January 1, 1978, which were not protected by statutory copyright, but had not fallen into *public domain*, now have automatic copyright protection for the author's life, plus 50 years, or, at minimum, for a term of 25 years (until December 31, 2002). For works *published* before January 1, 1978, copyright protection is automatically extended for an additional term of 25 years.

Works created on or after January 1, 1978 are granted a term of copyright protection equal to the author's life, plus an additional 50 years (though Congress was considering legislation in 1998 to extend this to life of author plus 70 years). For *works made for hire*, and for *anonymous* and *pseudonymous* works, the term of protection is 75 years from publication or 100 years from creation, whichever is shorter. All terms of copyright protection run through the end of the calendar year in which they expire.

Stave
Five horizontal lines used in *musical notation*, which, along with the spaces between the lines, serve to represent tonal pitches of a scale. Also called a staff.

STEF
The *performing-right society* in Iceland.

STEMRA
The *mechanical-right society* in the Netherlands, also covering Aruba, Dutch Antilles, and Surinam.

Step Deal
Also called an *option deal*. This is a variation of a *spec deal*, where a songwriter receives a partial payment towards a *creative fee* for writing a song for a film production, commercial, or other project. Upon completion of the song, the writer submits a demo to the company. If the company approves the song, a further payment is made and the song is recorded for synchronization. Final payment is made if and when the song is actually synchronized or otherwise used in the completed project. If the song is not used, the songwriter keeps the initial payment(s), and usually retains full rights to the work, though there may be conditions.

Stereo
Abbreviated reference for *stereophonic* (see below).

Stereophonic
A recording technique of mixing sounds down to two separate channels to create a natural audio image distribution. The simplest method of stereophonic recording uses two separate microphones to capture two recorded tracks or channels on *magnetic tape*. The sound is picked up separately from the left and the right sides of its source.

During playback, the sound is reproduced through two or more speakers that are placed so that listeners perceive music as coming from the left, right, and center. The effect creates a perception of depth that recreates as nearly as possible the conditions that would exist for listeners near the actual source of the sound.

Steward

(1) A union official or a union contractor who hires and supervises musicians and insures enforcement of terms in union agreements with producers. Also called a *shop steward*. (2) Person who supervises the property and business affairs of a club, hotel, convention center, arena, or resort, etc. (3) Person hired to help supervise or manage a concert or an event.

Stewart v. Abend

Known as the *Rear Window Decision*, a case decided by the Supreme Court, which concerned copyright renewal rights to a song used in the classic Alfred Hitchcock film Rear Window, starring Jimmy Stewart and Grace Kelly. The upshot of the decision affected songs written before 1978 (when the *Copyright Act of 1976* took effect). Prior to January 1, 1978, songs were given copyright protection for a 28-year term with the right to renew copyright protection for a further 28 years. The Supreme Court ruled that if a pre-1978 song was used in a motion picture during its initial 28-year copyright term, and the writer(s) died during the initial term, the *heirs* of the writer(s) are entitled to terminate the *synchronization license* during the renewal period. As a result, many film studios found themselves having to delete certain pre-1978 songs from film soundtracks if they couldn't get heirs to agree to new licensing terms. In addition, studios are reluctant to license pre-1978 songs for new films unless they can get heirs to co-sign synchronization licenses. See also *renewal expectancy*.

Stiff

(1) A *flop*; a recording that fails to make the charts or sell enough units to break even. (2) A wooden, lifeless performance. (3) To cheat; to renege on a promise, debt, or obligation.

STIM

The *performing-right society* in Sweden.

Stinger

An accented musical note or chord used in a film scene to highlight or dramatize an action or a character's emotions or reactions. Also called *sforzando*.

Stipulate

To demand, require, specify, guarantee, promise, or provide something as a condition of entering into an agreement. To require by contract.

Stipulation

A condition, guarantee, promise, provision, or demand required for the fulfillment of a contract or license.

Stock

(1) The *repertoire* of a theatrical company. (2) Theatrical productions taking place in locales away from major cultural centers (i.e., Broadway, London's West End), such as summer stock, provincial theaters, touring companies, etc. (3) A predictable or conventional storyline, plot, character, etc. (4) Inventory; merchandise kept on hand or in a warehouse by a store, distributor, or manufacturer. (5) A supply of parts, goods, songs, money, or other items kept on hand for future use. (6) Shares of ownership in a corporation.

Stock & Amateur Rights

The rights to stage a dramatic presentation away from a major theatrical center (i.e., Broadway or London's West End), such as plays performed in schools, summer stock, provincial theaters, touring companies, etc.

Stock Arrangement

An orchestration that is "off the shelf" or used generically (as opposed to material custom-arranged for a specific performance).

Stock Company

(1) A company of professional actors that stages plays, either at a single theater, or on a tour circuit. (2) A corporation whose ownership and capital is divided into shares of stock.

Stock Cover

A generic album jacket kept in inventory by a pressing plant or CD/tape manufacturer, which can be imprinted with any artist's name, album title, song titles, and credits at any client's direction.

Storyboard

A group of drawings arranged to illustrate the sequence of scenes, actions, or events to be filmed, videotaped, or animated.

Storyline

The plot of a book, movie, television show, dramatic work, or song lyric.

Street

Slang for public knowledge, colloquial language, casual dress, popular fashion.

Street Date

The scheduled release date for a phonorecord; date of publication. See *hit the streets*.

Strike

To clear a stage, set, or studio of props, equipment, instruments, scenery, lights, microphones, etc.

String

(1) A group of related businesses owned or managed by a single individual or company (i.e., a string of radio stations). (2) A series of achievements, as in a "string of hits." (3) To put strings on an instrument, such as a guitar. (4) To draw out, make longer.

Strings

A reference to stringed musical instruments as a group, particularly those played with a bow, such as violins, violas, cellos, etc.

Strip Show

A radio program broadcast daily at the same hour.

Studio

(1) A specially designed, constructed, and/or equipped room or facility used for (a) audio and/or video recording; (b) photography; (c) motion picture filming; (d) transmitting radio or television programs; (e) the study, creation, rehearsal, or instruction of dance, design, art, or music, etc. (2) A motion picture production company.

Studio Album

An album recorded in its entirety in a studio, as opposed to a *live* recording or a recording done from a *remote* location.

Studio Musician

A *session musician*.

Style

(1) An individual mode of expression. A unique quality, feature, fashion, or manner of expressing one's self through art, speech, writing, performing, etc. (2) A popular fashion. (3) Identifiable characteristics of an era, *genre*, type, or school of music, art, literature, etc. (4) Something done or expressed in a way that is reminiscent of someone else's work ("in the style of"). (5) A set of ground rules or customary practices for a particular mode of expression.

Stylus

(1) A needle on a phonograph record player tone arm, which picks up vibrations from the spiral grooves of a phonograph record as the record rotates on a turntable. The vibrations are converted by a *transducer* into corresponding electrical signals, which are expanded by an *amplifier* then converted to sound by a loudspeaker. (2) A needle-like tool with a sharpened point for cutting record grooves.

Subgenre

A narrowly defined type, category, or classification of creative style, form, content, or performance within a more broadly defined genre. *Examples*: *hard rock*, *soft rock*, *folk rock*, and *country rock* are all subgenres of *rock music*.

Sublicense

(1) A license granting certain rights to a third party from someone whose authority to assign those rights stems from a *direct license* from the owner or primary holder of those rights. (2) To make a secondary assignment of rights that were obtained directly from the rights holder. *Example*: A British music publisher licenses the European *subpublishing* rights to a song from an American copyright owner, then sublicenses the subpublishing rights for Germany to a German music publisher. See also *direct license* and *source license*.

Submix

Also called *ping-ponging*; a recording mixing technique designed to maximize the number of tracks available on a multitrack tape. For instance, instruments recorded on, say, four separate tracks may be mixed down to one track, thus freeing up the original tracks for additional *overdubs*.

Subpublish

To publish a work under license from the original publisher.

Subpublisher

A music publishing company that has full publishing rights to a work or catalog of works by virtue of a license from the original copyright owner. *Example*: An American music publisher grants the rights to its catalog in the United Kingdom to a London music publisher who then becomes the catalog's de facto publisher in that territory for the duration of the license.

Supublishing

The process of licensing copyrights overseas. When a foreign publisher licenses exclusive publishing rights to a song or catalog for its territory, it becomes the de facto publisher in the territory. The term *subpublisher* applies to a company that has full publishing rights under license from the original copyright owner.

Subpublishing agreements can cover an entire catalog or one or more specific songs only. There are, in fact, several types of subpublishing deals, including: (a) a *blanket* catalog agreement with one subpublisher for the world, excluding the original publisher's home territory; (b) blanket catalog agreements with one or more subpublishers for specific territories; (c) blanket catalog agreements covering the works of one or more specific writers; (d) specific song agreements covering one or more designated songs; (e) collection agreements (either blanket catalog or specific song agreements) whereby the subpublisher collects overseas earnings but does not actively promote the licensed copyrights.

Subsidiary

(1) A company controlled or owned and operated by another company. (2) Something that is subordinate to, or of secondary importance to something else, or which serves as a supplement, an auxiliary, or a backup to something else. (3) A subplot or theme that underlies and is subordinate to a main plot or theme.

Subsidiary Rights

Rights to use copyrighted material in areas that are *ancillary* to the purpose for which the material was originally created or intended. For instance, when a musical play is created, various subsidiary rights may become valuable once the play is successfully staged. These include movie rights, stock and amateur theater rights, touring rights, book rights, merchandising rights, etc.

Subsist

(1) To exist, remain, or continue. (2) To be maintained, supported, or provided for.

Subsisting

Something now existing and being maintained, such as the rights existent in a copyright.

Substantial Similarity

A standard for establishing an action for *copyright infringement*. Infringement occurs not only when someone makes an unauthorized copy of a copyrighted song, it also occurs when someone uses enough elements of a copyrighted song to be considered "substantial similarity." In other words, infringement is not limited to cases where copies are made note-for-note or word-for-word.

Successor

One who inherits or comes into legal possession of a property, asset, claim, title, or right. See also *statutory beneficiary*.

Suggested Retail List Price (SRLP)

Also called "sticker price," "list," "suggested retail price," and "published retail price (PRP)." A record company's stated retail price for product, which retailers may discount at discretion. Some companies use SRLP as a base upon which to calculate royalty payments; other companies base royalties on the product's wholesale price. See also *PPD, RRP*.

SUISA

The *performing-right* and *mechanical-right society* in Switzerland, also covering Liechtenstein.

Sunset Clause

A contractual provision setting a cut-off date to the rights of one party (such as participation in royalty income). For instance, a personal manager's contract with an artist might provide for the manager to receive a percentage of the artist's income from all contracts entered into during the term of the management agreement even after the agreement terminates. A sunset clause would limit such income participation to, say, three years after the termination of the management contract. Alternatively, a sunset clause could allow the manager to receive 100% of his commission for 2 years after termination, 50% of the commission for another 2 years, 25% for the fifth year, and none thereafter. Any number of variations can be negotiated between the parties. Sunset clauses can also be negotiated for music publishing contracts with regards to licensing of derivative works.

Superstar

A well-established star whose name and likeness are highly recognizable to the public. One who has proven over time to have consistent, widespread public appeal as a prime attraction and whose box office draw or marquee value warrants very high fees, royalties, or salary.

Superstation

A television or radio station that uses satellite or cable technology to reach a national audience.

Supervising Copyist

Person who oversees those engaged by an arranger to copy out individual instrumental and vocal parts of a musical score.

Supplementary Work

A *derivative work*. (1) A song or composition containing essential elements of one or more other songs or compositions and/or new material, such as a medley or a parody. (2) A song or composition that has been rearranged, translated, transformed, adapted, or otherwise altered from its original form. The setting of lyrics to an instrumental, for example, would constitute the production of a supplementary or derivative work. (3) A secondary use (such as a recording) of an original song. See also *derivative recording*.

Surplus

(1) A quantity or sum that is more than what was required or that is left over. (2) In accounting: (a) the total assets of a business less the sum of all its liabilities; (b) the value of corporate assets in excess of the capital stock's face value; (c) the margin of income less expenditures.

Surround Sound

A recording technique of mixing, encoding, and processing sounds down to several channels, which are played back over separate speakers so that voices or instruments seem to be spread out and to "surround" the listener. Originally introduced in movie theaters, and now available to consumers in home entertainment systems.

Survey
(1) An analytical report. (2) An investigation into opinions, reactions, habits, purchases, characteristics, qualities, etc. (3) Statistical projections taken from a representative market or audience *segment* in order to gain a general or comprehensive view of public opinion. (4) To conduct a poll. See also *performance survey* and *sampling*.

Surveyed Performance
A musical work that has been noted by a performing-right society has having been publicly performed (i.e., on radio or television, etc.). See also *performance survey*, *sampling*, *weighting formula*, *credit system*, *logging procedure*, and *credit weighting formula*.

Suspension
A contractual provision whereby a company can suspend the duration of the agreement due to *force majeure*, or the *disability* or *default* on the part of the other party (an artist, producer, songwriter, etc.). Usually, the suspension goes into effect upon written notice, which must be given within a specified number of days of the triggering event. During the suspension period, no fees or scheduled advances are paid, and the contract is automatically extended for a time equal to the period during which it was in abeyance. The suspension period ends when the other party's disability ends, when the default is *cured*, or when the disruption caused by force majeure is over.

SW
Abbreviation for *spoken word*.

Sweeps
A *survey* period during which radio and television audiences are polled to determine the number of viewers and/or listeners tuned into various broadcasts. See also *Arbitron*, *Nielsen*, and *ratings*.

Sweeten
(1) To add or layer strings or other instruments or voices to "soften" a musical arrangement. (2) To *overdub* strings or other instruments or voices to "soften" a recording.

Swing
(1) Form of ballroom dance music that achieved widespread popularity in the early 1930s. Its genesis was from 1920s jazz performed by small combos, which evolved into larger bands of 12 to 18 musicians playing written arrangements that were more melodic and harmonic. (2) To perform music with an intuitive rhythmic sense.

SXSW
Abbreviation for *South by Southwest*.

Sync
Abbreviated term for *lip sync*, *synchronization*, or to *synchronize*.

Sync License
See *synchronization license*.

Sync Right
See *synchronization right*.

Sync Track
A thin, vertical strip running the length of a motion picture film in which the sound recording is contained.

Synch
Alternative spelling for *sync*.

Synchronization
(1) A soundtrack, sound, song, or action that has been *synchronized*, or matched to a rhythmic beat or timed sequence, with filmed actions or other sounds. (2) The process of integrating music with visual images to produce an *audiovisual* work (i.e., a work with sound and sight combined). (3) A parallel occurrence.

Synchronization Fee
A one-off fee paid to copyright owners and songwriters for use of a work in a *synchronization*. Also called a *fixing fee*.

Synchronization License
Permission given by music copyright owners to *audiovisual* producers, authorizing the use of music in audiovisual works. Synchronization licenses are issued for movies, television productions, training films, travelogues, documentaries, promotional clips, advertising, how-to videos, electronic games, etc. New technologies have fueled a rapid expansion of visual media in recent years, so that licensing music for audiovisual works is an increasingly important source of music publishing revenue. See also *commercial synchronization license*, *television synchronization license*, *theatrical synchronization license*, and *videogram synchronization license*.

Synchronization Right
(1) The authority vested in music copyright ownership to use, or permit others to use, the work in an audiovisual recording, such as a film or videotaped production. (2) A license or permission to use a music copyright in synchronization with an audiovisual work.

Synchronization Royalty

A *royalty* paid to copyright owners on sales of a synchronized work used in a *videogram*.

Synchronize

(1) To occur, or cause to occur simultaneously. Also called *timed relation*. (2) To coordinate or match in exactly timed sequence the operation or occurrence of two or more things, such as an audio soundtrack with filmed visual action. (3) To combine, unite, or mesh two or more elements of a recording, film, or action into one seamless whole. (4) To calibrate the timing of something to match the timing or operative action of something else.

Syncopate

To shift the accent of an instrumental or a vocal phrase so that it occurs between the normal rhythmic beat or at a time when a normally weak metric beat is stressed.

Syndicate

(1) An association formed to promote a venture, further a shared interest, or pursue certain transactions. (2) An *agency* representing several writers, photographers, cartoonists, producers, publications, etc., that simultaneously sells articles, cartoons, features, photographs, television productions, radio programs, etc. to numerous publications or broadcast outlets. (3) A chain of newspapers or broadcast stations owned, controlled, and/or operated by one company. (4) To sell broadcast and/or publication rights to several outlets simultaneously. See also *satellite-syndicated transmission*.

Syndicated

(1) A television or radio program that has had broadcasting rights sold to several independent or non-network television or radio stations. (2) A newspaper column, article, cartoon, comic strip, feature, photograph, etc., that has had publication rights sold to several newspapers or periodicals.

Syndication

A radio or television program, or an article, a cartoon, a comic strip, a photograph, a column, etc. that is made commercially available to numerous broadcast outlets or publications by a *syndicate* or *syndicator*.

Syndicator

A *syndicate*; a company or individual who syndicates programs, photographs, articles, editorial columns, cartoons, comic strips, etc. See also *satellite-syndicated transmission*.

Synthesize

(1) To combine, layer, arrange, replicate and/or harmonize various sounds in order to create new sounds. (2) To combine, incorporate, integrate, adapt, arrange, and orchestrate various elements to produce a particular effect or a new product.

Synthesizer

An electronic, often keyboard-operated instrument used to manipulate and combine single soundwave forms and other sound sources, to create more complex, synthesized sounds, and/or to replicate the sounds of other instruments. See also *sequencer*.

Tag
(1) To label, identify, characterize. (2) A nickname, a descriptive reference. (3) The ending of a musical work during which an intro or hook is reprised.

Tail
On a reel of recording tape or film, the end is referred to as the "tail."

Tail In
Same as heads. A notation on a tape or film reel (or on the box containing the reel) indicating that the tape or film is wound so that the performance starts at the *head* of the reel.

Tail Out
Same as *tails*. A notation on a tape or film reel (or on the box containing the reel) indicating that the tape or film is reversed on the reel; the tape or film must be rewound to reach the start, or head, of the performance.

Tails
See *tail out*.

Take
(1) An uninterrupted version of a recorded, filmed, or videotaped performance. See also *final take* and *out take*. (2) The total amount of money collected from ticket sales and admission to a concert or other event. Also called the *gate*.

Talent Agency
An agent or service authorized to represent performers in booking personal appearances and other types of employment. Their function is much like that of an employment agency: finding work, negotiating terms of engagements, administering the flow of contracts. A specialized agency may be restricted to handling personal appearances, and might therefore be more properly called a *booking agency*. A *full-service talent agency*, on the other hand, might also represent a client in every conceivable area of employment, including commercials, endorsements, and ancillary activities (such as a recording artist branching into acting or writing books, etc.). Talent agencies are compensated with *commissions* based on a percentage of the fees received from employment they generate.

Talent Buyer
Person employed by hotels, clubs, casinos, and other venues to *book* talent.

Talent Development
The process of grooming and polishing new talent, of producing demonstration recordings and video audition tapes, of advising, guiding, consulting on career matters, and of helping to obtain contracts, bookings, appearances, publicity, etc. See also *development deal* and *demo deal*.

Talent Scout
An employee of a record company, music publisher, talent agency, booking agency, film studio, etc. who seeks out, finds, evaluates, and recruits new talent and material.

Talent Show
A presentation or *showcase* featuring new, unsigned, *semipro* and amateur performers, especially those hoping to gain fans, obtain contracts, or win talent contests.

Talkback
A communications device that links performers in

the studio with a producer, engineer or director in the control room.

Talkie
A motion picture with sound.

Tangible
Something that can be touched, felt, seen, and measured. Something that is quantifiable, which can be valued monetarily. See also *intangible*.

Tangible Asset
A property or something of value that has physical properties, which can be valued monetarily. Also called hard asset. See also *intangible asset* and *intellectual property*.

Tangible Medium of Expression
Any format by which a song, literary composition, performance, or other artistic work can be perceived, reproduced, or otherwise communicated, either directly or with the aid of a machine or device. *Examples*: compact discs, film, videotapes, audiotapes, books, photographs, paintings, sculptures, etc.

Tape
(1) To record audio, data, and/or video onto *magnetic tape*; (2) A thin, plastic tape coated with a layer of magnetic material, such as iron oxide, which is used to record electric signals or impulses of sound, video, or data. Magnetic tapes are manufactured in cassette, cartridge, or reel-to-reel formats. See also *digital audio tape*.

Tape Head
(1) In recording, the electromagnetic piece on a tape recorder against which a recording tape passes to receive and read data. See also *magnetic tape* and *head*. (2) The starting end of a reel of recording tape or film.

Tape Hiss
Unwanted high-frequency noise picked up on an *analog* audiotape during the recording process. Engineers often use one of several *Dolby* devices to suppress hiss, and *digital* recording systems eliminate hiss altogether.

Tape Op
A "tape operator," a recording engineer's assistant who operates tape machines, marks *takes*, cleans *tape heads*, splices tape, etc.

Tape Record
(1) To record onto tape. (2) A recording commercially produced on any *magnetic tape* format, such as *audiocassette*, *reel-to-reel*, *DAT*, etc.

Tape Recorder
An electronic device used to record and play back sound, video, and/or digitized information on *magnetic* or *digital* tape. An audio tape recorder requires a microphone or other input to pick up sound, which is transformed into an electric current. A transducer in the tape recorder's head magnetizes the tape as it passes across the recording *head*. When the tape passes across a playback head, the tape's magnetic field induces a current in the transducer, which is amplified to reproduce the sound through speakers.

Tape Vault
A place where master tapes are cataloged, filed, and stored for safekeeping; ideally, a climate-controlled, fireproof room or compartment.

Tapeless Studio
Recording equipment with the capabilities to record, store, manipulate, mix, and edit audio signals in digital format, rather than using magnetic tape.

Target
(1) To zero in on a particular audience or market when designing a product or a marketing strategy. (2) An object sought or a goal pursued. (3) An area within a television camera that is scanned by an electron beam to generate a signal output.

Target Demographic (Demo)
A specific radio audience or market segment. See *target market*, below.

Target Market
A segment of the population that is most likely to be interested in a particular product. The target market is defined by analyzing profile characteristics of a *market universe* and narrowing the field down to that specific consumer group whose attributes best match those for whom the product is designed to appeal. Profiles of a target market include age, sex, education levels, income range, lifestyles, etc. A market-driven company makes decisions on product acquisition and development, packaging, distribution, advertising, and promotion in line with how it has defined its target market.

TAXI
A subscription-based service for unsigned songwriters and artists who need to submit material to major record companies and other music users. TAXI acts as a pre-screening A&R service for companies who are reluctant to accept unsolicited material. Members receive bi-weekly lists of companies seeking material, together with full descriptions and guidelines of types of material needed. Members then make their submissions to TAXI, whose screeners will forward the submissions on to

the companies as "solicited material" if it is determined that the submissions are on the mark. Contact TAXI at 21450 Burbank, CA 91367. Tel: (800) 888-2111 or (818) 458-2111.

Taylor, Joseph Deems

Joseph Deems Taylor (1885-1966), an American composer, author, and music critic in whose name ASCAP presents awards to publishers and authors of books and articles about music.

TCH

Abbreviation for *The Clearing House, Ltd.*

Tear Sheet

Clippings or sample prints of photos and other publicity material.

Teaser

A short broadcast announcement touting a program to be aired later; a short press release or an abbreviated advertisement touting an upcoming release, concert, premiere, or other event.

Technical Director

Person in charge of set design, construction, and control during a performance.

Technical Rider

A clause, schedule, amendment or addition to a performer's contract detailing technical requirements to be provided by a concert promoter or venue with regards to lighting, stage crew, stage area, sound equipment, security, etc.

Techno

Modern pop/rock genre geared to dance audiences and characterized by *state of the art* electronic production technology, such as synthesizers, sequencers, etc. Has various *subgenres*, including *ambient* and *hardcore*.

Technology

The practical application of scientific discoveries, methods, and materials to the process of inventing, developing, producing, and/or improving goods, machinery, devices, or materials for commercial purposes.

Telecast

A television broadcast.

Telecommunications

The science and technology of transmitting messages, entertainment, and information over a distance, and the systems used for such transmissions, including radio, television, telephone, telegraph, cable, etc.

Television Producer

Person or organization that creates or causes to be created a program or series of programs for television broadcast, and which assembles, finances, guides, and shapes the elements of the program from concept through production to actuality.

Television Synchronization License

A license to *synchronize* copyrighted musical material with a taped television program. Television synchronization licenses are usually limited to five years (as opposed to movie synchronization licenses, which are normally granted *in perpetuity*). Shorter-term licenses (i.e., one year with options for one- or two-year renewals) may be requested for topical programs that aren't expected to be *syndicated* or re-run extensively.

Television synchronization fees paid to copyright owners for five-year licenses range from as low as $500 for a few seconds background use of a new or unknown song to more than $100,000 for important copyrights used as themes or featured performances in made-for-television movies. Reduced synchronization fees are usually expected for short-term licenses, with additional fees paid to renew or extend the licenses beyond their original terms. See also *synchronization license* and *free television license*.

Television, Videotape Agreement

Under the *AFM Television, Videotape Agreement*, musicians receive 75% of the basic scale amount paid for the original work when a program is re-broadcast the second and third time, 50% of scale for the fourth, fifth, and sixth reruns, 10% for the 7th rerun, and 5% for each additional rerun thereafter. Such payments are called *reuse fees* or *residuals*. AFTRA members receive *replay fees* for rebroadcasts of recorded performances, formulated on a *sliding scale* similar to AFM reuse fees.

Tempo

The rate of speed at which a musical work is performed; the beat or rhythm.

Ten-inch

Reference to the diameter of a phonograph record that is usually configured to play at 78 rpm.

TEOSTO

The *performing-right society* in Finland.

Term

(1) A fixed period of time during which a contract is in force, for which an assignment is granted, or for which a copyright is provided statutory *protection*. (2) A provision, clause, or portion of a contract or license relating to a specific condition of

agreement. (3) When used in the plural (*terms*): the specific conditions of an agreement or the various rights and obligations existing under an agreement or legal relationship.

Term Contract

An exclusive agreement, as between a songwriter and a music publisher, whereby all works created by the writer during the term of the contract are assigned to the publisher. The term of agreement is typically for one year with a stated number of *options* on the publisher's part to extend or renew the agreement for additional one-year periods. Term contracts usually call for a *nonreturnable advance* to be paid by the company, *recoupable* from royalties. Other common terms include a *delivery commitment* (the writer must assign a certain number of new works to the company during the term), and *performance obligations* (the publisher must achieve certain goals during the term, such as getting a stated number of songs recorded and released, etc.).

Term of Assignment

The length of time or period during which a license is granted or a copyright is assigned. A term of assignment may be longer than the *term of contract* under which the assignment is made. For instance, the term of a songwriter's contract with a music publisher might be for a period of one year, but all songs written by the writer during that period may be assigned to the publisher for a period of ten years. If a license or grant of rights does not specify a term, the assignment may be construed as being for the *life of copyright*, subject to termination under the *thirty-five year rule*.

Term of Contract

The length of time or period during which a contract is in force. See also *term of assignment*, above.

Term of Copyright

The length of time or period during which a copyright is afforded statutory protection, before it enters *public domain*. In the United States, the term of copyright protection is subject to the *Copyright Act of 1976* as amended. Protection extends for the life of the creator plus 50 years, or, in the case of works made for hire, for 75 years from the date of first publication. (As of 1998, Congress was considering legislation to extend the term of copyright protection to life of author plus 70 years.)

Terminate

To end, discontinue, stop, cut off, cease, break off.

Termination

The act of stopping, breaking off, ending, or bring-ing to a conclusion. The conclusion of something; the limit or end of a time period.

Termination Letter

A formal notice from one party to another declaring the end of an arrangement, assignment, or agreement.

Terms

See *term.*

Terms of Art

Certain words that come to have special meaning within a profession as a result of usage, contracts, and union regulations. Examples include *leader, contractor, cartage, doubling,* etc.

Territorial Block

A group of countries treated as one territory for licensing purposes. See *English Block* and *Continental Block.*

Territory

The geographical area, region, country, or group of countries in which a contract, license, agreement, or assignment has practical application and/or legal force.

Tessitura

The melodic range of pitch for a specific instrumental or vocal part, in relation to the complete range of that voice or instrument.

Test Marketing

The process of collecting and evaluating consumer reaction to a new product or service in order to determine the market's potential interest in the product or service. Testing is used to avoid squandering time, money, and energy trying to force an invalidated concept on an unenthusiastic public.

Testing is used not only to judge the commercial potential of a product or service, but also to evaluate the effectiveness of marketing strategies and tactics, and whether marketing materials, advertising copy, and promotional tactics are honed to do the job necessary for commercial success.

For instance, advertisements are tested by trying different presentations to determine the most effective headlines, copy, layout, etc. Focus groups may be used to determine which album track to concentrate on as the *A side.*

Products, services, and marketing methods are best tested on a small scale, fine-tuning until it is clear whether or not the proposition is a winner. *Regional testing* is normally carried out before committing to an expensive, national campaign. The best test region is usually the home base of the product, service, artist or songwriter that is being promoted. This is where there are already some assets in place, a degree of proven market identity or acceptance, and where there is the most knowledge of, and personal access to, media outlets and other marketing opportunities.

When test marketing doesn't succeed within the home region, either the marketer has failed to get the marketing concept properly focused or there is a product failure. Either case is a red flag, indicating barriers to success on a national level, and a clear sign that rolling out big bucks for a full-scale marketing campaign will be a wasted expenditure, since there is no proven commercial acceptance of the product or service. See also *market research*.

Test Pressing

An acetate or metal disc coated with lacquer made from cellulose resin, used in the disc mastering process as a reference to check the transfer quality of sound from a master tape to disc before approving the manufacture of vinyl records. Acetates are fragile; their sound quality deteriorates noticeably with repeated playings. Also called a *reference lacquer*.

Testing

See *test marketing*.

Text

(1) The complete words or lyrics of a song when written or printed. (2) A printed edition of a book, script, speech, poem, or set of lyrics. (3) The entire body of a written or printed work, as opposed to an excerpt, a paraphrase, a condensation, or a revision, and as distinct from headings and illustrations. (4) A subject, topic, or theme.

Texture

A distinctive, identifying characteristic, feel, or sound derived from the combined structure, arrangement, or composition of separate elements.

Theatrical

(1) A work created for a dramatic performance. (2) A stage performance of a dramatic work. (3) Exaggerated behavior, a display of dramatic gestures, affectations, or histrionics. (4) Pertaining to the stage or acting profession.

Theatrical Performance

(1) A staged, televised, or filmed dramatic work. (2) Music incorporated into the production of a dramatic work. See also *theatrical synchronization license*, *dramatic performance*, and *dramatico-musical performance*.

Theatrical Release

A feature film issued for commercial screenings in movie theaters.

Theatrical Synchronization License

A license to *synchronize* copyrighted musical material in a *feature film*. *Commissioned* movie *soundtracks* are frequently augmented by previously written songs licensed from music publishers. Film producers seeking a certain atmosphere will "drop" a song into the soundtrack. A well-known hit, for instance, might serve as a backdrop to a specific scene in order to evoke a nostalgic mood or establish a time frame.

A hit song might also be licensed to play behind the title or closing credits, for use as a running theme throughout the film, or featured as a performance by a character on screen. For a drop-in of a pre-existing work, the publisher retains full copyright, and issues the film production company a synchronization license to use the song in that particular production. Theatrical synchronization licenses are usually issued to film producers in *perpetuity*, and granted to cover all territories "throughout the world."

A theatrical synchronization license usually provides a one-time synchronization fee to the copyright owner (sometimes referred to as a *recording-right license fee* or *fixing fee*). The size of the fee depends upon the general importance of the song, and its importance to the film specifically. If the song is essential to the film, such as providing the film title, storyline, or theme, the fee can be substantially more. The amount of the fee also depends upon the *nature of use* (i.e., partial-length featured-vocal performance, full-length featured-vocal performance, background instrumental, etc.), the number times the work is used during the film, and the *duration* in minutes and seconds of each use.

The producer is granted *nonexclusive* permission to make copies of the film containing the recording of the song for import into any country covered by the agreement, subject to the terms of the agreement. Motion picture producers must also obtain *mechanical licenses* in order to distribute and sell videos and laser discs for home consumption. Frequently, motion picture producers will attempt to negotiate a very inclusive synchronization license, to take into account plans to rent or sell the film in all media, domestically as well as overseas.

Motion picture producers must also obtain *performance licenses* from copyright owners of any music used in their productions. Performance rights are licensed separately from synchronization rights in the United States, because *ASCAP* and *BMI* operate under consent decrees preventing them from requiring movie theaters to obtain *blanket* performance licenses for theatrical exhibitions. A flat performance fee for US theatrical exhibition is often included in the synchronization license, to be paid by the film production company. The performance fee is normally equal to the synchronization fee, though some publishers request up to 200% of the size of the synchronization fee.

In return for payment of a performance fee, the publisher gives the producer *nonexclusive* permission to perform or authorize others to perform the work as recorded in the motion picture, and in radio, television, and theatrical advertisements for the production. Permission for public performance of the work is limited to places of public entertainment where motion pictures are commonly exhibited, including television, and the production may only be exhibited on television stations or networks that have valid licenses from a performing-right society with authority to license and collect performance fees on the publisher's behalf.

Film producers do not need performance licenses for television broadcasts of movies. Television stations and networks are responsible for clearing performance rights for all broadcasts, which they do through blanket performance licenses with the performing-right societies. See also *synchronization license*, *television synchronization license*, and *videogram synchronization license*.

Theme

(1) The main topic, subject matter, or recurrent idea expressed in a song lyric, work of literature, screenplay, play, or other artistic work. (2) The principal melody of a musical work, or the main melodic line upon which a set of variations is based.

Theme-Oriented Album

An album of songs selected or recordings produced in order to achieve a specific ambiance, atmosphere, or mood, such as romanic, festive, etc., or as a representation of an era, performer, songwriter, or genre (i.e., "Honky Tonk Country," "Ladies Sing the Blues," etc.).

Theme-Oriented Folio

A printed collection of songs centered around one atmosphere or mood, such as romantic, festive, etc., or as a representation of an era, songwriter, or genre (i.e., "Classic Love Songs," "Blues from the Female Perspective," etc.).

Theme Park

An amusement park created around a central topic, where the settings and attractions are focused on creating a specific ambiance, such as the wild west, the age of chivalry, etc.

Theme Song

(1) The *signature song* used to open and/or close a broadcast program or feature film, or to identify a particular performer or group of performers. (2) A recurrent song featured in a musical play, program, or film, which becomes a signature song associated with the work itself or with one of the characters.

Third Party

A "stranger" to a transaction, meaning someone other than the two parties directly involved. A party that has no legal relationship to other parties involved in a transaction, contract, or license.

Third-Party Material

Songs recorded by an artist that were written by persons not directly connected to the artist or his/her record company, publisher, or producer-as opposed to songs recorded by the artist that were self-penned, or written by his/her producer, or by someone on his/her label's or publisher's staff. Also called *outside material*.

Third World

Reference to non-industrialized, undeveloped, or developing countries.

Thirty-Five Year Rule

Also called 35-year Termination Rule. Provision of the *Copyright Act of 1976* as amended, which allows authors of works created after January 1, 1978 (that are not *made-for-hire* works) to terminate exclusive rights, licenses, or grants assigned to another party within a five-year period beginning 35 years after date of publication or 40 years from the date of the grant, whichever comes first. To affect termination under this rule, the author must serve written notice on the assignee within the time period allotted.

Thirty-Three

Reference to a phonograph record format configured to play at 33 1/3 rpm, usually manufactured on twelve-inch discs.

Thomson & Thomson

Firm specializing in *copyright searches* and research information for the music industry. Located at 1750 K Street N.W., Suite 200, Washington, DC 20006. Tel: (800) 356-8630 or (202) 835-0240; Fax: (800) 822-8823 or (202) 728-0744.

Tie In

To coordinate, connect, or link two or more items, events, or activities. *Examples*: To tie an album promotion campaign in with a concert tour; to tie a soundtrack album release in with a movie release.

Tight

A solid, well-coordinated performance; together, well-rehearsed.

Timbre

The identifying quality of a voice, tone, or instrument, formed by the harmonic constitution of the sound generated.

Time

(1) A segment of a broadcasting period (i.e., *air time*); a broadcast interval during or between programs for commercials, announcements, and station I.D.s; a scheduled broadcast. (2) The *tempo* or rate of speed at which a musical work is performed; the beat, or rhythm. (3) To measure the length of a performance in minutes and seconds.

Time-and-a-Half

A payment scale for services rendered outside of, or in addition to, regularly scheduled hours (i.e., the normal rate of pay plus an additional 50%).

Time Buyer

Person working for an advertising department or ad agency who purchases broadcast air time for commercial spots on radio and television stations, networks, and cable systems.

Time Buys

Time slots purchased from radio and television stations, networks, and cable systems during which commercial spots are aired.

Time Delay

A signal-processing device used in recording and mixing to electronically adjust the delay of an audio signal, often to give the perception of "slap echo" or doubling (so that a vocalist or instrumentalist seems to be performing the part at least twice).

Time Signature

A sign or numerical fraction in musical notation that indicates the number of beats per measure and the note duration worth one beat.

Time Slot

A scheduled segment of broadcasting air time for a program, or a series of announcements and/or commercials.

Time Value

(1) The meter, or beats per measure and kind of note given one beat, as indicated by a *time signature*. (2) In finance, the cost of invested money to an investor waiting until the investment matures (i.e., returns a profit). Idle money loses value over time through inflation and the inability to put it to work earning interest or returns on investments.

Timed Relation

A *synchronization*. (1) To occur, or cause to occur simultaneously. (2) To coordinate or match in exactly timed sequence the operation or occurrence of two or more things, such as an audio soundtrack with filmed visual action. (3) To combine, unite, or mesh two or more elements of a recording, film, or action into one seamless whole. (4) To calibrate the timing of something to match the timing or operative action of something else.

Timing

(1) The coordinated pace or rate of speed at which a group of performers interact, exchange dialogue, or play or sing their individual parts in order to achieve a desired effect. (2) The process of regulating, refining, or adjusting the pace or rate of speed of a performance or of individual performers in order to achieve a desired effect. (3) The process of measuring the length of a performance in minutes and seconds.

Tin Pan Alley

Turn-of-the-century term associated with the districts where music publishers' offices were concentrated in New York and London, and of the music publishers and songwriters as a group who turned out the prevalent style of sentimental songs that achieved popularity at the time. The term supposedly originated as slang for the tinny sounds generated by cheap pianos used to demonstrate new songs in publishers' offices. See also *Brill Building*, *Soho*, *West End*, and *Denmark Street*.

Tip

A lead or a piece of information given by someone with inside knowledge, such as that of record companies, producers, and others needing new song material.

Tip Sheet

A newsletter, trade publication, or bulletin providing *tips* to subscribers. One type of tip sheet is aimed primarily at radio programmers, and features reviews of new recordings and summaries of airplay and sales activity around the country. Another type of tip sheet is circulated to music publishers and songwriters, containing tips about record companies, producers, and others needing new song material.

Title

(1) The name of a song, book, film, play, or other creative work, or of a division of such a work, such as a chapter or section. See also song *title*. (2) The name of a newspaper or periodical. (3) *Text* superimposed on a film or video or television program to present credits, translation, narration, or other information for viewers. (4) A legal right or justifiable claim to something. (5) Written evidence to a claim or right of ownership or control of something, such as a deed, bill of sale, copyright certificate, patent, contract, license, document of transfer, will, etc. (6) A preponderance of evidence supporting a claim or right.

Title Search

An inspection of public records in order to trace the owner of a copyright or piece of property, and/or to establish *chain of title*. Before making a major copyright asset purchase, a title search is usually conducted in the *Library of Congress*; other searches are made of court records for undisclosed loans, mortgages, or liens existing on any of the copyrights, and for filings of any litigation that is threatened, pending, or underway. See also *search organization*, *clearing house*, *copyright search*, and due *diligence*.

TM

Abbreviation for *trademark*.

Tone Arm

An arm-shaped device that extends over a record player turntable, and which holds a cartridge containing the *stylus* and electric conversion circuitry. Also called a *pickup*. See also *record player*.

Tonic

First note (or degree) of a major or minor scale from which the scale takes its name. For instance, C is the tonic note of the C major scale, and the tonic chord is the C major chord (C, E, and G). See also *dominant*, *key*, and *keynote*.

TONO

A *performing-rights society*, located in Norway.

Tony

An award, named for actress-producer Antoinette Perry, which is given annually in various categories for outstanding achievement in the theater.

Top 40

A radio station format geared to airplay of contemporary pop recordings that reach the upper 40 of a national Top 100 chart. See also *Contemporary Hit Radio (CHR)*.

Top 100

Tabulation of best selling recordings, videos, sheet music, radio airplay, etc., as in the "Top 100 Album Chart." The definitive national Top 100 charts are compiled by or for trade magazines such as *Billboard* by means of surveys of retailers (for sales) and radio stations (for airplay). Charts are frequently compiled to reflect most active sales or airplay in specific genres or market segments (i.e., Top 100 Country Singles; Top 100 R&B Albums, etc.).

Top Line

(1) *Music notations* containing a song's melody line, together with lyrics and chord symbols, but not fully orchestrated. Also called a *lead sheet* or *professional copy*. (2) Top billing as the featured star; most promi-

nent mention in a line of credits. (3) A recording marketed at the full retail price customary for *name artists*, as opposed to *budget line* or *midline*.

Top Spin

Positive momentum gained from marketing successes for a recording, film, or individual career.

Torch Song

A sentimental or romantic lament or plaint, expressed in song by a "torch singer."

Tour

(1) A trip with stops to fulfill engagements at various places along the route. (2) To travel on a planned route with scheduled stops in order to fulfill engagements, make promotional appearances, call on prospective clients, gather information, etc.

Tour de Force

A superb performance or achievement displaying great virtuosity, ability, talent, or skill.

Tour Merchandise Agreement

A *merchandising agreement* restricted to sales at concerts in a tour cycle (though there may be sell-off provisions for surplus merchandise at the end of the cycle). *Retail merchandise agreements*, on the other hand, allow merchandising through normal retail channels, as well as mail order. See *merchandising agreement*.

Tour Support

Financial and/or logistical resources given or loaned to a recording act, usually by its record company, so that the act can go on the road to promote itself and/or its new product when such an endeavor would not otherwise break even. Tour support funds are generally treated as an additional advance to the artist, and are *recouped* from artist royalties. See also *negative tour support*.

Track

(1) In recording, a discrete or distinguishable strip or path along the length of a *magnetic tape* (or a segment of a computer hard drive), on which data or sound can be recorded and played back separately from other tracks on the tape. (2) One of several distinct selections, works, or songs included on a compact disc, phonograph record, or audiotape (i.e., an album track, the title track). (3) To monitor the progress of something, such as marketing efforts.

Track Format

The physical arrangement of separate tracks on a *magnetic recording tape* (i.e., 24-track, 16-track, two-track stereo, etc.).

Track Listing
The line up of selections on an album.

Track Record
A summary, history, or *résumé* of experience, accomplishments, or performance.

Track Sheet
(1) Form used by recording engineers, mixers, and producers to plan, make note of, and identify which tracks on a *magnetic tape* are allocated or assigned to various instruments or voices. (2) Form used to organize and monitor marketing efforts for a commercial record release (i.e., radio adds, airplay, picks, chart entries, chart movement, sales, etc.). Also called "tracking sheet."

Tracker
Person assigned to check radio stations, trade magazines, record stores, distributors, etc. in order to monitor the progress of marketing efforts for a commercial record release, making note of weekly *radio adds*, chart entries, chart movements, airplay *rotation*, sales, etc.

Tracking
(1) Process of monitoring weekly radio *adds*, chart entries, chart movements, airplay *rotation*, sales, etc. (2) The line up of selections on a tape or album. (3) A recording technique in which a musician or singer doubles a performance on a separate track in order to achieve the effect of having used a larger ensemble. See also *double track* and *overdub*.

Tracking Scale
A union payment schedule for *AFM* and *AFTRA* performers requiring extra payment to union members for each additional track recorded on a particular song.

Tracking Session
A recording session scheduled for recording rather than mixing.

Trade
(1) A reference to the music business and/or entertainment industry as a whole, including companies, artists, performers, writers, producers, and others working in, or professionally associated, with the business and its customers. (2) A shorthand reference to a *trade publication* or *tip shee*t (i.e., *Billboard*, *Gavin Report*, *Radio & Records*, et al).

Trade Association
An organization formed by, and consisting of, companies and individuals who share professional interests, activities, and purposes. Trade associations generally seek to promote and protect the concerns of members, as well as providing members with information and education on matters regarding a particular trade. Many trade groups offer members marketing data and research sources, including *demographic* breakdowns of the market (by age, sex, region, education, income, etc.), as well as overseas markets and opportunities. Examples of prominent music industry trade associations include *AFIM*, *NARAS*, *NAIRD*, *NARM*, *NMPA*, *RIAA*, and *CMA*.

Trade Directory
A book containing alphabetical listings of companies together with names of personnel, contacts, addresses, telephone numbers, etc., usually grouped by classifications within a trade, such as recording studios, distributors, music publishers, radio stations, etc.

Trade Discount
A retail price reduction given to wholesale buyers.

Trade Journal
A *trade magazine*.

Trade Language
Terminology, slang references, and abbreviations commonly used and understood by people professionally engaged in a particular business, which may not be understood by those with little knowledge of the business. Also called *jargon*. See also *legalese*.

Trade Magazine
A periodical, such as *Billboard*, that focuses on news, articles, interviews, and other features of interest to people professionally engaged in a particular business or industry. See also *tip sheet*.

Trade Name
(1) The name by which a company operates and identifies itself to the public, or which is used to identify a commercial product or service. Also called *brand name*. (2) Terminology used by people professionally engaged in a business or industry as a reference to a particular type of product, service, or process.

Trade Practice
The customary way of doing something in a particular business; the usual methods of procedure; the accepted standards of quality; the schedule of prices, fees, or royalties customarily charged or paid for certain types of products, transactions, contracts, licenses, and copyright usages, etc. See also *industry norm*.

Trade Publication
See *trade magazine*, *trade directory*, and *tip sheet*.

Trade Related Aspects of Intellectual Property Rights (TRIPS)

A 1993 agreement concluded by members of *GATT*, which essentially applies international copyright protection standards to third-world markets. The treaty deals comprehensively with the roles of courts and customs services in over 120 countries in the fight against copyright *piracy*.

Trade Show

An exposition, fair, or marketplace where companies and individuals professionally engaged in a particular business meet to buy and sell product, demonstrate new product, establish contacts with prospective business partners, make licensing agreements, exchange views, etc.

Trade Union

A labor union formed to protect and promote interests of members employed in a specific type of industry, trade, or skill.

Trade Usage

(1) The usual manner, practice, or customary way of doing something, using something, or treating something in a particular business. See *trade practice*. (2) The manner of speaking or writing common to those engaged in a particular trade. See *trade language*. (3) The use of something, such as a demo tape or sample recording, for purposes of promoting, marketing, selling, and demonstration within a particular business arena, as opposed to offering it for sale to consumers.

Trademark

A distinctive *proprietary logo*, emblem, symbol, word, and/or *trade name* (or any combination thereof), which identifies a particular company, product, or service. As an *intangible asset*, a trademark can be protected from unauthorized use by others. Establishing legal claim to a trademark rests foremost with its continued use in commerce, though trademark applications are also accepted for registration based on a "bona fide intention to use the mark in commerce." The *Patent and Trademark Office* issues certificates of registration, good for 10 years, which may be renewed indefinitely for 10-year periods, provided the trademark is still in use at the time of each expiration date. The application fee is $210 per class. A trademark may be considered as abandoned if it falls into disuse. Federal courts have jurisdiction in trademark disputes.

Trademark Abandonment

A *trademark* may be considered as abandoned if it falls into disuse, if its owner fails to renew its registration, and/or if its owner knowingly allows others to publicly use it without permission, license, restriction, or claim for compensation, etc.

Trading Fours

When two or more musicians swap improvised solos every four bars.

Traditional

A term used to describe a method of performing, based on stylistic interpretations of a genre as characteristic of an earlier generation, and/or as handed down by one generation of performers to another. See also *folk music*.

Traditional Country Music

See *traditional*, above.

Traffic Manager

In a large recording studio, the person in charge of scheduling studio time for clients.

Trailer

(1) A brief preview of a coming attraction shown before the start of a feature film. (2) A blank strip of film on the end of a reel, which contrasts with the *leader* at the start of a reel.

Transact

To do business with others. See *transaction*, below.

Transaction

A business arrangement or dealings between two or more persons. An action that has taken place involving two or more parties acting with *mutual consent*.

Transcribe

(1) To record a performance or program for broadcast or public presentation at a later date. (2) To copy or transfer a recording from one format to another (i.e., from digital to analog; from tape to disc). (3) To take a part written for one instrument and rearrange it for another; to take a vocal part and rearrange it for an instrument; or to take an instrumental part and re-arrange it for a vocal. (4) To write down spoken words or lyrics that are sung.

Transcription

(1) A performance recorded for broadcast or public presentation at a later date. (2) A recording that has been copied or transferred from one format to another (i.e., from *digital* to *analog*; from tape to disc). (3) An adaptation or rearrangement of a musical part for a different instrument or voice. (4) A written record of something spoken or sung.

Transcription Library

A collection of prerecorded musical segments, themes, and melodies available for licensing in productions not requiring original music. Typical libraries contain instrumental fragments capturing a range of moods, such as lush orchestrations of romantic themes or music that builds suspense, tension, and fear. Users pay licensing fees to "drop" musical segments into productions, which range from training films to local radio programming. Also called *recorded music library*, *music supply house*, and *library service*.

Transcription License

Also called *electrical transcription license*. A license permitting the recording of music specifically for broadcast or *public performance*, but not for sale to the public. Transcription licenses combine aspects of *performance licenses* as well as *mechanical licenses*, because they involve (a) the public performance of music, and (b) the mechanical reproduction of recorded music.

However, most transcription licenses do not include the right to publicly perform the music, only the right to record it for the purpose of performing or rebroadcast. And an electrical transcription license differs from a mechanical license in that the latter permits the making of copies of a recording for sale to the public, whereas the former permits making copies of the recording only for public performance, not for sale. Unlike mechanical licenses, electrical transcription licenses are not subject to the *compulsory licensing* provision of the *Copyright Act*. Each license must be negotiated directly between the *user* and the publisher, or the publisher's agent.

Transducer

A device, such as a microphone or loudspeaker, that converts energy from one form to another.

Transfer

(1) To copy data, sound, or images from one source to another. (2) To convey, sell, give, will, or hand over possession of a title, right, claim, or property from one party to another. (3) A document, such as a deed or bill of sale, that validates the legal conveyance of title, right, claim, or property from one party to another.

Transfer Costs

Expenses incurred in transferring music from audiotape to the *mag stock* of a motion picture film.

Tranship

Also spelled *transship*. Discredited practice by independent regional distributors of undercutting distributors in other areas by selling product to retailers in regions outside their own designated sales territory. *Example*: An Atlanta-based distributor covering retailers in Georgia for XYZ Records sells XYZ product to retailers in California at prices lower than those charged by XYZ's California regional distributor.

Transition

(1) A *modulation* from one key to another; a key change. (2) A musical passage linking one element, such as key, to another. (3) A changeover, shift, transformation, progression.

Translate

(1) To change a text or set of lyrics from one language to another. (2) To simplify, explain, paraphrase, or interpret something said or written in order to make it easier to understand. (3) To forward, transfer, or transmit something from one place or medium to another.

Translation

(1) A text or set of lyrics that has been changed, transformed, or interpreted from one language to another. (2) Something expressed in terms other than those used in an original version. (3) Something forwarded, transferred, or transmitted from one place or medium to another.

Translator

(1) Person who interprets, explains, or rewrites a statement, text, or set of lyrics from one language to another. (2) A device used to forward, transfer, or transmit something from one place or medium to another.

Transmission

The transfer of information, sound, images, or data over a communications line from one location to another. A *broadcast*.

Transmission and Reproduction License

Also called *electrical transmission* and *reproduction license*. Any type of license granting permission for the online transmission and *interactive* reproduction of copyrighted musical works, as through *cyberspace*. Though such licenses do not yet have specific names that are accepted within the music industry, there are three licensing issues related to the use of music online. First, transmission of the music is a *public performance* and therefore subject to a *performing-right license*. Second, downloading transmitted music constitutes "copying" and is thereby subject to a *mechanical license*. And, third, combining music with visual images for transmission falls within the scope of a *synchronization license*. A permission for "transmission and reproduction," by whatever name, may combine aspects of all three licenses.

Transmission Program

A work produced solely for *transmission* to the public, or a body of works compiled in sequence for transmission to the public as one unit.

Transmit

To send, *transfer*, dispatch, deliver, *broadcast*.

Transmittal Letter

A cover letter sent with a document, contract, license, proposal, shipment, etc., summarizing the item or items being *transmitted* and/or the purpose of the *transaction*.

Transparency

A photographic image on slide film, which can be used for slide projection or for printing.

Transpose

(1) To rewrite, adapt, arrange, or perform a musical work in a key different from the original version. (2) To reverse, alter, transform, or change the order of something.

Transship

See *tranship*.

Tray Card

Also called an inlay card or backing card. A card cut to be inserted in a jewel box with a booklet and compact disc. It contains printed material corresponding to the backside of an album cover (i.e., song titles, bar code, etc.), and shows through the back of the transparent jewel box.

Treaty of Rome

A *copyright convention* of 1961 ultimately joined by 35 countries (but not the United States). The full name of the treaty is the Rome Convention for the Protection of Performers, Producers of Phonograms, and Broadcasting Organizations. The thrust of the agreement was to establish the legal concept that producers (i.e., recording companies) and performers are as much rights *owners* as they are rights *users*. That is, while they produce and perform licensed music and are thereby copyright users, the recorded performances themselves are copyrightable with inherent rights of control, protection, and compensation. The convention established copyright protection to recorded performances for a minimum 20-year period after *fixation*, which has since been extended to 50 years in most member countries.

Treble

(1) A high voice or high-pitched sound. (2) A control, especially on consumer audio playback systems, for increasing or reducing high end.

Tribute Album

A compilation recorded by either upcoming or established artists of hit songs previously associated with an icon of the music world. Examples might include current rock bands covering Beatles songs, or rising R&B artists doing their own arrangements of Sam Cooke hits.

Trip-Hop

A music genre associated with the *Bristol Sound*.

Triple A

A radio station format (*Adult Album Alternative*).

TRIPS

Acronym for *Trade Related Aspects of Intellectual Property Rights*.

True Pitch

The true position of a musical tone on a scale as defined by the tone's *frequency* of vibration (i.e., the true pitch of A above middle C vibrates at 440 cycles per second). True pitch may also be relative to another tone used to "tune" an instrument. A musician or vocalist who sounds a note slightly under or above an intended tone is "off pitch."

Trustee

An *executor* or appointee whose function is to control and govern the affairs or funds of an estate.

Tune

(1) To adjust the pitch of a note or instrument. (2) A melody.

Tuner

A radio receiver as a component of a *hi-fi system*. Standard AM/FM tuners receive signals broadcast from stations in the broadest band of the radio spectrum (i.e., 500 to 1650 kilohertz AM; 88 to 108 megahertz FM). A tuner works by isolating the frequency of the station selected by the listener (excluding other stations in the broadcast range), extracting the audio voltage of the transmission, and amplifying the voltage in order to activate the speakers of the high-fidelity system.

Turndown

A rejection.

Turntable

A round, rubber-coated platform of a phonograph *record player* upon which a record is placed to revolve at a constant speed so that a *stylus* touching the record's grooves can generate vibrations that can be picked up by the *tone arm* and converted into sound. (2) Term used as reference to a phonograph record player, especially as a separate component of a sound system (i.e., without amplifier or speakers).

Turntable Hit
A commercially released recording that has been successful in garnering radio airplay, but not necessarily successful in achieving significant sales in the marketplace.

Twee
British term for a song or record production that is too syrupy, schmaltzy, slick.

Tweeter
A small loudspeaker engineered to reproduce high frequencies.

Twelve-inch
Reference to the diameter of a vinyl record that is usually configured to play at 33-1/3 rpm (but see below).

Twelve-inch Single
A 45 rpm vinyl record with a 12-inch diameter containing not more than two track selections.

Twelve Tone Music
A modern classical music genre characterized by arrangements of tone patterns and repeated series of pitches, rhythms, or dynamics. Also called *serial music*.

Two-Track
A magnetic recording tape containing two discrete or distinguishable strips on which sound can be recorded separately and played back together to form a stereophonic effect.

TX Form
A form for registering copyright claim information with the Copyright Office. Under the Copyright Act of 1976, Form TX is used for registering nondramatic literary works.

Typeset
To fix, arrange, or compose written material into type for printing.

UC
Music format abbreviation for *urban contemporary*.

UCC
(1) Abbreviation for *Universal Copyright Convention*.
(2) Abbreviation for *Uniform Commercial Code*.

UCMR
The *performing-right society* in Romania.

U Form
Under the *Copyright Act of 1909*, song copyright owners filed a *notice of use* (Form U) with the Copyright Office once a song had been commercially recorded and released, so that anyone else wishing to record the work would be subject to the *compulsory mechanical licensing* provisions of the Copyright Act. Under the *Copyright Act of 1976*, there is no requirement for copyright owners to file a U Form.

UHF
Abbreviation for *ultrahigh frequency*.

Ukrainian State Copyright Agency (SCAU)
Performing- and *mechanical-right agency* in the Ukraine.

Ultrahigh Frequency (UHF)
The band of radio and television broadcast frequencies of very short wavelength, ranging from 300 to 3,000 megahertz.

U-Matic Video Tape
A digital audio video tape with a standard sampling frequency of 44.1 Kilohertz, onto which an original master recording is transferred in the *premastering*

phase of manufacturing compact discs. Also called a *1630*.

Under the Table
A secret payment, arrangement, or transaction, especially when made illegally, as in cases of bribery or *payola*, etc.

Underlying Property
A *property* on which something is based. For instance, a movie or musical play might be based on a novel or short story (the copyright of which is the underlying property).

Underscore
(1) Music composed and recorded for use as a background setting to a film or television production. (2) To compose and record background music for *synchronization* with a film, videotape, or television production.

Underwrite
(1) To support or sponsor financially; to assume the costs of a venture or project; to guarantee payment of the shortfall between income and expenses. (2) To support, endorse, and agree to a decision, arrangement, or agreement made by others.

Undivided Copyright
Though various rights associated with a copyright can be licensed separately, and copyright ownership can be shared among two or more parties, a copyright remains "undivided," meaning that all rights ultimately continue to vest in the work itself. When a work is eligible for *statutory* copyright protection, its owner is vested with a number of exclusive rights (the *bundle of rights*), including sole authority to publish, copy, reproduce, manufacture, perform, print, sell, distrib-

ute, display, broadcast, adapt, arrange, dramatize, or translate the work, or to authorize others to do so. The copyright is thus *divisible*, in the sense that the owner can license exclusive print rights to one party, while licensing other rights, such as mechanical reproduction, to other parties. However, there is always just *one* copyright in a work. See also *undivided interest*, below.

Undivided Interest

An share of ownership, right, claim, etc. in something as a whole. For instance, though ownership of a copyright might be shared any number of ways, there is still just *one* copyright in a work. So, if three songwriters equally contribute to the creation of a song, their individual contributions are merged and each owns an undivided one-third interest in all rights vested in the copyright. The ownership is divided three ways, but the copyright itself always remains undivided.

Each of the three songwriters might assign or sell their respective ownership shares to a music publisher, and each music publisher can further assign the shares they acquire. In other words, various rights to the copyright can be divided and transferred or shared, but each divided portion of the copyright remains a portion of the whole, and all portions, when added together, total 100% of one undivided copyright. Thus, if ownership of a copyright is "divided" into 10 equal parts, each owner is deemed to own an undivided 10% interest in all rights pertaining to the copyright. See also *undivided copyright*, above.

Unfair Competition

The illegal appropriation, use, or imitation of a trade name, brand name, trademark, service mark, logo, or design to induce the public to believe that a competitor's company, service, work, or product is one's own. Although song titles cannot be copyrighted, there may be cases where a song has become so established in the public mind that the Copyright Office will reject a new work with the same title, citing the principle of unfair competition.

Uniform Commercial Code

A set of laws, adopted by and applicable in most states, dealing with commercial transactions, particularly involving the sale, lease, and licensing of tangible and intangible goods, as well as financial transactions such as deposits, collections, securities, negotiable instruments, warranties, documents of title, lending, and investments, etc.

Union

A labor union formed to protect and promote interests of members employed in a specific type of industry, trade, or skill.

Union Card

An identification card with which the holder proves he/she is a current union member and is eligible to work on a union-regulated session.

Union Scale

Minimum wage rate(s) or forms of compensation for union employees and contractors as specified in union agreements for specific types of employees or specific types of work. Through collective bargaining agreements reached with record companies, both *AFTRA* and the *AFM* set minimum rates of pay for recording musicians, ranging from basic three-hour recording sessions, special 1 and 1/2-hour sessions, premium session rates (for after hours, weekends, and holidays), *double scale* for *leaders* and *contractors*, and supplemental payments for *doubling, overdubbing, cartage, resues*, etc. There are also scales set for symphonic work, casual engagements (one- and two-nighters), extended engagements, rehearsals, demo sessions, orchestrating, arranging, copying, and various types of work in motion pictures, videos, television, and commercials. See also *recording scale*.

Union Shop

A business whose employees are required to be union members, Also called *closed shop*. See also *open shop*.

Union Steward

Union official who supervises the working conditions of union employees or contractors (such as musicians), and who insures that terms of union agreements with employers are followed.

Unison

(1) The simultaneous playing or singing of one musical part by two or more performers, either on the same pitch or in *octaves*. (2) Two or more people speaking the same words simultaneously. (3) Complete agreement on all points of a matter by all parties involved.

Unit

(1) A single piece of product (i.e., one compact disc, one cassette, one phonograph record, etc.). (2) A collective reference to components making up equipment used to perform a specific function (i.e., an amplifier, a turntable, and a set of speakers making up a "stereo unit.") (3) A division, subsidiary, or branch of a company. (4) A band, group, or troupe of performers.

Unit Cost

The *prorated* cost to manufacture or produce a single piece of product. For example, if it costs $230 to manufacture 1,000 audiocassettes, the unit cost of each cassette is 23¢.

Unit Price

The wholesale price charged by a manufacturer or distributor for a single piece of product.

Unit Sales

The measurement of product sales in *units* as opposed to revenues.

Universal

Unlimited, unrestricted, total, entire, pertaining to all. *Examples*: a universal *partnership* is when individual partners agree to contribute everything they own; a universal *agent* is someone authorized to do everything the party he or she represents is legally entitled to authorize.

Universal Copyright Convention (UCC)

An international treaty on copyright, signed by the United States and more than 70 other countries in 1952, and which took effect in 1955. The purpose of the treaty is to eliminate discrimination against foreign copyrights by extending copyright protection in each member nation to copyrights originating in any of the other treaty countries. Every member nation must give all foreign UCC works the same copyright protection as given to domestic works. In order to qualify for copyright protection in UCC countries, works must be published with a *copyright notice*, which includes the symbol © (the letter C enclosed in a circle), the name of the copyright owner, and the year of first publication. Thus, though there is no such thing as an "international copyright," any author living in a UCC-member country is afforded copyright protection in all other UCC-member nations. With regards to current copyright notice requirements, see *Berne Convention*. See also *Buenos Aires Convention*.

Universal Product Code (UPC)

Also called *bar code*. A computer coding system used to identify products for inventory control, and to track sales and shipments. Product codes are patterns of vertical lines or bars representing a string of unique identifying numbers or letters that are assigned to each product and which are printed on each package containing a piece of product. The codes are read by computer-linked optical scanners, which provide and record information, such as price or quantity sold, etc. Most retailers require manufacturers to supply product with bar codes so that inventory control, pricing, and sales can be tabulated by in-house databases.

Universe

Term used in marketing as a reference to the scope or size of the population potentially interested a particular product. A defined market segment. (The *market universe*.)

Unlimited Liability

See *limited liability*. Owners of unincorporated businesses are personally responsible for all debts, obligations, and *liabilities* incurred by the business, including liabilities attributed to actions or negligence of any agents, partners, or employees. In the event of a successful claim against the business, the owner's personal assets can be seized to make up any shortfall between the company's assets and the amount of the claim.

Unsigned

An artist, performer, songwriter, etc. without a recording or publishing contract.

Unsolicited

Songs, master tapes, demos, audition tapes, etc. sent to a publisher or record company without being requested by the recipient, or without prior arrangement between the sender and recipient. Material that arrives *over the transom*.

Up Front

An advance, a *lump sum* payment, or a signing bonus, paid upon agreement to a deal, and/or before a production is started or completed, or before a service is provided, and/or before the recipient's commitments to the payer are fulfilled.

Up Full

A film, television, video, or stage director's instructions to an orchestra director or music editor to bring background music to a *crescendo* in order stress, emphasize, punctuate, or close a scene with intensity.

UPC

Abbreviation for *Universal Product Code*.

Update

To revise, modify, amend, reshape, or edit something in order to conform with current knowledge, technology, or fashion.

Upfront

See *up front*.

Up-front Exposure

The amount of money at risk from an investment in the initial stages of producing a recording, film, play, etc., before the production can be completed so that the investment might be recouped.

Uplift

In computing royalties to be paid on the retail price of recorded product, some record companies add what is called an "uplift" to their wholesale price in order to arrive at a *suggested retail price*. For instance, if the wholesale price on a CD is $12, an uplift of, say, 130%

would be added, resulting in a suggested retail price of $15.60, which would then be the starting basis of royalty calculations. See also *royalty base*.

Upload

(1) To transfer computer programs or data from a PC, peripheral workstation, or device to an online network, central computer database, or remote device. (2) Data or programs transferred from a peripheral device or computer to an online network, central computer database, or remote device.

Upstage

Usually, to steal the show from a featured performer.

Urban Music

A subgenre of contemporary R&B music popularized by African-American performers in major city centers. Also called urban contemporary (UC).

US Copyright Act

See *Copyright, Copyright Act of 1790, Copyright Act of 1909*, and *Copyright Act of 1976*.

US Copyright Office

Section of the *Library of Congress*, headed by the *Register of Copyrights*, which is charged with dealing with copyright matters. The Copyright Office is located at 101 Independence Avenue S.E., Washington, DC 20559; Tel: (202) 707-3000; Fax: (202) 707-8366.

For copies of publications explaining copyright matters, and for copies of *copyright registration forms*, call the Forms and Publications Hotline, (202) 707-9100, or write: The Copyright Office, Publications Section, LM-455, Library of Congress, Washington, DC 20559.

To talk directly with an information specialist or to request further information, call (202) 707-3000, or write: The Copyright Office, Information Section, LM-401, Library of Congress, Washington, DC 20559.

Usage

(1) A *trade practice* or *industry norm*: a linguistic terminology, practice, process, or procedure that has become firmly established and generally accepted within a trade, industry, or locality. (2) The method in which a copyright is used under license (i.e., a synchronization, performance, jingle, lyric reprint, transcription, etc.).

Usage Fee

(1) A fee or payment made to obtain permission to use a copyright. (2) An additional payment due a performer, producer, writer, or director each time their work (on a television show or commercial, etc.) is rebroadcast. Also called *reuse fee, replay fee*, or *residual*.

Used CDs/Records

See *used goods*, below. Sales of used records have long been a commercial reality, but the durability of CDs has spawned the growth of used CD stores to the extent that it is reckoned that used CDs account for some 5% of the $9 billion spent annually for recorded music in the United States.

Used Goods

Secondhand merchandise, product, or equipment. Copyright owners are paid on the *first sale* of products embodying their copyrights (i.e., CDs, audiocassettes). Purchasers then own the physical product, though not the copyright. But, as owner of the physical product, a purchaser can resell the product without additional payment to the copyright owner. For instance, a consumer can sell his/her CD collection without having to compensate the music publishers or recording artists. The concept of first sale is the legal basis video stores use to buy videos that they in turn rent out and ultimately resell as used videos. Many record stores also buy and sell used CDs on the same legal grounding. See also *used CDs/records*, above.

Useful Article

A legal term referencing an item or object having an inherent functional capacity or purpose, as opposed to something such as a photo or set of *specifications* portraying, describing, or providing information about a functional object.

Useful Life

The projected period of time that an asset will be profitable or productive. For instance, if a piece of recording equipment is depreciated for tax purposes, the number of years over which depreciation is taken equals the asset's estimated useful life. Also called "depreciable life."

User

Term for parties who license copyrights to perform, record, transcribe, broadcast, copy, print, manufacture, synchronize with film, etc. From a music publisher's perspective, for example, users include record companies, artists, record producers, broadcasters, film producers, advertising agencies, and software developers. The users, in turn, produce physical copies of the songs (i.e., CDs, videotapes, etc.) to sell directly to consumers (*end-users*).

User-Friendly

A device, such as a computer, or a computer program, designed and engineered to be operated easily by non-experts.

User Interface

The connection or meeting point between two or more distinct systems, groups, or entities, where communication and/or functional coordination is established. *Example*: A keyboard is an interface between a human and a computer.

VA Form

A form for registering copyright claim information with the Copyright Office. Under the *Copyright Act of 1976*, Form VA is used for registering visual arts (photos, models, prints, posters, album covers, designs, advertisements, etc.).

VAAP

The *mechanical-right society* in the former Soviet Union. (*RAIS* is the current name of the mechanical-right society in Russia.)

Valuation

An estimate, assessment, or appraisal of financial worth based upon analytical examination of financial records and/or condition of the object being valued and/or market considerations.

Value

(1) To appraise or assess financial worth through analytical examination of financial records and/or condition of the object being valued and/or market considerations. (2) Financial worth of an object or asset based upon analytical examination of financial records, condition, and market considerations. See also *market value* and *book value*.

Value Added Tax (VAT)

A sales tax included in the retail price of recordings sold in some countries. The VAT is deducted from the unit price when a *foreign licensee* calculates the *royalty base* of the product.

Vanity Label

A record label that distributes product commercially for producers or artists who pay all costs of recording, manufacturing, and promotion.

Vanity Publisher

A book publisher that distributes books for authors who pay the costs of design, printing, binding, etc. Also called "vanity press."

Variation

An alteration; a change, modification, disparity, deviation, digression, divergence, or difference between one thing and another. See also *version*.

Variety

(1) An assortment, a collection, a presentation, a mixture, or an offering of a number of miscellaneous things or different types of a thing. (2) A term for grading, typing, classifying, or categorizing. (3) A classification, genre, type. See also *variety show*, below.

Variety

A trade magazine catering primarily to the theatrical profession and the film and television industries, but also covering music industry news where the interests of the industries intersect. Located at 475 Park Avenue South, New York, NY 10016.

Variety Show

A revue, show, or entertainment presenting a number of different kinds of acts, such as singers, musicians, comedians, dancers, magicians, jugglers, dramatic skits, etc.

VAT

Abbreviation for *Value Added Tax*.

Vaudeville

In the United States, a widely popular forum for variety entertainment before being supplanted by radio, records, movies, and television in this century. Like *Music Hall* in Great Britain, vaudeville offered comedy skits, song-and-dance acts, magicians, jugglers, acrobats, mimes, etc. Today, the term refers to a musical style or type of act reminiscent of vaudeville's heyday.

Vault

A place where master tapes are cataloged, filed, and stored for safekeeping; ideally, a climate-controlled, fireproof room or compartment.

VCR

Abbreviation for *videocassette recorder*.

VDP

Abbreviation for *videodisc player*.

VDT

Abbreviation for *video display terminal*.

Vee-Jay

Also called *VJ*, the term is derived from *video jockey* (as in *disc jockey*), in reference to announcers who present music videos at *discotheques* or on television or cable channels, such as MTV, VH1, BET, CMT, etc.

Vend

To sell, trade, exchange. See *vendor*.

Vendor

A seller or supplier of goods or services, including manufacturers, importers, exporters, wholesalers, distributors, and retailers.

Venue

(1) An arena, an auditorium, a theater, a stadium, a convention hall, or other setting, where a performance takes place. (2) The legal *jurisdiction* in which a *cause of action* occurs. (3) The locality and setting for a trial. (4) The locality in which an affidavit is sworn or a deposition is taken.

Verbal Agreement

An unwritten, oral contract; a contract expressed in spoken words rather than in writing. In most circumstances and in most jurisdictions, verbal agreements are legally enforceable, except where real estate is involved.

Vernacular

A language, dialect, or style native to a particular people, country, region, or era.

Verse

(1) A division or section of a song in which the storyline is introduced, developed, or concluded, much like a chapter in a book. (2) One of the metrical stanzas, sections, or divisions of a poem or song, which precedes and/or follows a *refrain* or chorus. (3) A rhymed composition. (4) Poetry.

Version

(1) An adaptation, a *variation*, or a new interpretation of an original work. (2) A point of view. (3) A work that has been translated, paraphrased, edited, rewritten, or otherwise modified from the original. (4) A rendering or performance that is distinctively different from earlier renderings or performances of the same work.

Vertical Lyrics

Lyrics that deal directly with the subject, as opposed to *allegorical lyrics*. In popular Christian music, for instance, vertical or overt lyrics would speak directly to and of God or Jesus and/or about prayer and the Christian faith. Also called *overt lyrics*.

Very High Frequency (VHF)

The band of radio broadcast *frequencies* ranging from 30 to 300 megahertz, commonly used for *FM* and television transmissions. VHF waves cannot be reflected over the horizon, and VHF transmitters therefore have a relatively short range.

Vest

To give, sell, will, assign, bestow, endow, or place the control, rights, benefits, and/or possession of a property, or an interest therein.

Vest Pocket Publisher

Also called *desk drawer publisher*. The term refers to music publishers that keep their copyrights in their vest pockets (or a desk drawer), figuratively speaking, rather than dusting them off for active marketing. This type of publisher is entirely passive, or reactive, meaning that it licenses copyrights when requested by *users*, but makes no effort to sign new writers or promote new uses of the songs.

This situation arises when a small publishing company's owner retires without selling his catalog, but still receives royalty earnings from previous activity. It also happens when a publisher dies and his catalog is looked after by an *administrator* who fulfills licensing requests and collects royalties. (The administrator may be a surviving family member, lawyer, accountant, trustee, or hired manager.) Another example is that of an investor who acquires a copyright catalog and is content that the continuing income stream from the previous owner's activities is sufficient to pay back the investment and return a profit.

Vested

The condition of a right, title, interest, or claim that has been conveyed from one party to another.

Vested Interest

(1) A right, title, interest, or claim that has been or can be conveyed from one party to another. (2) A situation in which someone gains or is able to gain private benefits and personal advantage by controlling, promoting, or protecting a system, an activity, a thing, or a person.

Vested Interests

Parties who have a *vested interest* in maintaining the status quo, who resist any changes in a system or an activity that may diminish their power, control, influence, benefits, or profits.

VH-1

A cable television channel (*Video Hits One*), which programs *music videos* produced by record companies. Located at 1515 Broadway, 20th Floor, New York, NY 10036. Tel: (212) 258-7800; Fax: (212) 258-7955.

VHF

Abbreviation for *very high frequency*.

VHS

The current standard half-inch videotape format, introduced by JVC in competition with the Sony Corporation's *Betamax* format.

Victrola

A brand name for phonograph record players manufactured by the Victor Talking Machine Company (later, RCA Victor), which, for a time, became widely used as a generic term for record player.

Video

Term used for a visual broadcast, televised images, television production, or recording of visual images. Also refers to the visual portion of a television broadcast or an *audiovisual* production, or to the equipment and technology used in audiovisual recordings, productions, and broadcasts. Also used as a shorthand reference for videotape, videocassette, videodisc, or videogram. See also *music video*.

Video Buyout

An outright purchase by *flat fee* of the nonexclusive rights to use a copyright in a videocassette or videodisc, as opposed to paying royalties based on *per use* or *per unit* sale of copies.

Video Clip

A brief segment or extract taken from a complete videotaped performance or video production, used for promotional purposes, review, commentary, or news reporting, etc. See also *music video* and *promotional music video*.

Video Director

Person with supervisory control and management authority over the creative elements of a video production.

Video Display Terminal (VDT)

A computer monitor together with a keyboard, used to *interface* with a computer.

Video Game

A computerized game played by manipulating images on a display screen. Available in a variety of devices and formats, including large *arcade* models, CD-ROMs and floppy disks inserted into personal computer drives, peripheral devices attached to television sets (such as Nintendo and Sega), and compact, hand-held models, such as a Gameboy. Many video games use *synchronized* sound effects and music to enhance their entertainment value. See also *electronic game*.

Video Hits One

See *VH-1*.

Video Jockey (VJ)

See *VJ*.

Video Jukebox

A coin-operated device based on the same principle as a phonograph jukebox, in that a selection of music videos are available at the drop of a coin and push of a button.

Video Producer

Person or organization that creates or causes to be created a video product, that assembles, finances, guides, and shapes the elements of the video from concept to actuality. A provider, an originator, a maker, or a creator of videos.

Video Record

See *videogram*.

Video Rights

In a recording contract, provisions relating to the production and use of video performances by the artist of material recorded for the record company. Generally, the record company funds video production, and *recoups* the costs from artist royalties arising from commercial use of the videos. A negotiating issue is whether and to what extent the company might *cross-collateralize* recoupable costs against artist's royalties arising from sales of recorded product. Where videos are used for promotional purposes only, the artist receives no royalties, but for commercially exploited videos, a royalty schedule is negotiated to deal with various configurations, such as compilations, long-form video albums, etc. When the artist controls the song copyrights, a royalty and fee schedule is negotiated regarding *mechanical, synchronization,* and *performance* rights on commercially exploited videos (such rights are usually granted gratis on videos used only for promotion).

Video Rollover

An advance against royalties given by a video producer or distributor to a copyright owner as a previous advance is recouped. Normally, the advance equals an agreed royalty rate times a certain level of sales, with another like sum advanced each time that sales plateau is reached. For instance, a rollover advance to a music publisher on 15,000 unit sales at 6¢ per song would be $900 (6¢ x 15,000 units). When 15,000 units are sold, an additional $900 is paid; then, a further $900 is paid when the next 15,000 units are sold, and so on.

Video Software Dealers Association (VSDA)

Trade association organized to promote and protect the interests of video retailers and renters. Located at 5743 Corsa Avenue, Suite 122, Westlake Village, CA 91362. Tel: (818) 889-7148.

Video Vérité

A production technique for televising, filming, or videotaping scenes and subjects in an unstaged fashion in order to achieve a real-life effect, as typically used in documentaries.

Videocassette

A prerecorded or blank videotape enclosed in a *cassette* case.

Videocassette Recorder (VCR)

Device used to record and playback television programs, and to play prerecorded videotapes. See also *camcorder.*

Videocaster

A broadcaster of videos over television, cable, satellite, wired, or closed circuit delivery systems.

Videodisc

A type of *optical laser disc* capable of reproducing audio and visual images. Videodiscs cannot record television programs off the air for later playback, but their sound and visual reproduction is digital and therefore of better quality than that of *analog* videotapes used in *VCRs.*

Videodisc Player (VDP)

A device equipped with speakers and a video display terminal, used to play *videodiscs.*

Videodisk

Alternative spelling for *videodisc.*

Videogram

Term combining the words "video" and "program" referring to *audiovisual works* recorded, reproduced, and commercially released in *videocassette* and *videodisc* formats. Alternative terms for videogram include *home video, video record,* and *A/V film,* etc. Under copyright law, any type of videogram (whether promotional clip, music video, how-to, feature film, etc.) is defined as an audiovisual work. Producers of audiovisual works are required to obtain *synchronization, mechanical,* and (in some cases) *performance licenses* from music copyright owners or their agents. See *videogram mechanical license, videogram performance license,* and *videogram synchronization license.*

Videogram Mechanical License

Video producers, manufacturers, or distributors must get *mechanical licenses* from owners of music copyrights in order to make, distribute, and sell copies of audiovisual works (i.e., videos, laser discs, CD-ROMs). As in the case of phonorecords, mechanical licenses for audiovisual works may be handled by a publisher's *mechanical-right society,* such as the *Harry Fox Agency.*

Compensation to music copyright owners for phonorecords is limited to a maximum *statutory mechanical rate.* But, compensation for videogram mechanical rights is negotiated, rather than statutory. Negotiations between video distributors and music publishers may result in mechanical rights being paid for in one of three ways: (1) A *per unit royalty* for each video sold; (2) *buy-outs* (a one time payment, no matter how many videos are ultimately sold); (3) *rollover advances* (a set, non-returnable sum representing an advance on X number of units sold, with further non-returnable advances in the same amount as additional sales levels are reached).

Videogram Performance License

An exhibitioner who shows, broadcasts, transmits, or otherwise *publicly performs* a video containing music is required to obtain a performance license from the music copyright owner. In practice, permission to perform or show videos is obtained from *performing-right societies* under *blanket licenses* issued to the venue or broadcaster that exhibits, performs, or transmits the video.

Videogram Synchronization License

Under copyright law, any type of *videogram* (whether promotional clip, music video, how-to, feature film, etc.) is defined as an *audiovisual work.* Producers of audiovisual works using music are required to obtain synchronization licenses from the music copyright owners or their agents.

Typical videogram synchronization licenses contain provisions similar to those found in a *theatri-*

cal synchronization licenses, with the following differences: (1) the license is granted for a stated, limited term of years, rather than full term of copyright, and all rights granted to the producer terminate at the expiration of the stated term; (2) the producer is given permission to copy, sell, and distribute the song as contained in the specifically identified videogram; (3) the license is not valid for rental of videograms; (4) the producer pays the publisher a royalty for each videogram copy sold in the licensed territory.

Videotape

(1) A *magnetic tape* used for recording, playing, and broadcasting visual images and often sound. (2) To record visual images on tape.

Videotape Jockey (VJ)

See *VJ*. Also called *video jockey*.

Videotex

An interactive information system linking home television sets, personal and network computers, or other *video display terminals*, by television cables or telephone lines, to a central databank or to online services offering home shopping, E-mail, electronic banking, stock market quotes, news, etc.

Vinyl

(1) A compound forming basic materials for plastics used in the manufacture of phonograph records. There are several grades of vinyl used in the *compression method* of the *pressing* process, ranging from domestic (good) to Quiex II (better) and Teldec (best). The better the quality of vinyl, the cleaner the sound of the record. (2) A generic reference for any phonograph record format (i.e., 45 rpm seven-inch disc, 33 1/3 rpm twelve-inch disc, etc.).

Visual

(1) That portion of an *audiovisual* work capable of being seen by the eye. (2) A visible presentation or image; something that can be physically seen or perceived as an image in the mind. (3) A photograph, drawing, chart, graph, or other visible presentation prepared or used for illustration, promotion, marketing, etc. The term is frequently used in the plural, as a collective reference (i.e., the "visuals" used in album artwork for the front and back covers).

Visual Arts

Any of the arts associated with visual presentation (i.e., photography, cinematography, painting, etc.).

Visual Instrumental

An onscreen performance of an instrumental work (as opposed to music performed in the background by unseen musicians). Also called a *foreground use*.

Visual Vocal

An onscreen performance of a vocal work (as opposed to music performed in the background by unseen vocalists and musicians). Also called a *foreground use*.

VJ

Also called *vee-jay*, the term is derived from *videotape jockey* (as in *disc jockey*), in reference to announcers who present music video clips at discotheques, and on television or on cable channels, such as MTV, VH1, BET, CMT, etc.

Vocal

(1) A musical work with lyrics, to be performed by a singer or group of singers, often accompanied by instrumentalists. (2) A performance by a singer or group of singers, whether or not accompanied by instrumentalists. See also *a cappella*.

Vocal Rendition

The use of a song in a motion picture or television program with a vocal performance of the song's lyrics. An vocal rendition does not necessarily mean the synchronization fee should be more than that required for an *instrumental rendition*.

Voice-over

A film, television, or videotape *narration* provided by an announcer or actor who is not visible on the screen.

Void

(1) A contract or license that has no legal force, that has been invalidated, nullified, canceled, annulled, declared by a competent legal body to be *null and void*, untenable, etc. (2) To throw out (a contract) as invalid; to invalidate, cancel, or nullify a contract, license, or agreement, or any provision thereof.

Volume

(1) Term used in referring to the level of sales (i.e., "high volume"), whether expressed in terms of dollars or units. (2) One of a continuing series of books or phonograph albums (i.e., volume one, volume two, etc.). (3) A book, or bound collection of printed sheets, writings, drawings, music, etc. (4) A collective reference to all issues of a periodical published in one calendar year. (5) The extent, intensity, or range of the loudness of sound., which may be expressed in *decibels*, ranging from 0 dB to 120 dB (the maximum toleration). (6) The control device for adjusting loudness on an amplifier, radio, recorder, etc.

Volume Unit (VU)

A measure of sound loudness. See *decibel*.

VSDA

Abbreviation for *Video Software Dealers Association*.

VU

Abbreviation for *volume unit*.

VU Meter

A device used to display the volume intensity or loudness of sound.

Waive

(1) To voluntarily give up a claim or privilege, relinquish a right, dispense with a rule, postpone a deadline, or not enforce a penalty. (2) To defer or cancel a debt or obligation owed by someone.

Waiver

(1) A voluntary dispensation, deferment, relinquishment, or cancellation of a rule, penalty, right, claim, or privilege. (2) A document formalizing such dispensation, deferment, relinquishment, or cancellation.

WAN

Abbreviation for *wide area network*.

Warm-up Act

A performer who precedes the featured performer or act on a concert bill, and whose role is to enliven, enthuse, and excite the audience so they will be in a receptive mood when the featured act comes on stage.

Warpage

A condition in which vinyl records (for instance) are damaged or bent out of shape through improper *curing*, stacking, storage, shipment, or exposure to heat.

Warped

Phonograph records (or other items) that have been twisted or bent out of shape.

Warrant

(1) To assure a licensee, assignee, or purchaser that the licensor, assignor, or seller has clear title and right to transfer, sell, or assign a right, claim, title, or property. (2) To supply proof that one has the authority to enter into a transaction. (3) To guarantee something. (4) To *indemnify*. (5) To vouch for the quality, character, condition, or accuracy of something.

Warrantee

One who receives a *warrant* or to whom a *warranty* is made.

Warrantor

One who *warrants* or gives a *warranty* to another.

Warranty

(1) A guarantee of quality or accuracy. (2) An assurance by a party to a transaction that he/she has authority and legal right to enter into the transaction, and that his/her representations to the other party are true and accurate. (3) A *covenant* binding a party and/or his/her heirs, assignees, and successors to the terms of a transaction, and indemnifying the other party against damage or loss.

Warsaw Rule

Rule adopted by *performing-right* and *mechanical-right societies* belonging to *CISAC* regarding disposition of unclaimed *performance* and *mechanical royalties*. The societies pay such royalties to any songwriter or music publisher that can be identified as having a valid claim to them, but if no claimant is located, the royalties are put into a so-called *black box*. Each society maintains a black box containing unclaimed royalties. After a certain period of time, if no claimant comes forth, the royalties are distributed to music publishers belonging to the respective society. Some societies allocate black-box royalties to members based on membership seniority. Other societies prorate black-box royalties to members according to the percentage of their earnings vis a vis the gross royalties collected by the society.

Waveform

A *sound wave*, graphically represented to display its *frequency* and *amplitude* characteristics. Also called *waveshape*.

Waveshape
See *waveform*, above.

Wax
(1) Slang for phonograph record. (2) To record or make a phonograph record.

WB
Music format abbreviation for *world beat*.

Weighting
A statistical unit of measure derived from factoring or averaging variable numbers or values in a computation so as to reflect the relative importance of each number or value to the whole. See *weighting formula*, below.

Weighting Formula
A system of assigning a measure of relative importance to each variable in a combined group of variables. *Performing-right societies* use weighting formulas to determine the relative value of each performance category in which a musical work is publicly performed, in order to calculate royalties due songwriters and publishers.

For instance, *ASCAP* payments to members are based on *credits*. Each surveyed work is assigned a number of credits representing the kind of usage and the medium in which it is used. Credits are *weighted* to reflect the value of the performance, ranging from a low of 2% of one credit for some usages of copyrighted arrangements of *PD* works to 100% of one credit for a full-feature vocal performance on primetime network television.

ASCAP divides performances into several classifications, each of which is subdivided into *weights* (or percentages of one full credit) according to duration, medium, and nature of performance. At the end of each royalty distribution period, the number of performances surveyed for all ASCAP works are multiplied by the number of credits assigned to each performance; the total is then divided into the gross amount of collections available for distribution (i.e., total collections less administrative costs).

This calculation provides the dollar amount of each credit for the distribution period. The total number of credits received by each member's catalog is then multiplied by the dollar amount of each credit. The resulting amount represents how much performance income each ASCAP member receives for the distribution period.

For example, suppose $80 million is available for distribution at the end of one quarter, half of which is available for publisher members. And suppose there are 10 million credits earned by all publishers. $40 million ÷ 10 million credits = $4 per credit. A publisher that earned 20,000 credits during the quarter is then due $80,000. See also *credit weighting formula*.

West End
The main shopping and theater district in London, where the term equivalent to "Broadway musical" is "West End musical." See also *Tin Pan Alley*, *Soho*, and *Denmark Street*.

Whereas Clause
In a contract or license, a *recital* citing the underlying reason(s) for the transaction. See also *boilerplate*.

Wholesale
(1) The sale of merchandise in large quantities to a retailer for resale to consumers. (2) To sell product in bulk to an intermediary or retailer, which sells the product on to consumers at a higher price.

Wholesale Price
Price a retailer pays for merchandise. The retailer's profit margin is the price at which the retailer sells the product to a consumer less the wholesale price and *prorated* operating costs.

Wholesaler
One who buys goods in bulk from a manufacturer for resale to retailers.

Wide-Area Network (WAN)
A large number of computers or networks linked via communications equipment, in order to share data, exchange messages, and share hardware and/or software resources. See also *local area network*, or *LAN*.

Wild Spot
A television commercial shown between regularly scheduled network programming or which is shown on non-network programs or on non-network stations.

Window Display
An exhibition of merchandise in a retail store window, arranged so as to attract the interest of potential customers.

WIPO
Abbreviation for *World Intellectual Property Organization*.

Wireless
A radio receiver or radio transmission. The term originated from the fact that radio broadcasting through the airwaves eliminated the cable-wiring needed to link other forms of long distance communications, such as telephone and telegraph.

Withholding
(1) A sum deducted from a salary payment for taxes and/or pension contributions, and/or repayment of an employee loan. (2) A sum deducted from royalty

earnings for repayment of an advance, or placed in *escrow* because of a legal dispute, or held in *reserve* against potential *returns* of product on which royalties are earned.

Woofer

A large loudspeaker engineered for low sounds or bass frequencies.

Work

(1) The total creative output of a recording artist, composer, songwriter, etc. (2) An artistic creation, such as a musical composition or recorded performance.

Work Dues

Union membership fees collected from musicians, singers, actors, etc. for performance work done under union-negotiated contracts. Union members must authorize employers to deduct a portion (usually 1%) of all wages earned for direct payment to their *local*s.

Work in Progress

An unfinished musical composition, theatrical production, or other artistic endeavor, sometimes presented to backers, reviewers, or selected audiences for critical feedback, publicity, or to solicit financial support for completion.

Work Made for Hire

A copyright can be a work made for hire in one of two ways. In many exclusive songwriter agreements, for instance, the writer is "hired" (an *employee for hire*) to create songs within the scope of his or her employment. Officially, this means there must be a continuing business relationship during the creative process in which the employer guides, supervises, and oversees the writer and/or provides facilities, equipment, and materials.

The other approach is when an employer *commissions* a writer to create works for a specific use, such as a film or television production, a jingle, a translation, or an adaptation, etc. Once the commissioned work is completed, the relationship officially ends. The commissioned material is a work made for hire, though the creator is not an employee, since there is no ongoing relationship.

Normally, when a song is written, the creator is automatically *vested* with copyright ownership. The writer can assign copyright interest to a publisher, but still be eligible to recapture the copyright under certain conditions of statutory copyright law (i.e., after lapse of a prerequisite number of years, and/or other conditions of assignment between the writer and publisher). But, under a work made for hire agreement, the writer has no vested interest in the copyright. The writer was hired or commissioned to write the song *prior* to actually writing it. The writer is never eligible to recapture the copyright, because he or she never had it in the first place. If the employer or commissioner fails to meet all obligations laid down in the contract, the writer's only recourse is to sue for damages (although such a suit might include a demand that the copyright be assigned to the writer).

Though the publisher is credited as *author* in the copyright claim to a work made for hire, the songwriter receives full songwriting credit on all label copy, sheet music, film credits, registrations, licenses, etc. And, the songwriter's share of royalty and fee income is not normally affected when a song is a work made for hire.

Under the *Copyright Act of 1976*, a work made for hire has statutory copyright protection for a term of 75 years from date of publication or 100 years from date of creation, whichever comes first. This contrasts with the term or protection granted authors of works *not* made for hire, which is for the life of author plus 50 years. (Congress was considering legislation in 1998 to extend this to life of author plus 70 years.)

Work Permit

Also called *green card*. A United States government certification that allows a non-US citizen to remain and work in the United States for a certain period of time, subject to review and renewal.

Work Sheet

A form or checklist used to plan, manage, or track the progress of an activity, an administration process, a transaction, or a project.

Work Song

A rhythmic *folk* song performed by a gang of workers to set the pace or tempo of a laboring job.

WorksNet

Database maintained by *ASCAP* in New York, which is linked to *performing-right societies* throughout the world for registration of, and access to, *ISWC* numbers of music copyrights. ISWC stands for *International Standard Work Code*, a universally recognized copyright identification tool for songs. Upon registration of a song with a performing-right society, the society issues an ISWC number that is unique to the song. The number provides a method for identifying music copyright owners in order to insure fast, accurate, and efficient distribution of royalties earned by songs throughout the world.

The use of ISWC numbers is intended to slash administrative costs for mechanical- and performing-right societies, while increasing copyright protection for copyright owners. Any society in any country can access the WorksNet database in order to unlock ownership information and ensure royalties are distributed in timely and accurate fashion. See also *Common Information System (CIS)*.

World

Term used for assigning rights throughout the entire world in a contract or license provision dealing with the *territory* applicable to the agreement.

World Beat

See *world music*.

World Intellectual Property Organization (WIPO)

A standing committee of the United Nations headquartered in Geneva, Switzerland, which is responsible for administering terms of various copyright treaties (such as the *Berne Convention* and *Rome Convention*). WIPO holds hearings regarding needs to update or revise copyright conventions to accommodate technological advances in the methods of duplicating and distributing intellectual properties. In the United States, WIPO maintains an office at 2 UN Plaza, Suite DC2-560, New York, NY 10017. Tel: (212) 963-6813; Fax: (212) 963-4801.

World Music

Relating or pertaining to various types of music popular among different ethnic groups, particularly in *third world* cultures. Also called *world beat*.

World-Ex

In the provision dealing with the *territory* applicable to a contract or license, the term used for assigning rights throughout the entire world excluding the specific countries named (i.e., "World-ex The United States and Canada").

Worldwide

A reference to something, such as distribution or an assignment of rights, that extends throughout the entire world.

World Wide Web (WWW)

Vast network offering collection of information resources accessible through the internet using tools such as File Transfer Protocol (FTP), HyperText Transport Protocol (HTTP), Wide Area Information Servers (WAIS), TELNET, Usenet, etc. The term is sometimes used interchangeably with *cyberspace, information superhighway,* and *Internet* in reference to the electronic access and transmission of information through personal computers. Commercial online services like America Online reach an estimated 15 million subscribers throughout the United States. In addition, some 60,000 bulletin board operators link between fifteen and 20 million PC users nationwide. But cyberspace has no borders. PC users in Prague and Pretoria can access the same data at the same time as someone in Peoria.

The rapid development of Internet technologies for distributing information and entertainment has caused a scramble among copyright owners to upgrade international standards of copyright protection. The ability to upload, store, and download music affects copyright owners of sound recordings as well as owners of the underlying musical works contained on the recordings.

There are three licensing issues related to the use of music online. First, transmission of the music is a "public performance" and therefore subject to a *performing-right license*. Second, downloading transmitted music constitutes "copying" and is thereby subject to a *mechanical license*. And third, combining music with visual images for transmission falls within the scope of a *synchronization license*. See also *transmission and reproduction license*.

Wow

A slow oscillation, wavering, or pulsing of *pitch* in audio signals, caused by mechanical speed variations in recording or playback equipment. See also *flutter*.

Writer Development

Process of grooming a songwriter's creative ability, talent, and skill to the level required for commercial success. Also called an *artist development deal*, and usually entered into between a music publisher and a singer-songwriter. The publisher grooms (develops) writers as artists or producers, then takes an active role in securing record deals. See also *development deal* and *demo deal*.

Writer-Artist

A performer who writes most the material he/she performs or records. A *singer-songwriter*.

Writer-Owned Publisher

A music publishing company owned and operated by a songwriter, usually to publish works written and/or recorded by the songwriter, but often to also acquire copyright interests in works written by other songwriters.

Writer-Producer

A singer-songwriter who produces songs written by himself/herself, or a songwriter who produces recorded performances by others of his/her own works.

Writer's Share

Earnings due a songwriter from sales and performances of his/her work less that portion of earnings due by contract or license to a music publisher, administrator, subpublisher, etc.

WWW

Abbreviation for *World Wide Web*.

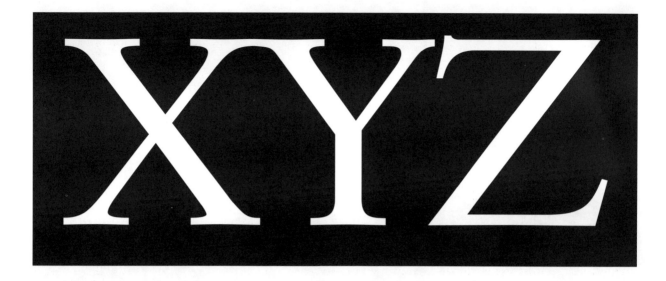

Yellow Pages of Rock
Annual *trade directory* published by *Album Network*. Located at 120 North Victory Boulevard, Burbank, CA 91502. (818) 955-4000.

Young Adult
A *narrowcasting* radio format aimed at the segment of the population ranging in ages 18 to 40. Musically, this market segment most favors pop/rock.

Youth Market
A narrowcasting radio format aimed at the segment of the population ranging in ages 13 to 25. Musically, this market segment most favors *alternative*, *rock*, *heavy metal*, *contemporary Pop*, *contemporary R&B*, and *rap*.

ZAIKS
The *performing-right society* in Poland.

Zimbabwe Music Rights Association (ZIMRA)
The *performing-right society* in Zimbabwe.

ZIMRA
Abbreviation for *Zimbabwe Music Rights Association*.

Zine
A DIY or self-published newsletter or magazine, the term derives from "fanzine" (fan magazine). Largely photocopied and distributed free to friends, aficionados of specific bands or music movements, and to various niche causes promoted by their publishers, zines have tiny circulations, but are reckoned to include between 30,000 and 50,000 existing titles at any given time, though home pages on the internet may ultimately replace their appeal.